A Little Taste of Freedom

The John Hope Franklin Series in
African American History and Culture
Waldo E. Martin Jr. and Patricia Sullivan,
editors

A Little Taste

The Black Freedom

EMILYE CROSBY

# of Freedom

Struggle in Claiborne County, Mississippi

The University of North Carolina Press Chapel Hill

© 2005 The University of North Carolina Press
All rights reserved
Manufactured in the United States of America

Designed by Jacquline Johnson
Set in Bulmer MT
by Keystone Typesetting, Inc.

The paper in this book meets the guidelines for
permanence and durability of the Committee on
Production Guidelines for Book Longevity of the
Council on Library Resources.

Portions of this work have appeared, in somewhat
different form, in Emilye Crosby, " 'Coming Back
At You': Challenging White Supremacy in Port
Gibson, Mississippi," *Mississippi Folklife* 31 (Fall
1998): 21–27; "Claiming the Law: Struggles Between
the Claiborne County, Mississippi, Civil Rights
Movement and White Resistance," *Arkansas
Review: A Journal of Delta Studies* 33 (Aug. 2002):
91–103; and "White Only on Main Street," *Southern
Exposure* 24, no. 4 (Winter 1996): 37–41, and are
reprinted here by permission of the publishers.

Library of Congress Cataloging-in-Publication Data
Crosby, Emilye.
A little taste of freedom : the Black freedom struggle
in Claiborne County, Mississippi / Emilye Crosby.
p. cm. — (The John Hope Franklin series in
African American history and culture)
Includes bibliographical references and index.
ISBN 0-8078-2965-x (cloth: alk. paper)
ISBN 0-8078-5638-x (pbk.: alk. paper)
1. African Americans—Civil rights—Mississippi—
Claiborne County—History—20th century. 2. Civil
rights movements—Mississippi—Claiborne
County—History—20th century. 3. Whites—
Mississippi—Claiborne County—History—20th
century. 4. African American civil rights workers—
Mississippi—Claiborne County—Biography. 5.
African Americans—Mississippi—Claiborne
County—Biography. 6. Oral history. 7. Claiborne
County (Miss.)—Race relations. 8. Claiborne
County (Miss.)—Biography. I. Title. II. Series.
F347.C5C76 2005
323.1762'285—dc22
2005011754

cloth   09 08 07 06 05   5 4 3 2 1
paper   09 08 07 06 05   5 4 3 2 1

for Kathy,

& for

Jean Louise

& her siblings

Contents

Illustrations

Preface

The early histories of the civil rights movement tended to be national in scope, with a top-down perspective that focused on major events, national organizations and leaders, significant legal decisions, and obvious political shifts. This perspective continues to shape the prevailing popular view and even much of the scholarship that portrays the civil rights movement as a reformist, interracial crusade where nonviolent protesters exposed the evils of segregation and convinced the country, especially well-intentioned white northerners, to live up to its ideals of freedom and democracy. This version of the movement is particularly egregious in popular culture, especially the still-influential 1984 movie *Mississippi Burning*, and in the education of middle and high school students. One of my students captured this perfectly with a short synopsis at Geneseo's 2004 Martin Luther King Day observance when he said, "One day a nice old lady, Rosa Parks, sat down on a bus and got arrested. The next day Martin Luther King Jr. stood up and the Montgomery Bus Boycott followed. And sometime later King delivered his famous 'I Have a Dream' speech and segregation was over. This is how the story was taught to me."[1]

Even more pernicious than this simplistic characterization of the movement (that denies the agency of Rosa Parks and the thousands of African Americans in Montgomery whose thirteen-month boycott highlighted the possibilities of mass action) is the *Mississippi Burning* rendition of movement history. Although the movie might be dismissed by some as irrelevant or extreme, this "wrongheaded attempt at a sympathetic portrayal of the movement," which features a heroic federal government defeating firebomb-throwing redneck white men while African Americans stand by as passive victims who are handed equality, remains disturbingly current, broadly accepted, and distress-ingly reflective of not just popular but scholarly assumptions and framing of the movement.[2] In fact, although historians and historical overviews typically offer a more complex version of the civil rights movement, collectively they have failed to adequately address or incorporate a new body of scholarship—particularly com-munity studies of local movements—that has emerged in the past decade. Indi-vidually and collectively, local studies, especially, are contributing details and adding complexity to our understanding of the civil rights movement and provid-ing the basis for reexamining important historiographical questions, especially those related to the implications of particular time and place; tactical and ideolog-ical differences and choices; gender and leadership; and the contours of white supremacy as a broad-based, national phenomenon. Despite the compelling findings of this relatively recent work, however, the outdated narrative of prog-ress, with its overemphasis on sympathetic whites and top-down change and its denial of African American agency, continues to dominate among all but a few specialists.

Reorienting this broad-based misrepresentation is important. Few students today understand how open and pervasive white supremacy was before the movement. They regularly ask why African Americans living through Jim Crow did not more directly challenge the status quo and commonly assert that they would have acted more aggressively. Reflecting the lack of historical depth that nurtures such views, another student, after reading one of my articles on the Claiborne County, Mississippi, movement, asked why blacks had not voted for sympathetic whites. She and others are just not aware of what may seem obvious to scholars and those who lived through the premovement era—that most blacks simply were not allowed to vote. As this suggests, students and the general public typically do not understand the extent of black disfranchisement or the white power structure's ability to retaliate against black activism. This lack of under-standing is exacerbated by the persistence of the triumphant narrative that most people absorb as movement history and by the accompanying assumption that our nation has actually confronted and solved the problems generated by segre-gation and white supremacy.

While historians engage over competing emphases and try to realign popular conceptions so they more closely match scholarly findings, those who still live in the communities most directly affected by the southern civil rights move-ment often hold onto competing interpretations. For many whites in the Clai-borne County, Mississippi, community I write about, especially those who lived through the movement as adults or children, the movement is "that old mess," something they do not want to think about, talk about, or examine. When pushed, they describe it as a hurtful time that damaged race relations and destroyed much that was good about their community. In contrast, Claiborne County African Americans who experienced the movement celebrate it, especially the feelings of possibility and togetherness that it engendered. However, they also point to stubborn and persistent problems, especially in terms of employment, public education, and continuing racial divisions, what they see as the movement's unfinished business. Almost forty years after the mass movement began in Claiborne County, there is little immediate hope for developing a shared understanding of the past. In fact, whites tend to see contemporary problems as stemming from the movement, while blacks see them as resulting from white determination to preserve the status quo.

This community study of the black freedom struggle in rural Claiborne County, Mississippi, extends roughly from Reconstruction to the present, with an emphasis on the post–*Brown* decision civil rights movement. Through this detailed history, I hope to address all of these audiences and versions of the movement by telling the story of a community and the people in it, including those who actively fought for full citizenship and those who struggled to sustain white supremacy. In the process, I explicitly engage with a number of historiographical debates, especially those related to chronology, the role of self-defense in a movement widely framed as nonviolent, the importance of economic boycotts, the implications of organizational and leadership styles, and the intersection between national change and local activism. This is a complicated and sometimes messy history that highlights and explores the primacy of African American activism, the forces driving change in the racial status quo, divisions between and within the black and white communities, issues of leadership and strategy, and the tenacity of white supremacy.

As a community study, this history offers insight into the movement and U.S. history generally, but it is also, fundamentally, about this particular place and the generations of people who have lived and died there, people whose lives typically centered around family, work, and church. In the midst of the daily demands of life, they also battled in large and small ways, and in arenas that ranged from the U.S. Supreme Court to the grocery store line, over definitions of citizenship and what it should mean for people on a day-to-day basis. African Americans insisted on dignified treatment and full inclusion in the community's public life, while whites clung to paternalistic notions of black inferiority and defended inherited privilege. In rural communities like Claiborne County, where lives were intertwined and most people knew each other, the civil rights movement generated both minor and dramatic shifts, many of them vividly illustrated by apparently mundane interactions between people going about their daily lives. In this close picture and these details, we see some of the problems of the dominant movement narrative and the ways that it is only part of a fuller, richer, and more complex story.

Abbreviations

AAUP	American Association of University Professors
AFL	American Federation of Labor
CCTS	Claiborne County Training School
CDGM	Child Development Group of Mississippi
CIO	Congress of Industrial Organizations
COFO	Council of Federated Organizations
CORE	Congress of Racial Equality
FBI	Federal Bureau of Investigation
FDP/MFDP	Freedom Democratic Party/ Mississippi Freedom Democratic Party
FHA	Federal Housing Authority
FSA	Farm Security Administration
HRC	Human Relations Committee
IWA	International Woodworkers of America
LCFO	Lowndes County Freedom Organization
MAP	Mississippi Action for Progress
MCHR	Mississippi Council for Human Relations
NAACP	National Association for the Advancement of Colored People
NLRB	National Labor Relations Board
SCLC	Southern Christian Leadership Conference
SNCC	Student Nonviolent Coordinating Committee
TPP	Tenant Purchase Program

A Little Taste of Freedom

CHAPTER One

Jim Crow Rules

Claiborne County, and its county seat of Port Gibson, located near the Mississippi River just south of the Delta, was one of Mississippi's first white settlements. On the eve of the Civil War, the community was dominated by cotton planters and mercantile traders, with Negro slaves outnumbering whites almost five to one. The Civil War and Confederate defeat brought a dramatic short-term reversal of fortune to both planters and slaves. In 1860, there were 3,339 whites, 12,296 enslaved African Americans, and 44 free blacks in the county. Seven years later, blacks had helped the Union army win significant battles, the Thirteenth Amendment had banned slavery, and black voters outnumbered white 1,015 to 9.[1]

In addition to being disfranchised by Reconstruction policies, planters faced huge debts and an uncertain labor force as they attempted to rebuild their plantations and economy. Adjusting to military defeat, they also had to confront a world in which blacks, whom they perceived as childlike, inferior, and dependent, embraced freedom, citizenship, and political participation. Dismayed when enslaved people left plantations to join Union troops, planters were further troubled by the post–Civil War political alliance of freedmen and white Republicans. During Reconstruction, black Claiborne Countians served in a number of important appointive and elective political positions, including mayor, sheriff, president of the county governing board, postmaster, and even U.S. senator, when Hiram Revels held that position in 1870. In 1871, the Reconstruction government of Mississippi purchased the campus of Oakland

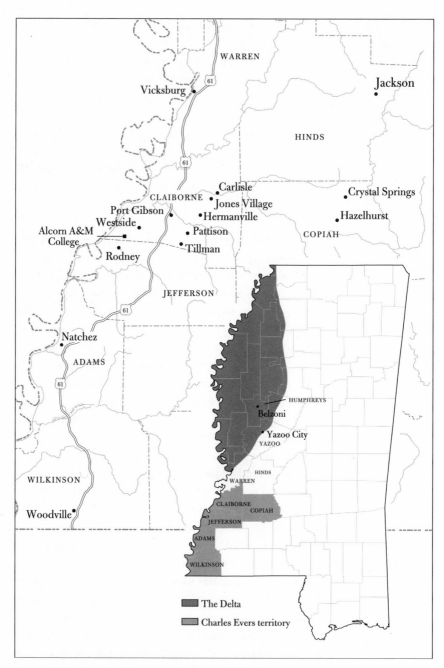

State of Mississippi and Claiborne County and Vicinity

College, a forty-year-old Claiborne County school for the sons of planter elite, which had closed during the Civil War. Built by slave labor, Oakland was re-named Alcorn (for the state's Republican governor) and became the first state-supported black college in Mississippi. Though Alcorn remained physically isolated and severely underfunded, it became an important source of opportunity for African Americans, especially those in the immediate area.[2]

Most black gains during Reconstruction were short-lived. White Mississip-pians used fraud, intimidation, and violence in the 1874 and 1875 elections to restore white supremacy and bring to power what became an all-white Demo-cratic Party. Though blacks and their Republican allies struggled to protect their political rights, they were overwhelmed by extensive violence and lawlessness. For example, in Vicksburg, about twenty miles north of Port Gibson, whites forced the black sheriff out of town and overpowered those who gathered to support him, killing as many as 300 African Americans. President Ulysses S. Grant declined to send in federal troops, and Adelbert Ames, Mississippi's Republican governor, was himself forced to leave the state. By 1877, Reconstruc-tion and the promise of racial equality had been destroyed nationwide.[3]

Well into the twentieth century in Claiborne County, black/white interactions were shaped by the legacy of slavery and the system of sharecropping that replaced it. Initially employed in Claiborne County in 1869, sharecropping was firmly established by the 1880s and varied little until the early 1930s. Sharecrop-pers contracted with planters to work a plot of land in exchange for a portion of the cotton and corn crops, usually one-half or one-third, depending on whether the landowner or tenant provided livestock, equipment, seed, and living ex-penses. Even when farmers around the country began using tractors and other forms of mechanization, cotton farmers relied primarily on their own labor, plowing, planting, chopping (weeding), and harvesting with only the most rudi-mentary of tools—plows, hoes, and mules. As late as 1930, 81 percent of African American workers in Claiborne County were involved in agriculture, and the demands of the cotton season shaped every aspect of black life—work, school, housing, food, religion, and recreation.[4] Sharecropping was ostensibly an eco-nomic contract and started out as a compromise between plantation owners who had little money for wages and former slaves who wanted land of their own to work in family units. A white planter reflected in the 1990s that he and other whites thought tenant farming was "a good system" that was "fair to everybody." However, planters had vast power and could intrude at will into the lives of their tenants.[5]

Claiborne County sharecropper Annie Holloway's interactions with white planter Leigh Briscoe Allen provide a good illustration. Before agreeing to move

Annie Holloway Johnson, landowner and voting rights activist, holding pictures of her second husband, Arthur Johnson, and an unidentified person. Photograph by Roland L. Freeman, courtesy Roland L. Freeman.

onto Allen's plantation, Holloway tried to ensure that she and her husband have a measure of autonomy. Since she intended to do most of the field work while her husband farmed around his day job at the Port Gibson Cottonseed Oil Mill, she asked Allen if he had to "see my husband in the field everyday." Her question reflects the common understanding that whites expected both a share of the harvest and to control their tenants' time. Allen agreed to Holloway's proposal, but, as she had expected, he still kept close watch over them and their crops. Holloway recalled that her husband "was working like I don't know what. He wouldn't let a vine get up on top of that cotton, 'cause Mr. Allen might ride down the road and see it." Once when Allen found the Holloways at home celebrating their first bale of cotton, he made it clear that only extreme illness could justify their midday absence from the cotton fields.[6]

Planters governed choices about crops, growing practices, and land use, such as whether tenants could plant a garden. Tenants generally subsisted on field peas, sweet potatoes, and corn. When they could, they planted a garden to supplement those staples with fresh vegetables in the summer and canned produce in the winter, providing a more varied diet and less need to purchase food on credit. However, planters often insisted that tenants plant only cash crops.

Children on the porch of typical sharecropper house in Rodney, Mississippi, just south of Claiborne County, 1940. Photograph by Marion Post Wolcott, courtesy Library of Congress, LC-USF 34 54956-E.

Until a New Deal government official promoting diversified agriculture intervened, Allen made Holloway plant cotton right up to the house. Another tenant asserted that her landowner was a good man to work for in part because he "didn't keep us from raising a garden."[7] Tenant housing was linked to the sharecropping arrangement and usually consisted of small, poorly constructed shacks full of holes and cracks. Almost all lacked plumbing and were difficult to keep warm in the winter. One sharecropper recalled that his family's calf once walked right through a hole in the wall. Katie Ellis described tenant houses as "barn houses" and said she was "dying for to have a place of my own." One black man became determined to "get my mama a little old place to build her house" when a white planter refused to let him cross a field to visit his mother. Blacks who were unable to buy their own homes often did what they could to improve the tenant houses. Annie Holloway, for example, covered the interior of Allen's tenant house with cardboard to try to seal it and then covered the cardboard with paper for decoration. She also purchased and installed glass windows after explicitly getting Allen's permission to take them with her if she moved.[8]

The white dominance that accompanied sharecropping helped planters tie tenants to their land and ensured a steady labor force. A former planter said that he preferred sharecropping to a simple renter's agreement for cash because "you had quite a bit more difficulty with that man that's paying cash," but "these fourth and half guys, they couldn't sell that stuff without you and him agreeing on it. That was a big difference, don't you see." He observed that cash renters were free to move if they wanted and concluded, "[If] he tells you goodbye, you see where you are, don't you see." However, whites' desire for control went beyond this profit motive. According to Jesse Johnson, the white man he rented land from resented Johnson's insistence on a business relationship as equals, including Johnson's determination to get receipts for the purchases he made on credit. "See, he just wanted you come there and get whatever you want, but don't get no receipt or nothing. And we didn't do it. And that's why he didn't like us." In fact, Johnson asserted that his independence and success bothered his landlord more than the poor crops of other renters. He explained, "Them other fellows, he told them how to farm, and grass overtook their crops," but "we told him we was renting this land, and all he was looking for was his rent. And we were going to work it like we wanted."[9]

Although plantations had much in common, tenants made distinctions based on things like a planter's willingness to permit their children to attend school, provide medical care, or allow autonomy. Katie Ellis, for example, contrasted her landlord, who "just rent the land to us and that was all," with those who "tried to keep you under their thumb." William Walker grew up in a sharecropping family and spent his adult life as a sharecropper on the Person plantation. He spoke positively of the whites his family associated with, including the family that "mostly raised" his father and "taught him how to read and how to tend to business." As for his own experience, he said, "[I] never have farmed with but one man and that was Mr. Person. And it was just like a home. We didn't own it, but we was at home." Despite concurrent memories of hard times and mounting debt, he described Person as a benevolent father figure: "Mr. Jimmy, he would always take care of us. And he'd send you to the doctor. You never had to worry about no doctor, and if you had to go to the hospital, he send you to the hospital. And he would foot the bill 'til we get up able to do so." Even though tenants had to repay the bills with interest, access to medical care was no small thing. When Minnie Lou Buck's two-year-old daughter broke her arm, all Buck could do was wrap the arm in clay and vinegar and a homemade splint. She recalled, "That child suffered. And that arm just swole up."[10]

The yearly account of charges made against the cotton crop (which included everything from groceries and doctor's bills to farm equipment and fertilizer) was a constant source of conflict. By harvest time, sharecroppers owed planters their share of the crops and payment for any advances of money and supplies, including interest that ranged from 15 to 25 percent. Whites generally kept the only records and resisted, sometimes violently, black efforts to keep their own accounting. In the best of circumstances, the debt and interest made it difficult for sharecroppers to make money, and few worked in an ideal situation. Planters could decide when and to whom tenants sold cotton, or they could buy it and store it for later resale, keeping any additional profit. Most important, however, planters decided how much tenants owed and what compensation they would receive for their year's work. Annie Holloway asserted, "You ain't gon' figure yourself, and they not gon' figure it for you. They gon' just give you something when it's all over with." She described a conversation that took place when she asked for an explanation of the yearly cotton settlement: "The one I was talking to that really fixed the paper and gave it to my husband, he couldn't say nothing. The other one said, 'That's what I say about you niggers: you doing better than you ever did in your life and you still ain't satisfied.'" Holloway concluded, "If you say anything to them about it, they go to cussing. He'd take the whole crop and give you something. Didn't settle up with you." Such white control could have dire consequences. In 1925, for example, after Frances Pearl Lucas's father was killed, she remembered, "The man would take all the crop from us, and Mama had six children . . . to feed and take care of. Didn't have nothing, didn't have no hogs or nothing to kill. And they'd take all we'd make. . . . My mother gave us away to anybody. She couldn't take care of us."[11]

There were rare exceptions when landowners based their settlements on written receipts and were perceived as relatively fair. G. L. Disharoon and his relatives had a reputation for being good to work for. Reverend Eugene Spencer, who became an important leader in the black community, described Disharoon as "the aristocratic type, a gentleman, so to speak, as he dealt with people." When Spencer was a young man, Disharoon told Spencer's uncle, "If you want Eugene to keep books for the records, it's all right with me." Spencer concluded, "He didn't want anything but his—and I did keep the records." Yet even Disharoon rarely came up with the same numbers as his tenants. Another one of his former sharecroppers recalled, "[He] kept an account of all that I got from him. I kept an account of what I got, [too]. Sometimes I go, I needed some things. . . . I had to wait on the charge. And he say, 'I ain't gonna charge you much.' See, when I get ready to pay him, it was more than I expect." A longtime tenant summed up sharecropping: "You do all the work, and then the man, at the end of the year, the man get the money. You wouldn't get nothing out of it. I didn't understand it. I never liked working on the half."[12]

Tenants had little choice but to accept the settlement given by planters. Most share agreements were verbal, though it hardly mattered. The inequities were protected by white supremacy and the closed nature of rural Mississippi. Historian Neil McMillen argues that, even after Emancipation, planters still "thought of the people who worked their fields as 'their niggers,' subject to their authority." When Reconstruction ended and the federal government adopted a hands-off policy in terms of southern racial issues, blacks had nowhere to appeal. The law was allied with the interests of planters and provided no relief. According to historian Nan Woodruff, "Wherever African Americans turned, they encountered a world circumscribed by constables and justices of the peace who constantly harassed them . . . [and] by plantation managers who also served as deputies, by planters who had the power to protect their workers from arrests or to send them to the state penitentiary, and by enough lynchings to remind them of the costs involved in defying the brutal instruments of domination."[13]

Unquestioned authority over the yearly crop settlements and final say over things like credit, medical care, and housing were part of the everyday, even mundane, manifestations of white supremacy. Violence produced the menacing backdrop that gave it potency. Blacks who wanted to protest their settlement or any affront at the hands of whites had to carefully calculate the possible costs. Between 1889 and 1945, there were six recorded lynchings of blacks in Claiborne County and adjacent Jefferson County. Moreover, white violence against blacks was sanctioned by the legal system and the larger white community. One black man recalled that when he was growing up, white children would "meddle with you." If whites "hit you . . . look like nothing you could say. They kill you back there in those days." In the 1940s, a white man killed a black soldier over $1.30 in a gambling game and teenaged white brothers killed a black youth in a dispute about a bicycle.[14]

In 1906, John Roan, a white man, killed Min Newsome, a prosperous black farmer and his former childhood playmate. According to his son, Newsome, who was successful enough to have a team of mules, a mare, a wagon, and a surrey, was working day and night to clear the 160 acres of swamp land he was purchasing. In a vaguely worded report, the local newspaper attributed the killing to self-defense after an argument, but Newsome's family maintains that Roan killed Newsome because he was jealous and believed the land Newsome was buying was "too good for a black man to have." The courts never indicted Roan, and despite the partial payment made by Newsome before his death, all the land ended up back in the hands of its original white owner.[15]

Similarly, in 1939, Farrell Humphrey killed a black farmer named Denver Gray. According to family stories, even as a young man Gray "didn't take no stuff off white folk." When he was sixteen, his family sent him to St. Louis because he had fired a shotgun at a white man who was "winking and beckoning" at one of his female cousins. When Gray returned to Mississippi, he still "didn't cow to white folks, and people thought he was crazy because if he saw a white man bothering anybody colored, he stop him. They didn't like that." According to Gray's daughter Hystercine Rankin, Humphrey shot her father in broad daylight on a county road, then went and told Gray's wife where his body was. Later, he bragged about killing an "uppity nigger." Evidently Gray's offense was talking back and buying his wife a new coat and stove, rather than purchasing second-hand ones from Humphrey.[16]

Humphrey was never punished, and in telling the story of her father's murder, Rankin began by explaining that white men had raped her grandmother and great-grandmother and both had conceived children as a result. She continued, "White folks could do anything they wanted to in those days, and if one of our men said something, they'd just kill him." She described her great-grandfather, Joseph "Daddy Joe" January, as a "fiercely independent man" who bought and cleared 100 acres of swamp land. When he learned his daughter had been raped, he "sat in the hallway . . . with a shotgun on his lap, and just cried like a little baby. . . . If he went for that white man, they would've killed Daddy Joe, probably burned his place and taken the land. That's just the way it was for us in those times." Whites could attack blacks capriciously and with immunity. With no protection from the law, blacks' every encounter with whites was potentially dangerous. Moreover, as historian Leon Litwack argues, success and independence offered no protection and could even make blacks targets. After shooting Min Newsome, John Roan reportedly went right to a magistrate and said, "I done shot that nigger, that nigger Min Newsome." Although the magistrate initially questioned why he would "shoot as good a nigger as that," Roan ended the exchange by asking, "You'd speak in defense of a nigger?"[17]

Although white authority was grounded in violence and political, economic, and legal dominance, it was sustained and expressed through social control and the concept of black "place." Segregation and black deference were two central pieces of the day-in-and-day-out experience of white supremacy. The result is what Neil McMillen has called a "social code of forbidding complexity." He observes that it was enforced in "often trivial ways" but argues that it "must not be underestimated." He explains, "If violence was the 'instrument in reserve'— the ultimate deterrent normally used only against the most recalcitrant—social ritual regulated day-to-day race relations. Within the context of a biracial social order based on white dominance, it served much the same function as 'good manners' in any society. For the most part, the code assured white control without the need for more extreme forms of coercion." In Port Gibson and Claiborne County, this control started with segregation. Schools, churches, buses, funeral homes, cemeteries, the theater, civic organizations, and even fund-raising drives were segregated. The hospital kept black and white patients apart. Bus stations, the courthouse, cotton gins, gas stations, and doctors either pro-vided separate waiting rooms, bathrooms, and water fountains or excluded Afri-can Americans from their facilities. Segregation extended to veterans' organiza-tions, bus-driver training, and contests for things like mailbox improvement and Christmas decorations. The county also had a white and a Negro county agent, separate clover tours for white and black farmers, and segregated 4-H clubs. When local businesses sponsored entertainment, they sometimes held separate showings for whites and blacks, but blacks were more often simply excluded from public spaces like the library and events, including the annual holiday church tour and the Fat Stock show. The *Port Gibson Reveille* almost invariably identified the race of blacks, but not whites. White newsman Fred Powledge writes that "the *normal* condition, according to the press and most of the rest of white society, was one of whiteness. Blackness was the exception."[18]

Courtesy and deference underscored the hierarchy implied by segregation. As historian Adam Fairclough explains, "Being civil to blacks as one might be to whites subverted segregation, because the caste system demanded an etiquette that made explicit, in *all* social interaction, the superiority of the white and the inferiority of the black." Forms of address, including courtesy titles like Mr. and Mrs., came to symbolize white supremacy. James Miller, who grew up in the 1950s and 1960s, recalled that there was a "certain way you supposed to talk to white folks. You saw them, you respected them. They were in charge. You knew your place." This was reinforced by whites' refusal to use courtesy titles to address blacks. Neil McMillen writes that a white postal worker marked out Mr. and Mrs. on envelopes directed to blacks, and another white man commented that it was "crazy mistering niggers in Mississippi." In 1944, Port Gibson whites insisted to blacks that it was "Impossible!" for a labor union to "make the boss call you 'Mister.'" The *Port Gibson Reveille* used courtesy titles for whites, but not blacks. Black teachers were turned down when they asked the bank to use titles on their checks, and a black business owner recalled that "a storm was raised" when she asked a bank clerk not to call her by her first name.[19]

African Americans have stark memories of this enforced system of racial hierarchy and the inferiority it implied. One woman remembered that at the theater, whites "had the nice, soft comfortable seats, and we were sitting up on the hard seats." In 1998, another woman still had the small, collapsible tin cup she bought over sixty years before to give her sick daughter a drink of water because whites "wouldn't want you to drink out of that fountain now [and] she was sick that day. . . . I was carrying her to the doctor." Referring to the requirement that blacks ride behind a curtain on public buses and the expectation that they use the back door at "white folks' houses," one black man said that he "resented" being treated like "a second-class citizen." Another man summed this up, saying, "There was black and there was white. We had been taught that by the water fountains, the bathrooms, [and] the doctor's offices with separate waiting rooms." He continued, "At that point, yes, we knew we were in Mississippi then, and Jim Crow ruled."[20]

Black children had to learn to negotiate the intricacies of interracial interaction at a young age. Juanita Burks Stewart's memories are typical. Though her family's white neighbors called her parents by their first names, Burks's mother always said "yes ma'am and no ma'am" in talking to the younger white woman. Moreover, whenever her mother sent her children over to help the neighbors, she would instruct them, "Go to the back now. Don't go to the front. Go to the back and yell out for Mrs. Price." Explaining that she "really really hated doing that," Stewart expressed frustration that since she never learned the neighbor's first name, even in telling the story she still had to refer to her as "Mrs. Price." As a child, Julia Jones called her family's landowner by his first name because she "hadn't learned to call them mister." As an adult, she speculated that he must have been unhappy with her refusal to call him Mr. but recalled that he "just laughed it off." She concluded, "I guess, he say, 'She'll learn.' And I did. I learned later on."[21]

Ken Brandon, whose father contracted to haul pulpwood for the white Callenders, remembered being confused about courtesy titles. On a trip with his father, he saw "this older black gentleman, he must have been 50 or 60, and he was talking to this younger white guy. He must have been about 20 years old. He was saying 'yes sir' and 'no sir.' And I didn't understand that." Shortly after seeing that interaction, Ken Brandon went with his father to the Callenders' house. Brandon, who was around seven years old at the time, recalled talking to a white boy who was about twelve and being unsure about how to address him. He remembered playing it safe and "saying 'yes sir' to him because that [was] what you supposed to do." Ken Brandon was confused, in part, because of his youth but also because his mother, Marjorie Brandon, had taught him that terms of respect should be based on age, not race. She flatly refused to use courtesy titles for whites her age and younger. Ken observed that one of his parents' few arguments was over his mother's refusal to say "sir" to one of the younger Callenders. According to Ken, his mother told his father, " 'He's the same age as I am.' She said, 'Mr. Hugh, he's old as my father, I'll say it to him.' Says, 'I'm not going to give him, or them . . . any more respect than I would give . . . a colored person.' . . . She said, 'I just can't say it.' My dad said, 'What do you mean you can't say it? You can.' She said, 'No, I can't.' "[22]

Black deference was also expected whenever blacks and whites shared public

Marjorie and Alonzo Brandon holding a 1960s photograph of themselves and their six children, Ken, Vivian, Carl, Maxine, Dennis, and John, 2004. Photograph by David Crosby, courtesy David Crosby.

space. In stores and banks, blacks were never served before whites. According to one man, "We had been taught, and even by parents, you know, that if you're around white folks, if you're in line at the grocery store, stand back and let them go on to the cash register and get checked out first." This was so much the norm that decades later a black man still remarked on the day in the 1930s or 1940s when the white sheriff actually waited behind black customers at the post office. A few restaurants had segregated seating for blacks and whites, but more commonly blacks who wanted food had to order at a back window and eat elsewhere. On public buses, blacks had to sit behind a curtain in the back or stand, if that section was full. Marjorie Brandon remembered, "You're trying to hold to keep from falling and they're sneering at you. 'Get back, I don't want to smell you.' I tell you we really had it." Her son Carl learned a hard lesson from his mother on one of the public buses: "I can remember getting on the bus and dropping down on the first seat that I saw vacant. Sometimes I wonder now if my shoulder is still hurting. I jumped down there and she immediately grabbed my shoulder and jerked me up. I was thinking [that] riding the Continental Trailways was kind of like riding the public school bus, you could sit wherever."[23]

James Dorsey, who became an important NAACP leader in the 1960s, recalled that when blacks encountered whites on the street, the whites "would occupy the whole street. And you had to get off to the side, wait, and let them pass." White control over ostensibly public streets was evident at a 1944 black Armistice celebration when the black organizers thanked whites for "giving them the privilege of parading through town." In a 1952 column intended to highlight the "friendly relations" between the races, *Port Gibson Reveille* editor H. H. Crisler revealed the implicit power relations that governed the streets. Crisler described how he set out on a Saturday, a day downtown Port Gibson was typically dominated by black shoppers, to find his "colored helper" at a black barbershop. Explaining that he believed the blacks gathered on the street "had prior rights there, especially on Saturday," he noted that "every one was as willing to give passage way as [I was] to recognize their rights." When Crisler reached the barbershop, the "colored helper" was not there, but the shop proprietor immediately left a customer to go searching for him, and when his efforts failed, the barber promised to continue looking and send the man to Crisler as soon as he was located. Noting that he was the "only white person on the street" and that he was "treated with perfect courtesy," Crisler interpreted these interactions as evidence of interracial friendship.[24] Perhaps they were, but it is more likely that they reflected black deference to his power as a white man.

Blacks in rural areas remembered having more relaxed relationships with whites, further illustrating the arbitrariness and complexity of interracial interactions. Civil rights activists who worked in southwest Mississippi explain that without the threat of "Black political challenge," whites and blacks shared "an intimacy, an air of easy familiarity." Ezekiel Rankin, a black man born in 1917, said "the atmosphere was good" in the rural area where he grew up. "Black and white got along well. We played together. We swum together. We worked together in the fields. . . . Folks were neighborly. It made no difference, if whites killed a hog, they'd send you a piece of meat. If we killed one, we'd send them a piece." He observed that sometimes they would even "sit down, eat at the table" with whites, but he concluded, "We really didn't know things as they really were." Nate Jones, his contemporary, had a similar experience in the Westside community near Alcorn College, recalling, blacks and whites "grew up together, and looked like to me we was friends."[25]

Whatever these relationships meant to the individuals involved, they did not eliminate white supremacy. Even those blacks who shared meals and friendship with whites in rural neighborhoods learned to act differently in town. After talking about his Westside-area friendships with whites, Nate Jones continued, "When we come to town, we know it was different. It was segregated. Had certain facilities we could use, had signs up, white and black. Same way on the buses and everything." Moreover, as southern children grew up, white supremacy inevitably intruded in their interracial interactions and destroyed any possibility for real friendship. According to Julia Jones, when white children "got twelve years old, ten or twelve years old," their black playmates had to begin addressing them with courtesy titles. Marjorie Brandon was deeply affected by her father's experiences with this practice on the Rodden plantation where he grew up: "My father had been there for years. He grew up on that plantation and the [Rodden] boys . . . was right along with my Dad. He said after they got a certain age that they were told 'Now look, you have to call this Mr. Percy and Mr. Willy, you can't just say Percy, Willy any more cause they getting up in age and you have to mister them.' That bothered me."[26]

CHAPTER Two

A Taste of Freedom

White dominance continued almost unchecked until the civil rights movement of the 1960s, but the Great Depression, New Deal, and World War II helped tear small holes in the fabric of white supremacy and set in motion large structural shifts that provided the impetus for fundamental change. The Depression era drop in cotton prices, combined with flooding and boll weevils, threatened cotton's centrality to Mississippi's economy. Even more significant, during the New Deal and World War II, the nation was considering fundamental questions about economic security and democracy that were essential to African Americans. President Franklin D. Roosevelt unleashed unprecedented federal activism, and the federal government slowly began to reverse its longtime abandonment of the Reconstruction amendments and their guarantees of black citizenship and voting rights. Congress considered legislation intended to regulate voting and make it more accessible to all citizens, and after blacks threatened mass protest in 1941, President Roosevelt issued an executive order banning racial discrimination in defense-industry employment practices. In 1944 in *Smith v. Allwright*, the Supreme Court ruled that the widespread southern practice of excluding blacks from the Democratic Party primaries, known as the white primary, was unconstitutional. Brought by the National Association for the Advancement of Colored People (NAACP), this case opened the door to expanded southern black political participation. The NAACP also won a series of school cases where the Supreme Court insisted that states do more to make educational opportunities equal, not just separate. These eventually culminated in the 1954 *Brown* decision, where the NAACP successfully challenged state-enforced school segregation.[1]

Powerful southern whites had mixed feelings about New Deal programs and the wartime policies that followed them. The New Deal saved many planters from economic ruin and essentially funded their subsequent mechanization, but whites feared the concurrent expansion in federal power. Southern Democratic congressmen made states' rights and white supremacy their priorities, and, according to historian James Cobb, southern planters chose a "pragmatic course," accepting federal money and rejecting "federal intervention in their affairs." This was true in Claiborne County, where whites used New Deal programs and wartime policies to channel resources into the white community and retain control over black labor and opportunities.[2]

Simultaneously, blacks sought to benefit from the changing circumstances of the New Deal and World War II. In Claiborne County, the Farm Security Administration (FSA) Tenant Purchase Program (TPP), in which the government facilitated tenant purchase of family-sized farms by locating land, financing loans, and providing ongoing support and supervision, offered one of the most significant opportunities. In 1930, roughly sixty-four black families owned farms, so the two dozen black tenant families who bought farms through the TPP from 1939 to 1942 marked a significant increase in black landowners. Participant Jesse Johnson insisted that outside of the program, whites "weren't going to loan you no money to buy no land. 'Cause they had all this land. They wanted you to farm like they wanted to farm, where they could get all the money." Another tenant purchaser recalled, "The bank wouldn't talk with you, man, what you talking about. They wouldn't talk with you. Oh, if they knows you, you might could get ten or twelve dollars out. . . . If you wanted a lot of money, you just going crazy. They loant you twenty dollars, man, you think you in luck." Katie Ellis pointed out, "If we make payment to the government every year on our land, we could [have] did the bank the same way." She concluded that, unlike local bankers, "the government project" gave blacks "a fair chance." Over the years, the blacks who did manage to buy land had to struggle to keep it; stories of blacks losing land through fraud and violence permeate Claiborne County oral histories. For example, Katie Ellis insisted that whites took land from her grandfather. "He paid for it, but they didn't give him no honor for it. They took it from him. And they say he never did pay for it. [Black] people didn't own no land much. They couldn't own it till the later days come up." These memories are corroborated by Neil McMillen's findings that across the state between 1890 and 1940 the "size and value of black-owned agricultural holdings declined substantially."[3]

Despite general white opposition to black landowning, few Claiborne County whites perceived the TPP as a threat. High black unemployment had created a labor surplus, and the agricultural economy was shifting away from sharecropping. A white planter on the FSA county committee that determined which applicants were accepted for the program explains that white planters knew their current system "was on the way out." The program also benefited whites. Two white families briefly participated, and the government's land purchases rescued two planters who were facing foreclosure. Moreover, the county committee stopped facilitating the purchase of farms as soon as World War II created more demand for labor.[4] Whites retained significant control over the TPP, including deciding who could participate. Applicants had to submit an application to the local supervisor and county committee (all of whom were white) and provide recommendations from three (white) businessmen. One purchaser recalled, "They said they wasn't gon' take nobody that the landowner didn't want them to take off their place." James Dorsey, whose family was evicted by their Jefferson County landlord for applying to the program, contended, "There were quite a few applications and a lot of them were turned down because the landowner called and said, 'Well, these are my best people and you just leave them alone.'"[5]

The oppressive nature of white supremacy was evident in some of the widespread black skepticism about the program. Some believed that participants would not be allowed to do things like sell eggs or go to town. Neither of these beliefs had any basis in the program's guidelines; instead, they reflected common experiences. Skeptics warned purchasers that they would never be able to pay off the loans, and one person compared moving onto government land to moving into slavery. The mortgages, which averaged $3,700, probably seemed like an enormous sum to sharecroppers who cleared only several hundred dollars in a good year. According to Katie Ellis, "Everybody was talking that we'll never pay for it. 'Oh, you under bondage, you'll never get out of debt. You'll never pay for it.'" These comments, too, reflected typical tenant experiences of inequitable settlements and unending debt. In fact, with access to reasonable interest rates and control over their land, most tenant purchasers paid off their loans ahead of schedule, providing a glimpse of black farming potential.[6]

It was also difficult for blacks to escape the widespread belief that white planters took care of their sharecroppers. James Dorsey remembered that landlords would tell tenants, "I'm treating you better than the government will. If you think the government gonna take care of you, then give me my house." Annie Holloway confronted this issue when her husband expressed reservations about leaving sharecropping. She told Alcorn professor J. H. Dean, "My husband backed out . . . [because] his supervisor say . . . if he feel like he need a suit of clothes, then tell him about it. And he see the place where he need one, well, then, he'll get one." Dean encouraged Rex Holloway, telling him, "Don't pay no attention to that man. He will be gone and ya'll will be here. You ain't gon keep no one supervisor. That man will be gone. It wasn't nobody but God give this to the people. This here is a God-given thing."[7]

Some tenant purchasers did receive a little help from whites, reflecting the paternalistic face of white supremacy. According to Eugene Spencer, planter G. L. Disharoon supported his decision to apply. "I told him [I was] gonna move. He said he never object to nobody trying to make a better step. He never objected to that. He talked mighty good. . . . He told me anytime I didn't like the program, as long as he had land, I had a home, to come back." In fact, the single largest group of participants came from Disharoon's plantation. This was due to his willingness to see tenants move on and his practice of working with tenants who were fairly autonomous (owning their own equipment and farm animals) and well situated to take advantage of the program. Both whites and blacks helped Annie Holloway, then a tenant on the Allen plantation. A neighboring black minister encouraged her to apply and drove her to Alcorn to learn more about the program. When she was preparing her application, she asked a white man to type it, telling him, "We want to try to get us a home and the government will loan us money if we qualify." Holloway recalled that he commented, "I ain't heard nothing about it." She told him, " 'Mr. Charlie, you just fix the paper.' And he got his paper. He was nice about helping you. You know, he was kind of special to the colored folk. When I got through I says, 'What I owe you?' He say, 'Nothing. I hope you be successful.' "[8]

According to folklorist Worth Long, these experiences were typical. The obstacles facing potential black landowners were so great that they needed some type of assistance. "Whether it was the resources of your own community or somewhere else, you needed something. See, you just couldn't come up and say 'Look I want some land.' It didn't work that way." However, "if you were . . . perceived as a good person in the community, a 'good Negro,' then you could get some help." Katie Ellis described the same practice, saying, "You had to go through the white folk hand. Those people that know you and give you a good reputation, they'd tell them, 'That'll be a good customer. You take him.' "[9] Though the vast majority of black farmers remained sharecroppers, the TPP's impact ultimately went far beyond the twenty-two black families who participated in the program. Tenant purchasers and other black landowners generally took the lead in supporting the NAACP, pursuing voting rights, and working to improve the black community's opportunities.

Even more than the New Deal, World War II had an immediate impact on

African American opportunities and southern race relations. Blacks took advantage of the war's focus on democracy and increased demands for labor, and black southerners who served in the military glimpsed alternatives to white supremacy and came home eager to claim full citizenship rights. Claiborne County veteran James Dorsey explained, "World War II came along and it opened up another avenue, another door for our people to really see that blacks could do . . . many things" that whites had said "they couldn't do." For Ezekiel Rankin, the war was "a turning point": "We got a chance to travel, go different places, meet a lot of different people from different backgrounds." He added, "You saw a lot of things that you normally never would have seen, and you saw in different countries, how people's culture, how they were living together, black and white. . . . It sort of helped a lot. It gave you something to look forward for. To hope for." Before arriving in the British Isles, for example, Rankin had been told that he would be treated better there than in the United States. He said, "It was a matter of fact because you were treated sort of like human beings, and here, at that time, you know, as I said before, Jim Crowism."[10]

Some soldiers even experienced integrated living and working settings. One of them was William Matt Ross, who later became one of the first post-Reconstruction black elected officials in Mississippi. He recalled his shock upon returning from military service. "I felt fine until I got to Camp Shelby [in Hattiesburg, Mississippi]. I was discharged at Camp Shelby and I got on the bus to come home and that man put me on the back of the bus, pulled that curtain across there. I think it was five years before I rode a bus again. I just couldn't, I couldn't undergo it. We had been living together and eating together and sleeping together and fighting together and everything until I was discharged." Few soldiers expected life in Mississippi to be dramatically changed. For example, though navy veteran Nate Jones subscribed to the *Pittsburgh Courier* and was influenced by the national black newspaper's aggressive advocacy of civil rights, daily letters from his wife let him know that in Claiborne County "things hadn't changed too much." Like Ross, however, Jones was changed, and he never gave up his commitment to pursuing a more equitable world. While he was still in the navy, he tried to prepare for voting by asking his wife to pay the required $2 poll tax. When a black man warned her that whites "gon' whup you if you do that," she backed off because she "didn't know what they might do to me." James Dorsey had more success, registering to vote as soon as he returned to Claiborne County. In the army he had encountered northern blacks who voted regularly and a white officer who encouraged black soldiers to vote. "When we were getting discharged, [he] told us that we ought to become, if we want, citizens of the United States, that we had fought for the country." Dorsey recalled that

Nate Jones, pictured here in his naval uniform during World War II, was a farmer, voting rights activist, and NAACP leader. Courtesy Nate Jones.

although few blacks were allowed to register then, "they let me register because I had been a soldier and therefore I didn't go through an examination."[11]

Not all black veterans returned home and pursued political rights. Asked about voting, another Claiborne County veteran responded, "Un-huh. I didn't think about that then. I didn't think about no voting or nothing like that see. I had never woke up." Whether or not they tried to register, many veterans were able to use the war and the GI Bill to improve their personal circumstances. Nate Jones and his wife combined his war wages and her farm earnings to buy 125 acres of land near Alcorn College, and Jones used the GI Bill to take a farm course that helped him improve his crop yields. Matt Ross graduated from high school through a night program specifically for veterans. Dorsey also completed high school, participated in several farm training programs, and attended Mississippi Baptist Seminary.[12] Like black landowners, many of these veterans played a critical role in pushing for voting rights and eventually leading the civil rights movement.

On the home front, the war's demand for labor threatened whites' customary control of black workers. With viable alternatives to picking cotton and doing domestic work, blacks either refused to do such poorly paid menial labor or demanded better wages. In 1944, *Port Gibson Reveille* editor H. H. Crisler bemoaned the difficulty of finding workers and waxed nostalgic about the recent past, when "a town denizen could pick up a workman on the street at any time to do his chores about the home." Contending that blacks were refusing to pick cotton during these "flush times," he expressed hope that "people will some day be hungry" enough to "accept an invitation to do a little labor." Historian Pete Daniel observes that as the "war industries and the military absorbed potential wage laborers, rural employers became obsessed with labor supply and control." For example, a Delta planter complained that he would have to pay $2 per hundred pounds to have cotton picked because black women "were loafing around town because they received money from their relatives in the service."[13]

In response, planters used their authority administering wartime labor policies to control the mobility of black workers. Historians Nan Woodruff and James Cobb found that planters "exaggerated their need for labor" to keep sharecroppers and day workers from moving, while local draft boards would "defer their prize tenants while shifting those who had moved away to the top of the induction lists." In Claiborne County, a black farmer received a draft notice about two weeks after he left to work in Chicago. Although he failed his physical, the local draft board denied him permission to return to his Chicago job. When he protested, they sent him another draft notice and inducted him into the army. In August 1944, the draft board immediately reclassified black workers at the Port Gibson Cottonseed Oil Mill who went out on strike. Facing induction into the armed services, the strikers went back to work the next week. Crisler editorialized, "We southerners do not handle striking factory workers with the same degree of tolerance they are handled up North."[14]

In July 1944, the Claiborne County sheriff threatened to jail people for refusing to work and the *Reveille* applauded him, writing that the sheriff's insistence that "no loafing" would be tolerated from "able-bodied persons" was the only way to "cope with this lush soldier-allotment life which too many of our people are enjoying." The sheriff made good on his threats, arresting two people for vagrancy before releasing them to work. He arrested another six for gambling, and, according to the *Reveille*, one of them quickly returned to the factory job that he had "deserted" the week before. A few months later, the sheriff published a notice in the paper: "Claiborne County farmers need labor to pick their cotton, therefore all persons able to work, should assist in this vital farm activity. Labor is very scarce, but we must get the cotton crop gathered. Any one knowing of any loafers, please notify me, and I will see that they work."[15]

These labor-related complaints and policies were influenced by whites' widespread assumptions that cotton picking was black work and that all black men, women, and children should be available to work for whites. One black woman remembered that when she moved to Fayette (about thirty miles from Port Gibson), a white man informed her that she had to go to work in the mayor's "cotton patch." She explained, "Back in those days the mayor had a man to visit each home and tell them that all black women had to go to the field." By October 1944, Crisler was insisting that blacks' refusal to pick cotton was fueling mechanization; he predicted that the South was on the "verge of losing one of its chief charms—the white cotton field with its army of colored pickers." The association between blacks and picking cotton was so strong that advertisers, who almost never used black images, depicted black men and women in advertisements for cotton-picking supplies. In contrast, neither the sheriff nor the editor expected white women to pick cotton. In fact, this image was so absurd that the *Reveille* periodically used it to entertain (white) readers. In September 1953, the editor described a group of white women who used scissors to gather 500 cotton bolls to give out to tourists and noted that one woman "didn't know a cotton field could be so hot." Asked if she ever picked cotton, another white woman laughed and said, "No, I didn't pick cotton. But, I tell you what. We did love to. We would try that, you know, and we would last about five minutes."[16]

The biggest labor-related conflict between Claiborne County whites and blacks came when black workers at the Port Gibson Veneer and Box Company organized a chapter of the International Woodworkers of America (IWA) and tried to win company recognition and a contract. The box factory assembled wire-bound boxes made of veneer and was Claiborne County's largest factory, employing 300–400 black laborers and a handful of white foremen, office workers, and supervisors. When IWA organizers initiated their drive in August 1944, black workers, eager for an alternative to the plantation-based work culture that dominated the factory and community, quickly responded. However, box factory owner Alex Wilson steadfastly refused to recognize or negotiate with the IWA, and white businessmen, law enforcement officers, and elected officials began a comprehensive and sustained campaign of persuasion and coercion intended to undermine the union effort. In mid-October, Hardy Wilson (plant owner Alex Wilson's father) insisted to workers who were assembled to pick up their pay that the company was helping them (by installing new machinery). He read excerpts from Booker T. Washington's writings that encouraged workers to be industrious and quiet, and he threatened that the plant would close if workers joined the union. Crisler used a similar approach in his editorials, insisting that workers should be grateful for their comparatively high $3 to $4 daily wages and threatening that labor agitation would disrupt "racial harmony" and force the plant to close and would do "no good for future congenial relationships between the races."[17]

Whites also used more explicitly coercive tactics. A white foreman told a black worker, "Your damn Union is going to get all you Negroes fired." Sheriff Malcolm Montgomery and plant superintendent J. C. Wheeless stood outside one union meeting to see which workers attended. At another, the sheriff threatened to run the organizer out of town. Montgomery also insisted that if there was "anything to [the union]," white leaders would have "let" the organizer hold a meeting in "the court house." The company tried to circumvent collective bargaining by reinstituting a policy of having workers sign individual job applications/contracts. Once standard practice, they had been discontinued during the war. When the company reintroduced the form during the union drive, workers were willing to submit to a physical exam and fill out the questions related to family, health, and past work history. They refused, however, to "assume all the risk and dangers" of the job or to concede that the company could fire them "at any time with or without cause."[18]

After a several-week standoff, plant owner Alex Wilson acknowledged the importance of the union when he included union president Luther Buie in a meeting where he issued an ultimatum, that workers who had not signed the form by Monday, October 23, would not be allowed to work. Wilson told the men, "This is my mill, and if whoever work at this mill, you are going to work and abide by my rules." However, bolstered by the wartime labor shortage and the union drive, black workers collectively refused to capitulate, and a few individuals openly challenged their bosses. Charles Marshall, for example, told Hardy Wilson that instead of new machinery, black workers needed better wages and access to skilled work. At a National Labor Relations Board (NLRB) hearing a year later, Marshall testified that he appreciated Wilson saying "how he liked the colored folks" but pointed out that Wilson "kind of switched around" and threatened that he would "make it bad for us." Eddie Thomas, a thirteen-year employee who had previously signed the application, refused to re-sign it, and testified that he objected to the provisions that allowed the company to fire him arbitrarily and made him responsible for his own medical bills in case of injury. He asserted, "That thing don't read right. I can't read and write that good but I read and spell enough to know that ain't good for me."[19]

Many workers saw the contract for what it was, a tool to disrupt their organizing effort. One objected to signing "all my rights away." After talking to Luther Buie, another decided he "wasn't going to sign if you all don't sign." The conflict came to a head Monday, October 23rd, when the company locked out employees who refused to sign. Fewer than 30 of the approximately 350 black employees were allowed to work, and a number of them had signed union cards. On Thursday, with workers showing no signs of relenting, Alex Wilson notified Buie that he would end his demand that workers sign the applications. Ironically, the day that Wilson asked workers to return, Crisler wrote an editorial commending him for his firm stand and warning workers that Wilson would close the plant before allowing "employees, under the influence of outside labor agitators, to dictate its policy." Even after Wilson's capitulation, workers continued to demonstrate their independence and refused to return to work that Friday. Many went instead to the courthouse for an NLRB hearing, where an examiner announced a November 22, 1944, NLRB election.[20] For workers, this was a major victory. They had won the right to vote on union representation, stood together in the face of a lockout, compelled Wilson to negotiate with their chosen representative, and forced him to rescind his demand that they sign contracts.

White leaders refused to concede, however. The day after the NLRB hearing, Alex Wilson told workers that, union or no union, the mill was his and he was "going to run it." H. H. Crisler, Port Gibson Bank president R. D. Gage Jr., planter L. B. Allen, and other prominent white leaders published a several-page appeal that asked workers to reject the union. Claiming that the union threatened the tradition of friendship between the races, the signers specifically addressed themselves to "wise" employees, called for "intelligent bi-racial leadership," and accused the union of being "unscrupulous" and of creating "racial friction." Ignoring workers' grievances and ability to act on their own behalf, these leaders argued that a "power-drunk labor organizer" was exploiting "the ignorance of colored men and women" and contended that the union and its representatives "do not care a Tinker's Damn about little black boys and girls becoming good citizens." They concluded by asserting that the future of the community's race relations was in the hands of the workers. "Workers use your head! Don't act too quick! You have plenty of time to join a union. Negroes should have an organization of their own. Negroes should have better pay and working conditions. Negroes must also have the intelligence and sanity to act with consideration and common sense." For these white leaders, good race relations required that African Americans accept white authority in exchange for paternalism. Although they expressed concern about black working conditions and wages both in this plea and in *Reveille* editorials, none of them addressed possible remedies. The appeal also took pains to explain how the loss of the plant (which they said would close if workers voted for the union) would hurt the entire community, especially merchants, bankers, and others dependent on the industry's payroll. Whites refused to concede that blacks could (or should) act autonomously, instead believing that blacks should put white interests first. Despite this, African Americans overwhelmingly chose to rely on themselves and their national union; in the November 1944 election, 199 workers voted in favor of the union and only 19 voted against.[21]

The IWA spent the next six months trying unsuccessfully to negotiate a contract and then appealed to the War Labor Board for a resolution. In July 1945, the board ruled that the company should raise workers' wages from forty to fifty cents an hour and adopted most of the union's contract requests related to seniority, work-place rules, and paid vacation. Even after this decision, the company still held out, refusing to implement the board's ruling or sign a contract.[22] Meanwhile, in November 1945, a year after the union election, the NLRB held hearings in Port Gibson to examine IWA charges that several workers had been illegally fired as punishment for union activity and that the company had violated the National Labor Relations Act when it used a lockout to try to force employees to sign the individual contracts.

One of the workers in question was Evan Doss, who was fired in February 1945 ostensibly for refusing to work overtime. His foreman, J. A. Gallman, asserted that he had left word with another worker for Doss to work an extra hour and Doss refused. Doss insisted he had never been asked to work and argued that he was fired for his union work. Several employees, including one woman who heard that the foreman "wanted to get rid of Doss anyway because he was connected with the C.I.O.," testified that Doss was targeted for his union activism. Although the NLRB expressed sympathy, they ruled that Doss's firing was not retaliation for union activism, in part because other union activists had retained their jobs. It is likely that both Doss's union activism and his insistence on standing up to whites contributed to his firing. During his NLRB testimony, Doss assertively contradicted his foreman's contention that he had been asked to work overtime, saying, "Mr. Gallman, I can't help what you believe. I said, I stand right here, and I will tell you and I will tell Oliver Brown, face to face and toe to toe, that he did not tell me and you either." In another typical exchange, Doss responded impatiently to a question he had already answered, saying, "Now you hear me say I don't know because I went home. I told you I went home." Other witnesses held their ground and found ways to assert their viewpoint, but none was as direct as Doss. The company argued that "the testimony of Evan Doss on the witness stand in this proceeding shows that he was discourteous to Gallman about said matter and assumed an attitude of insubordination which alone would have justified his discharge."[23]

Doss's experience also illustrates that even though workers had won union representation, the company retained virtually absolute authority over personnel decisions. Union representation did little to influence working conditions, and the NLRB would only intervene in firings that were directly connected to union work, something difficult to prove. Company officials employed an effective strategy of passive resistance, refusing to negotiate with the union and ignoring decisions made by federal agencies. In October 1945, almost a year after the workers voted for the union and three months after the War Labor Board directed the company to accept a contract that included pay raises, the company had still refused to comply. According to Leatha Doss, Evan Doss's wife and the union's recording secretary, workers were becoming discouraged and "falling back so fast." She wrote to union officials looking for "one or two words of encouragement" to "help us hold our membership together." In November 1945, the same month that the NLRB held its hearings about unfair labor practices, workers voted to strike but then continued to work, still hoping that the federal government would force the company to sign the contract.[24]

In December 1945, company lawyers asserted that, with the war's end, the War Labor Board, whose wage-related ruling they had been ignoring, no longer had any authority. With little hope that the company would sign a contract, box factory workers went on strike on April 8, 1946, about sixteen months after they had voted for the union. The context for the strike was significantly different from that of the August 1944 organizing drive. If Wilson's 1944 lockout had continued, workers could have easily found work picking cotton. Moreover, all of those who were fired or laid off after the union vote were able to find other work, including several who migrated for defense jobs. When workers went on strike in 1946, however, the wartime labor shortage was over and the nation was more hostile to unions. Facing threats from anti-union legislation and the emerging Cold War, the Congress of Industrial Organizations (CIO) itself was immersed in infighting and unable to sustain its many new southern locals.[25]

Claiborne County workers also faced aggressive repression. The box factory and Sheriff Montgomery publicized a Mississippi law designed to limit picketing, and the sheriff threatened workers, telling one man that "if he didn't go to work, he would put him in the grave yard." The sheriff tried to get the same young man to tell him about union meetings, and when he refused, he "hit him twice across the shoulders with a black jack." On another occasion, Montgomery told several picketers that if they did not move, he would make sure they never got another job and "shoot their brains out." In May 1946, Luther Buie appealed to his IWA contact in Memphis for help, writing, "We are needing some help from other locals as you know that our wages were so small that it wasn't much to be saved and our treasur[y] has just about gone. Everybody is holding out fine but are not willing to picket by themselves because a bunch of people are out there . . . with guns and high powered rifles. You know the South. These people with guns are not concerned in our strike but are threatening us with death threats."[26]

Although the IWA tried unsuccessfully to get unemployment benefits for workers, there is no evidence that the national union helped the local with financial resources or picketing. At least one other union refused their request to honor the strike. In August 1946 the NLRB ruled that the lockout imposed two years earlier constituted an unfair labor practice and insisted that the company reimburse workers for lost wages that week, but the company continued its strategy of inaction; it would take another two years and a U.S. District Court decision to force the company to comply. Despite losing this appeal, the company's policy of foot-dragging was generally quite successful in defeating workers' attempts to organize and win concessions. Even with the wartime labor shortage and active federal intervention, workers faced difficult challenges in their efforts to secure better wages and working conditions. Without the labor shortage and access to outside oversight, the striking workers had little leverage, and in the postwar years, plant management continued to dictate wages and working conditions.

CHAPTER Three

Adapting and Preserving White Supremacy

In the short term, the opportunities promised by World War II appeared somewhat illusory for African Americans, but, over time, the structural changes precipitated by the war contributed to the 1960s civil rights movement. In Claiborne County, one of the most important changes was the agricultural revolution that began with the Great Depression. Over the next three decades, planters diversified their crops—supplementing cotton with soybeans, timber, and cattle—and relied more heavily on tractors, pesticides, and cotton picking machines. These developments significantly reduced labor needs, and planters replaced sharecroppers with smaller numbers of year-round and seasonal wage hands. From 1930 to 1950, the number of black sharecroppers in Claiborne County plummeted from about 3,300 to fewer than 250. Blacks' involvement in agriculture also dropped from 81 percent of the black workforce in 1930 to less than 28 percent (which included both agricultural and forestry workers) in 1950. Despite this dramatic shift, Claiborne County's economic system remained racially segmented and strictly hierarchical. The work available to blacks generally paid little. In the mid-1940s, box factory workers earned forty cents an hour, or approximately three dollars a day. According to one woman, "If you could work out there, you were doing something." Agricultural workers typically earned fifty cents to a dollar a day, and, according to a 1961 economic report, most black farm workers could expect to work fewer than 150 days a year. In 1960, when 60 percent of white families earned more than $3,000 per year, only 10 percent of black families earned that much, and almost 48 percent earned under $1,000.[1]

Both sharecropping and the low wages paid to blacks throughout the first half of the twentieth century made children's labor essential to the survival of many black families. Asked about riddles and games from her childhood, Artemeasie Brandon responded, "[I] didn't have time for nothing like that. . . . [I was] working. Field work and house work, ironing and washing and cooking and things like that. . . . We had to hoe, pick cotton, set out potatoes." Hystercine Rankin remarked that there was always work to do and associated the passing seasons with her tasks—from working in the cotton field to quilting to gathering nuts and berries. Another black woman recalled, "As far back as I can remember, I went to the fields, and when I was big enough to hoe my row, I hoed my row with my mother." For J. L. Sayles, work began when he was a "little boy, about big enough to tote in stove wood." He and his siblings did chores for a nearby white family, and his mother "give us a dime and she take that other money and buy groceries or something with it, whatever she needed." Another man, who observed that he "was kind of small," was spending whole days cutting wood by the time he was eleven or twelve. "That's pretty rough to work all day. . . . I didn't like it, but this was a matter of survival." A woman who grew up in the 1960s reported that during the harvest season, she stayed out of school every other day to pick cotton. The rest of the year she worked for a white family after school, using the twenty-five-cent wages intended for her school lunch to buy cans of pork and beans for her family's supper.[2]

In contrast, white children's work was generally less integral to family survival. In a *Port Gibson Reveille* column about his 1940s childhood, E. T. Crisler wrote that "Saturday morning was never any holiday for me" and then described raking his front yard for fifty cents to spend on a movie and refreshments. Mott Headley, a white man who grew up on his family's plantation during the Depression, justified the poor wages paid African Americans by connecting them to his family's fears of losing their land (which housed twelve tenant families) and insisted that everyone was poor. "Back then nobody had anything." There was, however, never any danger that he would have to quit school to contribute to his family's support. Like Crisler, he had spending money for Saturday entertainment and even owned a car while still in high school. Other whites acknowledge having easy childhoods. One woman explained that white kids "didn't mature very fast" and another said, "I'm afraid I didn't do a whole lot of work."[3]

Whether blacks worked as sharecroppers or in factories, as day laborers, domestics, or pulp-wood haulers, they continued to do arduous, menial, sporadic, and poorly paid work. For example, box factory workers labored in primi-

African American Port Gibson Cottonseed Oil Mill workers, 1909. Photograph by Leigh Briscoe Allen, courtesy Mississippi Department of Archives and History.

tive conditions with only rudimentary equipment. One man recalled that when his mother loaded lumber in the winter, she wore long underwear and three or four pairs of pants to try to stay warm. In contrast, employees in the drying kiln had to withstand extreme heat. As in sharecropping, box factory bosses were demanding and capricious with the authority to layoff, fire, and discipline workers at will. They expected workers to comply with last-minute overtime demands and work overtime for the regular pay rate. When machines broke down, they docked workers' pay, sometimes for twice as long as the machine was broken. One worker recalled that a foreman asked him to do two jobs simulta-neously and promised to pay him the salary of two workers. The man did the work but never received the extra pay. Another worker testified that his super-visor was "half mad" and often refused to stop the conveyor belt when it was getting jammed up.[4]

White employers regularly insisted that blacks work long hours. According to one man, "It wasn't no such thing as eight hours. It was from sunup to sundown at fifty cents a day." A farmer remembered that "back then, they didn't allow us to

African Americans on the Allen plantation posing with cotton they picked, 1911.
Photograph by Leigh Briscoe Allen, courtesy Mississippi Department of Archives and
History.

put a watch on your arm. . . . When you couldn't see, that's when you quit. And
when you could see in the morning, that's when you went to work." Another
black man described how his white employer reacted when he and his brothers
stopped chopping cotton to walk the five miles home: "He say, 'What you all
doing knocking off?' [I] say, 'It time.' 'Naw,' he say, 'No, you all going back, work
till lightning bugs come out.' And we went back there and hoed. You could see
the lightning bugs, too. . . . We worked till the lightning bugs come out."[5]

The box factory followed the plantation model and gave employees advances
against their paychecks that could only be redeemed at a company commissary
that " 'furnished' what one needed until payday." Workers also had to rely on
personal relationships and employer goodwill instead of a formal procedure
when they applied for work, sought reinstatement after a layoff, or tried to get a
day off. A black woman whose mother worked at the box factory recalled that
"you had to know somebody" to get a job there. Her mother paid off her straw
boss to keep her job, and "that's how she worked for a long time." Although
factory work was usually more consistent than agricultural work, it was still

somewhat informal and sporadic. The box factory occasionally shut down for lack of work, and the Port Gibson Oil Mill was explicitly seasonal, pressing the yearly harvest of cotton seed into oil. Most black oil mill workers were also farmers and worked at the mill during the off-season or at night. During peak agricultural seasons, some box factory workers took days or weeks off to drive tractors or pick cotton.[6]

African Americans responded to the low wages and the irregular, dead-end nature of the available work by trying to piece together a living. Many raised gardens, hunted for food, and, according to folklorist Worth Long, relied on "ingenuity." When Annie Holloway was first married, she and her husband had no work and briefly subsisted on the food that they could pick, catch, or trade for. Nate Jones, who had fourteen brothers and sisters, remembered that during the Depression he and his brothers farmed during the day and took turns hunting at night. With the price of cotton down, he explained, they turned "to different things to survive," eating the meat and selling the furs. Many blacks, like Charlie Miller, worked multiple jobs. He worked nights for ten years at the oil mill while sharecropping during the day. He also helped build the Natchez Trace parkway, worked on a Quarter Boat on the Mississippi River, sold produce, and did a series of odd jobs for Port Gibson merchants. According to his son, Miller constantly sought the best possible living for himself and his family. For example, his work at the John Deere store helped him buy the tractor that freed his children from farm work so they could go to school.[7] A black man with a similar work history explained, "[I did] different things—cut sprouts, plow mules, hoe, set out potatoes, everything." He hauled logs out of the woods, rolled concrete in a wheel barrow, uprooted stumps with dynamite, and helped build highways and roads. Sharecroppers and small farm owners almost invariably did wage work during slack times. George Aikerson, who bought a farm through the Tenant Purchase Program, described how he supported his family and paid the mortgage: "Now I was young and logging. . . . Be about 8 o'clock [P.M.] and be farming time. I'd go out there and disk till 3 o'clock in the morning. Come back up here and wake her up. She cook my breakfast, and I'd get in the car and go back to the woods, and I could do that two nights and work in the woods longer than you." Lydell Page sold burial insurance and did farm, sawmill, and construction work before working as a paper hanger. His comment that he "scuffled" to make a living was probably apt for much of the county's black community. After describing his childhood and work life, another black man concluded, "I come up the hard way. It was so rough I reckon I wouldn't even talk about it. Pretty rough back then, rough."[8]

The legacy of slavery and the low wages paid African Americans allowed most white families to employ black maids and laborers to do domestic and yard work. As a result, white children grew up in close proximity to black people, sometimes with considerable intimacy. One white woman recalled, "I was raised by this colored woman with a daughter my age . . . and she breast fed me. I sat on one side and [her daughter] was on the other." Bill Lum's family employed a black "gardener and sort of a handy man" who "just kinda belonged to my father. He was raised there and his sister was our nurse." The black servant "built the fires in each fireplace every morning before daylight in the winter time." Lum explained that because the servant came in before his white employers were out of bed, he announced his presence by coughing "to let us know it was him coming in. The doors were never locked. He come on in like that." A white woman described the black families who lived on her family's plantation as "friends, as well as servants." These black friends/servants did the cooking, washing, and yard work and nursed the children. Another white woman recalled that "a large, wonderful black family, lived on our place as long as I can remember, probably before I was born." Her description illustrates the extensive nature of black service to white employers. "As a young man, John worked in the fields and as he grew older, helping around the house. He always turned the ice-cream freezer, made fires, fed the dogs, stayed with us when our parents went out for the evening, and was, in general, a great man to know." She concluded, "He was indeed, a devoted, trustworthy, kind, and gentle friend. John was like family to us." Another white woman said that she "had a wonderful black lady" who took care of her children. She insisted, "I loved [her] more than anybody I can probably talk about."[9]

At times, these relationships were helpful to blacks. Worth Long explains that "in white southern culture," the "people who work for you . . . became part of your family." As a result, "some white families helped in the education of . . . their servants' children. It's part of the system." A black woman who graduated from Claiborne County Training School in 1954 attended college with help from a scholarship acquired through a white Port Gibson church and a loan secured by her mother's white employer. Nate and Julia Jones developed important relationships with two white men, banker Eli Ellis and school superintendent Robert Segrest, who hunted on their property. Nate Jones believed hunting with Ellis facilitated his yearly agricultural loans from the bank, and Segrest encouraged Julia Jones to complete college; when she did, he hired her to teach. Nate Jones also worked for the school system, supplementing his farm income by driving a bus part time. Another black woman alluded to the assistance whites could offer when she recalled how her husband advised her brothers as they left Mississippi: "And Zeke, when he carried them, he said, 'Now, you ain't got Mr. Segrest.'

African American household worker with the white children in her charge, 1908. Photograph by Leigh Briscoe Allen, courtesy Mississippi Department of Archives and History.

That's them white people back out home that writes you a letter if you get in trouble or come to bond you out. And Zeke say, 'Now, you ain't got Mr. Shelton [Segrest] to help get you out of trouble.' "[10]

When white merchants described their interactions with black customers, they often framed them in personal terms. Mott Headley, who farmed and owned a small country store explained, "I paid [for] folks to get their tooth pulled. I paid midwives to come and get their baby out. And if it died, I paid to get it buried. Course I got my money back, I'm not talking about that. . . . That was just part of what I was doing. And my store was a country store; 90 percent probably of my . . . business was with blacks." In 1960, a merchant claimed that his business had "aided many of its customers, both white and colored, to obtain their own land and has acted as advisor and guardian angel to many of them in time of trouble." In the 1990s, merchant Rosalie Ellis Abraham insisted with pride that she told "black people how to do things. How to wait on their sick children and everything. . . . If they needed me for medicine or advice or anything, and I believe right to this day you could ask them, would I give them advice. And I would." Albert Butler, a black man who worked for the Piggly Wiggly grocery store owned by James, George, and H. B. Hudson, recalls that James Hudson was always "doing things for customers." For example, James Hudson charged people to fill out "their income tax form." Even though Hudson made money from this service, Butler insisted that both Hudson and his customers understood it as "a means of helping" and customers "was appreciative so they did business with him."[11]

Merchants and customers often characterized their interactions in terms of favors or kindnesses. They highlighted the service or merchandise more than the eventual repayment and usually failed to mention the high interest charges that were added to customers' bills. A former sharecropper who had credit arrangements with several members of the Ellis family described Jim Ellis as "real nice" and explained that when her husband worked on a Louisiana sugar farm, she relied on credit from one of Ellis's nieces. Although she paid her bills regularly, she still emphasized the merchants' willingness to extend credit, explaining that they "never did stop letting us have anything." Nate Jones developed ties with another member of the Ellis family when Michael Ellis gave him a pair of shoes on credit. Jones had twenty-five cents for a down payment and paid for the shoes fifty cents at a time. Based on that experience, he went on to buy most of his clothes, including expensive Sunday suits, from Ellis. Perhaps granting credit was understood as a gift or measure of friendship because it could so easily be withheld. Nate Jones got new shoes at the whim of Michael Ellis, who told him, "I believe you a good boy. I believe you will pay." In this instance, Ellis's act of goodwill, trusting a fourteen-year-old boy to make good on an approximately two-dollar debt, helped Jones. However, those conventions also reinforced blacks' dependence on whites for access to resources. As an adult, Jones explained that "the only way we could survive" was "through credit" from whites. During the box factory union drive, an employee testified that her boss said the union was "putting the white people against us so they wouldn't loan us anything."[12]

All these interracial interactions were strongly influenced by white power, and whites' claims of friendship with blacks were often embellished or inaccurate descriptions of more complex associations. For example, the "colored friends" who attended the funeral of white merchant Aaron Frishman would not have been invited to dinner. Melvin McFatter, a white man whose father owned a pharmacy in Port Gibson, saw some of these contradictions firsthand. He recalled that a black woman who worked for his family for many years "was treated almost like a member of the family as far as confidence. . . . Despite all of that, when we would sit down to eat . . . she ate in the kitchen and we ate in the breakfast room." The situation was even more ironic since the two rooms were connected by a small opening and while the black servant and white family ate in separate rooms, they conversed back and forth. Neil McMillen asserts that "whites generally read more into these acts of interracial humanity than did blacks." Yet he argues that "the personal affections and the frequent courtesies were nonetheless genuine and they form a small but important part of a very complex story." McFatter also noted this inconsistency, explaining, "Now black people and white people have worked together, you know, side by side and hand in hand, for years. That was alright, but nothing whatsoever on the social level."[13]

Claiborne County whites were bound together by similar attitudes about race and by the benefits of white supremacy, including the exploitation of black labor, disproportionate access to income and resources, and political power based on black disfranchisement. In 1960, for example, when 90 percent of black families earned less than $1,000 annually, white median family income was between $4,000 and $4,999. However, unlike blacks, most of whom shared similar economic circumstances, whites' income was spread through the census categories in roughly equal proportions. For example, sixty-five white families, or 9.3 percent of the total, made over $10,000, and fifty families, or 7.1 percent of the total, made under $1,000. The single largest group, ninety-one families, or 12.98 percent, made between $6,000 and $6,999. The wealthiest and most powerful whites were bankers, big plantation owners, and select merchants and professionals. Subscribing to the aristocratic or feudal traditions that shaped the community's race-based hierarchy, they claimed to speak and act for the universal good of the community, including whites and blacks. Moreover, they typically passed wealth and status from one generation to the next.[14]

The Gages provide an important illustration of the way leadership, occupation, and status were passed down through families. Robert Douglass (R. D.) Gage was born in 1861 in a Port Gibson house with adjacent slave quarters. His father was arrested briefly by General Ulysses Grant's soldiers and then removed from his clerk of court office in 1869 for being an "impediment to Reconstruction." After spending thirty-three years in Texas, where he worked as a lawyer, politician, and banker, Gage returned to Port Gibson and bought the controlling interest in the Port Gibson Bank, housed on Main Street in an antebellum structure built by slaves. He ran the bank with help from his son R. D. Gage Jr. (b. 1897), until his retirement in 1953. Judge Gage, as the older man was called, was a longtime trustee of the town's private boys school, Chamberlain Hunt Academy (CHA), and an avid participant in civic and community events. R. D. Gage Jr., who succeeded him as president and chairman of the board of the bank, was also on the CHA board of trustees, chair of the 1948 States' Rights Finance Committee, a regular on the county Democratic committee, and a leader in other civic organizations. R. D. "Bobby" Gage III practiced law in Port Gibson for five years and then began his own bank career in 1951. He continued the family tradition of political and civic work, leading the local Democratic Party Executive Committee for many years and working with the Lions Club and chamber of commerce. In the 1980s, Robert D. Gage IV became the fourth generation to lead the Port Gibson Bank. Joan Wheeless Beesley, whose family claimed similar power and status, observed that although bankers never "ran for public office," they were dominant community leaders. She described them as "sort of institutions" and explained that "leadership passed through generations in some families."[15]

Joan Beesley's grandfather G. W. Wheeless was a founder of the Port Gibson Oil Mill in 1882, served as a town alderman for over a decade, and gained the controlling interest in Port Gibson Bank before selling it to Judge Gage in 1918. His son (Joan Beesley's father), J. C. Wheeless, was the superintendent and part owner of the box factory and had one of the community's longest tenures on the board of aldermen, putting in over three decades after his first term in 1940. The Allen family also passed wealth and power through the generations. James Bennett (J. B.) Allen grew up on his uncle's cotton plantation, fought for the Confederacy, and developed a lucrative hybrid "upland long-staple" cotton. He was involved in the White Man's Party, which overthrew the integrated Republican Reconstruction government, and he had accumulated considerable wealth by the time he died, including an 800-acre plantation and a stake in Mississippi

Southern Bank. His son Leigh Briscoe (L. B.) Allen inherited a vast fortune, including the plantation that Annie Holloway lived on as a tenant farmer, and served as either mayor or alderman for more than a decade. When he retired, he was replaced by his son James (Jimmy) Allen, who, together with his brother, L. B. Allen Jr. (who served as alderman while Jimmy was away during World War II), kept the family represented on the board of aldermen for well over two decades.[16]

Other families, including the Drake-Satterfield lawyers and the newspaper owning Crislers, also had a strong multigenerational presence in the community's leadership class and elective offices. For example, J. T. Drake Sr. served as mayor and J. T. Drake Jr. as alderman. Their in-law, M. M. Satterfield, spent many years as alderman, mayor, and county prosecuting attorney. With most of the community's decision-making power centered in elite families and blacks essentially disfranchised, Claiborne County elections were marked by widespread apathy. In one extreme example, only thirteen individuals cast votes in the 1942 mayoral and aldermanic election.[17] In general, elective bodies were secondary to civic/service clubs in developing public policy. For many years, the *Reveille*'s account of the weekly Lions Club luncheon meetings contained the first public indication of impending community projects—like efforts to attract industry, pass bond issues for building schools, or establish recreation facilities. A county history described the all-white Lions Club, chartered in the mid-1930s, as serving the function of a chamber of commerce.

From its founding through the 1960s, the Lions Club was composed of about forty to fifty of the community's elite men, bringing together those who held political office and those whose leadership came through wealth and family status. Over the years, the Lions Club initiated or weighed in on a wide range of projects and issues. For example, club members passed resolutions asking the state board of trustees to retain a retiring Alcorn College president, condemning unions, and promoting states' rights. They evaluated proposals for a local sales tax, initiated Negro school improvement efforts in the late 1940s, worked to install lighting for night football games at Chamberlain Hunt Academy, encouraged the founding of a chamber of commerce, and endorsed bond issues for industrial plants. They entertained speakers from the local community and around the state, including politicians like Senator John Stennis and eventual governor Ross Barnett.[18]

White political and civic leaders took advantage of black disfranchisement to protect their economic interests. This is evident in their post–World War II efforts to supplement the declining cotton plantation system with new industry. In September 1952, the mayor laid out whites' rationale for securing an industrial plant, writing:

Merchants, banks, lawyers and so forth have subsisted upon what farmers and their farm workers spent. As long as cotton was the big crop, every plantation supported many people who had to buy things for their living and working. Now cattle are taking the place of cotton and the plantations don't need as many people to operate them. The result is that many are thrown off the land and have to leave the community to make a living. That means that there are fewer people left to buy from the merchants, fewer to do business with the banks, fewer to provide work for professional people, etc.

The mayor showed little empathy for the people "thrown off the land." His concern was with the white merchants and professionals who, as one said, "couldn't sell overalls to a cow." The drive for new industry was jump-started in August 1952 when Port Gibson Bank president R. D. Gage Jr. announced his support and reassured (white) farmers that the industrial drive was not intended to undermine the community's agricultural economy. In October 1952, Port Gibson voters followed the lead of their civic and political leaders and approved, by a 273 to 9 majority, a bond to build a factory site. In January 1954, the new company, American Paper Tube, began taking applications for employment from white men and women only, and the first new factory opened in just over three years.[19]

In April 1955, before the plant was running at full capacity, union organizers approached the white workers and won an NLRB supervised election. The white elite reacted with outrage, threatening that a union would force the plant to close, leaving taxpayers to repay the building bond without rent from an industrial tenant. Moreover, the mayor assured workers that the company would offer them a raise as soon as it was making a sufficient profit. Unlike the black box factory workers (discussed in Chapter 2), the newly hired white employees heeded the pleas of the community elite and, suggestive of their linked interests, asked the NLRB to cancel the election. The union disappeared, and the wages spent by the several hundred new factory employees bolstered downtown businesses. Based on this success, the same core of individuals, organizations, and businesses sought a second bond issue, built another industrial plant, and wooed a plastics plant to Port Gibson in late 1959. Although 525 of the 651 respondents to a 1957 labor survey done in preparation for the new plant were black, initially this plant, too, hired only whites. When the pool of available white workers proved inadequate, both factories began to hire black workers, though they continued to reserve the best jobs and shifts for white workers.[20]

Between 1954 and 1965, Claiborne County whites reinforced and extended their disproportionate access to resources and opportunity by building a swimming pool, a man-made lake for fishing and boating, and a country club. These all preserved segregation, in part, by diverting ostensibly public resources to the sole benefit of the white community. The pool project, for example, was started by the chamber of commerce, which urged people to donate money because "We owe it to our young people and to our community." Initiated just months after the *Brown* decision ruled school segregation unconstitutional, the pool was set up as a private, members-only corporation to exclude blacks. Jimmy Allen, at the time a member of the board of aldermen, the chamber of commerce, the Lions Club, and the local Democratic Party Executive Committee, explained later that as white leaders planned and developed recreational facilities, segregation was one of their primary considerations: "If we made it public, then it was gonna be an integrated situation. . . . Well for years and years and years that was the thing more or less that had to be considered. If you wanted a recreation, social event, and all, you had some undesirables you didn't want." Though the pool was financed primarily by private donations, whites referred to it as a community project and used public resources in its construction and maintenance. More-over, all whites, not simply contributors, were able to use the pool. African Americans briefly challenged this practice during the 1960s, but the pool has remained whites-only into the twenty-first century. Similar procedures were used to build private, whites-only Lake Claiborne, an artificial lake covering 110 acres, and Mosswood Country Club. At a Lions Club meeting, a member of the Fish and Game Commission offered to stock Lake Claiborne with fish and help in any other way that he could, while Mosswood Country Club was built with a Federal Housing Authority (FHA) loan.[21]

In addition to being discriminated against in jobs and excluded from recreation facilities and ostensibly public institutions, most blacks lived in poor housing and had inadequate public services. Black neighborhoods were typically located on narrow, poorly constructed streets, and many remained outside the town limits, where they were excluded from municipal water, sewerage, and garbage pickup. Streets in white neighborhoods were wider and better maintained, and most had sidewalks installed by WPA workers during the Depression. Some whites who lived outside the city limits actually had better public services than blacks in town. Few black neighborhoods had paved or maintained roads, and none had curbs or sidewalks. Blacks were disproportionately congregated in flood-prone areas. A 1945 legal brief described the typical housing of box factory workers as "two rooms of about 8×12 space" located in low-lying areas without running water or a sewage system. These housing conditions contributed to "a great deal of sickness," because "in low areas during the flood season or during heavy rains it is necessary for the occupants to move from their homes. After the high water recedes, of course, mosquitoes and other insects multiply greatly and create a very unhealthy condition." In 1968, a visiting attorney found similar conditions, describing one street as "quite incredible." He wrote, "Three houses have outhouses and/or cesspools," and on one side of the street "the connecting pipes are fitted with cement and quite inadequate. When the toilet is flushed a great deal of liquid waste escapes the pipes and flows behind the houses down into the ditch or stream."[22]

In the 1940s, when Port Gibson residents voted to borrow money for street improvements, black homeowners, whose tax rates increased, did not get to vote and did not receive the services. Moreover, the white electorate voted several times to institute and then increase a Port Gibson sales tax to support public services. One increase was explicitly presented as an alternative to an increase in property taxes.[23] Since whites owned more property with higher tax values than blacks, this diverted the tax burden to propertyless shoppers, many of whom resided outside of town. So not only were whites in Port Gibson disproportionately served by the town government, but blacks who lived in the county but shopped in Port Gibson subsidized the provision of those services for whites.

Blacks living in rural areas, governed by the board of supervisors, experienced comparable disparities. When Mott Headley was elected supervisor for District 2, he pledged to fix the roads in the poorest condition first. He found that the worst area was a "colored settlement" called Short Fork, which "was kinda unbelievable." He explained, "It was just dirt and water holes for the drain. And they had to walk out to meet the school bus when it was bad and all. And I got some criticism, but that's the first place I started." Headley insisted that he repaired Short Fork even though blacks "couldn't even vote then. It wasn't for their vote."[24] Though he offered this as evidence of his fairness, black electoral exclusion explains why there was such disrepair in the first place.

With no electoral power, blacks' only hope for influence or access to resources was through white benevolence or goodwill. A black man who went to school in the early 1960s remembered being acutely aware of the unequal "facilities and amenities" in the black and white sections of town. When he suggested to his teachers that blacks should present a petition to the mayor to procure change, one of his teachers said, "Well, you know, it's a little difficult getting their ear, but when you grow up, you can do that." Years later, he appreciated the way she handled his suggestion, concluding, "I guess it quieted the issue, but still was a way of reinforcing that these ideas were good ideas, but there wasn't a sympathetic ear or way to get these things accomplished." In several instances, black residents did petition whites. In 1950, newspaper editor H. H. Crisler wrote, "Some colored citizens have appealed to the *Reveille* in an effort to see if something could not be done to have the Board of Mayor and Aldermen improve their streets. They state that those residents of the back streets almost have to fight their way through weeds and grass to get to their homes. Added to this discomfiture, they are without street lights." Crisler supported their request, arguing that the town should encourage efforts, "by white and colored," to improve their homes and suggested that the town use those arrested on Saturday nights to do the physical labor. Evidently, neither the entreaty nor Crisler's proposed solution did much good, and he received another plea a year later. This time Crisler's editorial response included a much more active endorsement. Reporting that town officials claimed to have no money for repairs, he wrote, "Nothing has been done to these short streets for years, and it isn't fair to those living there to exact taxes without giving something in return."[25]

In the 1990s, H. H. Crisler's grandson emphasized that his grandfather had liked "all his helpers, black and white." Furthermore, he said, his grandfather was "slow to anger" and did not own a gun, borrowing one only when he thought the "Ku Klux Klan was going to storm the Claiborne County Court House and terrorize Black people and Roman Catholics." According to the family story, H. H. Crisler said that he had to "protect the many lovely Blacks and our Roman Catholic relatives." Crisler was one of the most consistent white advocates for improved educational facilities for African Americans. His protective attitudes can be seen in some of his political views as well. While he opposed antilynching laws, he advocated the prosecution and punishment of whites accused of crimes against black women and children. After a particularly egregious case in which accused lynchers were acquitted despite significant evidence, Crisler even conceded that a federal law might be necessary if southerners would not convict lynchers.[26]

Crisler's support for public services for the blacks who appealed for help is an example of his periodic advocacy for African Americans, but it also illustrates clearly the limits of the paternalism that he and many other whites believed in. Without power, blacks were dependent on white goodwill, and that goodwill generally failed whenever it competed with white economic interests. Moreover, Crisler's support did not extend to black equality or access to voting rights. During the World War II union organizing drive, he was one of the white leaders who discouraged blacks from joining the union, opening an appeal to black workers by writing, "the friendship of a host of Negroes throughout Claiborne County is valued highly and appreciated by the *Reveille*." Based on this and his claim that he had fought many "battles for justice and fairness for them," Crisler expected blacks to listen to his "straight reasoning" and, in this case, reject the union.[27] Even as he pushed the town's elected officials to repair a few black streets, Crisler assumed white superiority and believed, as did most of the community's elite whites, that southern whites should dictate race relations and control black opportunities.

CHAPTER Four

Working for a Better Day

Publicly, African Americans had to conform to white expectations in order to survive, but, privately, their responses were complicated and widely varied. Considering black life before the civil rights movement, Julia Jones, who became one of the county's earliest black elected officials, reflected, "I wonder how we could sing and dance and play at that time when . . . there was so much prejudice and I guess we just took it for granted cause we was born in it."[1] As Jones's comment suggests, although white supremacy was the context for black life, as much a part of Mississippi as the unrelenting heat of summer, it was not necessarily the focal point. Many African Americans accepted the outward limitations while simultaneously retaining an internal sense of self that nurtured a desire for a better life and more equitable world.

The psychological weight of white supremacy could be difficult to combat. One black landowner observed that some blacks "didn't think they could live if it wasn't on Mr. So-and-So's place." Charlie Miller, who worked multiple jobs to raise his family's living standard, described his understanding of how white supremacy was internalized: "See a child can't do no better than he taught. . . . When they brought us over here from Africa, the white man taught us what we know. . . . That grew up in you. He was more than I am. Hell, he better than me, see. That what come about." Miller's son James, who joined the civil rights movement as a high school student, called the premovement period a "time warp." He described how the inequities of the time seemed somehow normal to a child coming of age, insisting that it "didn't mean nothing cause that's the way society was. . . . If you never been exposed to anything else, you don't know that there is something else, so you assume that that's the way it is." A black lawyer and activist who worked with Miller in the late 1960s recalled having to combat the white power structure's ability "to influence the perceptions of reality that black folks had," including some blacks' persistent belief that "white folks were right."[2]

The notion that white is right may have been a side effect of the power whites wielded, but many black parents were able to instill a sense of self-worth and an alternative value system in their children. When white children spit on Marjorie Brandon from buses while she walked to school, her father tried to offer some consolation. He told her, "'Well that's just the way the whites treat the blacks.' He say, 'I read my Bible and I really do believe that the rail that's on the bottom is not going to always be on the bottom.' He would always tell me that cause I just could not understand it. I just feel like it was so cruel." Later, when she had her own children, Brandon was determined "that they would never, I didn't know how I was gonna do it, but I said that they would never be a servant for anybody." Her oldest son, Ken, recalled that she refused to let her children buy hamburgers during trips to Port Gibson because the café would only serve blacks out of a window in the back. "Mom couldn't stand that. And we got hungry. 'You can wait until you get home.' She would never allow us—. 'If I can't have it out of the front door, my money is not good as yours.' But that was part of her. 'I will not stoop to that.'" His father also emphasized self-respect and taught his children to "always look people in the eye."[3]

Other black parents taught their children similar lessons. One of Ken Brandon's childhood friends, whose parents were tenant purchasers in the Alcorn area, remembered that her father demanded that she and her siblings "always count the change" when they went to stores to "make sure we weren't short-changed, let people know we could count." When James Dorsey began to question segregation when he was about ten, his parents helped him understand white expectations. He explained, "We survived by our parents letting us know what was happening, what we should do in order to survive and get through this." Still, his parents refused to allow white supremacy to define their family, emphasizing to their children that "there would be a better day" and teaching them to be loving, honest, caring, and to "give out an honest day's work . . . [even though] we were underpaid."[4]

Blacks used a variety of strategies to improve their circumstances, and one of the simplest was moving. Many left the county altogether, sometimes to avoid trouble with whites and sometimes in pursuit of freer lives. From 1900 to 1920, the Claiborne County black population declined nearly 60 percent from 16,222 to 9,594. By 1960, it had dropped to 8,934. Another important black survival strategy was to avoid whites. According to Neil McMillen, most blacks tried "to minimize contact with whites wherever possible and to appear obedient when necessary." This was true in Claiborne County. One man asserted, "Most black parents at the time that could, tried to keep their kids away from some of the more obvious aspects of segregation. For instance, I don't remember ever going to a restaurant that had separate facilities for black people and white people. That was just, was sort of an insult . . . you didn't have to face." Hystercine Rankin reported that her great-grandfather "didn't want his children to ever work for any whites, especially his daughters, because he knew how the white men would be after them." At least part of Ken Brandon's uncertainty about the appropriate way to address a young white boy came from his personal "lack of contact with whites." Julia Jones said that as a child she was slow to learn about using courtesy titles with whites because she "didn't work around them." She explained, "We worked in the fields, but we didn't work in the house. If I'd worked in the house, naturally, I would have learned early to do it." Another black woman recalled being surprised when she encountered prejudice, because she "had never . . . been around [whites] or anything."[5]

In general, blacks sought refuge and autonomy in family and community. This separate world, centered around churches and schools, nurtured and sustained black people. Historian, singer, composer, and activist Bernice Johnson Reagon explains,

> Black people created in this land a world, and I grew up in that world. We really had to use whatever territory we could create, to take care of the business of making a people. And often that territory was not land, often that territory was cultural. And that's why African American culture is one of the most powerful in the world, because we had to get so much business done in that arena because it was an area we had control over. And the place where my people taught me the full range of my power as a human being was inside the black community and that took place in church, in school, on the playground.

In Claiborne County, churches provided social space and spiritual support. One woman remembered, "We practically grew up in the church." Another said, "I ain't never have no pleasure. Went to church—that was my pleasure." The yearly revivals, which coincided with the lay-by season (when the cotton crop had been hoed for the last time and was not yet ripe for picking), brought community members and relatives together for nightly meetings. One woman recalled visiting her mother's country relatives for the summer revival: "They never had just one preacher; it would be maybe two or three. I just loved the singing. One of the exciting things was at the end of the week when the revival meeting was over. Women started to cooking on Friday, you know. They take big boxes and baskets of food on that final Sunday, and oh, we used to love it."[6]

By 1951, there were four well-established black churches in Port Gibson and many more scattered throughout the county. The small, wooden buildings reflected the poverty and isolation of their congregations and African American determination to sustain their churches and ministers. One resident recalled with wonder that the small Westside community maintained three churches, and a minister remembered his congregation supporting him with food and twenty-five-cent payments.[7] Most of the community's ministers were poorly educated men who became preachers through "a call from God," and none of the pre-movement ministers in Claiborne County supported themselves solely through preaching. To supplement their earnings, they often served multiple congregations, with most churches offering services once a month and most blacks attending more than one church.

As one of the few gathering places available for blacks, churches were essential for meetings and sharing information. A white businessman peddled his funeral home and burial insurance in black churches, while black leaders used churches to organize a competing, noncommercial burial insurance to help poor families bury their relatives with dignity. Alcorn College professors and the Negro county agent advised congregations about federal programs and shared information about new farming techniques. Some ministers kept their congregations informed about current events, especially those that directly affected blacks. James Dorsey, who became a minister himself, recalled that when he was a child, ministers "would talk and preach and counsel and tell us about upcoming things." He explained that this was critically important because "we didn't know too much about the legislative bodies and what they were doing and everything." He added that most black people "didn't get very many newspapers and they didn't have very many radios and things like that," so they relied on getting information "through others."[8]

Some ministers also addressed practical issues related to self-improvement and community-building, encouraging their congregants to pursue education and landowning, for example. Reverend Eugene Spencer, who purchased land near Alcorn College and became the county's most prominent black minister in the 1950s and early 1960s, was one of those men who insisted that blacks not simply wait for the "rewards of heaven." He explained that his personal desire for education and material comfort, including things like a refrigerator and "a nice home to live in," influenced his approach to the ministry. According to Spencer,

Reverend Eugene Spencer, Tenant Purchase Program participant, community leader, and prominent minister, preaching at Mercy Seat Baptist Church in 1982. Photograph by Roland L. Freeman, courtesy Roland L. Freeman.

"In those years I was a little more radical than I am now. And I often said I didn't want the choir to sing 'You May Have All the World and Give Me Jesus' on Sunday Morning. I don't think you ought to sing nothing you don't believe. Well, I wanted some of the world and Jesus, too." He said that some people initially disapproved of this view. "You see, it wasn't too well accepted . . . from the preacher. He was suppose to get up and take his text and preach, and let those things alone. I soon convinced my congregation that all of it go together." He remained assured that his congregation was well served by his approach: "I think I'm responsible for a lot of people's buying land, educating their families and some of 'em often tell me so."[9]

Ministers rarely challenged the status quo directly, but black religious services did encourage black congregants to envision and strive for a world with different parameters. Ministers like Spencer fought against passivity and discouraged their congregations from accepting inferior material conditions. In addition, many songs and sermons could be understood in multiple ways. According to Bernice Johnson Reagon, many common phrases that emphasized movement and change, like "crossing over" and "in the morning," could apply to a spiritual nurturing of the soul or to "any everyday practical situation." Ministers often chose texts and sermon topics that emphasized freedom and transformation, returning again and again to the story of "Moses leading the children out of Egypt." As a result, Reagon argues that the black church played a critical role in "making a way in this world that would give us a chance to be different from the recipe that brought us here."[10]

Like churches, schools provided social space and spiritual nourishment. Year-end school-closing celebrations brought the community together for a communal meal and a program where children sang, gave speeches, performed in plays, competed in spelling bees, and showed off their learning. Folklorist Worth Long maintains that for Claiborne County blacks, education "was one of the dominant values." Before the civil rights movement, all blacks might not have agreed about the importance of "the right to vote and voting themselves." But if "you ask them about the value of education, as the central element past religion, past Jesus, then they would probably say, 'Yes, I think this is the most important thing . . . to my family historically, to myself now, and to my future generation.' "[11]

Despite blacks' support and even hunger for learning, their educational opportunities were extremely limited. Throughout the late 1950s, Claiborne County had two separate public school systems—one in the county and one in Port Gibson—and each of those operated separate schools for blacks and whites. The county system had no high schools, but when white students graduated from the eighth grade, they were bused to town to attend Port Gibson High School. Blacks who lived in the county and wanted to continue school after the eighth grade could go to either Claiborne County Training School (CCTS) in Port Gibson (which stopped at the tenth grade until 1942) or Alcorn High School operated by the college. However, they had to provide their own transportation or, more commonly, find a way to move nearby, living with relatives or paying for room and board.[12]

Until the 1950s, when threats of school desegregation and legal action led to new schools and bus transportation, most black students went to one of the nearly fifty rural one- and two-teacher schools that ended with the eighth grade. The school term for blacks was tied to the cotton crop and varied in length from four to seven months. Even with this shortened schedule, black children often had to miss school to work, and most dropped out well before their eighth-grade graduation. Few blacks could afford to buy school books, and many had a difficult time reaching school in bad winter weather. J. L. Sayles, who was only able to finish second grade, recalled, "We black folks, we didn't have anything. Just had to do the best we can and back there I didn't even have a chance to go to school. My mother bought me a book and that's the only thing that she ever bought. One book each and we was the ones to make a decision, what kind of book we wanted, speller, writing, mathematic." As late as 1960, almost two-thirds of the county's black adults over twenty-five had not completed eighth grade.[13]

Despite the persistence of inadequate resources and competing work demands, black school attendance began to improve in the decades after World War II. Influenced by wartime changes in the economy and by the national NAACP's attack on school inequalities, larger numbers of blacks graduated from both the eighth and the twelfth grades. In the 1944–45 school year, high levels of black attrition were reflected in the disproportionate numbers of black students in the lowest grades. For example, 32 percent of black students in the county system were in the first grade and only 5 percent were in the eighth grade. The numbers were similar in Port Gibson, with 32 percent of the black students in the first grade and 6 percent in the eighth grade. Only nine students, 1 percent of the total, were enrolled in the newly added twelfth grade at CCTS. By 1954–55, more black students were able to stay in school. For example, 9 percent of the students in the county system were in the eighth grade, and in Port Gibson, the number of students in the twelfth grade had increased to sixty in 1955.[14]

Although little more than shacks, the small schools scattered throughout the county were invested with the black community's collective hopes for a better world for their children. Blacks subsidized county education funds by supplying firewood, doing unpaid repair work, using church buildings for schools, providing transportation, and supplementing teacher salaries. Teachers and students were resourceful, making the best of poorly constructed schools and minimal facilities. At a school built on stilts, for example, the teacher had part of the class work underneath the building until it was their turn to recite the day's lesson. Students shared books, wrote their lessons in the dirt, and, in the winter, chopped wood for heat.[15]

Many students and their families made sacrifices to pursue education. Ezekiel Rankin explained that his parents "weren't educated, but they done everything they could to send us to school, at least through high school." He added, "I've heard my daddy say that he would eat corn bread and drink water, standing between the plow handles, if he could just see to it that we, you know, went to school." For Nate Jones, farm work came before school, but he was a motivated student: when he missed school, he did his assignments by lamplight after the day's chores. This was possible because his father could afford to buy him schoolbooks, and Jones remembered, "I treasured them. See, I always wanted to go to college and I never had the chance." In another family, a young man gave up his grade-school education to help a sibling attend college: "We had one sister, she went to Alcorn, and we had to stay at home to work to keep her in school." Such sacrifices were not uncommon, and one man asserted, "All the black folks understood that their passport to a better community was a good education. . . . It was a general position of my parents and other parents of that generation, that once we got an education, we would be free. Everything would be hunky dory."[16]

Teachers were almost universally respected in the black community. According to Julia Jones, aside from family, the teacher/principal of her two-room elementary school was the most important influence on her life: "I always looked up to him. He was very strict. He would beat you if he came by your house on Sunday afternoon and saw you playing ball or marbles. He would get you Monday morning. But that didn't matter, he was a hero in our community. Our family looked up to him." Another man emphasized the importance of teachers, insisting that "parents needed and wanted strong leadership for their children. That's when teachers . . . were right then, were accepted as doing things for the benefit of the students."[17]

In addition to creating more opportunities for black education, the economic changes triggered by the New Deal and World War II facilitated the growth of a black aspiring class. (Historian Michele Mitchell coined the phrase "aspiring class" to describe black workers between 1890 and 1910 who were "able to save a little money," were "concerned with appearing 'respectable,' " and typically "had normal school education or were self-educated." In the context of Claiborne County, the term "aspiring class" refers to those African Americans who had a measure of economic independence or a standard of living that went beyond survival. They also had some access to learning and the larger world and were among the community's leaders.[18])

Comprised primarily of landowners, teachers, and business owners who had access to more resources, education, and autonomy than most blacks, the aspiring class demonstrated the possibilities for doing nonmenial work and attaining a measure of prosperity. Many participated in civic activism, community-building, and racial uplift, using their individual status and achievements to access resources that benefited the larger black community. At a time when Claiborne County was still quite rural, World War II agricultural programs and civic fund-raising facilitated interaction between significant numbers of blacks in the aspiring class. For example, instead of focusing just on farmers, one farm program announcement invited "teachers, ministers, P.T.A. presidents, 4-H club presidents and other leaders." In addition to fostering contacts between blacks from all over the county, these meetings and civic projects offered leadership opportunities. In a pattern that continued after the war, a few black leaders chaired segregated meetings and fund drives and occasionally attended integrated meetings with their white counterparts. In the process, they honed fund-raising, organizational, and leadership skills while developing connections with members of the white elite.[19]

Within the race-based hierarchy inherent in these joint projects, blacks struggled to carve out autonomy and control. This is evident in blacks' differing participation in the 1942 and 1944 county war-bond campaigns. A white committee ran the 1942 campaign and worked through white planters to secure pledges (and payment) from sharecroppers; during the cotton harvest, the *Port Gibson Reveille* published a request by R. D. Gage Jr., president of the Port Gibson Bank and county chair of the war-bond committee, for landowners to "confer with their tenants and to obtain results." In 1944, black leaders asked for a separate war-bond quota and launched an ambitious bond-selling campaign within the black community. More than seventy black men and women worked on five district committees supervised by a seven-member executive committee. They promoted the bond campaign with a parade and a half-page newspaper advertisement urging "loyal Negroes" to buy bonds to support "democracy" and the country's "fighting men."[20]

The black war-bond volunteers provide a glimpse of the emerging black leadership class. The executive committee included two Alcorn professors, three public school teachers, Negro county agent J. C. Dunbar, and Reverend Eugene Spencer, who had recently purchased a farm through the Tenant Purchase Program. The district committees encompassed a broader range of the black aspiring class. Landowning farmers, including tenant purchasers, made up the vast majority of participants whose occupations are known. They were joined by teachers, several business owners, and a physician. Most of these men and women took part in fund-raising campaigns year after year, supporting, among others, the Red Cross, the March of Dimes, and the Cancer Crusade.[21]

In the postwar years, this aspiring class grew dramatically. From 1940 to 1960, the number of black professionals (almost all of them working at Alcorn College or in the public school system) expanded from 102, or 3 percent, to 252, or 12.9 percent, of the black workforce. The number of blacks working in retail businesses also grew from 46, or 1 percent, to 185, or 9.5 percent of the black workforce. Although most did menial work for white employers, a growing number operated their own businesses. By the early 1960s, blacks operated barbershops, cafés, small grocery stores, a shoe repair shop, a recreation hall, and several juke joints. Most black businesses were located on Fair Street, which connected Main Street, home to most white businesses, and Church Street, which was also Highway 61, the main road through town. Although blacks generally did the bulk of their shopping in white stores, many socialized on Fair Street. One woman recalled, "They had the Main Street. . . . They would call that the white people street. And they had Fair Street, they would call 'Nigger Street.' That's exactly what they would call it. We would go uptown and purchase items from the ten-cent store and stuff, but everybody black would hang on

Fair Street, the center of black businesses and widely known as "Nigger Street," ca. 1970s.
Courtesy Mississippi Cultural Crossroads.

'Nigger Street' which is Fair Street now." Black businesses rarely competed directly with their white counterparts. Instead, they typically drew customers by providing personal services, social space, or entertainment. Men went to the barbershops for haircuts and shaves but also to play checkers and swap stories. According to James Miller, they were full of talk about "what's wrong with the world and how you correct it." Grocery stores provided tables where customers could eat and visit, and even Carl and Marguerite Thompson's burial association offices offered "rest rooms, ice water, and lobby for your comfort and convenience."[22]

Shopkeepers, black and white, relied heavily on their Saturday business when black families poured into town. In 1956, Edgar Crisler Jr., whose parents owned the *Port Gibson Reveille*, wrote, "Saturday in Mississippi (Sat'dy in Negro dialect) means Negro Day, when the streets are so packed with Negroes that you can't walk in a straight line down the street for a quarter of a block. Saturday is by common consent their holiday, when the Negroes from the county come into town to mingle with their kith and kin, buy groceries for the next week, go to the show to see the shoot-'em-up Western and just loiter about the streets, gossiping and spending money." A sharecropper described Saturdays in town as "a joyful

Main Street (also known as Market Street), center of Port Gibson's white business district, 1940. Photograph by Marion Post Wolcott, courtesy Library of Congress, LC-USF 34 54859-D.

time" of window shopping and visiting: "We'd walk the street, look around, and we didn't have much money to spend, cause people didn't have much money in those times." A black woman who lived in town remembered that her cousins would visit and together they would run "around playing out there in the streets and stuff." She added, "Folks from all over the county would come in and drink, smoke cigarettes, and visit with friends. Whole families would come."[23]

James Miller, who grew up on the Disharoon plantation, remembered the Saturdays his father would give him a dollar, which "went a long ways then." He and his siblings would "just walk up and down the streets and buy stuff." He said, "You go to Mr. Norman Ellis['s Dry Goods Store] and you get a block of cheese and some salami and a big Barge pop, Man. Hog Heaven. They had the old guy that sold popcorn, peanuts, and candy." Miller also spent considerable time in his grandmother's café on Fair Street and insisted that the place to be in southwest Mississippi was Dannie's juke joint. Also on Fair Street, it had a "wild, cowboyish type of atmosphere" with bootleg liquor and "big-time stars."[24]

Black landowners were another important component of the black aspiring class. Though most land remained in the hands of whites and most black farmers continued to work as wage hands or sharecroppers, the number of blacks who owned their own farms tripled, from 64 to 186, between 1930 and 1945. Although landowners and their children did much the same work that sharecroppers did, they typically had larger land holdings, greater control over their resources, and a higher standard of living. In the mid-1930s, when tenants usually had access to about 30 acres, black landowners in Claiborne County had an average of 266.7 acres and tenant purchasers had an average of 99 acres. Land for pastures and extensive gardens supplemented the farmers' food supply and income. In addition, historian Gail O'Brien argues that "acquisition of land . . . was regarded as a social advancement, resulting in greater self-esteem for the individual farmer and his [or her] family."[25]

Hystercine Rankin's childhood experiences illustrate some of the differences between sharecropping and landowning. After her father was killed, she lived with landowning relatives and remembered working so hard that she never had time "to just sit at home and [be] free. You didn't have no leisure time for being free." Yet when she earned money picking cotton, she was able to spend it on school clothes instead of contributing it to her family for food and shelter. She also remembered that there "was always something good around," like popcorn or homemade candy. Moreover, landowners, with more financial means and autonomy than sharecroppers, typically made education a family priority, sending their children to school for the full session and through the eighth grade, regardless of labor demands. They were more able to purchase books, provide transportation in bad weather, and pay tuition and board so their children could complete high school and sometimes even college. As a result, a significant number of the county's earliest black teachers were from landowning families.[26]

There were ways that white leaders and the black aspiring class needed each other, and over the years they developed an uneasy but somewhat symbiotic relationship. Since whites controlled virtually all of the community's resources, blacks had to work with and through them. The interactions between black educators and white civic leaders provide a good illustration. Black teachers and principals were dependent on white school officials and voters for their jobs and for school funding. Despite the language of the Supreme Court's *Plessy* decision, separate was never equal in Mississippi and public money went disproportionately to support white education. In 1940, for example, Mississippi spent $51.71 per white student and only $7.24 per black student. In Claiborne County in 1953, the ratio was $387 to $40. From 1930 to 1940, the black schools in Port Gibson were overwhelmed by a dramatic population increase as farm laborers moved to town for box factory jobs. With no political power or outside authority to draw on, the black community had to do what it could with existing facilities or convince whites to improve them. Black educators tried to demonstrate that their students and faculty were diligent and worthy, and their efforts to cultivate white interest and cooperation translated into very small, piecemeal improvements. In 1942, the school trustees hired an additional teacher and installed "the gas heating plant removed from the white school." They extended instruction at Claiborne County Training School from ten to twelve grades and discussed plans to replace a burned down church that had housed an elementary school. These actions did little to satisfy the vast needs, however. At CCTS, a classroom designed for 20 students held 90, and some instructors were expected to teach as many as 125 students. The school was overcrowded, even with pupils attending in two shifts.[27]

In November 1944, school trustees began considering plans to improve black schools. H. H. Crisler wrote a supportive editorial, maintaining that educated people made better citizens and contributed more to their communities, concluding that "the Negroes of Claiborne County" were "entitled to better educational advantages" because they "are good, law-abiding people [and] they seldom give trouble."[28] Crisler's paternalistic advocacy was insufficient, and the school-improvement efforts stalled for several years, perhaps because they took place against the backdrop of black union organizing efforts. In this context, Crisler's support of the black schools based on "good behavior" could be construed as an effort to influence the union vote. H. H. Crisler and R. D. Gage were among the most important advocates for improving black schools, and they led the list of whites who unsuccessfully sought to convince box factory workers to reject the union. Perhaps when black workers chose the union, whites retaliated by refusing to address the problems of inadequate black educational facilities.

In fall 1945, Crisler renewed his advocacy for a new black school, arguing that CCTS's condition and overcrowding was "a shame" and that it was the "duty" of taxpayers to provide adequate facilities. That spring, when state-level black demands for an equal division of school funds evoked the possibility of federal intervention, Crisler commented that many elected officials "wanted to give the Negro a square deal but didn't have the nerve to do so" because they feared their constituents' reaction. Now, he said, if officials do not act voluntarily, the "federal government is likely to step in and compel the state to make a fairer distribution." This "outside pressure" and the availability of matching funds from the state legislature eventually prompted action in Claiborne County. In June 1946, R. D. Gage Jr. made a presentation to the Lions Club about the "inadequacies" of CCTS and the forty members present voted unanimously to ask the boards of education and aldermen to call for a school bond issue. A week later, those boards agreed and a group of elite whites, including H. H. Crisler, R. D. Gage Jr., and the owner of the oil mill, met with Claiborne County representative Russell Fox and the relevant legislative committee to discuss matching funds. A year later, amid advertisements and appeals from the Lions Club, the newspaper, and the governing boards, the bond vote passed 182 to 16.[29]

An H. H. Crisler editorial advocating the 1947 bond issue and improved facilities illustrates the combined incentives of federal encroachment and paternalism. "We want to show the northern critics of Mississippi that we can handle our internal problems far better than they can, with their unjust criticism. But above all, we appreciate our Negro population and we want to do all we can to give them educational advantages." The *Reveille* also published a letter from a committee of black citizens, including funeral home owner Carl Thompson, CCTS principal E. W. Reeves, union president Luther Buie, and several educators. Using statements by Crisler and Superintendent Roger Thompson to make the case for additional funding, the black committee appealed to white benevolence and displayed a posture that, at least publicly, accepted white authority. They wrote, "As a group we have tried to demonstrate our worthiness through loyalty and service in all efforts put forward for the betterment of our community. We do express our appreciation to you for your interest and for your willingness to help in this plan for improvement for our children. Therefore, we the colored people, solicit, plead, and beg the white citizens . . . [to cast] a favorable vote." After the bond passed, Crisler maintained that Port Gibson was "blessed by good Negroes" and that "the leading people of the race will appreciate what the white people . . . did to help them."[30]

Despite their assumptions of superiority, whites needed the cooperation of the black elite, especially teachers and ministers. Historian Nan Woodruff explains that by the late 1940s, white elites were preoccupied with "disciplining African Americans for a life outside of sharecropping but within the confines of segregation and disfranchisement. By utilizing black preachers and teachers, planters hoped to instill values that would make those who had left the land responsible members of the community and prevent their workers from joining unions and the civil rights movement." This alliance is reflected in the *Port Gibson Reveille*'s occasional coverage of the black aspiring class, in marked contrast to the paper's usual policy of reporting on blacks only when they were involved in violence or disasters. In a 1957 editorial, for example, Crisler praised "good Negro citizens" who had the "desire . . . to improve their farms and homes" and profiled a number of "good Negro farmers" in the paper's 1950 mystery farm series. He described the 1952 CCTS homecoming parade as "exceedingly creditable" and proclaimed that the entire program demonstrated the "wonderful development" of the black schools. Similarly, the *Reveille* reported on funeral-home owner Carl Thompson's leadership in black professional organizations and noted that world-renowned concert singer Rosa Page Welch's "white friends" were "proud of her accomplishments." A 1950 bank advertisement that advocated black savings, concluded by praising "the ever-present and sustaining influence of the teacher and the preacher, the school and the church."[31]

The white elite cultivated a more select group of black leaders to help mediate race relations. In his massive 1940s study of race relations, Gunnar Myrdal found that whites wanted a few blacks to "obtain as much prestige and influence in the Negro community as possible—so long as they cooperate with the whites faithfully." This type of black leadership was pervasive throughout the South, and the men who fulfilled that role have been called variously "accommodating," "liaison agents," "brokers," or "go-betweens." J. L. Chestnut Jr., a black lawyer from Selma, Alabama, remembered his revelation that black leaders were picked by whites and given "favors to dispense." Civil rights workers in Louisiana described older Negro leaders as "message carriers," while historian Glen Eskew characterizes black leaders in Birmingham, Alabama, as men who "petitioned and patiently negotiated with white officials." Black leaders were severely circumscribed, and there were few alternatives to this individualistic approach to achieving status or a more comfortable standard of living. According to Chestnut, "Any black leader who started criticizing the status quo would find no more morsels of power thrown his way." He explains that "for little crumbs of power, black preachers and other leaders could be counted on 'to keep the natives in line'—to cool off potential uprisings and to preach that blacks should clean up their own backyards rather than challenge the system." Myrlie Evers, whose husband, Medgar, was the NAACP's first field secretary in Mississippi, offers a similar analysis, writing: "In a segregated society there was always room for a few Negroes willing and able to justify their racial treason to work in the interest of the white man. Nor were all of them always conscious of the degree of their defection. Some, like the Negro minister whose church performed the function of draining off the frustrations of his flock, probably served a mental health function among Negroes while at the same time helping to keep the system working smoothly." She points out that many such leaders were acting largely on their drive to succeed and provide for their families and making the best of an unchangeable system. She concludes, "They were performing a service for the Negro community as well, even if that service were simply to supply a link in the chain of appeal to the white powers of the community."[32]

In Claiborne County, Reverend Eugene Spencer became one of these leaders. After he purchased a farm near Alcorn through the Tenant Purchase Program, Spencer's status in the community continued to climb. Accustomed to relative autonomy on the Disharoon plantation, he requested and received an exemption to the TPP requirement that every check written against the loan be preapproved by the program administrator. He paid off his forty-year loan in only seven years and was a leader in the county wartime and farm programs. Pastor of several churches, by the 1950s Spencer was the county's leading black minister and moderator of the Claiborne County Baptist Association, a position that gave him about 2,000 constituents and considerable prestige. In 1958, he was elected vice president in the statewide Negro Baptist Convention and held the presidency the following year. In that capacity, he hosted the fall 1960 State Baptist Convention, an event that included speeches by the Port Gibson mayor and banker R. D. Gage III.[33]

Even as a tenant farmer, Spencer commanded a measure of respect. He remembered that when Disharoon wanted him to move into a house that was "raggedy looking" and had no windows, he told Disharoon, "I couldn't move in that kind of house." Spencer explained that Disharoon agreed to provide materials to fix it up because "I was considered a top farmer at that time. . . . It was to his advantage to, shall we say, keep a top man. If we didn't make nothing, then he wouldn't get nothing. And I think he wanted me also for an example, because more or less on your large plantation, people try to do what they see somebody else doing." Spencer believed that his insistence on keeping his place "neat and nice" led to his inclusion in the FSA program; he reported that the Alcorn professor who encouraged him to apply said, "There's a man that ought to be on his own farm, with that kind of ambition, willing to fix up somebody else property." Spencer fully embraced middle-class values, including the importance of saving money, abstaining from alcohol, and pursuing education, and he used stories from his own experiences to encourage these values in his congregations. For example, he described how a banker approved his first bank loan, although he had nothing to secure it with, because the banker trusted him to repay it. Not willing to rely solely on the banker's goodwill in the future, Spencer immediately began a savings account, which he used as collateral for his next loan.[34]

In the black community, Spencer was respected as a successful farmer and minister and for his ability to negotiate small favors from whites. Spencer appealed to whites to support his churches, including Spring Hill Baptist Church, which was built on land donated by the Allen family. Several times through personal appeals Spencer was able to secure additional land for the church from the Allens and regularly used Allen Lake (and others around the county) for baptisms. Jimmy Allen, who eventually inherited the land, agreed to subsequent land donations and lake access because he liked Spencer. He remembered him as "a fine fellow" and contended, "He was a little bit more progressive than the average black preacher. I'll put it that way. A little more, I don't know how to say it. Not as emotional. And more down to earth. Very reasonable."[35]

In 1948, when Alcorn president J. H. Pipes threatened to close the college's high school department, arguing that the school needed to use all its resources to support the college program, Spencer and several dozen black Westside residents protested. Spencer had moved near Alcorn to facilitate his children's education and threatened to file a lawsuit if they were denied a high school education. It did not come to that, however, in part because black parents' interests coincided with those of white taxpayers and school officials. The latter group worked out an agreement to keep Alcorn High School open by paying tuition for Claiborne County residents. As a result, blacks continued to have access to the school and whites saved money, since this arrangement cost far less than expanding the already overcrowded CCTS and providing transportation to rural blacks. In telling the story of his fight over Alcorn High School and subsequent battles for buses for black children, Spencer described himself as "an agitator," saying, "I was in all that fight. Quietly."[36]

In addition to their visible work with members of the white elite, a number of black leaders also pursued NAACP membership and voting. For rural blacks interested in civil rights, the NAACP was *the* organization to join, and it claimed the allegiance of many, especially after the onset of World War II. Historian Patricia Sullivan explains, "The NAACP provided the essential vehicle for meeting the escalation of black expectations and militancy that accompanied the war." Southern NAACP membership grew from 18,000 in the 1930s to almost 156,000 by the end of the war and "created an infrastructure of support for black protest and politics." Ernest Jones, a black farmer born into a landowning family in 1886, founded the Claiborne County NAACP branch, probably in the early 1940s. After attending Alcorn, Jones returned to the Carlisle community in the northeast corner of Claiborne County where he and his wife Sarah Dotson raised seven children and farmed more than 300 acres of land. Jones also taught school and Sunday school, was a church deacon, and founded a countywide Baptist Aid program that provided inexpensive, noncommercial burial insurance. Before that, he built coffins "so that people could get a decent burial." In 1960, a white state employee wrote that Jones "is an advisor for other Negroes in this area," telling them "their rights [and] how much to charge white people for their work." The community where Jones lived is now named Jones Village in his honor because his land sales made it possible for so many blacks to build homes of their own. One of his daughters recalled, "He sold it all to the black folks so they could have somewhere to stay. He almost gave them the land for what they paid for it, but he was trying to help."[37]

Though Jones's combination of community involvement, financial success, and independence were unmatched in Claiborne County, his values and pri-

Ernest Jones, farmer, community leader, and founder of the Claiborne County NAACP. Courtesy family of Ernest Jones.

orities reflected those of the larger black community. His daughters emphasized his commitment to and faith in religion, education, and voting rights. The Joneses held family prayer meetings around the fireplace and insisted that their children work hard and contribute to the family's well-being. Despite this emphasis on work, one of the children explained that her parents "never took us out of school for anything." The only time her father ever punished her was when she could not answer his question about what caused the American Revolution. "And I never will forget it. He got my hand and he told me and I know today. I know today what was the cause of that war. I haven't never forgotten it. He said, 'Taxation without representation.'" When Jones's children graduated from the eighth grade, they boarded with a black family near Alcorn so they could attend high school and college.[38]

Jones cofounded the NAACP branch with fellow farmer Dan Newman. The two men met through church work, and over the years their families became intertwined through marriage. Most of the early NAACP members had similar profiles and strong community and kinship ties. Of nineteen known members, fourteen were farmers, and all but two of those owned the land they worked. The majority lived in or near Pattison, a small village in the southeastern portion of the county. The Pattison-area members included cofounder Dan Newman, who owned 240 acres of land; Floyd Rollins, a teacher, farmer, and disabled World War I veteran with a pension and a good deal of financial independence; and six people who bought land through the TPP, including Annie Holloway, Jesse Johnson, and Roscoe Johnson, who was also Dan Newman's in-law. There were two farmers in the Westside area near Alcorn, Reverend Eugene Spencer and Reverend A. L. Martin. Four others owned businesses in Port Gibson, and one was a laborer in the local icehouse. The merchants were Eddie Lee, who was of Chinese and black ancestry and operated a small grocery store founded by his parents; Carl and Marguerite Thompson, who, in the mid-1940s, bought part of a funeral home that Carl Thompson had worked in for his white father; and barber Alexander Collins.[39]

Twelve of the nineteen members were related to at least one other member. Alexander Collins illustrates these interconnections. His brother married one of Ernest Jones's daughters; Dan Newman was his uncle; and his sister married Roscoe Johnson. Because the members feared repercussions, the local branch was organized exclusively through these personal contacts and was relatively secretive. James Dorsey first learned about the NAACP when he was fourteen and his father A. N. Dorsey, a Pattison-area TPP farmer, bought him a membership and took him along to the group's meetings. Dorsey explained, "I was the eldest of the boys [and] he thought I should know and be exposed to some of the things. In case something should happen to him that at least one of the members of the family would know." Most of the group was extensively involved in civic, community-minded work, including fund-raising, farm programs, community development, church work, and school support. Twelve were on the 1944 War Bond Committee, and at least four were Masons.[40] Along with their civic orientation and relative prosperity, several were well educated. Most were aware of alternatives to Claiborne County's plantation society and actively worked to expand the boundaries of their world, seeking information and pursuing opportunities. Given the initiative and independence necessary to successfully apply to the Tenant Purchase Program, for example, it is not surprising that almost one-third of the black TPP participants were among the county's first NAACP members.

In 1951, Jones and Newman decided to expand the NAACP and recruit enough members for a charter from the national organization. At the time, the NAACP's Supreme Court victories in school and voting cases had made southern whites wary of the organization, but they had not yet launched the all-out attack that would follow the 1954 *Brown* decision. According to historian John Dittmer, in Mississippi the early 1950s showed some "signs of gradual improvement in the racial climate" because whites believed they had survived World War II's threat to the racial status quo. Even before *Brown*, however, Claiborne County blacks were cautious and did not follow the 1952 suggestion of Gloster Current, NAACP director of branches, that they hold "a well-advertised mass meeting for the purpose of putting the work of the branch before the public in order to secure as comprehensive . . . and large a membership as possible." In fact, the Claiborne County charter never arrived and, in requesting a duplicate, local members asked that it be sent without NAACP on the return address.[41]

There is no complete list, or even a full tally, of those who joined the NAACP during the 1951 drive. However, there were at least seventy members and possibly more. This expanded group had much in common with the original nucleus and were probably recruited in the same circles of farmers and other black leaders. Of the fifty-nine listed on the charter and another fourteen who were members during the early 1950s, at least one-third were landowning farmers or merchants, well over half were involved in civic activism, and many had ties to other members.[42] For example, Nate Jones, who learned about the NAACP through the *Pittsburgh Courier* and had been searching for a local branch since he returned from his naval service, joined during the 1951 drive. His former teacher Annie Martin, whose husband, Reverend A. L. Martin, was the local secretary, told him about the NAACP branch. Once he was aware of the branch, Jones began cautiously recruiting others who he "had confidence in." One of those was his nephew's wife, Marjorie Brandon. Brandon's son Ken remembered his mother's determination to belong to the NAACP and Nate Jones's visits to deliver news and the yearly membership card, though it was "hush hush" even at home. Marjorie Brandon recalled that she was cautious because "I was always told that the white people would threaten you or maybe they might kill you and so once you got your card, you didn't make them visible. . . . I believe I burned [mine]." Her husband worried about the consequences and tried to talk her out of joining, but she "just kept convincing him that, you know, that was the only way that we were going to be free or only way we were going to have any rights." She explained, "I just felt like someone had to take a stand. Life itself is just a chance. Who knows what's going to happen tomorrow."[43]

CHAPTER Five

Reacting to the *Brown* Decision

Black and white Mississippians responded very differently to the 1954 *Brown* decision. It inspired many blacks to redouble their efforts for full citizenship. Myrlie Evers recalls that "suddenly there was a voice, more impressive and resounding than that of any Negro leader, the voice of the highest court in the land, and it was saying in unmistakable language that segregation was wrong, was illegal, was intolerable, and that it must be ended." She continues, this "voice of change, of impending liberation, of challenge to the central fact of any Negro's life . . . echoed through Mississippi's Negro communities." White Mississippians, on the other hand, reacted with outrage and embraced what John Dittmer calls a "siege mentality" that "encompassed virtually every citizen and institution in Mississippi."[1]

White Mississippians were among the most vocal leaders of a southwide massive resistance campaign that aggressively defended segregation and white supremacy. The state legislature pushed improvements to black schools (called "equalization") in an effort to slow federal enforcement of desegregation and to appease blacks. The white Citizens' Council, founded in October 1954 to maintain segregation and protect "the southern way of life," was more explicitly threatening. Composed primarily of "upper-middle-class leaders," the organization had 25,000 dues-paying members within three months and quickly spread to other southern states. Although the council portrayed itself as law-abiding, scholar Charles Payne observes that the organization pursued "the agenda of the Klan with the demeanor of the Rotary," and John Dittmer argues that it "fostered and legitimized violent actions by individuals not overly concerned with questions of legality and image." Lawmakers also created the state Sovereignty Commission, which generated propaganda, investigated black activism, and funneled public money to the Citizens' Council.[2]

While the state geared up for war, Claiborne County whites publicly emphasized paternalism, in keeping with their traditionally moderate approach to race relations. H. H. Crisler contended that desegregation would hurt both blacks and whites and that the "constantly growing friendship between the races would have brought about a far better condition between them than can possibly be produced by this unfortunate court decision." He also insisted that "this paper has been a staunch friend of the race" and has "done everything possible to help the race with the education of its children." None of his editorials acknowledged the vast inequities that were at the heart of the *Brown* decision. In January 1956, a *Port Gibson Reveille* columnist expressed similar views in a long letter addressed to "our Colored friends." Referring to "proposed changes that can bring about a crisis," she argued that the only way to avert this was for "the colored people" to be "taught what is right in this matter." After expressing a desire to "see everyone treated fair," she lectured blacks:

> Do not listen to high-sounding talk from organized groups who promise you things which they never purpose to grant. You, the colored race, will be the victims of their ungodly schemes. Don't fall for the fancy chatter, and be proud that you are a race, separate and apart from all others. The thing so many are trying to force upon us, would not make you happy. It would only cause confusion, unhappiness and heartbreak for you, and for the rest of us. . . . Don't be taken in by outsiders who are not even familiar with your problems, who would turn you against the people who proved through the years to be your friends.[3]

Although few African Americans shared this perception of the community's race relations, the county was not as brutal as some others in the state. Before the *Brown* decision, the Claiborne County NAACP operated in a semi-open fashion. Reverend Eugene Spencer insisted to an interviewer that whites knew about the early NAACP meetings and offered this as evidence that Port Gibson was "an unusual town." He claimed, "We had no radicals [and] the white people know that we were just trying to help our people." In 1956, NAACP leader Dan Newman must have had some hope that NAACP members could talk with *Reveille* editor E. T. Crisler, since he asked the national organization to send fifty copies of a pamphlet called "A Southerner Looks at Moderation" to distribute to members and the newspaper editor. This is in stark contrast to the experiences of black World War II veterans in neighboring Jefferson County who faced explicit, violent threats when they joined the NAACP and registered to vote. One of them recalled, "Sheriff Willie Winters said, 'He'll wade in blood up to his neck before he see a nigger vote.' " Bill Minor, a white reporter known for his fair coverage of the civil rights movement, contends that Port Gibson "had good solid [segregationists]," but "it didn't have the reputation that some of them had of being a mean town. . . . [Port Gibson] had the antebellum kind of atmosphere or something [that was] less threatening."[4]

Despite this apparent moderation, Claiborne County whites were still determined to maintain the status quo. They organized a local Citizens' Council that, according to E. T. Crisler, was led by "the finest men." These were the same men who dominated public offices and political decision-making, including state legislator Russell Fox; Fox's eventual replacement, Robert Vaughan; state senator P. M. Watkins; banker R. D. Gage III; chamber of commerce president Louis Ellis; and car dealer and alderman Jimmy Allen. Four of the six men on the 1960 county Democratic Executive Committee were also publicly identified as council members. In the late 1950s, the Claiborne and Jefferson County Citizens' Councils' public activities included raising money for private schools in Little Rock and hosting a series of speakers, including Congressman John Bell Williams and Ross Barnett, soon to be governor.[5]

Local white leaders participated in a southwide pattern of repression that eliminated 226 NAACP branches in fourteen southern states between 1954 and 1956. Several known NAACP members faced harassment and, according to Eugene Spencer, the organization "had to go underground. You were a bad person if you were a member of the NAACP. You couldn't get a job." A white woman who had hired Lydell Page to hang wallpaper questioned him about the NAACP. He recalled, "I was up on the ladder, she was on the floor and she said, 'Page, stop a minute,' and I stopped, looked around. She said, 'I want to ask you a question.' I said, 'What is it?' She said, 'We understand that you are with the NAACP.' " Instead of answering directly, Page told her there was no local branch but added, "If I'm a member in it, I don't see no harm in it." Then he turned the tables. " 'Now, I'd like to ask you a question.' She said, 'What is it?' I said, 'Are you a member of the Citizen Council?' [Laughter] . . . And that killed that right there.' " On another occasion, a white police officer warned Page that a white man was threatening to kill him because "they say that you belong to the NAACP."[6]

When NAACP president Ernest Jones tried to hire a white man to lay gravel, the worker refused, telling him to "let the NAACP lay" it. In another instance, whites burned a cross at the end of Jones's driveway. Most of the people he had recruited to the NAACP in the early 1950s quickly fell away, and, years later, he emphasized how difficult it was to sustain enough members for a branch charter. "We'd go around to houses and they would join, pay their fee, and I wouldn't see 'em no more. They wouldn't even attend meetings." Jesse Johnson asserted that members "got scared after they was questioned by some of the white people," while another early member recalled that when whites sent word "that they wanted names of members," the organization "stopped meeting." Nate Jones concurred, noting that "word got out that if anybody got caught with [membership cards] you might lose what you got or make your house burn down or something like that. That put a lot of fear." He contended that when whites discovered an NAACP membership card in the wallet of a black man who was in a car accident, the man's family was denied the insurance benefits they were entitled to and "didn't get justice." His wife, Julia, remembered struggling with fear every year when Nate went to pick up their membership cards. "It was definitely a tragedy if you were caught with a civil rights card. You might lose your job, or you might get beaten up, or both, you know. And so when he would bring it home, I would be frightened about it."[7]

Under scrutiny and facing intimidation, the number of people willing to join the NAACP declined in the early 1960s, and most members kept their affiliation secret. In 1961, branch cofounder Dan Newman reported to the national office that Claiborne County had twenty-seven paid-up members. But, he explained, "Our people . . . are under pressure and will not work. We did not have a meeting in '61." When he sent in payment for six memberships in May 1963, Ernest Jones wrote, "We are no longer operating as a branch." In October 1963, seven more people had paid dues, but the total of thirteen was still significantly below the twenty-seven of two years before and the 1952 high of around seventy.[8] Although a few individuals continued to pay dues and maintain their connection to the national organization, until 1966 the Claiborne County NAACP had essentially no program; its only role was to provide a relatively quiet way for a few determined people to act on their commitment to civil rights, facilitate contacts between like-minded individuals, and promote communication with outside civil rights activists like NAACP field secretary Medgar Evers.

Before the *Brown* decision, Claiborne County whites had commonly allowed a few African Americans to register to vote. For blacks, voting was essentially a privilege, not a right of citizenship. James Dorsey insisted that "there was no way in the world" blacks could complete the voter registration form "the way" the white registrar "wanted it" but explained that officials were occasionally "lenient" with a few blacks, "because they figured that twenty or thirty folks wouldn't make a difference." A white woman similarly noted that a few black leaders, "usually property owners and very responsible citizens," were allowed to register because of "who they were, their place in the community." She explained that "they had the respect and trust of the powers that be in the community." Nate and Julia Jones argued that whites allowed some leaders to register "to deter the others. That was so they would persuade the others not to go. Somehow, [the leaders] didn't try to help us. Most time they would say that, 'We the leaders,' and they kept their secret about [registering]."[9]

Even that measure of access to the franchise was revoked in 1955. After the *Brown* decision, the Mississippi legislature passed a law requiring all voter registration applicants to fill out a twenty-two-question form and interpret a section of the state constitution. When an NAACP-sponsored voter-registration drive from January 1, 1954 to March 1955 succeeded in raising the number of black registered voters in Claiborne County from 87 to 140, local whites initiated a re-registration campaign and used the new state law to purge black voters. Eugene Spencer, one of those disenfranchised, characterized this period around 1955–56 as a "red hot" time when the Ku Klux Klan and the Citizens' Council were "there watching us." He recalled that whites "scatter[ed] pamphlets all round through the town of Port Gibson" and "discouraged our people." Although the registrar (who had complete authority) allowed whites to re-register by simply signing their names to the poll book, blacks had to fill out the new, complicated form and were almost invariably failed. As a result, the number of black registered voters dropped from its historic high point of about 140 to fewer than two dozen.[10]

The registrars and their staffs often used delay tactics or refused to allow blacks to complete the complicated form. Those blacks who did manage to apply were almost invariably failed, often for unstated reasons. World War II veteran Matt Ross, for example, testified, "I had tried to register so many times and was turned down, I almost gave up trying." When his wife tried to register, the circuit clerk refused to give her a form and told her to "go read up" on the constitution. Because of this aggressive resistance, many people simply accepted that "black people wasn't allowed to vote." Asked when she first registered to vote, one black woman said, "I was good and grown." She explained that the circuit clerk "wasn't too particular about colored folks coming in for to register."[11]

Despite white hostility, however, a number of African Americans tried repeatedly to register or re-register. The most persistent were usually land or business owners and NAACP members. Annie Holloway Johnson went to the registrar's office at least five times between 1956 and February 1959. Twice a clerk told her there were no forms, and three times her application was rejected. On one occasion, the clerk stopped her midapplication, saying she had to leave for lunch.

After lunch, Holloway Johnson started the application over, and it, too, was rejected. William Owens, a Pattison farmer who had registered in 1952, was also repeatedly rejected despite persistent efforts to re-register. His brother-in-law Eugene Spencer tried to intercede on his behalf, talking to newspaper editor E. T. Crisler. Spencer explained, "I mentioned the fact to him that here's a man owns two hundred and something acres of land that they wouldn't let vote." Spencer insisted the editor was sympathetic, but Owens remained unable to register and Spencer acknowledged that "there were those [whites] who tried to hold the line on voting."[12]

Even when blacks were able to register, they were typically prevented from voting. Between 1954 and 1962 when the Justice Department intervened, eight was the highest black vote total recorded in Claiborne County. At one polling place, a prospective voter was told to wait for a police officer, who never came. After several hours, he gave up and left. When James Dorsey's father and several other Pattison farmers tried to vote, the election officials sent them to Jackson. In Jackson they were sent back to Pattison. When the farmers stopped again at the Pattison polling place, they were told that "their time would come, but at this particular time, they were not allowed to vote." Merchant M. M. McFatter was one of the white men who rejected black voters. He recalled, "There was a colored man that I had quite a bit of respect for, always stopped and talked with him. I had been up here and we had denied some colored people the right to vote. So, when I saw him the next day, he said, 'Mr. Mac, why won't you let us register and vote?' I said, 'Well, if ya'll start voting, you'll put people in there that will destroy this town. You'll put people in there that don't know what they're doing.' "[13]

One of whites' most effective strategies was the white primary, the practice of excluding blacks from the Democratic primary. Although the white primary had been ruled unconstitutional in 1944, whites used it on at least a dozen occasions between 1954 and 1956. State legislator Russell Fox, for example, told Ernest Jones that he could not vote because he "wasn't in harmony with the Democratic Party because of his being President of the NAACP." When Annie Holloway Johnson tried to vote, a white man at city hall asked her if she belonged to the NAACP. When she said she did, he told her there was "no way in the world for her to qualify to vote." An election official told Eugene Spencer that to join the Democratic Party and vote he would have to sign an affidavit denying membership in the NAACP. He also explained that if Spencer signed such an affidavit, white officials would "bring perjury charges against him." Spencer, who was familiar with the Supreme Court decision outlawing the white primary, explained later, "I was aware, abreast of what was going on. It just hadn't quite happened here, and we were trying to bring it about."[14]

Lydell Page registered to vote when he returned from military service in World War II but recalled that white officials only let him vote "for senators and presidents" and "they didn't let me put [the ballot] in the box. . . . I couldn't vote for no local officials." He described how election officials would call in "little Bobby Gage" (R. D. Gage III, of the Port Gibson bank family dynasty) to question him about his attitudes on race and segregation. Page crafted his responses carefully. "Well, you know, I wasn't gon' say I wanted [social mixing]. But I believed in it. They asked about segregation. I said this about segregation. I told 'em I said, 'Now, if I didn't believe in segregation, I wouldn't be here. I wouldn't stay here in the South. I'd be gone on.'" Although he was circumspect in his answers, white Democratic officials would always conclude that Page did not subscribe to the state Democratic Party's creed and repeatedly refused to let him cast his ballot.[15]

Encouraged by NAACP field secretary Medgar Evers, in February and March 1959 Annie Holloway Johnson, Eugene Spencer, and three other blacks complained to the Justice Department that they were being prevented from registering to vote because of their race.[16] In April 1959, the Justice Department directed the FBI to interview the complainants and determine whether they could identify "qualified Negroes who have been denied registration for racial reasons." The FBI turned up two more names and interviewed both people, but they ignored the Justice Department's request that they interview Medgar Evers. When one of the Justice Department lawyers tried to renew the request that Evers be interviewed, his supervisor overruled him. Instead, the Justice Department closed the case, concluding that the "victims do not look strong." Federal voting rights laws were weak, but proving discrimination was made virtually impossible by the Justice Department's failure to compare the requirements for white and black applicants and by the FBI's reluctance to cooperate. Moreover, in justifying the FBI's refusal to interview Medgar Evers, one Justice Department lawyer ignored the existing complaints from Claiborne County blacks and concluded, "To solicit such information from the NAACP representative at this time would be contrary to policy since we would not be investigating actual complaints but would actually be on a fishing expedition."[17]

In addition to suppressing the local NAACP and blocking black access to voting, white leaders acted to head off any attempt at school integration. Russell Fox, Claiborne County's longtime representative to the state legislature and an active participant in the statewide massive resistance movement, led this effort. Alderman Jimmy Allen claimed Fox "fought a whole lot for the underprivileged, you might say. And for the blacks." He recalled, for example, that when the legislature was debating fishing licenses, Fox argued, "This poor black fellow out here that's gonna sit on the bank and fish in the pond, it's no reason that he's got to have a license to do it." Allen, whose own family's political power relied on black electoral exclusion, asserted that Fox "had a lot of black friends out there. . . . Of course, they couldn't vote for him then. This was before the voter registration period." In contrast, journalist Bill Minor characterized Fox as "vicious" and emphasized that he worked closely with Walter Sillers, the powerful segregationist Speaker of the House. He explained that Fox had a "quick mind" and an excellent understanding of all the "parliamentary tricks that existed." When Fox and Sillers "didn't want to hear any more about some bill they didn't like, Russell Fox would be the killer. . . . There might be a dozen people standing, but [Sillers would] recognize Russell Fox." Minor described how Sillers and Fox derailed legislation that would have equalized black teacher salaries. When the bill was presented, "Russell Fox got up and he [said], 'Speaker, gentlemen,' he didn't wait. He'd go right into it. Said, 'Does it mean that those Nigras can be paid the same as whites in this bill?' And poor old Elmer [McCoy] said, 'Well it just applies to teachers in general.' [And Fox replied], 'Mr. Speaker, I move we indefinitely postpone this bill.' That's the way they did that."[18]

By 1954, Fox had become a supporter of school equalization in the hopes that it would forestall integration. At a Lions Club meeting, he compared equalization to the 1890 state constitutional convention that effectively disfranchised African Americans. In a June 1955 political advertisement addressed to the "members of the Mississippi white Democratic party," Fox argued that maintaining segregated schools was the most pressing problem facing the state and pledged to "furnish . . . additional revenue, and to see that the children of Claiborne County, both colored and white, receive their fair share of the funds necessary to carry out . . . our present system of segregated schools." Led by Fox and the Lions Club, Claiborne County whites joined the statewide attempt to avoid desegregation by improving black schools. By 1959, the community had spent $900,000 to convert Claiborne County Training School to Richardson Elementary, named after a former black teacher, and build a new black junior and senior high school, named Addison after a former black principal.[19]

White leaders also helped the state Sovereignty Commission keep track of black voter registration efforts, NAACP memberships, and "potential trouble makers." In May 1959, for example, Port Gibson police chief L. L. Doyle invited commission investigator Zack Van Landingham to speak at a Lions Club meeting. While in town, Van Landingham talked with the police chief, the sheriff, Bobby Gage, and several other white leaders who all assured him that they had no trouble with "the Negroes." In fact, they said they had been "amazed" when they learned that blacks had complained to the Justice Department about voting rights violations, and they "promised to try and determine the names of these 5 Negroes" and pass that information on to the commission. In a June 1960 report, written several months after the sit-in movement started in Greensboro, N.C., commission investigator A. L. Hopkins identified Annie Holloway as one of the people who had complained to the Justice Department, described Ernest Jones as a "race agitator," and assessed the activism and attitudes of Eugene Spencer, Floyd Rollins, Alexander Collins, and Carl Thompson. He asserted, for example, that Thompson "is not a known race agitator, but he is believed to agitate under cover when the opportunity presents itself." As evidence, Hopkins noted that "the Chief and Sheriff had information that Thompson attempted to have students from Addison School in Port Gibson demonstrate or participate in sit down strikes at the drug store in Port Gibson."[20]

The Sovereignty Commission warned local officials of impending federal investigations and recorded the license numbers of blacks who attended Jackson NAACP meetings. They observed that William Owens (and/or others in his car) attended an NAACP meeting at the Masonic Temple in May 1959 when NAACP leader Roy Wilkins spoke. After the freedom riders arrived in Mississippi in 1961 amid much national publicity, investigators asked Claiborne County whites if "the NAACP had stepped up its activities or if the Negroes were making a special effort to vote." White leaders almost invariably assured the Sovereignty Commission that there were no racial problems. In June 1960, for example, circuit clerk Pauline Easley reported that "everything is quiet." Six months later, police chief L. L. Doyle said that "everything was getting along smoothly regarding racial conditions in Port Gibson."[21]

One of whites' best sources of information was Negro county agent J. C. Dunbar. In March 1959, school superintendent Robert Segrest passed on Dunbar's report that there was an eighteen-member NAACP branch and the names of eight probable leaders, asserting that "Dunbar is a good Negro and one that can be depended on for reliable information." When the commission investigated Alcorn College professor Jesse Morris after he applied to be a notary public, Segrest turned to Dunbar to find out if Morris was "connected with the NAACP or any organizations friendly to integration." As a reward for his cooperation, Dunbar was named principal of Addison High School in 1964, although he had not taught school in over four decades and had no administrative experience. In 1965, Dunbar was appointed to the Claiborne County Farmer's Home Administration board, becoming the first African American named to a community board without being explicitly in charge of a separate black effort.[22]

Blacks were not happy about Dunbar's close ties to whites. A teacher remembered people saying that "he wasn't even qualified to be a principal" and only got the job "because he was in with the whites, and all of that kind of stuff." Robert Segrest's secretary reported that NAACP activist Floyd Rollins "was very unfriendly to Dunbar because of his attitude regarding the race situation." Moreover, in 1960, at a time when local whites believed that "most of the talk regarding integration and other racial problems originates from this Negro Masonic Lodge," the Masons evicted Dunbar and he relocated to the superintendent's building.[23]

The conflict between Dunbar and the Masons was emblematic of growing divisions among black leaders. The early NAACP coalition, which brought land and business owners together with teachers and ministers, became increasingly strained as whites escalated their use of both rewards and coercion to control black activism. While a few farmers led voter registration efforts and kept the NAACP branch alive, if barely, teachers and ministers grew more cautious. Reverend Eugene Spencer, for example, allied himself more and more with the white community. Although he was included on a Sovereignty Commission list of NAACP members in Claiborne County, whites did not perceive him to be a threat. Concerned that "radical Negroes" might take over the Negro Baptist Convention after the death of Sovereignty Commission informant and longtime convention leader H. H. Humes, the commission tried to influence the organization's 1958 election. An investigator reported success when Spencer, whom he described as "trustworthy and friendly," was elected vice president (which meant he would be president the following year). In September 1965, white Claiborne Countians named Spencer to a tricounty antipoverty executive board seeking federal money.[24]

In case enticements were insufficient to secure continued cooperation from black leaders, whites backed them with threats. The school superintendent provided the Sovereignty Commission with a roster of black teachers, presumably to check against its "agitator" index. Reverend Alexander Martin, one of the community's first NAACP members and longtime secretary of the organization, dropped his membership when Segrest threatened to fire his daughter. In an era when white southerners consistently equated civil rights with communism, the 1958 Claiborne County Grand Jury insisted that teachers were responsible for combating "communistic views and policies of government [that] will utterly destroy our American way of life" and concluded their annual report by commending "both colored and white [teachers] for the most excellent manner in which they are conducting themselves." A year later, the state attorney general told the Lions Club that he did not "think these [black] teachers will let out of state agitators deprive them of their jobs."[25]

Abandoned by the federal government and facing widespread coercion and intimidation, Claiborne County African Americans engaged in little overt activism. In fact, Alcorn students initiated the first dramatic civil rights action in Claiborne County. In 1957, they protested a series of articles written by history professor Clennon King. When King, a controversial man whose father was an NAACP branch president in Albany, Georgia, criticized the NAACP and defended segregation, Korean War veterans and NAACP members led the student body in boycotting his classes. They demanded a retraction and connected their protest to the emerging civil rights movement. One student sign claimed, for example, that Clennon King was trying to "tear down" what Martin Luther King Jr. was trying to "build up." Many faculty and administrators supported the students, and one drove to Jackson to personally inform state NAACP field secretary and Alcorn alumnus Medgar Evers of the protest. Evers contacted local and national newspapers, which began daily coverage of the campus events.[26]

White officials responded quickly. On Tuesday, the second day of protest, the Sovereignty Commission asked black informant Reverend H. H. Humes to investigate. Assuming that "these incidents are being caused either by members of the faculty or by outside pressure," they instructed Humes to "determine exactly who sparked the incident." As the protest continued, white authorities became concerned that the boycott might spread to other black colleges and began to suspect that Alcorn president J. R. Otis was "a primary instigator of the student walk out." On Thursday, the board of trustees tried to convince students to return to classes and threatened to close the college if they refused. One student responded angrily to their threats, saying, "We don't give a damn if you burn [the college] down." After this unproductive meeting, the student body voted unanimously to withdraw from school Friday morning and the student council president wrote an emotional explanation of their refusal to capitulate to the trustees' demands. "It would be trite to attempt to describe the sorrow that we feel as we chant the 'Alcorn Ode' for the last time and watch eighty-six years of our history come to a close. However, our sorrow is not unmixed with the solemn pride that comes from knowing that we have done what any honorable American either Negro or white would have done under similar circumstances. If it must be our fate to see the institution that we love be destroyed, we can think of no better altar upon which we might be sacrificed than upon the altar of self-respect." On Saturday, the board claimed that the student "withdrawal [had] not [been] made in good faith" and expelled them all instead. The trustees also fired President Otis, charging that he had "wholly failed" in his duties and that the students had taken over with the "acquiescence, if not the consent and approval of the President."[27]

Even before the protest against Clennon King, Otis was in trouble with the board of trustees. He had already resigned under pressure, effective at the end of the school year. Publicly, his resignation was attributed to poor health, but O. W. Moses, who worked in the college's business office, believed that Otis was actually fired because he was "real outspoken and in the hole." In addition to overspending the college's limited resources, Otis had connections to the Regional Council of Negro Leadership and the NAACP and was noticeably missing from the group of black college presidents who supported Mississippi governor Hugh White's plan for continued segregation in exchange for additional resources. According to Moses, Otis's strong academic leadership and the school's educational successes counted little with the trustees. Although Otis was already on his way out, his support for the Alcorn students cost him the remaining months on his contract and a promised paid vacation.[28]

Moses's account of Alcorn's relationship to white administrators illustrates the extensive white oversight of black institutions, including their day-to-day operations. Purchase orders, for example, had to be approved by Jake Scott, a white employee in the administrative offices of the Institutions of Higher Learning. According to Moses, "I always called him the president of the black institutions. . . . Jake [Scott] was in there to oversee the black institutions." Scott's responsibility for black colleges was evident in 1960 when Sovereignty Commission investigators were alarmed that a teacher at Jackson State, another Mississippi black college, was holding a discussion on a book about poll taxes. Scott investigated the matter and assured them that there was "absolutely no need to worry about where [the professor] stood." After the passage of the 1964 Civil Rights Act, Scott instructed Alcorn administrators in how to respond to inquiries from U.S. Commissioner of Education about the institution's admissions policies regarding race.[29]

When the trustees replaced Otis with John Dewey (J. D.) Boyd, who had been the superintendent of Utica Institute, a black junior college about fifty miles from Alcorn, they expected him to keep tight control, eliminate dissent, and maintain the status quo. A light-skinned man who several employees claimed "thought he was white folks anyway," Boyd had already proven himself willing to endorse school segregation even when other black leaders refused to. As an Alcorn graduate and one-time instructor, Boyd was familiar with the campus, and he had reopened the college within a week of assuming the presidency. Each student had to go through a readmission process that involved bringing a parent or guardian to a meeting with Boyd and signing a pledge renouncing both past and future protests. The students identified as protest leaders were refused readmittance, and the boycott was effectively ended. Within two weeks, Boyd reported that "students are taking part in class work, and various activities at the college, in a normal way, and our cooperation is very good."[30]

Through his decisive actions, Boyd reassured those whites who feared the civil rights connotations of the student strike. E. T. Crisler wrote that Boyd "is going about his difficult duties in a systematic and conscientious manner," and the *Pittsburgh Courier* reported that "Boyd will stay clear of the NAACP and the desegregation question." Over the years, Boyd developed a reputation for being a "tough task master" who could "handle them niggers." He cemented his ties to the trustees by squashing dissent and controlling students and employees through fear of expulsion or firing. According to one employee, Boyd had a "very positive" and "very strong relationship with the Board." He explained, "Their attitude was they were going to stay out of it. 'As long as you control your situation, . . . we won't bother you. Only time we gon' get involved is when you lose control.'" In early 1959, when the Sovereignty Commission considered developing a network of black leaders to "funnel information" and handle "any incident or development that might threaten segregation in the state," they listed Boyd among the potential members.[31]

In exchange for maintaining the racial status quo, the trustees paid Boyd well and allowed him a measure of autonomy in directing campus operations. A faculty member who came to work at Alcorn after the 1957 protest said that Boyd "could do no wrong because he brought Alcorn back to life after the strike." He also recalled that "the powers that be . . . gave him a free hand to do the things that he thought were necessary to do." Although Alcorn remained underfunded relative to the state's white institutions, during Boyd's tenure, the college received a major infusion of money. Beginning with a gym, completed in 1959, there were at least twelve major new construction projects in Boyd's first ten years at Alcorn. Although this building program corresponded with a dramatic expansion of the student body and was part of Mississippi's attempt to circumvent the *Brown* decision, many people attributed the additional resources to Boyd's talents and thought that he was working miracles.[32]

Despite his close ties to the trustees and other whites, Boyd did not automatically follow the wishes of white authorities. For example, in 1963, when the Sovereignty Commission tried to arrange a speaking tour at the state's black colleges for Uriah J. Fields, a black minister critical of the Montgomery bus boycott, the president of Jackson State readily agreed, but Boyd turned them down, arguing that it might "cause confusion and disruption with the students." In fact, he suggested that permitting Fields to speak would obligate him to allow students to invite other speakers, including "Martin Luther King Jr. or other agitators that planned on creating strife and disruption." Here, Boyd used his proficiency at keeping Alcorn separate from the civil rights movement to claim the authority to reject an anti–civil rights movement speaker. At the same time, he emphasized to the commission investigator that he had "perfect harmony with all white people." He pointed out that he used chartered buses "in order not to subject" the students to public transportation, explaining that this prevented "any kind of racial disturbance that might give the college a bad name."[33] Boyd's rejection of Fields and his rationale for chartering buses contained considerable ambiguity. The Sovereignty Commission and board of trustees could interpret these decisions as Boyd's attempts to avoid controversy, but they can also be understood as protective measures intended to shelter students and faculty from white supremacy as much as possible.

O. W. Moses, who worked in the business office during both Otis's and Boyd's presidencies, disagreed with those who characterized Boyd as an "Uncle Tom." According to Moses, "He didn't back down from, bow to, the board. He told them just what he thought. So, I said he considered himself . . . as the white person and we were still the black people, the Negroes. [That's] the way he handled it." Moses recalled a meeting between Boyd and the trustees about how to handle reopening the college after students had been sent home for participating in a demonstration. Some board members thought Boyd should call all of the students, but Boyd insisted that students had to initiate the readmission process. Despite pressure from the board, Boyd "sat there and held face."[34]

Under Boyd's leadership, conditions at Alcorn continued to reflect whites' ability to use black representatives to maintain the status quo. In October 1959, Boyd responded to a student protest over "stringent regulations" and the "expulsion of a student" by calling in more than thirty-five highway patrolmen and sending the students home on chartered buses. After a three-day cooling-off period, most of the students were readmitted through personal interviews. When the trustees instructed the administration to organize a committee to hear student grievances—most of which centered on Boyd's severe social restrictions and arbitrary disciplinary procedures—Boyd used the committee's investigation and report to punish faculty who supported the students' efforts to promote a more open campus.

One of these faculty members was Corinne T. Carpenter, an assistant professor in the business school who, according to a colleague, was "well thought of." Carpenter was a consistent advocate for civil rights and student freedom, and she and her husband were both registered voters. After teaching at Alcorn for nineteen years, she was one of twelve employees notified in May 1960 that her contract would not be renewed. Boyd justified his action by claiming that Carpenter was "not with him" and that she took notes during grievance committee meetings in such a way that he was unable to identify his critics. Carpenter insisted that she was covered by tenure and appealed her dismissal to the American Association of University Professors (AAUP). When he was questioned by an AAUP investigator, Boyd refused to address the substantive issues but maintained that given the 1959–60 student protests, the campus would have "fallen apart" if he had given Carpenter and the other faculty earlier notice of their pending dismissal. Moreover, he directly attributed the lack of student protest in the fall of 1960 to Carpenter's absence. The AAUP censured the college, but as one of the faculty members noted, the AAUP "didn't really carry that much weight at black schools at that time." The fired employees essentially had no recourse.[35]

After the faculty purge, the faculty and staff who were left learned to keep their opinions to themselves. According to one, "You couldn't talk about [student protest or civil rights] cause if you got involved, you got fired. It was just that simple." Most of the faculty assumed a defensive attitude and protected their jobs by distancing themselves from anything related to the civil rights movement. During the 1960s, they stopped leaving campus to attend fraternity and other social events for fear they would be suspected of civil rights activity. One faculty member insisted that when Boyd expelled students for activism, "There was empathy, sympathy, but there wasn't anything faculty could do to save them. They were gone."[36] In the 1960s, when college students across the South energized the movement with sit-ins, Alcorn students remained on the sidelines, cut off by Boyd and the college's rural, isolated location.

CHAPTER Six

Winning the Right to Organize

In 1961, the escalating national movement provided Claiborne County blacks some help in their efforts to secure voting rights. When Jackson NAACP activist Reverend R. L. T. Smith became the first black Mississippian to run for Congress since Reconstruction, Student Nonviolent Coordinating Committee (SNCC) field secretary Robert Moses acted as his campaign manager. Smith and Moses traveled the congressional district, encouraging black voter registration, surreptitiously passing out campaign literature, and conducting workshops, including two in Claiborne County. Nate Jones was one of about twenty men who attended the first, and he recalled, "We had a young man from New York come down, and his name was Moses, I never will forget it." Whites found out about the meeting and, according to Jones, "[When] we came downstairs, I bet it was fifty white people down there and they was checking everybody that come out. . . . When we came out, I did hear them call out some people, but I didn't hear my name. But it started falling out." In a bit of an understatement, Jones concluded that whites "didn't like the idea of us meeting"; only he and two others returned the following Friday.[1]

At roughly the same time, the Justice Department reopened its investigation into Claiborne County blacks' allegations of racial bias in voter registration, instructing the FBI to reinterview the five 1959 complainants, along with ten other blacks who had also tried unsuccessfully to register. Prodded by Medgar Evers and inspired by Moses's literacy classes and the investigation, a number of blacks renewed their efforts to register. Barber Alexander Collins made at least five attempts to register in 1961 and 1962, many of them in February and March when Moses and Smith were campaigning. Annie Holloway Johnson tried again to register on April 9, 1962, accompanied by two friends, Thelma Crowder and Estelle Collins Johnson. The latter was her neighbor (Roscoe Johnson's wife and Alexander Collins's sister), and all three attended Mercy Seat Baptist Church, where Eugene Spencer was pastor. In fact, they made their plans to register at Sunday school and Crowder thought she "had it made" and would pass the test because their "Sunday School lesson was centered around" the Mississippi Constitution. However, Crowder recalled that Circuit Clerk Pauline Easley said her application "didn't make enough sentences" and "she balled it up and threw it in the waste can. And she didn't give the others an opportunity to pass either."[2]

The three women described their experience to "some of the head leaders" and to Justice Department investigators who interviewed eleven African Americans about their registration experiences from April 8–10. According to Crowder, "We all were questioned separately. And I told him I was reluctant in answering his question for the simple reason [that] I live here and I didn't know what might would happen. And I was afraid. He said, 'You need not be afraid, this is confidential.' . . . And a short while [later] we were informed to go on down and register. We went on down there and she registered us." Despite the Justice Department's assurances of confidentiality, within two years, Crowder had been identified by name in court documents. Her experience exemplifies the problem articulated by state NAACP president Aaron Henry when he explained that it was easy to find blacks who had been discriminated against, but "it was terribly hard to find a person who was willing to become part of a federal suit and thus run the risk of sacrificing everything."[3]

In August 1962, based on Crowder's experience and other evidence, the Justice Department filed suit against the state of Mississippi and six registrars, including Claiborne County's Pauline Easley. The suit alleged that "the county registrars have used the broad powers given them in administering the interpretation test to discriminate against Negroes" and challenged the constitutionality of a number of Mississippi's voting laws. Easley's ability to fend off black voters is evident in Sovereignty Commission and Justice Department tallies. The number of blacks registered to vote in Claiborne County went from fifteen in 1960 to sixteen the following year and seventeen in April 1962. However, with the lawsuit pending and the Justice Department scrutinizing completed applications, Easley probably felt compelled to pass the most persistent black applicants. Consequently, the total jumped to twenty-six by January 1964. In 1963, Alexander Collins and Nate Jones, who both maintained their NAACP membership even when others began dropping off, became registered voters after repeated attempts. Jones followed up Moses's literacy classes with his own study of the state constitution. Despite this, he remembered having trouble when the registrar asked him to interpret the 92nd section. "That was, look like, the longest section in there. And then interpret on paper and then she would ask questions. And . . . when I would pass it in, she would say, 'Well, you didn't make it this time. I'm just write void on this and try it again.' And she just voided it and told me to try again. I would go back. But finally . . . I was registered."[4]

The Justice Department also provided some assistance for the handful of blacks who had already succeeded in registering by insisting that white officials stop using the white primary as a tactic to limit black voting. In April 1962, they informed Claiborne County Democratic Executive Committee chair Bobby Gage that the Democratic Party must stop keeping black ballots separate, questioning "prospective voters about their beliefs," and requiring "statements affirming belief in principles of racial segregation or disaffirming participation in organizations." Under threat of legal action, white officials agreed to conduct the June 5 primary "in accordance with the Constitution and laws of the United States." Moreover, they acknowledged "their obligation to permit Negro citizens to vote in the primary." As a result, thirteen of the seventeen black registered voters were able to cast their ballots for R. L. T. Smith.[5]

Whites in Claiborne County resented the Justice Department's intrusion and consistently tried to undermine its investigation. Editor E. T. Crisler criticized the lawsuit as an attack on states' rights. After quoting Mississippi senator John Stennis, who said [Attorney General] Robert Kennedy was "engaged in a systematic search behind every fence post and under every rug, seeking some evidence of wrong-doing," Crisler added, "Yes, his men have been in Claiborne snooping all over the place." When FBI agents interviewed white citizens about voter registration on two separate occasions, they received little cooperation. Of the ninety-nine whites the Justice Department asked the FBI to interview in July 1963, only eight were willing to provide signed and written statements; forty-three were completely unresponsive. Ultimately the FBI received some cooperation from fewer than half of those on their list. Public officials were no more helpful. White farmer and politician Mott Headley expressed hostility toward an interviewer who, he said, "wanted to know what I had done to keep any of them from registering." Headley recalled telling him, "Look, let me tell you something. . . . I really don't even have time to talk to you. If you want to come late this evening and sit on my porch and talk to me about farming, that's all I know. I'll be glad to visit with you, but unless . . . I'm under arrest, you and I don't have anything to talk about."[6]

In April 1962, when investigators asked to look at the voter registration forms, Easley refused. In response to a formal November 1962 demand, she balked again and insisted on having additional information "before any consideration of any inspection or copying of any records." Among other things, she wanted the "names and addresses of such persons to whom alleged distinctions based upon race or color were made." With the help of a court order, the Justice Department did eventually copy some records in March 1963, yet Easley still defied both the letter and intent of the law, failing to provide applications made before June 29, 1962.[7]

Despite this comprehensive resistance, whites persistently denied that they were preventing blacks from registering and voting. In 1964, a *Washington Post* reporter wrote that E. T. Crisler said blacks "haven't shown much interest" in voting and that he "denied that there have been official efforts to discourage them." According to the reporter, however, Crisler would not "estimate how many years would be needed for whites to 'gradually' tolerate a shift in voting patterns" or whether they would accept such change. Crisler's comments make it obvious that, despite his denials, he assumed whites controlled black voting. Mott Headley's memories are similarly contradictory. In the early 1990s, when he recounted his conversation with the FBI agent, he sighed heavily and said, "You know, I don't remember there being a whole lot of opposition to them registering. I really don't. I tell you what now. I had a lot of black friends." Yet Headley also noted that he was elected to office before blacks voted.[8]

Despite white reticence and obfuscation, the Justice Department found considerable evidence of racial discrimination. Examination of white applications showed that many people with low literacy levels were registered and that there was a striking similarity among many white responses to a question about the duties and obligations of citizenship. Several whites reported receiving assistance, and one woman, who did not know how to answer the question on citizenship or interpret the constitution, said that Easley gave her the answers. Whites were consistently assigned shorter and more understandable sections of the constitution to interpret. The investigation uncovered whites who were allowed to reregister by simply signing the book, some who voted without reregistering, and others who registered for the first time without taking the registration test. A few reported experiences like that of one white man who told an investigator that he registered simply by giving his "name, age, residence and occupation." Moreover, in contrast to their treatment of black applicants, registrars were never too busy for whites, and those who came in groups were allowed to fill out their forms simultaneously.[9]

While Easley did her best to deny the Justice Department access to her records, she regularly supplied the Sovereignty Commission with lists of black voters and reassurances about their limited numbers. In September 1961, she reported that only two blacks had registered since she had taken office in January 1960. This was juxtaposed with her assessment that "relations among the races were very good at this time." When Carl Thompson and Jesse Morris applied to be notaries public, she provided detailed information to the commission about their registration, poll tax, and voting histories. The Sovereignty Commission offered its own assistance to Easley, including a March 1961 warning that Justice Department investigators were asking questions around the state. In February 1965, the Sovereignty Commission director ordered investigators to remove references to their investigations of black voter registration from their files. He directed them to cover up, not stop, these illegal investigations.[10]

The Justice Department investigation and Bob Moses's workshops briefly provided Claiborne County blacks some contact with the emerging Mississippi movement. However, those connections never really developed. By the summer of 1962, SNCC workers had decided to concentrate their voter registration work north of Claiborne County, in the Mississippi Delta, where the majority of the state's black population lived. SNCC often recruited organizers and volunteers from black college campuses, and their decision not to initiate a project in Claiborne County was influenced by Alcorn's isolated location and President J. D. Boyd's dictatorial control. After visiting the campus, they believed the college would be an impediment rather than a help to organizing the local community. According to Worth Long, SNCC found "some good individual folk [at Alcorn], but by and large they were there to get a degree and then go out and teach people what they know." He added, "The administration and the conservatism among black people in that area, especially among the preachers, teachers and preachers, was such that you wouldn't want to even think about" trying to organize there. A former Alcorn student concurred, explaining that few students were willing to risk crossing Boyd: "When you are coming from a cotton field where you out there picking cotton and doing things like that, and then you have an opportunity to go to college, of course you're going to be conservative. . . . You better protect it because that might be your only shot."[11]

SNCC's assessment of the difficulties associated with recruiting Alcorn students was borne out in April 1964 when students initiated a protest over Boyd's policies governing campus social life. The protesters tried to pressure Boyd to meet with them by convincing most of the student body to spend the night on the football field, ignoring a campus curfew that was one of the rules they objected to. Instead of capitulating, Boyd suspended all of the protesting students, and most stayed home the rest of the semester, learning firsthand the power of state repression and the futility of campus protest at Alcorn. Despite support for the students from parents and alumni, the board of trustees refused to consider students' grievances and insisted that they "must learn that boycotts, sit-ins, demonstrations, and other civil disobedience against the State of Mississippi will not be permitted."[12]

Since the protest took place on the eve of the highly publicized 1964 Summer Project, state officials were particularly concerned about whether the Alcorn protest was explicitly related to the civil rights movement. An investigator for the highway patrol concluded that there was "no racial connotation; it was apparently just a rebellion against authority." Although reassured, state officials worked to further isolate Mississippi college students. In 1964 and 1965, the trustees passed several resolutions aimed at keeping civil rights workers off state campuses, ordering the presidents of each institution to "prohibit from the campuses . . . any person actively engaged in, or connected with, the 'Mississippi Project' now being conducted by COFO [Council of Federated Organizations]." Moreover when two SNCC workers began planning to go to Alcorn early in 1965 to build on the 1964 protest, a black informant notified the Sovereignty Commission. The commission warned state administrators, Boyd, and the governor and then instructed its informant to "terminate [the] possible movement at Alcorn College." A few days later, the informant reported that he had successfully talked the SNCC workers out of trying to organize the campus.[13]

With SNCC's earlier decision to focus on the Delta, the NAACP and its field secretary, Medgar Evers, remained the most important link between Claiborne County and the statewide movement. Claiborne County activists occasionally drove to Jackson for marches and NAACP meetings at the Masonic Temple, and Evers did what he could to encourage the underground NAACP branch. He facilitated the late-1950s complaints to the Justice Department and the 1960s Justice Department investigation. Alexander Collins's wife has strong memories of one of Evers's visits and recalled that her husband "was just carried away with the strength and the depth that he had in helping the black race to survive."[14] Even this tenuous tie was severed with Medgar Evers's murder in June 1963. Essentially cut off from outside help and worried about the repercussions of explicit protest, Claiborne County blacks remained on the sidelines from 1963 through late 1965.

During that period, the story of the Mississippi movement was primarily the story of SNCC and COFO, an umbrella group that coordinated civil rights work in the state from 1962 to 1965. COFO was composed of SNCC, the Congress of Racial Equality (CORE), the state conference of the NAACP, and local movement organizations, though SNCC had the most workers and was the "dominant partner." COFO organized voter registration projects throughout the Delta, co-ordinated a 1963 Freedom Vote campaign where blacks unable to register to cast protest ballots, and initiated the large-scale 1964 Summer Project, which brought about 1,000 mostly white volunteers to Mississippi. Extensive press coverage of the project and accompanying white violence exposed the depths of the state's massive resistance and ensured the passage of the 1964 Civil Rights Act. The summer ended with the Mississippi Freedom Democratic Party's challenge to the all-white Mississippi "Regulars" at the Democratic National Convention in Atlantic City. Though the MFDP was unable to unseat the Regulars, the challenge did draw attention to blacks' continuing electoral exclusion and helped generate support for subsequent voting-rights legislation.[15]

Around the state, many NAACP activists were enthusiastic participants in the COFO coalition, but the national NAACP refused to join. The NAACP's competition with other civil rights organizations was a recurring story, especially after the early 1960s explosion of sit-ins, freedom rides, and mass demonstrations brought growing prominence to SNCC, CORE, and the Southern Christian Leadership Conference (SCLC). In particular, SNCC's emphasis on developing local leaders and preference for collective decision-making put the organization at odds with the national NAACP, which was decidedly hierarchical and bureaucratic. The NAACP seemed to want loyal followers, not independent thinkers and actors. Relations between SNCC/COFO and the national NAACP became increasingly strained during the 1964 Summer Project. According to John Dittmer, NAACP executive secretary Roy Wilkins and Director of Branches Gloster Current "continued to view COFO with suspicion, if not alarm." Current criticized state NAACP president Aaron Henry for his close ties to COFO and for failing to make the NAACP, as an institution, his priority. Although some local NAACP activists did have occasional difficulty with COFO, at times feeling excluded from decision-making and overlooked by impatient younger radicals, the national organization's primary concern was competing effectively for publicity and prestige. This is evident in the NAACP's high-profile July 1964 tour designed to test Mississippi's compliance with the public accommodations portion of the newly passed Civil Rights Act. A delegation of state and national NAACP officials traveled with reporters to perform a limited testing in larger towns where they met minimal opposition. While the tour was covered on the front page of the *New York Times* and deemed a success by the NAACP, most of the establishments that accommodated the NAACP delegation remained closed to blacks as soon as the media and the national figures left.[16]

Following the tour, the NAACP's director of voter registration, John Brooks, filed an extensive report critical of COFO, especially its appeal to "lower-income people who want to gain freedom but lack leadership ability and influence in their community." Brooks argued that "a three- to four-week power play is needed" to "put the NAACP in Mississippi in the driver's seat." He proposed using a voter registration program to "build up our NAACP membership and branch structure in Mississippi." He concluded parenthetically that "voter Registration will be secondary; our primary aim will be to build the NAACP Organizational Structure." The 1963 death of Medgar Evers and his replacement by his older brother Charles Evers exacerbated the NAACP's conflict with SNCC/COFO and further limited its role in the Mississippi movement. According to John Dittmer, "The emergence of Charles Evers was a setback for the Mississippi movement. Although Medgar had initially been wary of the young organizers in SNCC and CORE, and they of him, by late 1962 there had developed a mutual respect. Medgar had been comfortable working within the COFO framework, where Charles ignored COFO leaders and tried to undermine their programs. From the summer of 1963 on he began to chart his own course for the state NAACP, which frustrated and infuriated grass-roots activists and national NAACP officials alike."[17]

Both Medgar and Charles Evers were World War II veterans and Alcorn graduates who fiercely resented racial injustice. Otherwise, their values and personalities were quite different. Charles Payne argues that "the transition from Medgar to Charles Evers illustrates the statewide change to a more morally ambiguous climate." When Medgar was nurturing the NAACP in Mississippi, Charles, by his own admission, was in Chicago pimping, running numbers, and bootlegging. Even before his brother was buried, Charles Evers claimed his job with the NAACP by telling several reporters that he was replacing Medgar. Evers later wrote that NAACP head Roy Wilkins "almost slit his throat" shaving when he heard on the radio "that the NAACP had picked Medgar's successor: Charles Evers." Evers added, "The last thing Roy wanted was Medgar's rough, tough big brother coming out of the Chicago rackets to soil Medgar's memory and tarnish the NAACP." However, despite his reservations, Wilkins conceded Charles the job rather than risk a public confrontation with the slain martyr's brother. Charles Evers asserted, "With the memory of Medgar's murder so close, he just couldn't refuse an Evers." This incident exemplifies the opportunism and ambition that characterized Charles Evers. Earlier, as a twenty-three-year-old freshman at Alcorn, he had declared himself class president. Although another student insisted on a vote, he was no match for Evers, who told the assembled students, "I fought in the war, risked my life overseas. I got three businesses going. I've stood up to white folk all my life. Can you match that?" In a 1990s memoir, Evers asserted, "I was a born leader, proud, and without a scared bone in my body. I was born to get rich and rise in politics. But I hit a brick wall saying,

'Niggers got no business making money, being proud, or going into politics.' I had to struggle so hard to take my place out front."[18]

Three months after Evers took over as the NAACP field secretary for Mississippi, Gloster Current observed to Wilkins that although Evers was "not as well prepared and grounded in our movement as we would like," he was "impressed by his aggressiveness and willingness to move out in several directions and not wait to find out what he should do. In other words, he believes in erring by doing rather than erring by inaction." Despite this hopeful tone, Evers and the nation's oldest civil rights organization were a bad match. Evers never saw himself as a cog in the NAACP machine and consistently ignored national policy, embarrassed the organization with his speeches, refused to follow its guidelines for submitting reports, and issued press releases with typing, spelling, and syntax errors. His controversial style and propensity to act on his own without consulting his superiors kept him in hot water. NAACP officials alternately ordered and cajoled him to consult with the national office and have speeches preapproved; they questioned his judgment and, where possible, gave him explicit instructions for handling controversial situations, like the trial of Byron de la Beckwith, who was accused of murdering his brother. Within a year of Evers's hiring, Gloster Current's cautious optimism had evaporated and he wrote Evers, "There are times when I despair of ever being able to obtain from you a clear understanding of how an executive functions in the NAACP."[19]

When Charles Evers began his work as NAACP field secretary, the organization had a tenuous presence in Mississippi, with about a dozen branches. While COFO workers moved into communities, encouraging voter registration, teaching in citizenship and freedom schools, and organizing the MFDP, the NAACP had little to report. During his first two years as state field secretary, Evers was a popular guest speaker around the country but did little at home. A handful of schools were desegregated (a legacy of Medgar's work), and Evers occasionally issued press releases or sent letters and telegrams of protest to the state and federal governments. Ultimately, though, there was little growth in branches and almost all NAACP activism came from individuals working with COFO. Evers's rare reports, a continuing source of contention with the national office, had little to say about NAACP activity, and he initiated little in the struggle for civil rights. A Claiborne County man recalled that when a group of farmers sent a man to meet with Evers, he told them, "Be quiet and hold off. Don't do anything." One of the few things Charles Evers did was try to undermine SNCC and COFO. Sovereignty Commission informant reports are filled with details and speculation about conflict between Evers and COFO. In February 1964, Evers warned Jackson State College students "not to have anything to do with" the SNCC workers trying to organize a protest. Despite several letters of protest from NAACP members, Current praised him and suggested that he might finally be getting the "hang of things."[20]

Despite their shared antipathy toward COFO, Evers's conflicts with Wilkins and Current escalated in October 1964 when he defied explicit orders and used a Buffalo, New York, NAACP speech to endorse Robert Kennedy in his Senate race. Current complained to Wilkins's assistant, John Morsell, that Evers was acting as "if he were God's appointed savior" and contended, we have "a very real problem which we are going to have to deal with." In June 1965, when Evers again blatantly ignored the NAACP nonpartisan policy, Current wrote him, "I do not think you are naive. I have found you to say one thing to us in the National Office . . . and another to people to whom you later talked separating yourself from National policy. You have indicated that you did not agree with or obey such and such a National policy because of your differing opinion." A little over a month later, Current made a case for firing Evers for "gross misconduct" and "incompetence." Current charged that in addition to his repeated violation of NAACP policies and procedures, Evers had failed to cooperate with "top level staff" working on a voter registration project.[21] It appeared that Charles Evers's connection to Medgar and his work to undermine COFO were no longer enough to appease the national office.

Ironically, the decline of SNCC/COFO and an August 27, 1965, Klan car bomb attack that injured Natchez NAACP branch president George Metcalf gave Evers a reprieve and the opportunity he needed to save his job. Although he had little or no prior involvement in the Natchez movement, he took the community by storm, articulating widespread black anger and publicly warning whites that blacks were armed and ready to retaliate. His bold statements and charismatic speaking captivated many Natchez blacks, who flocked to hear him at mass meetings. Many people in the area were immediately receptive to him as Medgar's brother and because he had ties to the area from his college days at Alcorn, when he operated several businesses. After quickly winning popular support, Evers moved to take over the Natchez movement and destroy rival organizations.[22]

Evers also increasingly followed the NAACP party line (perhaps because his job was on the line or because at a fundamental level he had more in common with the New York staff than was initially evident). After his explosive statements about black retaliation were widely publicized, Evers issued a press release calling for peace. Evoking the "ambush killing" of his brother Medgar, he concluded by arguing, "This is a time for reason, a time for honest communication, a time for constructive working together to build a better community. This is not a time for violence." Not surprisingly, the formal statement coincided with a visit from top NAACP officials and reflected their reasoned language, not Evers's angry and impulsive commentary. Similarly, although Evers led several protest marches in defiance of court orders, he called off others and generally undermined sentiment and action directed at massive demonstrations and civil disobedience. In this and in his willingness to negotiate with white leaders, Evers's actions were in line with the program laid out by an NAACP administrator who urged Natchez blacks to avoid demonstrations and use their initial demands as "negotiable goals" rather than as an ultimatum.[23]

Evers won favor from the national NAACP by undermining the MFDP and emerging as the undisputed leader in Natchez. According to John Dittmer, "The Natchez movement was in turmoil. SCLC, NAACP, and FDP organizers were competing for the allegiance of the black community, . . . [and] Charles Evers was at the center of the controversy, skillfully playing off one faction against the other, establishing himself as *the* leader of the Natchez movement." He explains that Natchez blacks cared little about the behind-the-scenes struggles among movement organizations and activists. "They had found their leader in Charles Evers, and through October [1965] they continued to pack the nightly mass meetings and answer *his* call for demonstrations." Evers easily mobilized several busloads of partisans to lobby on his behalf at the NAACP convention at which the board was considering his firing. His obvious popularity gave credence to his threat that he would start a competing organization if he were fired. Moreover, by winning control of the Natchez movement, gaining favorable national press, and downplaying mass protest in favor of boycotts and negotiation, Evers had made himself, as Dittmer writes, "indispensable to the national NAACP."[24]

Despite his earlier ineffectiveness as a movement leader in Mississippi, Evers used his Natchez triumph to initiate successful local movements throughout southwest Mississippi. Dittmer and Charles Payne compellingly demonstrate that by this time, late 1965, the movement had won the right to organize. Despite the persistence of violence and continued collaboration between state officials, law officers, and terrorists, the monolithic defiance that Mississippi was known for had eroded. Historian Neil McMillen explains, "Although Mississippi's segregationists were no more ready to embrace the black citizens as their equal than they had been a decade before, a growing number of them recognized by the mid-1960's that last-ditch defiance was utterly futile." Moreover, Evers faced little organizational competition. The COFO coalition had disbanded in July 1965, and in a chapter titled "Battle Fatigue," Dittmer points out that a significant number of key SNCC organizers had returned to school or left the state. Many of the remaining workers struggled with the organization's structure and direction. Payne writes that in the aftermath of the 1964 MFDP challenge, "SNCC was trying to resolve a staggering number of questions, many of them products of the organization's disillusionment with American society." Meanwhile, the MFDP, the primary organization carrying on the SNCC/COFO tradition, was putting most of its 1965 resources into a national-level Congressional Challenge and few people were involved in community-based organizing. Moderate whites were seeking out more conservative, NAACP-oriented black leaders, including Aaron Henry and Charles Evers, trying, according to Dittmer, "to establish themselves as the authentic voice of the 'new' Mississippi."[25]

While SNCC was struggling for direction and COFO was disintegrating, the Voting Rights Act (VRA), signed by President Lyndon Johnson in early August 1965, opened the door to widespread black voter registration. In an article chronicling black enfranchisement in Mississippi, Neil McMillen acknowledges the Selma campaign as the immediate catalyst for the VRA but argues that "the need for this revolutionary measure was nowhere more compellingly demonstrated than by the civil rights alliance in Mississippi." Yet, as he points out, COFO had been disbanded by the time of the law's passage and was thus unable to use it as an organizing tool. Similarly, the MFDP, whose Congressional Challenge had provided Congress with an ongoing reminder of the need for strong voting rights legislation, ended 1965 with few resources left to pursue voter registration or any coordinated civil rights program.[26] Ironically, Charles Evers, who had played little positive role in the Mississippi movement, was now positioned to take advantage of the new laws and Mississippi political leaders' grudging acceptance of the inevitability of some change in the status quo.

CHAPTER Seven

A New Day Begun

Even while they remained on the sidelines, Claiborne County blacks followed news of the movement elsewhere. When he was still a young child James Miller heard adults in his family discuss the Little Rock desegregation crisis. "I can remember my grandmother, dad's mother, saying that, 'That stuff ain't never gonna come here. We alright here.' My grandmother, on my mama's side was saying, 'Well, Dr. King is saying what's right. It's a lot of stuff wrong, need to be dealt with. Colored folks are just as good as white folks. And everybody ought to be treated equal.'" Trying to explain how far away the national movement seemed, he compared it to the 1980s anti-apartheid movement in South Africa. "It's just that far away. So never ever would that upset what was going on here." By fall 1965, that had begun to change. Mass movements just down Highway 61 in Fayette and Natchez sparked additional conversation and made a Port Gibson movement seem possible, even likely. In a street corner conversation, for example, one man heard about the NAACP for the first time when his coworkers mentioned the organization's efforts to "get a better deal for black people in Fayette." In another case, a black woman who commented that blacks "was marching down to Fayette" sparked a heated confrontation with a white storekeeper, who became "kind of furious." According to Julia Jones, "hearing about the movement sparked the desire here" and led people to believe that it was "on [the] way up here."[1]

The nearby movements provided the immediate impetus for the Claiborne County movement. In November 1965, NAACP attorney Marian Wright (later Marian Wright Edelman), Rudy Shields, a thirty-four-year-old black man from Chicago, and several other Natchez activists initiated efforts to launch a voter registration project in Claiborne County. Their first stop was the Baptist Ministerial Association, led by Reverend Eugene Spencer. Although the ministers promised their support, Spencer immediately expressed some reservations, telling the visitors that Claiborne County blacks "could handle" their push for civil rights "without anybody coming in, without any uproar" and insisting that "everything was going along fine."[2] He also organized a group called the Human Relations Committee (HRC), which sought to achieve moderate change through negotiation. The founding of the HRC had the approval of local whites and was intended to head off the outside organizers and control civil rights activism.

While Spencer was pulling the HRC together, Rudy Shields quickly became the most important civil rights organizer in Claiborne County. After meeting with the ministers, he sought out other black leaders, including farmers and business owners who were part of the network that had nourished the county's NAACP branch and sporadic voter registration efforts. Born in Columbus, Ohio, Shields served four years in the army during the Korean War and worked in Chicago putting undercoating on cars before moving to Mississippi in 1965. He later explained, "They were having difficulty getting black folks to register to vote, so I came down to volunteer my services." By the time Shields began working in Claiborne County, he had served a quick movement apprenticeship, helping with voter registration and a boycott in Natchez and organizing an NAACP branch across the Mississippi River in Ferriday, Louisiana. His most extensive experience came in the Fayette (Jefferson County) movement as Charles Evers's point man. In less than two months, he, Evers, Natchez volunteers, and Jefferson County activists had founded a new NAACP branch there and were hosting weekly mass meetings. They initiated an effective boycott of white merchants and, with help from federal registrars, increased the number of black registered voters from a handful to over 3,000. During his first Claiborne County trips, Shields was accompanied by Steve Marsaw, a Natchez native and NAACP activist. Described as a quiet man who was active with youth, Marsaw probably eased Shields's way by introducing him to some of the Claiborne Countians he knew. Nate Jones, whose nephew played against Marsaw's baseball team, asserted that "by him being a baseball manager, he knew how to organize."[3]

Shields was articulate, inspiring, and effective. He quickly became well known and popular throughout the black community. James Devoual, who was a high school student, described Shields as "a very personable guy. I mean, he felt right at home even though he had never been to Port Gibson before. He felt at home among us." He explained, "He'd walk up and start a conversation, talk about the NAACP. He'd talk about the organizing efforts. He'd talk about racial pride, self-worth, doing something, getting involved, changing the system, and he just motivated you to want to be a part of that." Part of his effectiveness came through his ability to "recognize local leadership and push it out front." George Walker, a Korean War veteran and ambulance driver for Thompson's Funeral Home, vividly recalled the day Shields came by asking for a list of people who "wanted to see the black race go from where we at." Walker continued, "This is the way he came to me. 'Do you want to go to the front of the bus or the back of the bus?' and stuff like that. He had something like that to talk to you about. That's the way he came to you. He never said what you should do. He never told me what I should do. He put it on your mind, and once you would say that [you agreed], then he would have you obligated. 'Well, we gon' have a meeting next week, why don't you come out?' " Reverend J. L. Sayles asserted that Shields gave people courage by letting them "know who he was and what he stood for." Other movement supporters described him as "hard working," "single-minded," "fearless," and a "diehard believer that change would come." James Miller remembered that Shields "looked like a hobo" with "raggedy" shoes and clothes but insisted that when he "opened his mouth, Jesus Christ, he got to you. And I mean, he was dedicated to what he was doing."[4]

Though Shields developed his reputation among blacks over a period of months, many people were immediately receptive to both his message and his style. Nate Jones remembered that when Shields and Marsaw "sneaked in," people "got to singing those freedom songs and everything and the house got packed and they got interested." He concluded, "That's how [the movement] got going. They slipped in and set it up." Shields and Marsaw rejuvenated the NAACP, bringing back former members and recruiting new ones. At a December 12, 1965, meeting, fifty-seven people joined the organization and the group applied for a new branch charter. Despite some fear, at Shields's urging they agreed to operate openly instead of in secret. With the revived NAACP and Spencer's HRC, Claiborne County blacks appeared to have two vehicles for dealing with their collective grievances. A few NAACP members even met with the HRC to prepare a list of demands to present to the white community. Despite this brief cooperation, however, Spencer was almost certainly collaborating with white leaders and using the HRC to prevent the emergence of an active NAACP, minimize black protest, and keep Evers away from the community. Spencer told James Dorsey that the HRC needed to "get some things going" to "ward off" a mass movement and later explained that "whites didn't want an 'outsider' coming in." HRC member F. A. White Sr., a school principal nearing retirement, shared Spencer's view, explaining that "white people didn't care much about talking to the NAACP" and preferred using the HRC, to settle things "without confusion or misunderstanding." Another man insisted that whites wanted to work with black leaders like Spencer and J. C. Dunbar (then principal of Addison) who they thought had "control over the lower classes."[5]

The members of the HRC and five white men appointed by the chamber of commerce formed what became known as the Bi-Racial Committee. In addition to Spencer, the HRC members were Reverend James Dorsey, a World War II veteran, longtime NAACP member, and new pastor of Port Gibson's First Baptist Church; three of Spencer's Westside neighbors, farmer and onetime NAACP member Reverend Alexander Martin, TPP farmer Reverend O. S. Burks, and former box factory union activist Reverend Evan Doss, who was farming on Spencer's land; Pattison farmer, teacher, registered voter, and NAACP activist Floyd Rollins; Alexander Collins, whose barbershop was the unofficial NAACP headquarters; a school principal; a store employee; a prosperous carpenter/ farmer; and three ministers who served Claiborne County churches but lived outside the community. All the white members were well-established bankers and merchants. R. D. Gage Jr. and Richard Hastings were presidents of Port Gibson's two banks and among the community's "first families"; similarly, lawyer J. T. Drake traced his family history to the county's antebellum settlement. James Hudson and M. M. McFatter, who owned prosperous local businesses (the Piggly Wiggly grocery store and McFatter's Drugstore), were newer members of the white elite. Though none of them were officeholders, these men consistently served in leadership positions in the local civic organizations and played an active role in shaping public policy.[6]

The Bi-Racial Committee, chaired by Gage, met twice and considered a petition that the HRC had developed in consultation with the NAACP. Whatever the origin and purpose of the HRC, their thirteen demands resonated throughout the black community. They included requests for a Bi-Racial Committee (which was redundant by then); a black appointee to the school board; a black police officer and a black deputy sheriff with full arrest authority; the desegregation of public facilities, specifically including the library; the hiring and upgrading of black employees in "governmental positions" and "all job opportunities"; the upgrading of city services in black neighborhoods; the building of a youth recreation facility; and for whites to "give Negroes the proper title and courtesy." The HRC petition ended with an allusion to the NAACP-led boycotts and demonstrations in Fayette and Natchez and implied that if Claiborne County whites would address their complaints, blacks would reject the NAACP and Evers: "Due to the many bad situations in which our towns and cities are

Collins Barbershop, the Fair Street meeting place and informal headquarters for the NAACP, ca. 1970s. Courtesy Mississippi Cultural Crossroads.

undergoing that have brought about bad relationship [*sic*], we the members of the Human Relations Committee, feel that our problems can be settled in our local district around the conference table."[7]

The black participants in the negotiations expressed considerable goodwill toward their white counterparts, but their recollections are almost entirely of rejection. Spencer emphasized that "there were no disparaging remarks" and that "everyone was treated with courtesy." However, whites contended that they "weren't quite ready" for integration and that "both races had to be educated in such matters." One participant remembered that the bankers agreed to use courtesy titles in their mail, but whites still refused to use them in face-to-face interactions with African Americans. Ultimately, white negotiators agreed to little and insisted that any changes would "take time" and that "their people were harder to handle than Negroes." Whites did ostensibly comply with two of the HRC's demands, forming the Bi-Racial Committee and hiring a black police officer. Yet whites had actually initiated both of these actions *before* they were formally requested by black leaders, making it clear that whites were not making concessions in response to the independent actions of Spencer and the HRC but were offering the black community a few carefully chosen tokens through the vehicle of the HRC. This contributed to many blacks' ultimate conclusion that whites had encouraged Spencer to form the HRC to preempt protest.[8]

Despite whites' refusal to address blacks' fundamental concerns, Spencer called a December 21st meeting at the courthouse to present the HRC's negotiations to the black community. A mass meeting of African Americans at the courthouse for a public discussion of racial grievances was big news. Facing a Confederate statue, the courthouse was in style and use a monument to the antebellum era. Whites, not blacks, used the courthouse for meetings and political rallies. Spencer later explained that the meeting was held at the courthouse to let blacks know that whites had approved it and "there was nothing to fear." At least 300 blacks crowded into the large upstairs courtroom for the meeting, which had been publicized by ministers, Shields, NAACP branch members, and word of mouth. Spencer recalled that whites even "let their servants . . . off, and they came to the meeting."[9]

When he opened the meeting, the sixty-year-old Spencer was at the pinnacle of his career. Starting as a sharecropper, he had achieved landownership and prospered through the Tenant Purchase Program. Spencer was universally acknowledged as the county's top black minister and was active in the state Baptist organization. He had recently fulfilled a lifelong goal by graduating from Alcorn. His children, too, had graduated from the institution, and one son worked at the college. His standing with white leaders was at its high point. Two months earlier he had been named to a three-county antipoverty committee, serving with Piggly Wiggly owner and Bi-Racial Committee member James Hudson, among others.[10] The emerging civil rights movement and whites' antipathy to the NAACP enhanced his bargaining power, and he was in an unprecedented position to parlay his standing with both communities into racial progress.

It is unclear whether the white members of the Bi-Racial Committee were present at the courthouse meeting, but Spencer was clearly in charge. After opening with a prayer, he skillfully directed the meeting, emphasizing that whites had hired a black police officer and formed the Bi-Racial Committee. He reported that one of the banks would hire a black cashier if they could find someone qualified and that whites had tentatively agreed to desegregate bathrooms and cafés. (Desegregation was actually mandated by the now-eighteen-month-old Civil Rights Act of 1964.) However, since whites had been vague in their promises, Spencer had little to say about when these changes would be implemented or about the other grievances on the petition. Instead, he emphasized that change "would take time," argued against "outsiders," and urged the crowd not to "be hasty."[11]

A few people expressed skepticism. Nate Jones, Spencer's friend and neigh-

Claiborne County Courthouse with Confederate statue, 1940. Photograph by Marion Post Wolcott, courtesy Library of Congress, LC USF 34 549000-D.

bor, recalled, "[I asked,] 'You mean they got Alcorn college down there and you can't find nobody in that college to work as a bank teller.' And he kind of ignored my question. And, somebody told him, I don't know [who], 'Hear him. Hear what he has to say.' And I asked the question over and directed it to Reverend Spencer. He shook his head and [said] 'I'm afraid to say no, we can't find nobody down there to work at the bank.' " Jones and the other questioners were a distinct minority that night. With almost universal consensus about the grievances, the excitement of the courthouse meeting, and the previously unheard of possibility that whites would entertain any collective black requests, Spencer was able to win over the crowd. The more than 300 people voted, in the words of *Reveille* editor Crisler, to "endorse the committee plan and the petition" with only three dissenters. Most blacks probably thought they were voting to have all of the grievances addressed. However, since the white committee members had not agreed to the demands in the HRC petition and the larger white community had not even met, it seems clear that the issue before blacks at the courthouse meeting was not really the grievances themselves but whether to accept the guidance of the HRC and, by implication, to reject the NAACP and outside organizers. This is implicit in Spencer's insistence, in describing that night, that "we could handle our own problems without the civil rights people coming in."[12] Nate Jones was one of the dissenters. After years of associating with the NAACP and attempting to register to vote, Jones, more than most, saw a viable alternative in Shields's organizing and the mass movements in neighboring communities. He was unwilling to accept either Spencer's authority or vague promises dependent on white goodwill. Though he stood virtually alone, his questions and concerns resonated with many in the audience; less than a week later others would speak up at a mass meeting hosted by the NAACP.

Meanwhile, on December 23, the *Port Gibson Reveille* announced a meeting for "all white merchants, . . . officials and other white citizens interested" in hearing "a report of the white members of the Bi-Racial Committee." Referring to the "discord prevalent in communities in our area," Crisler offered his endorsement and praise for the local people who were trying to "solve problems by sitting down together." He concluded with a familiar refrain: "Friendly relations have long existed here between white and Negro citizens, and we certainly would not want any disruptive actions which would injure all citizens to take place. Therefore, we urge that differences and problems be handled through the committee composed of members of both races." A front-page letter from Sheriff Dan McCay and Mayor E. D. Davis to the "Colored Citizens of Claiborne County, Mississippi," insinuated that "outside agitators" were threatening "Colored people" and encouraged anyone who felt threatened to contact local law enforcement or the "Colored Committee on bi-racial problems," who could "explain to you your rights." None of this coverage or commentary addressed any specific grievances. Instead, like Spencer at the courthouse meeting, the *Reveille* and white officials were evasive about everything except the importance of keeping the NAACP and movement workers out of the community.[13]

A showdown around the authority of the HRC came on December 28, when the Claiborne County NAACP hosted a "jam-packed" mass meeting at St. Peter's AME Church the same night that whites met at the courthouse. With HRC members attending the white meeting, Shields and Marsaw conducted the NAACP meeting. Unlike Spencer, they encouraged questions, discussion, and audience participation. Calvin Williams, the chief of security at Alcorn, was at the meeting as an observer to keep Alcorn president Boyd apprised of the movement's plans and get information "on things that would hurt Alcorn." Yet when the discussion turned to public services (like street-paving and water lines) that had bearing on his neighborhood, he began questioning Shields aggressively. In his typical style, Shields saw Williams not as a threat but as a potential leader. James Miller described their exchange: "[Shields] posed the question to the crowd and Calvin Williams spoke up and when Calvin Williams spoke up, he challenged Rudy on something and Rudy—I guess the way Rudy said it—that's what he wanted him to do, challenge him. . . . and [when] Williams challenged him again, [Rudy] said, 'Okay, you come on up front.' And from that point on, [Williams] was anointed on the head as a leader."[14]

Meanwhile, according to the *Reveille*, the whites meeting at the courthouse had voted to support the negotiations of the white members of the Bi-Racial Committee. Crisler's coverage did not include any specifics, and it is unclear what that vote of support was actually for. There is nothing to suggest that whites offered any concrete proposals. They either failed to recognize the strength of the NAACP or were simply unwilling to consider any substantive redress of black grievances. Instead of sincere negotiation, they relied on the lasting power of white supremacy. In an act rife with symbolism, they sent the HRC members to act as literal go-betweens and speak for them at the NAACP meeting a few blocks away. Nate Jones recalled, "They sent a group of blacks from the other side down there to ask us not to let the NAACP get established here." When Spencer arrived at the NAACP meeting, he was invited to the front. In addressing the crowd, he emphasized his connections to the white committee members and described them as "some of our top men." He insisted that whites in Claiborne County were better than those in other places and that if blacks followed their lead, the community would have "peace and harmony." As he had in the earlier meeting, Spencer stressed that whites had agreed to take down the signs marking segregation in public facilities and that the bankers "indicated that they would probably start a training program for cashiers and such." Despite having so little concrete to offer the crowd, he urged them to accept this start and reject the NAACP.[15]

This time, however, Spencer faced persistent, aggressive questioning. Calvin Williams told a historian later that Spencer was "taking shit" and "it was tough that night." Away from a white audience and in the midst of a spirited discussion facilitated by Shields, African Americans openly argued with Spencer and insisted that "the power structure had to do more than promise." Despite Spencer's efforts to put a good face on the negotiations, white leaders had put him in a difficult spot by refusing to offer a specific time frame for potential changes and by rejecting outright many of the black community's requests, including key ones calling for more courteous treatment and better jobs. Even Charles Groves's appointment as the first black police officer had significant limitations. His duties were restricted to directing traffic in front of the black public schools, and he had no authority to arrest whites. Whites chose Groves, probably with the approval or recommendation of Alcorn president Boyd, without considering the wishes of the larger black community, some of whom considered Groves an "Uncle Tom" and an inappropriate choice.[16] Moreover, Shields and Marsaw had already discussed voter registration and economic boycotts, two strategies that local blacks could use to achieve power and to pressure the white community for additional concessions.

Finally, the biggest sticking point that night was the black community's insistence on choosing its own leaders. HRC member James Dorsey recalled that the audience "wanted some of the other folks to be on the committee and they thought the NAACP . . . should have a voice." Nate Jones recalled that whites "picked the group of blacks. Pointed them out. I don't know who did it. But it wasn't done, you know, by the majority of the people." Before the night was over, the HRC had lost its standing and virtually the entire black community came to believe it was simply a "tool to be used by the power structure." Several people recalled that even Spencer's son Harold "stood up and told his daddy that he thought the committee had been chosen wrong." James Miller described an exchange between the two men about the black community's concerns about leadership and the need for specific commitments from whites: "Harold Spencer was trying to convince his father that he needs to deal with these things. And I think Harold wanted to take that aggressive leadership as well, this new emerging leadership. His father told him, 'No.' And I could see his expression on his face, as he's sitting there puzzling, wondering, 'Well, why Pop? Cause this makes sense.'" It was a long night, and before it was over the NAACP asked the HRC to join with them. They refused and disbanded instead. Spencer left the meeting and went to tell his white allies what had happened. Years later, Jones described begging Spencer to stay and affiliate with the NAACP: "I had so much respect for him. I just said, 'Please don't go back up there.' But he said he had made his commitment. He went back down there and let them know the NAACP had organized." Most of the HRC members followed Spencer, though Alexander Collins and Floyd Rollins, the HRC members who had worked most closely with the NAACP over the years, stayed and reaffirmed their allegiance to the NAACP.[17]

In the *Reveille*'s last issue of 1965, Crisler editorialized about the contest between the HRC and the NAACP, emphasizing his fear that "friendly relations" would be "severed." Putting the onus entirely on the black community, he wrote, "The Negroes have the choice to make." He framed this choice in terms of well-intentioned "local negotiation" versus disruptive "outsiders" who would bring "tension, fear, and hatred," concluding, "We trust our Negro citizens will think seriously on this important matter. Those who sincerely believe that mutual understanding can be achieved by the races working together, will let their thinking be known."[18] By the time Crisler wrote his editorial, however, the black community had already chosen the NAACP.

CHAPTER Eight

Moving for Freedom

The Claiborne County mass movement matured in the context of persistent racial violence. The August 1965 car bomb attack on NAACP leader George Metcalf in Natchez was followed by other serious incidents in southwest Mississippi. In November 1965, a bomb exploded near a movement freedom house in Vicksburg, and Hattiesburg activist Vernon Dahmer was killed by a Klan firebomb for advocating black voter registration in January 1966. In 1967, a Klan car bomb killed Natchez NAACP treasurer Wharlest Jackson. Nearby Fayette had a strong Klan presence and a history of unpunished murders of African Americans, including one in August 1965, another in June 1966, and a third in August 1967.[1] Claiborne County whites undoubtedly benefited from this violent atmosphere, but they relied primarily on economic intimidation and threats in their efforts to suppress movement activism.

Whites initially targeted visible black leaders, especially those who had served on the HRC or had ties to the NAACP, to keep them from associating with the movement. A Port Gibson merchant changed his credit terms and demanded that HRC member Reverend O. S. Burks immediately pay his grocery tab in full. Burks's daughter recalled, "The police came to collect the money that night. I never will forget that as long as I live. The police had never been out to our house before." Whites "dissuaded" Reverend Alexander Martin from resuming his NAACP affiliation, and Principal F. A. White refused to join because he thought it would jeopardize his son's teaching job. Calvin Williams lost his job as security chief at Alcorn when he became a leader in the NAACP. Williams later insisted that Alcorn's president, J. D. Boyd, had actually sent him to the NAACP meetings and that "all of my calls were accepted with great praise until the night I asked Rev. Spencer questions that a leader of the Negroes . . . should have known." Williams asserted, "In my opinion this is the point where the President's feelings changed." On January 20, after Williams was nominated to chair an NAACP negotiating committee, President Boyd demoted him from head of security to patrolman and gave him a work schedule that made it impossible for him to attend NAACP meetings. A month later, Boyd wrote Williams that he would not be rehired when his contract expired on May 31.[2]

Many blacks feared economic repercussions. Reverend Burks and J. C. Dunbar, friends and neighbors to Nate Jones, warned him that he would be denied bank loans and fired from his job driving a school bus if he joined the movement. Jones said, "They tried to discourage me that all of this [access to credit] wouldn't be there anymore if I fooled with 'that thing.' That's what they called it at the time." Jones recalled that Dunbar got very emotional, telling him, "You don't know what you doing. You better get out of that." But Jones refused to back down, telling him, "Naw, Professor Dunbar, I'm not going to get out of it." After Dunbar and Burks were unsuccessful, Eli Ellis, Jones's banker, who had hunted on his land for many years, called him in to Mississippi Southern Bank. "He said, 'I heard that you was teaching hate down there.' I said, 'Naw, I never done anything like that.' . . . He said, 'Well, we been good to you. We let you have, been letting you have anything you want.' I said, 'Why sure, I been good to you.' I said, 'I paid my debt. I been just as good to you as you been to me. I don't teach any hate, but I want my rights, just like you want yours.'" According to Jones, as he was leaving, Ellis told him, "I know you a pretty good person. I didn't think you'd be caught up in a mess like that." Jones replied, "Well, I am. I'm in it." Years later, Jones explained that he stood publicly in the face of these threats while his friends chose a different path because "I just didn't see it like [they did]. . . . Naturally I had been out of the country and been different places and had got a little taste of freedom and knowed what it was like. I just couldn't stoop to what they was trying to get me to do."[3] Despite Ellis's threats, Jones never actually had trouble with his current or future bank loans.

James Dorsey also stood up to white intimidation. At a mid-January 1966 meeting, the onetime HRC member and pastor of First Baptist Church agreed to serve as NAACP president when field secretary Charles Evers "couldn't get anyone else." Initially reluctant, Dorsey accepted out of a sense of duty that was heightened by seeing whites try to "shut out" the NAACP and Evers. Dorsey recalled that "Mr. Evers was there. He pleaded with them and others, because at that particular time, most of the branch presidents was being harassed, being shot at, and some was being killed. Because [Vernon] Dahmer at Hattiesburg had [been killed] and he was the president out there. So, I told them I would do what I could if I could get some good [executive] board members who would follow." Dorsey was well prepared for the NAACP presidency. In between military stints, he had finished high school and taken classes at the Mississippi Baptist Seminary. As a younger man, he had joined his father at NAACP meetings and watched him try to vote. Like many veterans, his military experiences exposed him to the world outside Mississippi and convinced him that blacks could do anything whites could. Although his commanding officer encouraged him to move North and seek better personal opportunities, Dorsey was more influenced by his parents' teaching that "if there are changes to be made, they should be made within your own home." He said that when the movement began, he felt that "I had given my life—at least I had offered it—for my country. . . . It was something greater then, to offer it for reform and change for the people who really need it."[4]

Longtime NAACP activists Nate Jones, Alexander Collins, Floyd Rollins, Jesse Johnson, Walter Griffin, and Dan Newman agreed to serve with Dorsey as NAACP board members. They were joined by newcomer Calvin Williams, who, though he had no previous ties to local activists, shared many of their experiences. He was a World War II veteran and Alcorn graduate, joined the NAACP as a young man, and tried unsuccessfully to register to vote in the early 1950s. Although most of these men were already somewhat prominent in the black community, their leadership status flourished when they publicly affiliated with the movement and they supplanted more prestigious leaders who failed to embrace the movement.[5]

Eugene Spencer is the most obvious example of a displaced leader. He went almost overnight from being at the height of his career to carrying the label "Uncle Tom" the rest of his life. Though he remained a popular pastor, one man observed that Spencer "killed himself" the night he publicly rejected the NAACP. Reverend J. L. Sayles, who was active in the Claiborne County movement, asserted that Spencer and others on the HRC chose a "bizarre friendship" with whites instead of the NAACP. In a conversation with historian Jack Chatfield in 1969, Spencer was clearly bitter and sounded much like the white leaders he had been close to. He insisted that the NAACP had "a way of brainwashing the colored people" and "preaching hate." He expressed dismay at movement activism, commenting that "there were children six years old marching around Port Gibson talking about they wanted their rights. I can't describe how they carried on." In fact, despite his years of pursuing voter registration, Spencer was reluctant to support universal suffrage, asserting that the majority of Claiborne

Reverend James Dorsey during World War II. A community leader, Dorsey was NAACP president from 1966 to 1968. Courtesy James Dorsey.

County blacks were "untrained in politics and would ruin our county." J. C. Dunbar, who had fed whites information about the underground NAACP, shared many of Spencer's views, including opposition to rapid change and the belief that premovement race relations in Claiborne County had been the "best in the country." After failing to convince Nate Jones to avoid the movement, he tried, also unsuccessfully, to use his leverage as principal of Addison High School to discourage Ken Brandon, son of early NAACP member Marjorie Brandon, from integrating the white public schools in August 1966. He used his position as the first black man on the countywide Farmers Home Administration committee, which administered housing loans, to threaten another activist, telling him that if he "didn't back off" he might lose his financing and have his house "taken away."[6]

Although some traditional black leaders were displaced, the local movement, reinforced by both Charles Evers's personal preferences and the national NAACP's elitist culture and hierarchical decision-making, employed a similar authoritative, top-down approach to leadership. An NAACP adviser's criticism of a 1964 Jackson negotiating committee for presenting a report to a mass meeting before privately discussing it with other leaders illustrates this style. "The committee . . . erred in allowing the community at large, through the mass meeting, to vote on matters which should have been presented to them in a positive manner as policy established by the leadership. The followers are not intricately involved in the day to day operation of the program and lack the ability to intelligently evaluate its assets and liabilities. Therefore, any conclusions reached by the masses are based on emotions and not on logic."[7] Though Claiborne County NAACP leaders never articulated such elitism, the movement largely followed this model, and movement work followed a fairly clear hierarchy related to age, gender, status, and personality. Collectively, the NAACP officers and the most visible movement leaders were better educated and of a more secure economic class than their constituents. Most of the NAACP board members had more in common, in terms of age, class, and education, with the members of the Human Relations Committee (which some of them had been) than with other movement participants. Most had traveled outside Claiborne County, especially through military service. Moreover, they all had a measure of community status through some combination of education, landowning, family connections, or economic success. Except for Calvin Williams, all had been affiliated with the underground NAACP and involved in community activism; perhaps most important, during the first months of the movement, they were self-selected volunteers who could command respect and were willing to take a public stand.

Despite opposition from some notable ministers, Claiborne County's black churches and ministers were essential to the movement's success. All of the weekly mass meetings were held in area churches, most of them in James Dorsey's First Baptist Church, which was centrally located in Port Gibson and the county's largest black church. Dorsey replaced Spencer as chair of the Baptist Ministerial Association and urged other ministers to encourage their congregations to join the movement. Lesser-known ministers, especially, flocked to mass meetings, and movement leaders utilized black religious traditions, consciously conducting mass meetings like church services. SNCC field secretary Worth Long observes that mass meetings were "structured in a traditional way, almost like a church service but there was freedom, the word 'freedom,' instead of a religious reference." According to SNCC worker and scholar Bernice Johnson Reagon, one of the things that made Mississippi activist Fannie Lou Hamer so effective was her ability to place "Jesus where his experiences, as passed through the traditions of the Black church, could be used in the freedom struggle." James Miller noted that in Claiborne County "most of the preachers would be singing out the same hymn book on Sunday morning," preaching "something kinda like liberation theology." Moreover, "a large percentage of blacks who went to church . . . were involved in the movement."[8]

In response to Charles Evers's widespread appeal and the organizing efforts of Rudy Shields and local NAACP leaders, by the end of January 1966, hundreds of blacks were attending the Tuesday night mass meetings. Entertaining, educational, and uplifting, these meetings combined singing, prayer, and Scripture reading with speeches that emphasized movement goals, encouraged voter registration, and pushed NAACP memberships. They were forums for exchanging information, recruiting volunteers, and discussing the mechanics of the movement. Participants looked forward to meetings and packed the church from "front to back," with people standing against the walls and spilling out onto the church grounds. One woman recalled that meetings were so good she "just deserted my church." Doubling as NAACP branch meetings, mass meetings pulled people into the organization, and by April 1, the branch had 495 new members. One woman explained that she joined because it "stands for colored peoples." The spirit and fervor of the meetings was contagious. Ken Brandon remembered "feeling inspired." He stressed the revelation that came from being part of "a room full of other people who are voicing some of the things you are kind of thinking. . . . And you just get all fired up." A very serious student, he particularly enjoyed the intellectual stimulation, commenting that speakers "expanded your mind" and forced you "to stretch and go beyond what you had originally thought about." His mother, Marjorie Brandon, emphasized that speakers "would motivate and give [you] courage to . . . stand up for your rights."[9]

Meetings helped combat fear and break the paralyzing grip of white supremacy. The spirituals and freedom songs that nurtured faith and defiance played a critical part. Worth Long claims that although it "sounds irrational . . . you can answer a question of fear with song. You hear your strength when you sing loud in a group of three hundred people. There is a certain kind of feeling of strength

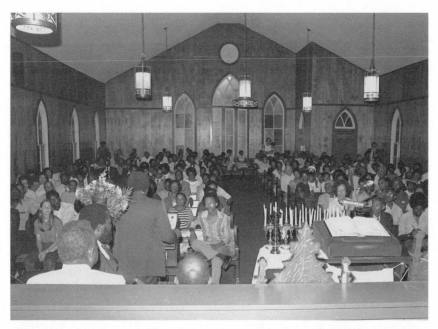

First Baptist Church, pastored by James Dorsey and home to civil rights movement mass meetings, pictured during a 1982 NAACP celebration of a movement-related Supreme Court decision. Photograph by Patricia Crosby, courtesy Patricia Crosby.

that you have that is unlike anything else that I know." Bernice Johnson Reagon, who sang in the Albany, Georgia, movement and with the SNCC freedom singers, explains that "singing voiced the basic position of the movement, of taking action on your life." One of the organizers who came to Claiborne County later in the decade remembered that meetings always "started with singing." She "came to see how the music helped set the tone or set the stage for any discussion that came after." The music "was a working part of the agenda."[10]

In mass meetings, singers confronted white authority figures by calling the names of the sheriff, the mayor, and other visible white leaders in songs like "Ain't Gonna Let Nobody Turn Me Around." Similarly, speakers often told stories and "made reference to some, some lowdown white person, you know, . . . making some kind of outlandish remark about somebody" to build courage and "get a fire under you." Years later, one man still had vivid memories of a speaker who told a story about a man riding a train without buying a ticket and how one train employee after another tried to make him get off the train. Finally, the rider "came up with a .38 and told them, said, 'Look,' said, 'I got a mother that's dead and in heaven. And I got a father that's dead and in hell. And I got a sweetheart in

Alabama.' Say, 'I'm gonna see one of them tonight.' What he is saying, . . . Freedom. Freedom. Heaven and hell or freedom."[11]

Charles Evers was usually the featured speaker, and his brash fearlessness and flashy oratory made him wildly popular. According to James Miller, "He would make his grand entrance, walk down the aisle, everybody would just stand up and cheer, clap, go on 'ooooh!' and the choir would start singing one of the freedom songs. 'Ain't Gonna Let Nobody Turn Me Around. Ain't Gonna Let [Sheriff] Dan McCay Turn Me Around,' that kind of stuff. And you know, by the time he would get up to speak, the crowd would be at a fever pitch." In October 1966, a reporter for a Vicksburg black newspaper observed that "whenever Mr. Evers enters the meetings, young people scream with delight and elderly ladies, who can reach him, shower him with hugs and kisses." The author added that Evers's "magnetic personality seems to radiate [through] the church." Here Evers was at his best—teaching, encouraging, inspiring. As one man put it, "He got the folks built up to where they were ready to go." Reverend Sayles said, "Charles Evers wasn't scared of the Devil . . . [and] he could talk. . . . He would tell those white folks just what he wanted them to know." Others remembered that he was a persuasive communicator who gave "local folks . . . a sense of what they could accomplish." A movement worker recalled that "when Charles came in here, he brought it all. . . . He knocked a lot of fear out of a lot of us." One of his closest supporters in Fayette practically deified him, saying, "He came, and we just used him as an earthly God. You know how when you're thirsty, you're hot, you're thirsty, you're run down, and somebody gives you a cool drink of water?"[12]

At the same time that Evers and mass-meetings were energizing the black community and creating a sense of communal solidarity, Rudy Shields spear-headed the movement's first big initiative—an exhaustive black voter registration drive. With close to 4,000 unregistered blacks of voting age, it was a major undertaking, which was often tedious and sometimes dangerous. Shields and his volunteers worked systematically, enlisting the help of churches and civic groups, passing out informational fliers, making home visits, and providing transportation. Some—like George Walker, the Thompson Funeral Home employee whom Shields approached during his first days in Claiborne County, and Leesco Guster, a young woman whose husband was a successful contractor—worked virtually full-time. Others joined in for a few hours or days, loaned their cars, or contributed gas money. A Pattison man, for example, caught a ride to work so others could use his car during the day. At night he drove around himself, talking to people about voting. Nate Jones recalled that between farming, driving a school bus, and canvassing for voter registration, some nights he only got two or three hours of sleep.[13]

Canvassers typically had to explain the registration process and try to quiet fears. Prior to the movement, virtually all African Americans shared the reality that blacks were not "entitled to vote." George Walker recalled that the registration drive required "a total turning around of education of minds to get them to want to come out and really see what you were talking about." Leesco Guster, who spent five weeks driving Shields "all over Claiborne County," observed that while a few blacks resisted, "most of them we got." According to NAACP board member Walter Griffin, one of the most important ways to counter fear was to point out, "I've been down and registered and didn't nobody kill me or drag me or hang me." He explained, "Your example would be reassuring to those who had been afraid."[14]

Canvassers had the most difficulty reaching the men and women who still lived on plantations. Walker remembered, "You had to face down guns from the white plantation owners to go in the place. We did that a lot." Reverend Dorsey recalled, "A lot of the plantation managers or owners didn't want [Rudy Shields] to bother so called 'his people,' because they were doing fine." In fact, stories about Shields sneaking onto plantations are told and retold. One woman recounted how he "crawled through the bushes to the people's houses." It was a triumphant story, ending with success. "They got them, though. They registered. They sneaked out there." Guster described a particularly harrowing experience when some sharecroppers promised to go register if she and Shields would come back the next day to give them a ride. When they returned, they were met by an armed white man who accused them of trespassing. "Mr. Shields cited some part where we had the right to go on property to ask people to go and register. And so, one of the black peoples there [said]—I never will forget this— 'Us don't want to lose what us got.' This just the way she said it. Mr. Shields said, 'What do you have? You don't have a damn thing.' He said it just like that." When Guster and Shields left, without the people, they had to get past their white adversary. "This man . . . parked on the other side of this little one-way bridge and, talk about scared, I was. Cause I was driving. Mr. Shields had got, he was in the back with my old .45. When I got along near the bridge, I said, 'Mr. Shields, there he is parked. What should I do?' . . . He said, 'You just drive.' I say, 'But if . . . he get to shooting, don't I have to duck?' And I was so scared. But we had to go across the bridge."[15]

Shields and Guster made it safely home that day, but fearing the implications of a major shift in political power, whites persistently fought to undermine black voter registration. A white merchant explained, "The white people didn't want to surrender their politics, and they felt like it was self-preservation. Because the black people would control the government and they didn't want to turn it loose.

It was just as simple as that, the way I see it in retrospect." Some white actions were trivial, like the Gage family's refusal to let federal registrars use their parking lot. Whites also made threatening phone calls and harassed people who came to town to register. Circuit clerk Pauline Easley, who had been sued by the Justice Department, did what she could to obstruct the registration drive. Dorsey recalled that she "slowed down the process . . . [and] wouldn't take but so many a day or hour. A lot of time you go there and the office would be closed." Nate Jones noted that "Rudy Shields and them would carry people up in droves and she refused to register them." However, federal registrars limited Easley's authority. George Walker enjoyed describing how they forced Easley to register blacks. "We would keep . . . [the courthouse] full and keep her frustrated, and all based on the way she had treated us in the past. And then we would say we gon' only register this many today, and we'd get in two times that many, and she would have to register them if they were there before five and in the courthouse." In fact, by April 1, 1966, 1,500 blacks were registered to vote, suggesting that from January to April, blacks registered at a rate of about twenty per day. On April 16, the first day the Justice Department's team of federal registrars worked, more than 100 people were lined up at eight A.M. when the doors opened, and 300 had registered by the end of the day. By May 17, the 2,600 black registered voters, well over half of those eligible, gave blacks the electoral majority.[16]

Throughout February, the NAACP branch steadily gained new members and attendance at mass meetings averaged about 400 people. Starting on March 1, the movement began holding marches once or twice a week. In pairs, hundreds of blacks walked the several blocks from First Baptist Church to the courthouse through a gauntlet of hostile and sometimes gun-carrying whites. These marches offered a public declaration of support for the movement and articulated dissatisfaction with the racial status quo. Leesco Guster explained, "In marching, you letting people know just how you feel. You don't have no other way to let them know. And when we in the church they don't be in there to see or hear, so you just bringing it out there, but you doing it in a peaceful way. And if they see that you are all together, then they'll know the strength and know we mean business. Cause that was the only way we had to let them know how we felt."[17]

Marching was dangerous business. White law enforcement officers were always present, taking pictures, identifying participants, and writing down license numbers. Heavily armed, untrained auxiliary police carried their weapons openly, while other white residents watched from doorways and second-story balconies. The threat of violence and retaliation gave this white presence ominous undertones. Thelma Crowder eagerly embraced the movement but recalled that she joined the first march very reluctantly. Worried about arrest or physical

Marchers returning to First Baptist Church after marching to the courthouse, 1966.
Courtesy Mississippi Cultural Crossroads.

violence, she said, "I was shaking. . . . I was so scared, I didn't know what to do."
Julia Jones, anxious about her teaching job and assuming that whites would
"retaliate one way or another," resolved to leave the marching to others. Talked
into joining by Alexander Collins, whose wife was also a public school teacher,
she found that "marching [and] seeing courage in other people, gave me courage." She stopped worrying about being fired and concluded that "God had all
the jobs." Many blacks found similar courage through their religious faith. When
Thelma Crowder was asked to sing at a courthouse rally, she recalled, "I tried to
sing 'Amazing grace how sweet the sound that saved a wretch like me.' Oh, I was
trembling, scared and crying. But I led the hymn, and the people sang it. And on
and on my fear went away."[18]

In general, singing, praying, and listening to bold oratory at the courthouse
rallies that accompanied marches helped dissipate fear. In particular, Reverend
Evan Doss reassured many marchers. Doss was a large, physically impressive
man who, as J. L. Sayles put it, "was strong and wasn't scared of a tiger." He
continued, "That man could pray. Look like make your hair get to quivering on
your head and I know those white folks, . . . I imagine they felt good over it too.
That man could pray sure as you're born. People . . . was on the street down

there shouting. . . . Oh, we would have a time there. Sure would." When the movement began, two decades had passed since Doss and his wife helped organize the box factory union, but he was still willing to stand up to whites. During one of the first mass marches in Port Gibson, participants thought whites were spitting on them from the upstairs balconies. Doss looked up and said, if "something else fall down here, we all coming up." Describing the incident, Sayles said, "He wasn't joking either. . . . And they knew he would come up there, too. And the rest of them were gon' follow him. . . . You couldn't hear them whimper up there."[19]

In the midst of this thriving movement, the black community prepared a second list of collective grievances and presented them through March 14th and March 21st letters from the NAACP to white leaders and public officials. Written at Collins Barbershop, the letters were signed by Evers, NAACP board members (James Dorsey, Alexander Collins, Calvin Williams, Nate Jones, Floyd Rollins, and Walter Griffin), and Reverend Mack Tisdale, a last-minute recruit who played little future role. The Port Gibson letter was based on an NAACP model and was quite similar to one presented by the Fayette NAACP a few months earlier and to others used later by southwest Mississippi movements associated with Evers. The almost identical letters all called for employment of African Americans as clerks and cashiers in local businesses; desegregation of public schools, hospitals, businesses, courtrooms, public facilities, and bus stations; employment of black policemen and deputy sheriffs to work on an integrated basis with full arrest authority; employment of blacks in the welfare offices to demonstrate "good faith and impartiality"; the addition of blacks to the board of education and all other boards and commissions; crossing guards for Negro schools and police escorts for African American funerals; black jurors and election officials; improvements to black neighborhoods; white business, church, and political leaders to denounce all "extreme groups"; and the extension of courtesy titles to all African American citizens.[20]

In addition to these relatively uniform requests, the Claiborne County letter included a few demands related to public school policies, housing and public services, and the hiring of black home demonstration and county agriculture agents. The NAACP leaders ended by asserting that the "objectives of the Negro citizens of Port Gibson and Claiborne County are, simply put, to have equality of opportunity, in every aspect of life, and to end the white supremacy which has pervaded community life." They pointed out that "Negroes now constitute a majority of registered voters" and "will have a powerful voice in the future affairs of the City and County." They insisted that "progress in inter-racial cooperation cannot wait for elections of the future, since all citizens now are entitled to free exercise of their rights." Letting whites know that they would use pressure if necessary, they asserted that "peaceful demonstrations and selective buying campaigns" are "inevitable unless there can be real progress toward giving all citizens their equal rights."[21]

Unlike the Human Relations Committee's vague references to possible protest, the NAACP explicitly threatened to boycott white merchants if their demands were not addressed by April 1. This put merchants on the front lines of the struggle. Although many of them later claimed to be innocent victims, they had traditionally played an important role in maintaining the mores of white supremacy through their extensive contacts with African Americans. They typically served whites first, no matter how long blacks had been waiting, maintained whites-only eating facilities, refused blacks access to bathroom facilities, and often insulted black customers. Merchants were also an integral part of Port Gibson's close-knit white civic and political elite. They belonged to the civic groups that served as informal policy boards and typically determined communal projects, including the building of segregated recreational facilities, new black schools (to hedge against integration), and factories (to provide a customer base to sustain the town's merchant and professional elite). When the chamber of commerce appointed the white members of the Bi-Racial Committee, all of them were merchants and bankers. James Dorsey commented that whites picked those who "would see blacks everyday, like your bankers and your head merchants" because "they figured that these people more or less had control of certain people. But they were wrong."[22]

Moreover, long before the movement began, blacks had struggled individually for decent treatment from area merchants. Faye Davis recalled her frustration with a Piggly Wiggly clerk who "would always throw your money on the counter." She felt "misused," and from the time she was about twelve years old she refused to shop there. Thelma Crowder had a similar experience at the Piggly Wiggly. "I rolled my buggy up, and the cashier beckoned to the white lady to come on around. And she pushed her basket in front of me. I stood there for a few minutes and I thought, 'I ain't got to take this.' . . . I just . . . walked on out." Julia Jones, bothered by the abusive language a white store clerk used when a black employee answered the woman with a simple "yes" rather than the "yes ma'am" the clerk expected, also left a cart of groceries in the Piggly Wiggly. Many blacks had similar experiences, and some tried to avoid shopping in white-owned grocery stores, trading instead at the small black-owned stores or at Lee's grocery, owned by a Chinese-black family. One woman who shopped exclusively at Lee's explained that she did so because some whites "can act sort of nasty with you."[23]

Between the March 14th letter and the NAACP's April 1 deadline there were at least two unproductive meetings between NAACP leaders and their white counterparts. Though Evers skipped the first meeting as a concession to whites, who opposed his involvement, it made little difference. Whites refused to seriously consider any of the NAACP's demands. There are no available copies of the white community's formal response, but it probably had much in common with the town of Fayette's reply to demands presented by that community's NAACP. The Fayette letter opened with vague language about "peace and good will" and then quickly dismissed each of the demands by obscuring the issues and denying responsibility. According to Sovereignty Commission director Erle Johnston, Port Gibson whites claimed that "they had no power to grant the majority of the demands."[24] However, the two most important demands, for better jobs and respectful treatment, were actually within the immediate control of individual merchants.

A young activist insisted, "The issues for the boycott were not major kinds of requests. 'Call us "Sir" and "Ma'am." Give us the clerk jobs and cashiers.' Basic decent rights. That's all we were asking." In the 1990s, a Claiborne County white woman offered insight into whites' view of hiring black clerks, contending that it "stuck in the craw of everybody." Several merchants insisted that they had no need for additional workers and they were unwilling to fire white employees in order to hire black ones. Mayor E. D. Davis told blacks he had already "given" them a police officer and would not hire any others, while Piggly Wiggly owner James Hudson and banker R. D. Gage vowed never to hire blacks to work as cashiers. Jitney Jungle owner Rosalie Abraham maintained that she "didn't feel like it was a good idea" to hire a black cashier because blacks would lie and steal. In a telling contradiction, she also explained that when she had young children she was able to work at the store because "you could get help pretty reasonable. And they were pretty dependable." She was referring to black women who "cooked your food and washed your clothes and fed your children and all." One black woman, referring to whites in general, pointed out the paradox in this kind of attitude, declaring, "I definitely wouldn't see myself letting somebody cook for me if I couldn't trust them."[25] That Abraham and other whites trusted black women to cook their family's food and nurture their children but refused to consider them for jobs as cashiers was one of the ongoing contradictions inherent in white supremacy.

Historian Adam Fairclough notes that many of the Southern Christian Leadership Conference's battles "concerned issues that were mainly symbolic"; however, he contends that "the tenacity with which whites defended these symbols of domination suggest that in attacking" them "the civil rights movement struck at the heart of the southern caste system." Persistent disrespect of blacks was a crude and constant reminder of white dominance and Claiborne County blacks repeatedly emphasized the indignity of being called "boy" or "girl" or "auntie" or "uncle" while having to address whites as Mr. or Mrs. William Owens, a landowning farmer from Pattison who spent years trying unsuccessfully to regis- ter and vote, testified, "We are used to people saying, 'Hello, ole Nigger.' It bothers me. M-A-N spells any kind of man, white or whatever color his is. But I had to take being called it. I had no protection." In 1997, Charles Evers summed up the importance of courtesy titles, writing, "This long list came down to one simple thing: We're as good as you. Treat us right! The hardest demand for the bigots to swallow was giving Negroes courtesy titles: 'Mr. Evers,' 'Mrs. Evers,' or 'Miss Evers'—no more 'boy,' 'girl,' and 'nigger.' "[26]

Whites' memories provide a glimpse of this divide from another angle. A woman who worked with the black PTA in the 1950s and considered herself open-minded explained that she was raised in an atmosphere of paternalism very similar to Port Gibson's. As a child, she was taught to treat black household servants with respect: "You didn't snap out. You never raised your voice, and you did not sass anybody. And we were made fun of [by other whites] for saying, 'Aunt,' and 'Uncle.' But the reason we did—they could have been our aunt and uncle, probably—but, it was a term of respect." Thus, even as she and many other whites believed that by saying "aunt" or "uncle" they were being respectful to blacks, blacks were insisting, in the words of Charles Evers, that "if a person's old enough, [call them] Mr. or Mrs., not auntie, uncle, we not your auntie, uncle." Whites were very slow to hear blacks and even slower to change their ways. In the early 1970s, merchant Waddy Abraham acknowledged that "in 1966 it was a common practice among whites to refer to blacks by names they found offensive."[27]

As with the Bi-Racial Committee meetings, the best that could be said of the late March meetings between the NAACP and white leaders was that, as several participants observed, they were "friendly" and there was "no antagonism." NAACP president James Dorsey described the meetings as mostly civil, explain- ing, "There was very few who was arrogant in the meeting. Most of them would sit and listen too." However, he insisted that whites were not really there to negotiate. "I think their attitude was just to send people there, we would air our grievances, and maybe we would just get tired of coming and nothing being done. It seemed to me that that was a wait and see attitude . . . that these people took." He added that white leaders persisted in their belief that they had treated blacks fairly and that black leaders were "too forward." The negotiations were almost certainly hampered by whites' expectation that they could choose, or at least approve, black leaders. In 1964, after the Democratic Party offered the MFDP two compromise seats and named the delegates who could fill them, Aaron Henry commented, "This is typical white man picking Black folks' leaders, and that day is gone." Only months before, highway patrolman Charles Snodgrass reported that in Natchez, "There is no person or group in the Negro community with the necessary prestige to control and direct the Negro citizens." He suggested that "the white community should take advantage of this opportunity to pick and groom a local leader or a local group of Negro leaders." In Claiborne County, whites had hoped to work through Eugene Spencer and the HRC and perhaps had not yet acknowledged how completely that effort had failed. According to George Walker, "The black ministers thought they had the power, so . . . the whites had come to [them] and say, 'I thought you had it.' In the end, okay, they found out they didn't have it." Not only that, Walker continued, whites had expected Dorsey to support their efforts and when he "came over [to the NAACP] . . . they were looking at him in different eyes. They . . . felt they had been stabbed in the back."[28]

Dorsey noted that white leader R. D. Gage had always relied on "certain blacks who" he believed "had influence and therefore he had a safe posture by knowing the right persons in the community to call." With whites unprepared to acknowledge black autonomy or accept independent black leadership, Dorsey had a difficult time convincing them that the NAACP represented most of the black community. "They really thought that . . . we was satisfied. They thought we was not speaking for the masses. . . . They attributed our coming forward to them as a result of these other persons. They called them 'outside agitators,' you know, like Mr. Evers. . . . They say like if it wasn't for these people it's possible you wouldn't be asking for these things." Few whites believed that African Americans had the unity or staying power necessary to mount an effective challenge to their authority. One black activist remembered that "at first" whites thought "it was a joke." When asked about the movement, store owner Rosalie Abraham said that she did not believe it would come to Claiborne County because she was "so optimistic." In fact, she had thought whites could keep it away through the strength of their hopes: "Well, I think, if they just thought it *wasn't* going to happen, it wouldn't have happened. You know, it can be so much in your *feeling*, so *much* in what you *feel*. I *do* believe that way. If you *believe* in something, it's bound to come around. Because if you believe in Jesus, isn't Jesus going to take care of you?"[29]

Whether or not they shared Abraham's faith that they could prevent the movement from arriving, most whites did believe that if they waited long enough, the outsiders would leave and the status quo would prevail. This belief, too, was based more on wishful thinking than reasoned analysis. Whites had surely followed the movement's numerous court victories, protest successes, and passage of major congressional legislation through the nightly news and the *Reveille*'s editorials. Closer to home, they had seen blacks take to the streets in large numbers and initiate effective boycotts in Fayette and Natchez. Yet whites had reason to believe they could withstand blacks' insistence on change. Whites in the area had so far conceded little and had deflected most demands. Port Gibson whites had yet to experience enforcement of the Civil Rights Act or face the impact of the new black electoral majority. Similarly, the public schools remained entirely segregated over a decade after the *Brown* decision declared that unconstitutional. Finally, the strategies of foot-dragging, overt resistance, intimidation, and ignoring undesirable federal rulings and court orders had worked extremely well for white leaders during the World War II union drive and postwar strike at the box factory. World War II had also threatened (or promised, depending on one's perspective) considerable change in the status quo. Yet whites outlasted and withstood it. Commenting on the failed negotiations, one NAACP activist remembered that whites "sat there right until that particular day and stood right out on the street, cause they didn't think [the boycott] was going to happen."[30]

CHAPTER Nine

It Really Started Out at Alcorn

In April 1966, the movement intensified dramatically. On Friday and Saturday, April 1 and 2, hundreds of blacks gathered for mass meetings and marches to publicize the boycott, which began at noon on April Fool's Day. On Monday and Tuesday, April 4 and 5, more than a thousand demonstrators gathered near Alcorn to join Charles Evers in protesting the college's inferior resources, poor staff working conditions, and Boyd's restrictive policies. NAACP executive secretary Roy Wilkins called Alcorn's problems (including inadequate budget, deficient physical plant, and low teacher salaries, all of which lagged far behind the state's white colleges) an "indictment of Mississippi's segregated educational system, [where] . . . Negroes run a gamut of inferior schooling."[1]

Evers had begun focusing on the college in his February speeches, and on Friday, March 4, three days after the first public march in Port Gibson, he led more than 200 demonstrators (most of them from Natchez and Fayette in Adams and Jefferson counties) along State Highway 552 toward the east entrance of Alcorn. They were stopped short of the campus by a large assembly of law officers, and after a brief confrontation between Evers and Alcorn's head of security (who had just replaced Calvin Williams), the lawmen arrested all the marchers and took them to Port Gibson for booking. The conditions in jail were unsanitary and extremely unpleasant with crowding, lack of food, and some abusive guards, but no one was seriously hurt and everyone was released by the next evening.[2]

With help from the Lawyers' Committee for Civil Rights

Charles Evers (front left), leading marchers on Highway 552 toward Alcorn A&M College, March 4, 1966. Courtesy Mississippi Cultural Crossroads.

Under Law, a group of civil rights attorneys who provided much of the legal work for the Claiborne County movement, the NAACP secured a court order permitting a march at Alcorn on Saturday, March 12. Although only 200 people were allowed to march, more than 800 gathered at the campus for an outdoor meeting. During the march, Evers presented President Boyd a list of thirty-two grievances that he prepared with the Claiborne and Jefferson County NAACP branches. The petition focused primarily on five areas: staff work conditions and pay; student activities and social restrictions; free speech, due process, and reinstatement of fired staff members; facility hours and salaries; and student loan access and procedures.[3] In the subsequent weeks, when neither the Alcorn administration nor the state board of trustees responded to the NAACP's petition, Evers repeatedly attacked President Boyd and called for broad-based demonstrations.

In a Port Gibson speech after the March 4 arrests, Evers told the crowd that Boyd "is blacker and burrier headed than I am and he called his great white father and had us arrested and put in his filthy dirty jail." He went on to say that only a "low down Negro or an Uncle Tom" is lower than a white man. During his

Charles Evers (front left) leading marchers during a court-protected march at Alcorn A&M College, March 12, 1966. The March and April demonstrations gained considerable national media attention and were featured on all three television networks. Courtesy Mississippi Cultural Crossroads.

March 12 speeches at the court-protected Alcorn march, he called Boyd "ignorant," "no good," "arrogant," and a "dictator." Telling the crowd that "the students and faculty live in a prison at Alcorn," he emphasized, "We are here to help the school, not tear it down. We are not going to see Negroes removed from white slavery and put into black slavery." During an April 1 speech calling for protests at Alcorn, Evers claimed demonstrators would stay at the college until Boyd was gone and called for people to bring "cheese and crackers, peas and cornbread and blankets." He concluded that "this is not a civil rights matter; this is Negro against Negro." On Saturday, April 2, he continued his assault on Boyd, telling a Port Gibson crowd, "We are going to walk on Boyd until he is as low down as our shoe soles." He called Boyd the biggest "Uncle Tom" in the state and predicted that they would teach him a lesson.[4]

On Monday, April 4, and Tuesday, April 5, while lawyers battled in court over whether demonstrators had a right to march on the public highway that ran through Alcorn, hundreds of blacks gathered on the edge of campus. The state responded by blocking the highway with a massive force of lawmen, including sheriffs, deputies, Sovereignty Commission investigators, more than 200 members of the Mississippi Highway Patrol, and a contingent of the National Guard. Years later, NAACP president James Dorsey pointed out that although the movement wanted only to hold a peaceful march, the state sent "tanks and armory . . . and the whole National Guard." Public school students, who were boycotting their classes at Evers's request, tried repeatedly to march through the campus. Turned away by lawmen, they cut through the woods onto campus, where they reassembled around Boyd's home, singing, dancing, and clapping. On Tuesday, campus security chief Vernon Maxwell dispersed one such crowd by using fire hoses and tear gas, but he failed to dampen the young people's enthusiasm. According to a highway patrolman, they "continued their shouting and whooping and hollering and slurring and intimidation of the members of our Department."[5]

The demonstrations were initiated and conducted almost exclusively by community members, not students, and college administrators did their best to keep the college students isolated from the protests. They made Patton's store, the demonstrators' gathering place, off-limits and renewed threats to suspend any students who joined the demonstrations. However, with the public school students roaming the campus, it was impossible to keep the Alcorn students completely separate. On Monday morning, several were beaten by highway patrolmen, and that afternoon a few students hurled bottles and insults from the dorm windows. Lawmen shot tear gas directly into one of the dorms (making it uninhabitable for several days) and arrested thirty people.[6]

On Monday and Tuesday evenings, hundreds of adults joined the younger people, and the crowds off-campus swelled. On Monday night, Evers and movement lawyers appealed to Sheriff Dan McCay and an assistant state attorney general for permission to hold a silent march, but the lawmen refused, citing an injunction issued by the Claiborne County Chancery Court that enjoined Evers, NAACP board members Nate Jones, Walter Griffin, Calvin Williams, and "others acting in concert with them" from "organizing, leading, conducting, and/or participating in any demonstration and/or march of any size, character or description on the campus of Alcorn." Denied permission to march and effectively blocked from the campus by the hundreds of lawmen standing in the road, the protesters held an outdoor mass meeting. At one point, Evers led demonstrators toward the wall of lawmen, stopped for a brief prayer when they could go no further, and then retreated. As marchers approached, the lawmen donned their gas masks but did little to interfere, and the rally ended before 9 P.M., when Evers urged everyone to go home. On campus, 600 students marched to Boyd's home and requested a meeting. In typical fashion he refused.[7]

Standoff between protesters and lawmen at an Alcorn demonstration, April 1966. Courtesy Mississippi Cultural Crossroads.

On Tuesday, April 5, Evers left the campus area around noon for a Jackson meeting with members of the board of trustees. Very little came out of the meeting, but Evers accepted the board's request that, starting the next day (Wednesday), he call a temporary end to demonstrations while the trustees investigated the grievances. After returning from his meeting, Evers tried again to gain permission for a march before the next day's moratorium. As he had the night before, Evers led the enthusiastic crowd of more than 1,500 people toward the campus until they were stopped by the waiting patrolmen. Standing between the supportive crowd and the lawmen blocking their way, Evers alternated his comments between the two groups. His speech ranged from Boyd and conditions at Alcorn to school segregation and local politics, returning repeatedly to the highway patrolmen blocking the protesters. Evers told the lawmen, "You wouldn't stand for what we are standing for. You wouldn't take it if it was you being suppressed and denied as we have." He asserted, "I don't believe you even know that there is a God up there. How could you hate us so bad, how, to destroy us physically without a cause? You are not to be hated, you are to be pitied, because you know not what you are doing. May God have mercy on your soul." He told the crowd that the highway patrol had "no right to block the march," insisting, "It's not their highway, it's ours. We have a right to march. We'll march anyway." Turning back to the patrolmen, he tried again and again to convince them to step aside and allow a march. Denouncing the overwhelming presence of "all these men armed as they are, knowing we are unarmed," he repeated to the crowd, "You have a right to march" as long as you "march peacefully and quietly and return back to our destination."[8]

At one point, Evers directed the highway patrolmen to "just stand aside boys and let the men go through. We're not going to argue with you tonight, we're not going to fight with you tonight. We have a right to march." By this time, hundreds of students had left the main campus area—some standing behind the patrolmen and others slipping through the woods to join the community demonstrators. Evers's next comments, which were met with loud yells of support, were addressed to the students behind the lawmen, offering, "If you can't march to us, we will march to you. We'll make a sandwich of the highway patrol." Then he told the patrolmen, "You can call your boys out but we're coming. We aren't going to let anyone turn us around—we outnumber you down here."[9]

Shortly after Evers made these comments, Giles Crisler, the highway patrolman in charge, gave the crowd two minutes to disperse and completely clear the road. Although the troopers had themselves already kept the highway closed to traffic for two days, they refused Evers's request for additional time. Evers immediately asked people to step back off the road and move their cars. The crowd responded as well as they could, but with close to 2,000 people and their vehicles on a narrow two-lane highway bound closely by thick woods, it was an impossible request. Moreover, highway patrolmen almost immediately attacked the crowd with tear gas, billy clubs, and rifle butts. One man recalled that they "began coming in a huddle, pushing, shoving, hitting, kicking, shooting tear gas, firing rifles, breaking people's car glass, hitting cars with sticks, shooting gas in people's cars and causing old people to fall down; some of them to get run down cause people was in such a panic behind all that commotion."[10]

Nate Jones remembered that when Giles Crisler gave his men the command to move into the crowd, he explicitly instructed them not to hurt Evers. "That what they said, don't harm Evers. . . . They [said use] tear gas, but they told him don't hit him." That prohibition did not apply to the rest of the crowd, however, and before it was over, many people were injured. Jones saw patrolmen attack a minister from Hattiesburg and Reverend R. L. T. Smith, the NAACP leader who ran for Congress in 1962. A black cab driver from Port Gibson suffered one of the worst beatings and spent two weeks in the hospital. According to Julia Jones, "They liked to killed him. They did him bad. [He was] in bad shape." Many others suffered from the tear gas. A minister who was forced by the crowd into Patton's store recalled, "After we got inside of the store, we got teargassed. Oh yeah! I hadn't never been teargassed, my lord. They filled it up and then they . . . blocked the back door to keep anyone from coming out. . . . And we were just about suffocating there." Another participant who helped the injured said that "some of them we had to send to the hospital because their head was beat in and some of them was choked up with gas, eyes burning and everything." Julia Jones remembered the terror she felt when one of the lawmen pointed a gun directly at her. "It was amazing that they didn't shoot me cause I was outside on the right-hand side of the store facing the road, just walking up. I was in the crowd, but when I looked, everybody had gone and I was just standing there and they let the gun right at me and my mind said walk over to the side and I did. . . . But I was looking for a bullet any time."[11]

In subsequent litigation, the highway patrolmen defended their attack by arguing that the crowd was violent. They isolated Evers's most inflammatory rhetoric and juxtaposed it with the bottle- and brick-throwing that had occurred earlier on campus. They made much of having confiscated one gun, a loaded .22, and of having seen someone holding an ax handle. They stressed Evers's threat to make a sandwich of the patrolmen but failed to note that the moment had passed peacefully and the crowd had already moved away on its own. They also claimed that Evers told the crowd, "If you have any grievances against any highway patrolman, catch him by himself and beat the hell out of him." However, that particular quote is not on newsreel soundtracks. Moreover, Evers had combined his confrontational statements with others urging the crowd to act peacefully. He had maintained that protesters had "no fight" with the patrolmen and urged the crowd not to "throw any rocks or bottles." He had also insisted to the crowd, more hopefully than accurately it turned out, that "there'll be no bloodshed" and "nobody's trigger-happy."[12]

Troopers and demonstrators both agreed that some students had earlier dropped things on troopers from their dorm windows and some community demonstrators did throw bottles and rocks at troopers. Protesters, however, insisted that it was the troopers' decision to clear the road that had precipitated conflict. This claim is borne out by the state's own account. According to the troopers, when several hundred lawmen moved to clear the road, some members of the crowd responded by throwing "large numbers of bottles and other objects" and one man wrestled a carbine away from a patrolman. According to the patrol, at this point they "had no alternative other than to use tear gas to disperse this unruly crowd."[13] Demonstrators counter that the patrol attacked and used tear gas at the same time they moved to disperse the crowd. Their interpretation emphasizes that the bottle-throwing came after the troopers charged the crowd and that the trooper's carbine would have remained in his hands if he had not waded into the crowd.

Furthermore, Nate Jones concluded that patrolmen used tear gas out of anger when they were unable to trap the students who had come off-campus. According to Jones, when the patrolmen "closed in to catch those students," he used his knowledge of the area to lead them away from the troopers, through a pasture, and back to one of the men's dorms. He recalled, "And they got back on campus behind all the patrolmen and got in the dorm and talking about screaming and hollering at Patton's. And see that made the man mad and that's when he started the tear gas and teargassed our crowd . . . after them students got back on campus." For their part, neither the state nor the troopers ever tried to explain or justify the order to clear the road. It was probably just the excuse they needed to vent their frustrations after several days of almost around-the-clock duty. Sheriff Dan McCay observed years later, "You get enough people together, somebody is going to get to fighting or something. So, as soon as they got a disturbance, they gassed them."[14]

It would seem from the lawmen's perspective that the use of force worked. Despite the mass mobilization and widespread publicity, the state of Mississippi quite handily stopped this instance of movement activism. In addition to using force, the state secured favorable injunctions and court decisions from federal judge Russell Moore. On April 13, Moore "enjoined plaintiffs from demonstrating on or adjacent to campus" until several pending cases were decided. The state sued protesters for damages, and the demonstrators sued the state for the right to conduct peaceful protest along the state highway that ran through campus. The hearings were completed in July that year, but with the temporary injunction prohibiting protest, Moore waited two years before entering his decision, on July 24, 1968. He found against demonstrators and issued a permanent injunction outlawing peaceful protest near the college. By this time, neither Evers nor anyone else had the resources or interest necessary to appeal the decision, and the ban on demonstrations is probably still in place.[15]

The community demonstrations at Alcorn reveal both Charles Evers's strengths and weaknesses as a leader. Hundreds of people answered his call to demonstrate, and the large numbers of protesters and Evers's emerging national reputation generated considerable publicity, including coverage by all three television networks and the *New York Times*. However, once he had mobilized supporters and attracted attention, Evers seemed unable to capitalize on this interest. He did not try to organize the many parents, alumni, and Alcorn supporters around the state who were dissatisfied with campus conditions. He made little attempt to document the deficiencies of the campus or substantiate the thirty-two grievances presented to the board of trustees, and he made no effort to work with other people and organizations. Moreover, his rivalry with SNCC kept the community-initiated protests cut off from the efforts of a handful of students who were in contact with SNCC workers and trying to organize other students.[16]

Similarly, the demonstrations earned Evers an audience before the board of trustees, but when the board dismissed all the grievances in a perfunctory manner and simultaneously commended President Boyd and instructed him to continue his "usual disciplinary proceedings," Evers had no response. Later, Evers spoke of shutting down the campus for summer school, called for further demonstrations outside the campus, and proposed a march in downtown Jackson, but he never followed through on any of these. Reflecting on the Alcorn protests, James Dorsey, who worked closely with Evers for many years, concluded, "I think this was a time that [we] was kinda ill prepared." In addition, most of those involved remember the protests as a battle between Evers and Boyd. In fact, it seems evident that Evers became blinded by his obsession with J. D. Boyd and lost sight of the state's blame in generating the tremendous problems at the school. One participant recalled being confused: "It was like Evers was fighting against Boyd. The same things he was saying about white folks, he was saying about Boyd." While Boyd was clearly a dictatorial administrator who obstructed civil rights activism, trampled on free speech, and ran Alcorn in an arbitrary and capricious manner, he was also a representative, and to some extent a creation of, the white power structure. Evers made this connection in his speeches, but he did so primarily to insult Boyd, and his focus was on Boyd's removal rather than a change in the system that produced him and used him as its proxy.[17]

The demonstrations themselves also proved somewhat distracting. Media coverage quickly focused on the state's refusal to allow protesters to march on the public highway and its use of violence to disperse demonstrators. And when Evers and the Lawyers' Committee initiated legal action, it focused on the right to protest and on securing damages because of police brutality. Ultimately, neither the media attention nor the legal action addressed the more fundamental question of the state's role in perpetuating race-based educational inequality in its institutions of higher learning. This issue was not raised in court until 1975, when, in what became known as the *Ayers* case, a black parent filed suit on behalf of his son and others, demanding that the state redress the inequities in higher education. Perhaps there was little that Evers and his companions could have done to successfully attack the problems at Alcorn, but the tactics Evers chose were clearly limited and ineffectual. Moreover, after the brief period of intense confrontation, he and local community residents quickly turned their attention elsewhere, leaving the Alcorn battles in the hands of the Lawyers' Committee and a few students on campus. The latter tried to organize a widespread student-based movement but had little success. Alcorn students, faculty, and staff who challenged the status quo were still easily isolated and controlled, and the activist students were quickly suspended. In fact, Alcorn faculty and students remained cut off for the duration of the civil rights movement.

While little changed on campus as a result of the demonstrations, they did have a profound effect on the Claiborne County residents who took part. Sheriff Dan McCay claimed that the movement "didn't start in Port Gibson. . . . It started at Alcorn, black against black, and it just flew over, boiled over into Port Gibson. . . . That's exactly right." Many would agree with him. The large gatherings near campus introduced many people to the mass movement and extended the collective experience of listening to Evers's oratory, singing freedom songs, and challenging white supremacy (here in the form of lawmen). Even seeing and experiencing the state troopers' violence firsthand seemed to solidify commitment, rather than intimidate people. Julius Warner, who had been only marginally involved in the Port Gibson movement before the Alcorn demonstrations, saw state troopers beat his father. Recalling the incident, Warner commented that the troopers "really thought they had put [protesters] on the run, but I guess it only made them mad." Warner himself became one of the movement's most dedicated workers and a leader in a black self-defense group. He recalled, "That was the first time I had really seen violence and that was the beginning of the movement here in the county. They really started down there."[18]

CHAPTER Ten

Everybody Stood for the Boycott

The Alcorn demonstrations helped publicize and reinforce the boycott of Port Gibson merchants that had started just days before. The formal decision to boycott came on March 29 at the NAACP's regular Tuesday night mass meeting when Charles Evers reported that the white community had failed to offer any concessions. Virtually everyone present enthusiastically endorsed the boycott. At noon on Friday, April 1, Charles Evers and more than 450 African Americans marched from First Baptist Church to the courthouse to announce and promote the boycott. After that, NAACP board member Walter Griffin recalled, "word [of the boycott] spread like wild fire." He continued, "I am sure someone there told the attendees to spread the word to other black people who weren't there. The word must have been passed around because they didn't crowd in town like they once had." A woman who never attended meetings remembered that it was easy to follow news about the boycott: "People that were going to the meeting, they'd tell me about it."[1]

The second day of the boycott fell on a Saturday, the traditional shopping day for blacks, and offered a glimpse of what was to come. Under the scrutiny of thirty highway patrolmen in town because of the boycott, the NAACP again combined a mass meeting and a noon march to the courthouse "to demonstrate the seriousness of the matter." As Evers concluded his speech and headed back to the church, he yelled to Piggly Wiggly owner James Hudson watching from the doorway of his store, "You better take a good look . . . because this is the

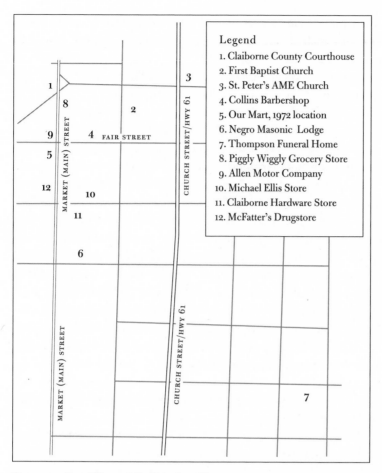

Downtown Port Gibson, Mississippi, 1966

last time you'll see this many black people in front of your store for a long time." According to George Walker, except for the twenty men, women, and children who volunteered to picket that afternoon, "After they marched that day . . . the streets was clear."[2]

By week's end, virtually everyone in Claiborne County was aware of the boycott. Not only did news of the boycott spread by word of mouth and the Port Gibson meetings, marches, and picketing, but Evers referred to it repeatedly during the Alcorn demonstrations and the weekly edition of the *Reveille* was filled with boycott-related editorials and letters. Moreover, Evers's prediction to Hudson proved quite accurate. Hudson later recalled, "We were busy and packed in the store up until the noon speech [on April 1]. After the crowd dispersed, there wasn't a single black person that came inside our door for a week at least. Not even somebody who tried to come in for at least a week. Even little kids that used to come in and buy penny candy all during the day, nobody came in." Jitney Jungle owner Waddy Abraham observed, "There was no trade," just "marching out front, signs and everything." Awareness and support for the boycott spread so rapidly that Hudson did not have a prospective black customer until the following Saturday, April 9. When a black man who had been out of town approached the store that day, he was surprised when picketers surrounded his truck and asked him not to patronize Hudson's business.[3]

The boycott coincided with the height of the Claiborne County movement. Only a few months after the tentative decision to found an open branch of the NAACP, most Claiborne County blacks were supporting the movement and participating in some way. Julius Warner recalled, "Everybody pitched in and worked together. You've never seen people so organized and so sincere about working together with each other." He described the black community during that time as "very close knit," noting that even those who "set back and watched" and "didn't want to be seen . . . were really in favor and we knew that." The few available numbers bear this out. In mid-April, Charles Evers reported that the NAACP branch had more than 1,300 adult members, and by year's end, another 400 had joined. More than 40 percent of the county's black residents over the age of 21 belonged to the NAACP. By mid-May there was also a youth branch with almost 500 members and more than two-thirds of the county's eligible black population was registered to vote.[4]

During this period of intense activism, roughly from March 1966 through February 1967, the vast majority of African Americans enthusiastically supported the boycott. Marjorie Brandon explained, "Everybody stood for the boycott. It was very united." One participant testified that when the boycott began he "avoided all white merchants like the plague," while another explained her support in terms of racial solidarity, saying, "I wanted to stand with black people." An activist who began working in Claiborne County in the 1970s remembered that the boycott "was a part of people's identity, what they had or hadn't done during that boycott. I remember that very clearly. It was an identifier."[5] By requiring sustained, widespread, and virtually unanimous cooperation from the black community, the boycott played a vital role in building and extending active engagement with the movement. Unlike voter registration, which was a one-time act, the boycott relied on a daily commitment, making it fundamental to the lives of most blacks. Boycotting was also widely accessible because it usually did not demand open defiance of whites or a high level of physical or financial risk.

The boycott offers a good illustration of the multiple layers of movement participation. While organizer Rudy Shields and a core group of workers over-saw the daily details necessary for making it work, Evers and NAACP board members were the leaders, determining strategy, sharing information, and moti-vating others. Leadership was male oriented; there were no women in this inner circle, known as the "leading mens." During marches, Evers implied that women needed protection, typically asking men to march in front and back, with women and children in the middle. When the court allowed 200 people to march at Alcorn, Evers called for ministers and business men to demonstrate and everyone else to wait on the sidelines. Descriptions of NAACP mass meetings are filled with the names of male speakers and officers. Marjorie Brandon observed that "mostly men would speak. Most women, just, I suppose, didn't speak out." Even at a meeting sponsored by the "Ladies Auxiliary," most of the speakers were men who, according to one report, "commended the ladies for their efforts."[6]

Age was also an important prerequisite for leadership. Across the South many local movements were started by young people initiating direct-action cam-paigns. When SNCC began organizing in Mississippi, high school and college students were among the organization's earliest and most committed recruits, and many became organizers and leaders in their own right. In Port Gibson, youth energized the local movement and made significant contributions as workers, but they rarely took the lead. At thirty-eight, James Dorsey was the youngest recognized leader. James Devoual, who was a teenager at that time, recalled, "Back in those times we had a cliché that we used to use. Old men for counsel, young men for war. So in the main, in the NAACP itself, we had very little say-so. Of course, back then, kids were seen and not heard."[7]

The hierarchical nature of the local movement was clearly reflected in mass meetings and the ways most blacks deferred to the authority of the NAACP branch. Most people in Claiborne County who attended mass meetings came to be an audience. Everyone joined in singing and usually some people offered their opinions or ideas, but there was little public or collective decision-making. Moreover, as the movement became established, the NAACP became almost a de facto government for the black community, making decisions and establishing rules. NAACP president James Dorsey explained that mass meetings were used to "inform peoples" and James Miller observed that "it all came from the top. Very little came from the bottom." He added, "People came there to get informa-tion and to get instruction. They didn't come there to participate and offer different strategies. I don't even remember any mechanism that was put in place, by which they could decipher opinions from the masses." The passivity of most movement participants was at the heart of a conflict between COFO activist Ed King and Charles Evers. When King was running as an MFDP candidate in the

1966 Democratic primary, the first election where significant numbers of Claiborne County blacks were eligible to vote, he wanted to campaign at a Port Gibson mass meeting. According to King, Evers "didn't want me to speak. I kept insisting and he said, 'You don't have to come. I'll tell the people who to vote for.' And I said, 'Charles, I don't want people in Port Gibson voting for me because you tell them.' . . . And, he said, 'What's politics all about? I control these people. They'll do what I say.'"[8] King eventually spoke at a mass meeting, but he remained at odds with Evers because of their philosophical differences.

While Evers and a few male leaders made decisions, movement workers—who were mostly women, younger, less elite men, and teenagers—carried them out and were responsible for most of the day-to-day work of the movement. NAACP branch president James Dorsey noted that many who did the "actual organizing work" "did not have the high titles." One of Marjorie Brandon's sons observed that movement workers were "young people and old people, mostly women. I guess the civil rights movement was centered around a few men, women, and the children." Teenagers who were drawn to the movement would check in with Shields after school and do whatever chores he had lined up—picketing, voter registration canvassing, soliciting NAACP memberships, or passing out informational fliers. For them, the movement was a mix of hard work and play that provided an outlet for teenage rebellion and a constructive way to attack white supremacy. According to James Devoual, movement work "gave us a pride, a new sense of pride, of self-worth, of equality." He added, "We enjoyed . . . being able to rebel, being able to take a stand. . . . We had always been deprived of that."[9]

Some young participants had to contend with worried or skeptical parents. According to one, his parents would always tell him, " 'Don't go out there and get hurt. Leave that mess alone.' I'd say, 'Okay.' and be gone." James Devoual's parents were members of the NAACP, but they were "more of the passive members" who "believed in praying. They believed in 'God is gonna make it right.' And they were prepared to wait for that long gradual change as opposed to getting out there for that quick change. . . . Revolution, I think that was a word we were using then." Devoual's parents thought the young people should stay home, because they feared "something terrible was going to happen" at the Tuesday-night meetings. James Miller observed, "In a lot of cases, the kids challenged their people about whether or not they were going to take part in the movement." Jimmy Ellis connected his activism to his growing realization that "we are all human beings, created by the same God and everything and we should be treated fairly too." Although his parents initially worried about his safety, he "never had any problem out of them" after he explained that he was "participating in the movement to make it better for our race."[10]

Looking back, many of those brash young activists now have a better apprecia-tion for their parents' worries. Talking specifically about their role in challenging state troopers on Alcorn's campus, one explained that their only "fear was you were somewhere you shouldn't have been and if you get put in jail, what will be the reaction of your mother and father. At that particular time . . . I don't think we had a real fear of death." James Miller stressed that "it was a season in which you had to make decisions about what you were going to do." Years later he realized that those were "serious decisions" that could have a "profound impact on the rest of your life," but he concluded, "It was not that intense at that particular time for each individual. Most of it was spontaneous."[11]

Sometimes movement work imbued typical teenaged pastimes with a sense of purpose. Miller observed, "It was about the movement, but it was also about an excuse to get out and socialize. It would afford you the opportunity to be able to rap with some little girl you're trying to go with." Another participant explained, "I was a country boy raised on the farm, and I wanted to do something. And all the country boys, they would be involved, and we would look forward to coming into town." Another man recalled that during the movement he was most con-scious of "having fun, really having fun, laughing, and clowning. I tell you cause several of us was friends and cousins involved and we were mostly having fun." James Devoual added that one of their jobs was to "kind of hang around in the streets to see what was going on. . . . We were just kind of the eyes and the ears." Activities like the Alcorn demonstrations gave teenagers a chance to break the traditional rules governing race relations. Miller insisted, "Being young, you seize upon every opportunity you could to confront the police. We loved to challenge authority. You got a kick out of doing that." He described the situation when troopers and high school students faced off on either side of the fence around campus: "[The troopers] were at attention with their guns like this and two or three of us would walk up to the fence and talk about their mamas and they daddies and their wives and we would say these derogatory things about their families. . . . They stood at attention. I have to say, they were very disciplined, ones that I had an encounter with. Because under normal circumstances, given that I was a little black boy, talking to a grown white male like that, they would have knocked the shit out of me."[12]

Rudy Shields and George Walker were the teenagers' most important teach-ers and role models. James Devoual said that Shields "gave us self-worth. He showed us how its done. He showed us where it was done. And then he gave it to us to do." George Walker grew up sharecropping in Claiborne County and worked in the box factory before being drafted for military service during the Korean War. When the box factory refused to rehire him, he went to work for

Thompson's Funeral Home, a job that gave him more security than most other blacks. When Shields arrived, Walker immediately embraced the movement, working side by side with him on voter registration and the boycott. After Shields left to work in other communities, Walker took on the job of mentoring young people. One teenager explained that Walker "acted like he cared" and helped young people "feel motivated" and like they "really were contributing." James Miller, who became a community organizer himself, said that Walker appealed to young people by "involving you. He did it by involving you. Cause you know, I think we were trying to figure out how the hell, where we fit. . . . How can we get involved? How can we make change, make things happen? What was our, what was our niche in the movement. And George helped us young people find out where that was." Evers also encouraged their participation. One teenager remembered her pleasure when Evers met them after a day of working from "sun-up to sun-down" on voter registration to recognize their efforts. "That's what really made us feel good—that he felt enough to come himself and thank us." One volunteer, who was an eighth-grader at the time, observed, "There was something in the air and Charles Evers was a real good motivator and if it took dying then we were ready to go. It was just worth it."[13]

The young people's picketing and publicity work was important, but the boycott's success ultimately depended on dramatic shifts in black shopping patterns. Many shoppers turned to local black businesses, which experienced a major boost in sales. They could not adequately handle the shopping volume or fill the diverse needs of the black community, however, since most were grocery stores and all were small businesses with limited stock and high prices. The NAACP also exempted three white businesses from the boycott: Salter's gas station, Meyer-Marx Drugstore, and Stampley's, a small grocery store/gas station just outside of town. This was partly a practical decision, allowing local access to prescription drugs and gasoline, but these particular choices also highlight the ways blacks assessed white merchants. Meyer-Marx was the only white store that employed a black clerk and was the first business to desegregate its eating facilities. Salter's had desegregated its bathrooms. Harvey Stampley operated a small business with his wife and probably desegregated his bathrooms. At least one movement activist considered him "a good man," and in 1967 when Matt Ross became the first black person elected to the board of supervisors, Stampley bought him a pistol for protection. In summing up the rationale for these choices, Evers explained that these white store owners "showed us courtesy and respect."[14] Since few white merchants fit this profile, most blacks began to do the bulk of their shopping in Vicksburg (about thirty miles away) and Jackson (about sixty miles away). They also traveled to Fayette (about twenty miles away) after

Left to right: Community organizer James Miller, 1969 NAACP president Reverend Eddie Walls, community organizer George Walker, and William Matt Ross, first African American elected to the county board of supervisors (1967) since Reconstruction, pictured in 1994 with artifacts from "No Easy Journey," a permanent exhibition commemorating the Claiborne County movement. Photograph by Patricia Crosby, courtesy Patricia Crosby.

1967, when Evers opened a shopping center there. Thus, the boycott required that blacks deal with the inconvenience of shopping further from home, the sacrifice of doing without spontaneous purchases (like ice cream on a hot day), and the more fundamental problems of finding transportation and securing credit.

Women typically took on the extra work and planning necessary to shop almost exclusively—with limited transportation and income—about forty-five minutes from home. They also did much of the behind-the-scenes work that was essential to the ongoing success of the boycott and the movement. For example, Leesco Guster, who was already heavily involved in the voter registration drive, was one of several women who took care of the details associated with picketing and store-watching. She and others bought posterboard, made signs, and initially made sure there were picketers most afternoons and every Saturday.

Based on instruction from civil rights attorneys and guidelines from the national NAACP, they taught picketers what was legal and what was not, making sure they kept a tight formation and did not block the sidewalk or go on private property. James Miller insists that in Claiborne County "women carried the movement. There's no doubt about it. I mean, there were some men who stood up, but it was a minority. Women were the backbone of the movement. I'll stand on that." Similarly, an older minister explained, "We do a lot of talk, we men, but the lady folk is a doer. They don't do much talk, but they doing. We'll do a lot [of talking about] what we gon' do . . . and the ladies gon' on getting the job done." Another activist made a similar assessment: "Women . . . they quicker to do the work than the fellows. Lot of fellows don't want to be standing out there." This testimony is supported by Claiborne County's voter registration drive, where 80 percent of the first 1,500 blacks who registered to vote were women.[15] Women's involvement in Claiborne County activism mirrors the pattern throughout the South, where, despite their less visible roles, women participated in the movement in greater numbers than men.

Many of the most active movement women had spent years doing social welfare work for the community's well being and some were fairly elite with the resources to spend considerable time on movement work. Thelma Crowder (Wells) was one of the most prominent of these women. By the time she was born in 1908, her grandparents, who had been enslaved, were fairly prosperous, owning farm land and a cotton gin. Living on their land with her parents, Crowder attended school full time and was able to graduate from tenth grade (the highest available) in 1924. She supported herself as a seamstress, and was married with grown children when the movement began. Crowder's family had a strong tradition of community service; her grandparents donated land to their church, and both her father and a cousin supervised the local one-room elementary school. She carried on this legacy, serving on committees and fund-raising for charitable causes. Well-read and knowledgeable about the NAACP, she quickly applied her sense of civic responsibility to the movement, attending meetings, marching, leading songs, raising money, cooking food, helping with picketing, supporting young people, and soliciting NAACP memberships.[16]

The experiences of women in the movement reflect the complexity of prevailing assumptions about gender. For example, Leesco Guster and others explicitly identify the car she used to drive Shields around as belonging to her husband. In discussing her premovement job, she said that her husband "allowed" her to work for a white family. These comments suggest that she, her husband, and the surrounding community assumed some measure of gendered hierarchy within her marriage. And while her movement work was extensive, it was largely that

Leesco Guster, a dedicated activist during the civil rights movement, 2004. Photograph by David Crosby, courtesy David Crosby.

typically done by women: canvassing, housing workers, selling NAACP member-ships, singing in the choir, working with the youth chapter, raising money, and picketing. At the same time, however, some aspects of the Gusters' participation seem more ambiguous in terms of traditional gender norms. Although she and her husband, Harry, were both activists, Mrs. Guster took the lead. She partici-pated in marches, but said she would not "allow" her husband to because she worried that he could not handle being jailed because of high blood pressure. Moreover, although most of her work was associated with repetition and tedium, it also exposed her to danger. She faced armed whites while canvassing with Rudy Shields, and she joined armed men protecting her house. Historian Anne Standley, writing about several relatively well known black women civil rights leaders, notes a pattern that Claiborne County women appeared to follow. She argues that many women's behavior "showed contradictions—on the one hand a boldness in initiating protests and applying pressure on whites in power, while at the same time a submissiveness in their acceptance of the authority of the black male clergy."[17] In Claiborne County, Guster and other women stepped up to do the work that needed doing—whether it was canvassing, challenging whites through public marching, or defending their homes with weapons—and simultaneously accepted prevailing gender hierarchies.

Though women and high school students did much of the movement's mundane work, a group of men labored alongside them in the trenches. A few were longtime NAACP members like Nate Jones, but most of the men involved in the day-to-day work were younger than the prominent NAACP leaders and had few ties to previous activism. George Walker was one of the most visible of these. Most of the others worked in factories in Port Gibson or Vicksburg, and almost all of them had roughly a high school education. For example, James "Pluty" Whitney, who first got involved by answering Evers's call for volunteers to picket on the first Saturday of the boycott, was thirty years old with an eleventh-grade education and worked at the American Paper Tube factory in Port Gibson. Elmo Scott, Whitney's thirty-one-year-old half-brother, was a high school graduate who worked at the Port Gibson Allied Chemical factory. Twenty-seven-year-old Julius Warner, whose father was beaten by patrolmen at Alcorn, was a high school graduate saving money to attend college. (He eventually taught social studies in the public schools.) Warner, who, like Whitney, worked at American Paper Tube, recalled that a number of his coworkers got involved together. He explained that although "most place of employment did not let the blacks get involved" in the movement, American Paper Tube "didn't bother you about what you did after you got off work." Those who worked the night shift, like Ernest "Tullos" Brown, a forty-year-old Baptist minister, were available for movement work during the day. One merchant remembered that Brown "stood across the street in front of my store for the entire duration of the boycott. . . . He worked at Le Tourneau's at night, and I heard him say many times that it was awfully hard to watch the stores all day and work all night."[18] Like those who belonged to the earlier underground NAACP this generation of movement workers was connected to each other through ties of kinship and work. They attended meetings, marched, worked on voter registration, canvassed for NAACP memberships, picketed white stores, and helped protect the black community.

Although a vast majority of blacks enthusiastically supported the boycott, a few continued to patronize white stores. Blacks who violated the boycott became targets of enforcement, including ostracism, name-calling, destruction of property, and, on rare occasions, physical violence. A high school student testified, "The rumor was if you violated the boycott you would be punished. Some black people feared that and some didn't." Most blacks believed the movement's goals were important enough to justify these coercive tactics. Jackson minister and longtime NAACP activist R. L. T. Smith later acknowledged that "those who purchased goods . . . from the white stores were under a threat of bodily harm," but he also argued that their actions were harmful to "the spirit, to the dignity of man, to the aspiration of the people around there." Another person argued that boycott enforcement was worthwhile because it "afforded blacks a chance to look at themselves and ask themselves what direction do you want to go." After noting that a man was beaten for violating the boycott, Reverend J. L. Sayles asserted, "He had no business in there. . . . If they said, 'Don't do it,' don't do it." A teacher described boycott violators as "hard-headed" and justified the coercion: "See, we're trying to get this done, and they're going to sneak in behind your back. And every time they got in there to get something, we had somebody there to get them. And they would beat their behinds, good. That's a fact."[19]

Though most Claiborne County blacks were receptive to using coercion, the impetus for this practice came from Charles Evers. He set the tone during his April 1st courthouse speech, telling the crowd, "If we catch a Negro at any store, we will get his name, address, and phone number and take care of him later. Claiborne County is off-limits to Negroes. Don't even ride around town in your cars." He regularly insisted that boycott violators would be "taken care of" and suggested it was acceptable for the black community to use these coercive methods to police itself. In his 1971 autobiography, he claimed that he had learned these intimidation tactics during his "Chicago underworld days." In a 1990s interview, he reiterated, "If you broke the boycott you might have to be chastised a little bit. Our way of chastising, now I'm not going to say what that was, but we did chastise."[20]

Evers appears to have introduced this type of boycott enforcement to the Mississippi civil rights movement; there is no evidence of physical intimidation in the NAACP- and COFO-led boycotts that took place in the early 1960s. However, within six months of Evers's arrival, there were reports that coercion was being used to enforce the Jackson boycott. In a 1990s interview, Ed King, who had worked closely with Medgar Evers and the Jackson movement, contended that before Charles Evers's arrival, "nobody ever thought of doing this kind of thing. I mean, the purpose of a boycott wasn't to have 100 percent black participation." Instead, he argued that the boycott was a way for blacks to gradually (and anonymously) become more involved in the movement, giving people a way to take "the first step towards fighting for their own freedom." Somewhat bitterly, King concluded that because Charles Evers "would use threats and violence" and "have somebody beat up a few blacks who violated and crossed a picket line," he "had more successful boycotts than Medgar did or Martin King."[21]

Although absent from earlier Mississippi civil rights boycotts, intimidation found more widespread acceptance in the post-1964 period. According to one of her biographers, Fannie Lou Hamer's speeches in the spring of 1965 called for "retributive or retaliatory violence." She used language much like Evers's, insisting in one speech, "We got to stop the nervous Nellies and the Toms from going to the Man's place. I don't believe in killing, but a good whipping behind the bushes wouldn't hurt them." Charles Payne notes that in 1965, the Greenwood, Mississippi, Freedom Democratic Party began emphasizing boycotts, a tactic "that SNCC was not particularly known for." By the fall of 1967, the boycott had become the "focal point of movement activity in Greenwood" and "a small secret group" called the Spirit used enforcement tactics against "the most recalcitrant" boycott violators. Payne believes that this was "the first time local activists took any form of reprisals against non-activist neighbors."[22]

Claiborne County blacks' acceptance of boycott enforcement was bolstered by the hierarchical nature of the local movement. Deferring to the NAACP as if it were a government, they accepted the decisions and policies handed down by the group's leaders. According to Marjorie Brandon, "Most people was a member and they abided by our decisions." Ferd Allen, who was president of the Fayette NAACP, justified the practice of reading the names of boycott violators at meetings by asserting that "they were violating the rules and regulations that had been set up by the NAACP." Matt Ross explained, "The purpose of calling the individuals' names was to let the rest of the community know that these individuals were not respecting the organization that had protected them so far as their rights were concerned." Evers responded to criticism by insisting, "That was the law of the movement. You have to follow the law." Many accepted this view. A Claiborne County woman who was a passive movement supporter explained, "When the boycott was on, I just obeyed the laws, the rules and I didn't go in [the stores]."[23]

The movement's most important tools for convincing recalcitrant blacks to cooperate with the boycott were peer pressure and persuasion. NAACP president James Dorsey maintained that movement supporters would "try to talk to peoples and explain to them what we were trying to do, and what it would mean for them and for their childrens and grandchildrens, you know." One enforcer also insisted that their first step was to talk to people who violated the boycott: "Some of them appreciated us telling them and not bothering them and some of them had the big head and wanted to do what they wanted to do themselves. . . . Them that had the big head, we tried to take care of them." Evers testified that he would "discipline black people" who violated the boycott with "a good tongue-lashing and [by] embarrassing them and showing them how backwards they are to do such things." Implying a similarity between the NAACP's actions and the Citizens' Council's, he concluded, "We would ostracize those people socially, like the whites in Mississippi have ostracized other whites whose actions they didn't approve of." According to Marjorie Brandon, this tactic worked so well that violators would be "standing out to themselves. [People would] say, 'You just go on over there, you [act] white, why don't you go on over there with the whites.'" Evers's description of the Natchez boycott in his 1997 autobiography applies just as well to Port Gibson's: "We held that boycott the spiritual way: preachers and church choirs, sermons and speeches. But if a Negro bought from the wrong grocery store, we might take his groceries. If he bought gas at the wrong filling station, we might drop sugar in his gas tank. We threw brickbats through some windows at midnight, wrapped in paper with a warning. . . . Our brickbats said, THE NAACP IS WATCHING YOU. We never caused permanent injury, but some folk must be scared into doing right. If they break a boycott, you belt-whip them. I got many belt-whippings as a boy. No harm done." In Claiborne County enforcers sometimes took and destroyed groceries or packages. Occasionally they threw bricks or shot at homes or cars belonging to persistent boycott violators. More rarely, they beat people up.[24]

Although Evers introduced enforcement, he left the implementation to others and it became one of Rudy Shields's trademarks. Wherever he worked, blacks and whites associated enforcement with Shields. In fact, some people believed that Evers explicitly brought Shields into the state in order to do this type of dirty work. Rims Barber, who worked with the Delta Ministry (founded by the National Council of Churches in the wake of the 1964 Summer Project), remembered that Shields "was accused of all sorts of mischief." He said, "I don't doubt that Rudy carried on some excesses, that if he was walking the picket line and you broke the boycott and went in, and came out with a bag full of something, he'd knock it out of your hand if he happened to be walking by as you exited the building." Shields visited people at home and warned them that if they did not stay away from boycotted stores they would be "in trouble. Now whether he meant it or didn't mean it, who knows, but people felt intimidated. Absolutely." Rick Abraham remembered that Shields "took a hard view on his own people, people in the black community, who, in his view, would sell out the movement." He added, "When Rudy said we need to boycott this store, you know there were people who would boycott that store, not always because they understood the issue, but because it was Rudy Shields who was saying it. And that was out of respect and in some cases, maybe even out of fear, but Rudy had a reputation of being tough." A Claiborne County activist offered a similar assessment, describing Shields as "kind of rough" and insisting that he "shaked them up. . . . They was scared of Rudy." Nate Jones recalled that people sometimes "said Rudy was too rough on them," and Julia Jones added that Shields would "push people kinda rough if they didn't respond." A minister contended that Shields "was really, really strict." Even when he engaged in enforcement, however, Shields was careful. Sheriff McCay, who desperately wanted to disrupt and discredit Shields's work, described him as a "very smart" "professional agitator" who "knew exactly how far to go and never break the law."[25]

The targets of boycott enforcement included some members of the black elite, especially teachers and ministers, and the poorest blacks who were most closely tied to whites. The black elite's lukewarm support for the boycott was related to a number of factors. As a group, they were typically less engaged in the movement. Most were treated more respectfully by white merchants and had less personal experience with some of the grievances driving the boycott. A black man who was a high school student at the time explained, "Those blacks who had kind of like made it on their own were not serious advocates of the movement." Moreover, their preferential treatment by merchants was actually part of what distinguished them from other blacks and reinforced their status. Accustomed to respect and deference from the black community, some were taken aback when picketers and store-watchers of a lower class insisted that they change their shopping patterns. A teacher explained that though she supported the goals of the boycott, she believed that she should be able to shop wherever she wanted. In the end, she chose to observe the boycott because, "They would tell you *not* to go in there. And say, 'If you are seen going in there, we'll get you.' And they would have somebody to beat you up. . . . Uh-huh. And you'd be so scared. I didn't ever go in them. (Laughter.)"[26]

Though many poor blacks actively supported the movement, a few, usually driven by fears of losing jobs, credit, and access to white favors, did not. One man explained, "A lot of black people were like afraid of losing their jobs, basically being maids or working on the plantation or something like that." James Dorsey observed that, in addition to being "solely dependent" on whites for wages, "people that worked closely with whites, like maids, and things like that [sometimes] . . . felt like this person was their savior." James Devoual explained that you "had those diehards" who "were just kind of white oriented." Searching for the "correct words," he continued: "They had lived with white folk all of their life. They had been kind of conditioned to think in that slavery mentality, and I don't care what or how you tried to reason with them, it was . . . embedded too deep for you to do anything about it. Those were the ones that were kinda like 'Uncle Toms.' And I don't think it was all their fault, it's just all of their lives and from their parents it was passed down from generation to generation. Some things you don't do. 'Mr. Billy Bob is okay. I knew his granddad and his family. I worked for him and yeah, I'ma go in his store.' " Melvin McFatter, son of druggist

M. M. McFatter and a high school student during the movement, argued that some older blacks were "happy" with "their niche." A black minister thought that some did not believe they could "make it without doing what other people tell them to do, especially [when] some of the white people [would say things like,] 'I been knowing you all my life and you can come up in my store' and something like that. I think a lot of them listened to that." Access to credit was a serious problem for some blacks who might otherwise have chosen to observe the boycott. Reverend J. L. Sayles explained that some people would "say, 'Well, I can go to Mr. So and So and he let me have some on credit.' Those folks up yonder won't let him have it and that make a difference, makes a person kinda will slip in a place, you know, cause he know if he get in there, he can get it on credit. He doesn't have the money, but if he get in there he can get it on credit."[27]

Though boycott violators were few in number, some became notorious for their persistent disregard for the boycott. One of these was fifty-six-year-old Emerson Davis, characterized by one activist as being "totally influenced by whites." He made his living doing odd jobs, and it seems that merchants cultivated Davis as a symbol of antipathy toward the movement more than as a legitimate customer. They rewarded him for coming in their stores by giving him merchandise, paying his rent, and offering him work. He testified later, "I really have to live off of rich people, I can't live this way alone. I was trying to protect my business. I shop in white stores because I was given credit there." Davis was also something of an informant. He "gave a civil rights paper" to a white man who asked for it and, in a half-hearted denial of his habit of running to whites with information, insisted, "I don't report to anyone about things I see unless they ask me."[28]

For their part, most blacks dismissed Davis as an "Uncle Tom" who acted out of short-term self-interest. One pointed out, "See he wasn't working. Didn't have no job, but he'd come around and white folks would give him stuff, handouts, give him some tobacco, some snuff to chew." Julius Warner concurred, explaining that Davis "had a pretty large family. I guess he was doing that to, you know, help support his family, basically. . . . Once he started, he got all the odd jobs that most other blacks had been doing." Dorsey observed that blacks who violated the boycott "would get a reduced price or . . . get foods or something of this nature." Melvin McFatter and Sheriff Dan McCay acknowledged that white merchants sought to entice black customers by giving them "free stuff if they came to the store." Blacks ostracized Davis for his refusal to support the boycott, though it did little to change his behavior. He testified that NAACP leader Alexander Collins convinced his black landlord to evict him and another black man to fire him. Davis also said that "Shields and some of the youngsters, called me 'Uncle Tom' because I was going into stores." In June 1966, Davis accused Shields and three other black men of beating him up outside a black café on Fair Street. At a subsequent mass meeting, Shields announced that Davis was a "Tom receiving his medicine." (Though Shields was convicted of beating Davis, the conviction was overturned on the grounds of jury discrimination and he was never retried.)[29]

Laura Cullins, a fifty-nine-year-old black woman who worked as a maid for M. M. McFatter and a local doctor, also persistently violated the boycott. Charles Evers dismissed her as "confused" and someone who "thought she was white," testifying that "we just wrote her off as one of those . . . little colored folks that's going in there, they ain't enough to keep them in business, so don't worry about them." Despite Evers's claim, some boycott supporters did harass her, shooting at her house and calling her names. She testified that she was labeled a "half-white cracker" and that a caller told her, "You got home this evening safe, but how many evenings you'll get home safe I don't know. . . . We're not going to put our hands on you other than to tie you up and [put you] in the Grand Gulf swamp and let the mosquitos devour you."[30]

Cullins and Davis were the most visible targets, but there were others who faced onetime or occasional consequences for refusing to observe the boycott. To some extent, the method of enforcement varied between those, like Davis and Cullins, who violated the boycott to gain favor with whites or to flaunt their hostility to the movement, and those who, for convenience or other reasons, occasionally evaded the boycott. Leesco Guster described several examples of enforcement that were probably typical. When Priscilla Duck violated the boycott by going into McFatter's Drugstore and defiantly told Guster that she would "spend her money anywhere she want to spend it," Guster "turned her name in." Duck's name was announced at an NAACP meeting, and shortly afterward her picture window was broken. Guster interrupted her story with a laugh, saying, "I'm not supposed to be saying all of that" and quickly clarified her role in this incident. "I didn't do it, I just told it." But then she made it clear that she fully supported the act of retaliation, saying, "I didn't have any mercy on anybody. I told on my own sister." She explained that when her sister continued to buy candy from a white merchant despite her efforts to persuade her not to, Guster asked Shields to talk to her. "Mr. Shields didn't break nothing, but he did go there and talk and gave her a little scare. If I told on her, you know I'd tell on anybody."[31]

In another situation, Shields turned to Nate Jones for help. A dignified man with considerable respect for divergent viewpoints, Jones also laughed as he told the story. "Rudy Shields came to me and told me, 'You go see your pastor and tell him, that we not going, we not going to break his leg this time. We gon' pistol whip him this time.' That's what he told me. I went to my pastor and told him exactly what he said." Jones explained that, earlier, Shields and several other men had picked his pastor up to warn him about violating the Fayette boycott and he had hurt his leg jumping out of the truck. Jones concluded, "I scared my pastor. Scared him bad, too. I told him exactly what [Rudy Shields] said." Attempting to explain why their pastor refused to support the boycott, Nate and Julia Jones speculated that he identified with whites and enjoyed some privileges from his ties to whites. "He was almost half white just about. And he had been around white folks all of his life. . . . He didn't want to leave that because it felt good to him. They would give him tips and different things and he wanted to keep all that friendship and everything going."[32]

Although ostracism and even some physical punishment appears to have been widely accepted in the black community, a number of people take pains to minimize the extent of the violence. A man who was in high school at the time insisted that "they never would hurt anybody, just whup 'em enough to scare 'em." Julius Warner explained that there was "no real violence" but that people "would throw bricks at the houses at night, maybe break a few windows and things of that nature. Beating people up and things like that, that was rare." The NAACP Executive Board's position on enforcement remains murky. A man who acknowledged using enforcement observed that the NAACP leadership would "come in there talking about nonviolence," but when people were arrested for enforcement-related offenses, they "didn't have to worry about getting out. They'd be there to get you out." On a number of occasions, people who were victims of boycott enforcement turned to NAACP leaders for help. George Walker tried to convince Laura Cullins to observe the boycott, but when she refused, he advised her to talk to movement leaders about ending the harassment she was experiencing. Her son later testified that the harassment stopped after he spoke with NAACP leaders Calvin Williams and Alexander Collins. James Dorsey handled complaints by directing people to the police, telling them, "We have no control over this element."[33]

Ultimately, the idea or threat of enforcement was probably as important as the individual acts of violence. Asked about violent enforcement in 1969, George Walker, who was by then one of the community's most important leaders and someone people often turned to for help, estimated that over the three years of the boycott, about ten or fifteen people had bricks thrown through their windows. In June 1973, Sheriff Dan McCay testified that he was aware of about 100 incidents related to boycott enforcement, though there were far fewer charges and arrests. A Hinds County judge who ruled that the boycott was an illegal conspiracy enforced by violence could identify no more than twelve acts of enforcement, only three of which involved physical violence. A man whose support for the movement was only lukewarm implied that boycott enforcement was not a big deal: "Someone, I don't remember who, once indirectly threatened me for continuing to trade with whites, but I attached no importance to it. The message was just to remember a boycott was on." Others who persisted in trading with whites reported that it cost them little. Jasper Coleman, who testified that he continued to buy from whites because he needed them for work and credit, concluded, "I never lost any friends, no one ever called me a traitor." Willie Myles insisted that he always shopped with whites but testified that he experienced little harassment and what he did experience (his wife got one threatening phone call, his name was read aloud at an NAACP meeting, he was called an "Uncle Tom," and he was told that some men were going to beat him, though they neither threatened nor touched him) did nothing to change his practice of shopping with whites.[34]

In fact, some blacks probably used whites' perception of boycott enforcement to obscure their reasons for boycotting, finding it easier to let whites believe that their new shopping patterns came from fear of retaliation rather than support for movement goals. Celia Anderson provides a useful illustration. A sharecropper, she was also a strong movement participant. She went to meetings, marched, registered to vote, and canvassed among her neighbors and friends. She was called Mama Celie because of her fierce protection of the younger activists, including her own children and grandchildren. James Miller explained, "Mama Celie, she was a grassroots kind of person. She was the kind of woman that would go out here and throw a brick." He added that she "almost demanded" that her children "be a part of the movement, and she had a bunch of them." In fact, he claimed that one of her sons was among those involved in violent enforcement and "did a whole bunch of stuff that he ought to be in the pen for, in the movement." Although she bought nothing new during the boycott, Anderson made regular payments to merchant Barbara Ellis for previous credit purchases. She later explained how she allowed Ellis to believe her observance of the boycott was due to fear of retaliation. "Miss Barbara [would] come to the door and get it. 'Celie come on in here. Come on in here.' I say, 'No, Miss Ellis. I ain't going to let them whup me, you know.' We'd have a big laugh and I'd pay her and she'd give me a receipt. Something I already owed her for. Paid her out." Despite her comments to Ellis, Anderson never considered breaking the boycott. A May 1969 Sovereignty Commission effort to catch several men using coercion also illustrates how blacks hid behind the threat of enforcement. An investigator had a white merchant send an employee to drop shirts off at a dry cleaners while he stood watch, hoping to catch black store watchers threatening or attacking him. The employee never actually tried to go into the store and instead went out of his way to talk to movement activists on the street. Yet he told his employer that he was unable to drop shirts off to be cleaned because enforcers "wouldn't let him go in."[35] Unaware that he was being watched, this employee used the excuse of coercion to justify his observance of the boycott.

In recalling the boycott, most Claiborne County blacks insist that it succeeded because of widespread support, not because of violent enforcement. Though Evers is not a particularly reliable source, he dismissed boycott violators as insignificant, saying, "If a black person . . . is mistreated by any individual and denied and he ain't got no more sense than to go in there and spend his money and his time, then, yes, sir, I still say . . . we just don't need him." Leesco Guster contended that "everybody was just together," while another woman explained, "We wasn't worried about that part [enforcement]. We wasn't going in because these people was out there marching, and they was trying to get things better for the black people." Marjorie Brandon noted that the boycott "was really well enforced" and then amended her statement: "Well, really wasn't too much enforcement because people just didn't go in there. Just didn't go in there. Everybody believed in it and this is what everybody wanted. 99 percent of them felt like you know, if they getting our black dollar then they should have some black people in there working for them."[36]

CHAPTER Eleven

Clinging to Power and the Past

The Claiborne County movement exposed the vastly different perspectives and attitudes of blacks and whites and generated both subtle and dramatic shifts in race relations. The movement forced whites to come up against some of the ways they were dependent on blacks—as customers, employees, and props in their ideology of good race relations. Whites responded to black activism with shock and surprise and initially tried to halt the movement by appealing to blacks through traditional paternalism. When that failed, the white community employed more coercive tactics, including economic intimidation, the misuse of the legal system, wide-ranging threats and harassment, and occasional violence.

Rudy Shields, who was repeatedly arrested for his movement activism, frequently used his trials to speak for the civil rights movement and challenge whites' racial views. The white prosecutors often facilitated this practice by focusing more on Shields's impact on the community than on the specific charges against him. In particular, the encounters between Shields and District Attorney T. J. Lawrence, a World War I veteran who spent his boyhood in Claiborne County and lived in nearby Sharkey County, reveal the competing worldviews held by movement participants and opponents.

Lawrence used his questions to portray a premovement world of racial harmony, once asking Shields, "Now did you know, before you came to this county, that peace and happiness and order, and love and charity, prevailed among the races, did you know that?" Shields retorted, "I know that it was quite the contrary and still is . . . otherwise why would they boycott? Why would ninety-nine percent of the Negroes be out of the stores if they were so happy?" Shields consistently contested Lawrence's assertions that he was singlehandedly disrupting the community against the wishes of blacks, as well as whites. When Lawrence charged that Shields had been sent to Claiborne County to "disturb those people," Shields responded, "Since when is getting people registered disturbing people? That's a man's Constitutional right, to register, and not only that, it's a civic duty to register." Shields refused to allow Lawrence to set the terms for black-white relations. When Lawrence asserted that a white merchant had helped and befriended several black women who were among her customers, Shields insisted, "If Mrs. Bearden was helping those ladies, well I think that's fine. But by the same token, I still hold to my conviction, that if Mrs. Bearden had loved colored people so much it seems only obvious that she would give the Negroes jobs as a cashier, or a job with some dignity to it."[1]

Years of asserting and believing that blacks were satisfied left many whites truly bewildered by movement activism. One black woman recalled that "a lot of [white] people thought colored people should be satisfied to stay like they was." Shortly after the movement began, a white welfare worker told her, " 'I don't see what the black people's fighting about. . . . Ya'll seems like ya'll happy. Every time we see you, you laughing, happy. Look like you happy all the time.' I say, 'Yes, I guess we laughing to keep from crying.' That's right. I say, 'I know I'm not happy.' . . . She thought black people was satisfied the way things was." One white woman insisted that she never thought about race growing up and expressed regret that her children would not share her experience. She said that during the movement, "You pulled back just a little bit" from "people, maybe, that you had felt really comfortable with and trusted." In May 1966, a merchant wrote to the *Port Gibson Reveille*, "I am astonished and deeply hurt to see what is actually going on in our town. Friends seem to distrust friends; neighbors are against neighbors and most of all the colored people are against the white. You can look into eyes and faces of people that you once considered friends and find a look of distrust and hatred." James Miller observed, "Everybody became very sensitive about anything that happened between black folks and white folks."[2]

Writing about the civil rights movement in St. Augustine, Florida, Taylor Branch argues that a black newcomer to the community had an easier time engaging in confrontation because he "did not see a life's story behind most faces in town." Certainly blacks and whites in the Claiborne County area had their share of uncomfortable surprises as people behaved in new and unexpected ways. Focusing on Charles Evers's influence, druggist M. M. McFatter recalled that "he had a way of stirring up, raising the temperature you know, and we had people the white people would just swear by. For instance, Mr. Hudson, he swore that his main man, he ain't going with that, but he did." In describing the response of Fayette's white mayor, Turnip Green Allen, to a question about Ferd Allen, the community's NAACP president, Evers captured the essence of white surprise and ambivalence about many black activists. "Someone asked Turnip Green Allen what Ferd Allen was doing. Turnip Green gave Ferd a good reference: 'He's a very good nigger. In fact, he used to work for my father-in-law. But he turned out to be the President of this thing.' Turnip Green Allen never understood why good old Ferd Allen would boycott Fayette."[3]

Blacks, too, faced revelations about those they lived and worked among. Florence Mars, a white native of Neshoba County, Mississippi, observed that "Negro citizens . . . found it difficult to understand the intense hostility directed against them by people they had known all their lives." George Walker remembered his surprise when whites refused to grant the Human Relation Committee's requests. "I had known most of the white people and they was always nice. Anything we wanted, we get it, and then when the demands came down . . . I say, 'That ain't gon' be nothing.' . . . When they said no, it was a shock." Describing the antagonistic onlookers lining the streets during marches in Port Gibson, Julia Jones recalled, "I just looked right in this Ellis boy face and I was surprised. But probably not as surprised as he was." After explaining how she and her husband had shopped with the younger Ellis's parents and relatives for years, Jones emphasized he was on the street, "*With a gun*. And that really surprised me, him having a gun. I would have thought he wouldn't do that." Nate Jones added that he had not thought "they was that type of people."[4]

Unwilling to accept that blacks had never been content, let alone happy, whites repeatedly blamed the new militancy on outsiders. White leader Jimmy Allen said, "I remember the agitators coming in from outside. They used churches you know, which was a good place for to get their attention. . . . Some outside preacher would come in and make these talks and all. Of course, the fact that it was actually turning blacks against whites, we didn't appreciate it a whole lot. We had been getting along with them for years. There were some people who abused them, there's no doubt about it, but generally, in this area particularly, there was enough respect back and forth where there wasn't any complications." One white merchant testified in the 1970s, "We had a happy relationship among blacks and whites until this happened." Another merchant insisted, "The locals here were not really doing anything. It was the outsiders that came in here and organized the boycott." A black man who acknowledged the importance of outside influences put a different twist on this, pointing out, "We *seem* to have gotten along well together, but that's because we accepted where we were. And then when someone came by and said, you can have something better. That caused us to want to do that."[5]

Unita Blackwell, a COFO and MFDP activist from nearby Mayersville, emphasized that the Port Gibson boycott was psychologically devastating to the white community and explained that they had "conned" themselves into thinking that they had their own self-contained economy and instead found out that they were dependent "on a bunch of 'niggers.' That's what they said. . . . They was so . . . in denial until they didn't realize that their economy was the so-called niggers. Their whole livelihood was the so-called niggers." Nate Jones reflected that when he paid off his bill with white merchant Michael Ellis, "It hurt that man. It hurt that fellow so bad to see me go. I had been one of his customers for years." Before the movement, Jimmy Ellis remembered, the black Ellises and white Ellises had a good relationship because "we wore the same last name." Michael Ellis gave Jimmy Ellis school clothes and "used to say that we were all related, part of the same family. Cut off the same family tree." Once the high school–aged Jimmy Ellis became active in the movement, however, he recalled, Michael Ellis "told me to get out of the store and don't ever come back and what he said about family, that's a lie. 'You nothing but a no good nigger like the rest of them.'"[6]

During the early days of the boycott, the NAACP pushed for blacks who worked in white homes to quit their jobs in order to reduce the problems created by informants and to make sure whites realized how much they relied on black employees. It is not clear how many blacks actually left their jobs, but whites found the prospect upsetting. M. K. Davenport recalled that her maid quit and told her that the NAACP "wanted to show us what it was like not to have any contacts of help and friendship from the black community. They thought that we didn't—and they were right—we did not realize." She remembered that "all of a sudden, all over town," whites felt a "loss" and a "great shock." Saying that she and her maid "loved each other," she insisted that she "wasn't really hurt" and "it wasn't such a blow to me" because "I wasn't totally dependent on it." Her children were mostly grown, she said, and "I knew how to do all the work. I'd washed and ironed and done to take care of my own children."[7] Moreover, Davenport remained convinced that her maid would not have quit if she had really needed her. These comments illustrate the dual nature of the loss white women faced—of labor, and of their sense of emotional connection to the black women who worked for them.

An April 1966 letter to the editor by merchant Ronnie Hulbert reveals a similar sense of betrayal and demonstrates how his personal feelings and business decisions intermingled. Hulbert wrote that the previous Christmas he and others in the Kiwanis Club had collected "several hundred dollars worth of food, clothes and toys" and "about 90 %" of it "went to the colored community." He bitterly concluded, "Now, to show their appreciation they are boycotting the same ones that helped them! Should we continue to help them after this?" Hulbert apparently believed that blacks should collectively accept several hundred dollars of charity instead of full citizenship rights. He also insisted that after the boycott he would provide repair service only to blacks who traded with him during the boycott and that "it will be easy for me to tell Negroes 'No Credit.' "[8]

Albert Butler, a black man who worked at the Piggly Wiggly, argued that owner James Hudson developed intense opposition to the movement because he felt betrayed. He had not believed "that blacks would actually stop shopping with him because of the relations that he felt he had with us. Then when he found out that they would, I think he, that kind of got him upset." Moreover, Butler maintained, "had individuals known how to deal with him," they would have had more success "in trying to get some of the things that we as blacks were asking for." Hudson blamed the boycott on outsiders and "was the type of person that did not like to be dictated to or told what to do." Like many of their white counterparts, James Hudson and his siblings grew up with blacks. Their father was a preacher who passed out Gideon Bibles in black churches, and the Hudson family, which started out relatively poor, was befriended by a black neighbor who "would always make sure they had something to eat." The youngest brother, George Hudson, recalled later, "I was born and raised and I played with my black friends." By 1966, when the boycott started, the Hudson brothers were prospering and had moved into a more commanding relationship with blacks. They offered credit and services through the Piggly Wiggly, worked with the FHA to build and sell houses to blacks, and employed blacks in their grocery store and construction business. Although they did not inherit the mantle of leadership like the Gages and Allens, they had achieved some status. The brothers were active in community affairs, and James, who was a World War II veteran, former high school teacher and coach, and member of the county Democratic Executive Committee, later testified that other merchants deferred to him in regard to the boycott, telling him, "Whatever you decide, we'll go along with you."[9]

After the boycott began, James Hudson was involved in several confrontations with picketers, and Evers testified that Hudson stood "out in front of his store with his gun" and made hostile or obscene finger gestures to black marchers. Leesco Guster observed that Hudson spent a lot of time "meddling" and picking at blacks. She was particularly bothered by this because she had heard James Hudson tell her husband "that black people was the ones that supported his store and he was gonna do whatever, you know, whatever it took" to resolve the conflict. Echoing Hudson, she insisted, "Black folk were the ones that supported his store. Even if he were not gonna do it [make concessions], he could have just not meddle us." During testimony about the NAACP's efforts to negotiate with white leaders, Evers singled Hudson out, describing him as "a terrible fellow" who was "a little angry. We tried to keep him cool, but he wouldn't let us do it." During one meeting, Hudson "left like a whirlwind almost." Albert Butler insisted that this behavior marked a change in Hudson, and that before the movement he consistently acted as peacemaker, smoothing over conflicts generated by his older brother, who treated black customers poorly. Moreover, Butler believed that James Hudson was actually more "liberal" about race than some of the other business owners in town and that "it wasn't until later that . . . James was labeled as being one of the [worst racists]."[10]

Whites were bothered by many of the changes that came with the movement, including the presence of black voter registration workers, demonstrators, picketers, and store watchers on the streets. Business owner Jimmy Allen described marches as "an irritation," and another merchant criticized black mass meetings: "They'd carry on about what they gon' do, how the thing is going. You couldn't get down that street for the cars and the people. I'm talking about men, old folk. They were hardly could walk, they'd be there. Like a big family reunion. They want a good time, they go there. . . . And you know how they are, like to shout and carry on anyway." James Hudson testified that he became afraid to let his daughter walk down the streets because of his experiences of "having to push or go around a bunch of young blacks." He explained that blacks "would be walking two or three abreast or just crowding the sidewalk and you would have to get out in the street to go around them. They wouldn't let you by. Nothing like this had happened before the boycott was put on. After the boycott, it happened hundreds of times." Pharmacy owner Q. H. McDaniel's description of picketers conveyed similar hostility. "They picketed up and down the entire business district, not just my store. They made noise; they would stomp, like storm troops."[11]

An encounter between movement activist Calvin Williams and several Port Gibson white men in April 1966 illustrates how whites believed they should control public space and struggled to hang onto that authority when it was challenged by the movement. Williams and several companions were walking down Main Street to investigate rumors of a movement-related confrontation when they encountered Police Chief L. L. Doyle standing with several other white men. Though Williams responded cooperatively to Doyle's request that the group disperse, and even asked those with him to walk in twos, he was later

Picketer in front of McFatter's Drugstore, 1966. Courtesy Mississippi Cultural Crossroads.

arrested and charged with "disturbing the peace" and "blocking the public sidewalk and entrances to stores." James Dorsey contends that whites arrested Williams because they "didn't want a lot of blacks to assemble together." In fact, the white men who believed Williams acted improperly failed to identify any unlawful behavior. Collectively, they testified that Williams and his companions had walked in a group down the street and stopped on a corner. None of them reported that Williams physically blocked the sidewalk or any store entrances. Chief Doyle, for example, justified Williams's arrest by testifying, "This group of Negroes were utilizing almost all of the sidewalk." Moreover, he and the other white men saw no irony in the fact that they, too, were standing in a group on a sidewalk corner. One of the things that appeared to bother Doyle most was that

White men lounging on steps of Port Gibson Bank, located on Main Street in a building constructed by enslaved people, 1940. Photograph by Marion Post Wolcott, courtesy Library of Congress, LC-USF 34 55016-E.

he believed Williams had violated an earlier agreement that blacks would not conduct any marches without explicit white permission. Like officials in a Louisiana town who conveyed ownership of the streets to merchants so they could arrest picketers for trespassing, Port Gibson white officials believed the streets belonged to them and blacks could only use them with permission.[12]

In general, whites reacted to the boycott and the mass movement with the same combination of paternalistic appeals and coercion that they had used to halt the union drive twenty years earlier. They refused to accept that the boycott represented the black community's collective dissatisfaction, instead attributing it to outsiders and insisting that it was entirely dependent on boycott enforcement and intimidation. The April 7 edition of the *Reveille* was filled with letters, editorials, and advertisements imploring local citizens, "white and colored," to "shop at home." The mayor and board of aldermen urged blacks to shop in white stores, because it "aids the general economy of our town." Editor E. T. Crisler claimed that "all responsible citizens, whites and Negroes," disapproved of the boycott. A merchant later reiterated that "the locals here were not really doing anything. It was the outsiders that came in here and organized the boycott." An advertisement for the Southwest Mississippi Discount store blamed "outside instigators" and those who "would sell out their own mothers if it would give them more power and money," and the aldermen offered protection from the "destructive forces at work in our community." In a late April letter to the editor, a white man claimed, "The Negroes in this county are publicly admitting they can't think for themselves! They are paying Charles Evers and his goons to think for them." Crisler directed a long editorial at the black community, writing, "Plain talk to our Negro citizens: Many of you sing and talk of 'wanting our freedom.' Then allow yourselves to be enslaved by intimidation, and lose a basic freedom, which is spending your money where you want to. We doubt very much that you are happier because of ill-will engendered, the disruption in your normal buying, and the prospect of lost jobs."[13]

Like Crisler, many whites articulated a seemingly altruistic concern for blacks and implied that the boycott was more damaging to blacks than to white merchants. The aldermen urged "full cooperation of all our citizens" (meaning that blacks should shop in white stores), because it would prevent "inconvenience to the buyer." One store advertisement maintained that boycott leaders "care not about the misery and hardship they heap upon their own people," while another letter writer insisted that blacks "are suffering more than the whites, because we still trade locally and at less expense, and move with freedom." Reflecting on the boycott, Jimmy Allen argued that "it was just as hard on their race as it was on the merchants," and Sheriff Dan McCay claimed that "lots of the old black people, it was really hard on them."[14]

Whites failed to see the validity of black grievances, rejecting moderate change and good-faith negotiations with the NAACP. Many years later, McCay still characterized black demands as "unreal" and "impossible," and one merchant testified that when Evers "asked what we had to offer, we offered nothing." Rosalie Abraham contended, "My husband and I weren't going to give in. . . . And none of the other stores around here wanted to give in either." Evers observed that merchants resented the implication that blacks were telling them what to do and that merchants insisted, "We're not going to let ya'll make us do nothing." Evers explained that "they were just set in their way and determined not to give in 'cause they knew that once they gave in, then blacks outnumbered them." Marjorie Brandon thought merchants acted like they "would rather . . . go out of business, sacrifice their business than to kneel to change."[15]

Along with paternalistic appeals, whites relied heavily on coercion and intimidation to undermine the movement. Merchants appear to have been particularly active in striking back at black activists, and they dominated the Friday night meetings at the courthouse where whites discussed strategies for breaking the boycott and getting "back to normal." In his April letter to the editor, radio repairman Ronnie Hulbert encouraged more whites to attend these meetings, writing that the white leaders had compiled "a list of Negro carpenters, plumbers, painters, handy men, and etc., who are active in agitating." He urged, "Let's get that list and hit them in the pocket book—fire them, don't hire them! Use white folks!" He reported that "merchants are cutting off credit, foreclosing on past due accounts, moving Negroes who formerly did not pay rent off their property, and firing Negro employees due to lack of business." It is difficult to determine how many people experienced direct reprisals, but blacks' fears of economic retaliation were pervasive. One organizer recalled that into the 1970s, the white power structure "permeated the lives of black people in that county" and many blacks still worried that "they'd lose their job cleaning somebody's house. There was such a dependence, economic dependence." Rick Abraham described how whites used similar intimidation in Yazoo City, Mississippi, in the late 1960s when blacks participated in demonstrations. "The white folks they worked for would come down the street, and just glare at them and come say things to them like, 'You ought to be shamed of yourself,' like very condescending, talking down to them like they were children you know. And I could just see that some of these people were worried about losing their jobs. If you stood up and spoke out and you became part of the effort to change things, you could become a target. You could lose your job, you could really suffer."[16]

As soon as Leesco Guster began working with Rudy Shields on voter registration, she was fired and whites began boycotting her husband, Harry, who was a successful contractor. More as a favor than because she wanted the work, Leesco Guster had cleaned house for the daughter of one of Harry's most important clients. One morning while she was working, her employer came home talking about the NAACP and the movement: "She walked in and she said, 'I'm tired of this damn shit.' And the next thing, she told me that, you know, that's okay, she wouldn't need me any more." Guster explained, "I knew what was happening. It was the people getting to her." Whites stopped hiring her husband at the same time. "They got together and must have agreed not to hire. Nobody, I mean nobody, gave him nothing to do. Even, he used to work out of town, look like they cut down on him too. Nobody." This attempt at intimidation failed, and being unemployed just gave the Gusters more time to devote to the movement. Leesco Guster remembered thinking after she was fired, "She coming here falling right in line with her people, why can't I fall in line with mine? I wasn't afraid. I wasn't afraid." The Gusters were protected by a measure of financial security. Harry Guster received enough money through a VA pension and social security that they were able to live without "strain," and they even had enough resources to provide bond when Shields and others were arrested on movement-related charges. In fact, another movement activist connected Harry Guster's practice of posting bond to his inability to get work: "He'd post bond, so many bonds till he couldn't even get no job in Claiborne County."[17]

Thelma Crowder lost work as soon as she became involved in the movement; a number of white people asked her to return material they had given her to sew. Matt Ross, a city employee and movement supporter who owned a small grocery store/gas station, recalled that when the boycott began, "the city said there were certain things I couldn't sell unless I renovated. That went on for about 3–4 months. They would not keep me insured unless I made improvements." His wife, who ran the business while he was working his day job, remembered that whites immediately stopped patronizing their store. She observed, "Black folks were attempting to advance themselves, and whites disliked us and stopped coming around." Horace Lightfoot, an electrician who was later the first black person elected to the Claiborne County Board of Education, testified, "After the boycott went into effect, whites withheld their trade. . . . In April 1966, I didn't get any money."[18]

A number of blacks were suspended from school or lost their jobs for participating in the various Alcorn protests. In addition to Calvin Williams, President Boyd fired the other four staff members who joined the March 4 protest, where almost 200 people were arrested. He suspended the seven student participants, all of whom commuted to campus from Claiborne and Jefferson counties. Two of them, Dorothy and Nettie Brandon, were related to NAACP activists Marjorie Brandon and Nate Jones. Immediately after their suspension, their mother, Artemeasie Brandon, lost her job babysitting for an Alcorn professor when Boyd threatened to fire him if he did not fire her. Like the Gusters, several of the suspended students, including both Brandons, became even more active in the movement. After protesting at Alcorn, three men employed at the Le Tourneau factory near Vicksburg lost their jobs. Le Tourneau employees were also fired for more general "civil rights activity" and for violating the company's informal policy mandating segregation in the lunchroom. A number of Port Gibson merchants fired black employees movement activism. According to Nate Jones, Herbert Becks "lost his job for participating." A Piggly Wiggly butcher was fired immediately after attending a courthouse rally during his lunch break, and Dorothy Brandon insisted that the boys and men who worked bagging groceries at Hudson's grocery store knew that "if they got involved any kind of way, they would lose their job." Merchants acknowledged that they fired black employees but claimed they did so because they had so little business. One merchant testified that although his "help tried to dissuade my customers from coming in my store," he "didn't fire them on account of that but fired them on account of lack of business."[19]

Merchants and bankers punished movement activism by manipulating blacks' access to credit. NAACP president James Dorsey asserted that "the principle figures" were often targeted and would get notices that creditors were changing payment agreements and wanted "all our monies now." Like the fear of being fired, the threat of losing credit was widespread and affected most of the black community whether or not they experienced personal retaliation. After describing how her white customers withdrew their dressmaking orders, Thelma Crowder added, "I haven't had any trouble with the banker. . . . I heard others say they were turned down but I haven't [been]." Although it turned out to be a false alarm, Guster remembered that a black man told her husband that they should "check about our house note . . . because Bobby Gage said he was going to foreclose us."[20]

Whites also manipulated the legal system to suppress movement activism. According to scholar Steven Barkan, "The entire legal machinery of the South became a tool for social control of civil rights efforts." Speaking in McComb, Mississippi, in 1962, SNCC's Bob Moses made essentially the same point, explaining, "The law down here is law made by white people, enforced by white people, for the benefit of white people." Whites arrested a number of blacks for boycott-related activities. On the second day of the boycott (April 2, 1966), Ann Marie Collins was arrested when a white store owner objected to her efforts to convince several blacks not to shop with her. After the owner tried to push her away, Collins was charged with public profanity and breach of peace and convicted of the latter. Two weeks later, fifteen-year-old George Lee Weddington was arrested by a state trooper for obstructing traffic when he stepped onto Highway 61 to get around a patrol car parked on the roadside. The justice of the peace subsequently dismissed the charges, but not before Weddington was arrested, taken away from his picketing duties, and jailed. Rudy Shields was the most frequent victim of movement-related arrests. His first arrest came on April 2, after he had spent the day coordinating picketing. He was charged and found guilty of assaulting a young white woman, although the alleged victim said she was not aware of being attacked. In subsequent months, he was charged with assault, threatening, cursing, trespassing, and interfering with trade.[21]

There was little evidence to support movement-related arrests. Shields's assault case is a good example. Not only did the woman Shields was convicted of assaulting testify that she "did not know any crime had been committed," but the highway patrolman who eventually filed the charges did not do so until hours after the alleged incident. Shields's attorney, John Biasucci, commented, "The extraordinary incredibility of this is fascinating. A white officer sees a Negro male forcibly strike or push [a] pretty, blond, pregnant, southern girl—and does not make an arrest or do anything at all for hours." After Shields was convicted but only fined $25, Biasucci concluded, "The amount of the fine underscores the absurdity of the whole proceeding. If [the] defendant had indeed been guilty of assault and battery on a blond, pregnant, pretty, white girl, the $25.00 fine would be ridiculously low. In effect, I believe it was the judge's way of making clear that Shields was guilty of being a boycott agitator, but that he was really innocent of that criminal charge." Talking to a historian three years later, Port Gibson's first black police officer Charles Groves volunteered a remarkably similar story and interpretation. Groves said that the police produced a "fake affidavit" that Shields had bumped a pregnant white lady and that Groves was supposed to testify that he had witnessed the incident. Groves refused and was fired almost immediately. Groves concluded (as did Shields's lawyer) that whites were "trying to upset all the pickets."[22]

There were other instances when police and prosecutors manufactured charges and manipulated procedures to disrupt the movement. Thomas Watts (who would use his case to challenge jury discrimination in Claiborne County) was charged and convicted for carrying a concealed weapon when patrolmen stopped him and *saw* his gun sitting out in the car. Klan supporter Ronnie Hulbert used a gun to make a citizen's arrest of black teenager Daniel Giles, alleging that he broke a store window. The window had not actually been broken, but Giles was still charged with (and then convicted of) breach of peace. In another instance, Port Gibson attempted to use the same lawyer to prosecute *and* defend Emerson Davis, the black man who refused to observe the boycott, when he was accused of threatening Rudy Shields.[23]

Because of their shared interest in opposing the civil rights movement, white judges, prosecutors, and lawmen typically acted in concert and abandoned the separate roles traditionally delineated for the various participants in the legal system. After one case, a Lawyers' Committee attorney noted, "Once again

[District Attorney] T. J. Lawrence and [Circuit Court] Judge [Ben] Guider colluded in a disgraceful manner." Even before they were tried, Guider pressured defendants to plead guilty by predicting that they would face high fines and jail sentences if they did not. In one instance, he told an attorney that you "might find it to your advantage" to accept a guilty plea. Untrained justices of the peace were particularly susceptible to pressure from prosecutors. After one trial, an attorney observed that the justice of the peace "abdicated to the prosecuting attorney" and even commented that "he had no choice but to find the defendant guilty." The lawyer believed the justice was alluding to white animosity to the civil rights movement and speaking literally.[24]

Local whites' hostility toward the civil rights movement was evident in their courtroom behavior and comments. Longtime district attorney T. J. Lawrence addressed a white civil rights attorney in a condescending and derisive way, referring to him, as he did to black witnesses, as "boy." Lawrence also launched aggressive verbal attacks against Rudy Shields that were unrelated to any of the issues before the court. In one diatribe, he called Shields "filthy, slimy, vulgar, indecent, [and] inhuman." White officials typically interpreted civil rights lawyers' legal objections as personal attacks. Moreover, judges regularly made comments about community crisis or instability as the context for convicting African Americans. One referred to the current "trouble," while another said that these "[are] not normal times." Travis Vance, acting as prosecutor in mayor's court, closed one argument by emphasizing "the dangers of mob violence of Negroes."[25]

Claiborne County's lawmen worked closely with the highway patrol and the Sovereignty Commission. Sheriff Dan McCay estimated that there were fifteen highway patrolmen and two investigators "stationed in Port Gibson for about four months." He explained that whenever there was a hint of conflict, the patrolmen would arrive "en masse" with about "30 to 50 highway patrol cars [and] at least two patrolmen in each car." Although Sovereignty Commission director Erle Johnston has claimed that by 1966 the organization was no longer acting as a watchdog for segregation, but was instead devoted to ensuring a peaceful transition in race relations, he and his investigators continued to ally themselves with whites, offering information, advice, and strategies for disrupting the movement. For example, investigator Tom Scarbrough reported in January 1966 that Johnston sent him to Fayette, Mississippi, to "work with public officials and businessmen . . . to determine some way of breaking a boycott by Negroes." Johnston himself characterized black leaders as "agitators" and once advised Fayette whites that in order to create some bargaining leverage, they should counter NAACP demands by insisting that the black community "eradicate venereal disease in their race and also secure legal status for the common-law marriages that I am sure are wide-spread."[26]

Highway patrolmen, Sovereignty Commission investigators, and local lawmen actively harassed movement workers. NAACP president James Dorsey reported that highway patrolmen frequently tailgated and stopped him, sometimes making him wait in his car for more than thirty minutes while they ostensibly checked his license. When Sheriff McCay offered Dorsey a gun permit to carry a weapon for self-protection, Dorsey declined. Even if McCay did not intend to set him up, Dorsey feared that highway patrolmen would seize on the presence of a gun as an excuse to attack or arrest him. Dorsey recalled that in one encounter, a patrolman asked whether he had a gun. Dorsey replied, "Yes," and, referring to the number of chapters in the Bible, said, "It shoots 66 bullets." Laughing as he recalled the incident, Dorsey explained that the trooper "thought sure I was coming up with a real one. He thought he had me."[27]

Officers regularly ticketed movement activists for what Marjorie Brandon referred to as "little picky stuff." She explained, "They would harass people" and use "any kind of excuse" to try "to make an example" out of people who "had the nerve to stand up for rights . . . so the next person wouldn't try." She said, for example, that "if you go in Port Gibson and go by the light and it was on caution, they give you a ticket and say you ran a red light. Things of that sort." Her niece Dorothy Brandon remembered that highway patrolmen would follow and stop voter registration workers "for no reason," and NAACP board member Calvin Williams observed that they "would walk right straight on at the picket[er]s, with their billies in their hand." Another movement leader complained to the FBI that excessive patrolling by the highway patrol upset "people waiting to register."[28]

In many Mississippi communities, auxiliary police forces provided official sanction for white men who wanted to use vigilante tactics against the movement. Florence Mars argues that although not all members of the auxiliary police were Klansmen, the auxiliary police were "the legitimate police arm of the Ku Klux Klan." Port Gibson whites responded to the movement by using armed auxiliary police to try to intimidate blacks, especially those who came downtown for mass meetings and voter registration. The auxiliary policemen often aimed guns out of their car windows as they patrolled the Port Gibson streets, and many blacks believed they would carry out the persistent rumors that First Baptist Church "was going to be bombed." During the period when the auxiliary police was most active, white men (probably auxiliary policemen), shot out Rudy Shields's bedroom window in a house several blocks from where the NAACP hosted its weekly mass meetings. Shields was keeping watch that night and returned fire from "some bushes near the highway."[29]

Overall, the climate was tense and hostile as whites used widespread threats and harassment in an effort to suppress the movement and frighten blacks. Several crosses were burned around the county. Matt Ross found Ku Klux Klan signs near his house, and there were rumors "that the Ku Klux Klan was going to start rioting and killing." The most visible leaders and activists were the most common targets, and many received threatening phone calls. After recounting how he and his family were inundated by harassing calls, NAACP president James Dorsey reflected that if "you don't believe with all your heart, you would actually quit. Because they would come up with some tactics." When a white man who identified himself as a Klansman phoned Leesco Guster and asked whether she was "tired of living," she "gave it back to him, you know, and told him he would be a dead one if he came down here." Despite her bold words, she remembered, "That was a night because you couldn't sleep [for being] in fear. From then on you had to be on watch." She, her husband, and Shields stood guard all night with help from some men in an informal self-defense group. Whites made similar threats against Calvin Williams when he ran for sheriff in 1967 and Floyd Rollins when he was elected the county's first black election commissioner in 1968.[30]

When Marjorie Brandon's six children and three of their cousins (younger siblings of Dorothy and Nettie Brandon who were suspended from Alcorn) desegregated the formerly whites only public schools, all the children and both families faced persistent harassment, including name calling, threatening phone calls, and menacing visitors. Brandon recalled, "We went through some rough times, some sleepless nights." The constant harassment grew more intense leading up to the May 1967 graduation, when her oldest son Ken became the first black student to graduate from Port Gibson High. "They would call. Call. And if you were on the streets, anywhere, they would yell out after you. And then it came to time for graduation. We got threats, and saying they were gonna kill our son when he went up to get his degree." When Brandon complained to the sheriff, he gave her implicit permission to defend her home, telling her, "Everybody supposed to protect their home." Sometimes alone and sometimes with help from others, Brandon did keep watch and assured the sheriff that if anyone "come on this property, somebody gonna come get somebody." Ken remembered that "when things started to get kind of rough, Mom put a gun in the car. She put a gun in the car and we took off." Brandon explained, "You felt like you didn't have any other choice. Cause all these whites had guns, you had nothing. . . . And I know that's why I felt like I had to carry mine."[31]

According to Fred Tisdale and James Dorsey, on two occasions white men showed up intending to kill black leaders. Fred Tisdale recounted that, after his father Mack Tisdale signed the NAACP's March 1966 demand letter, white men came looking for him, saying, "We need to see him. We want to teach him a lesson." Tisdale continued, "Well then, it occurred to me what they were looking for him for, because they was harassing many blacks at that time." Concerned that they intended to hurt his father, he headed for his trailer to pick up a weapon. The two men left then, but Tisdale insisted, "If they come in here to kill my daddy, they would get to hell, quick." Dorsey believes that only a case of mistaken identity kept him from being killed one day. He explained that if Reverend Evan Doss was still living, "he could tell the story" about the day an armed white man who, "wasn't of this area," went to Doss's house and pulled a gun on him. Doss told Dorsey that, after comparing Doss's face to a picture, the man "said, 'My God, I got the wrong man'" and quickly left. Locals pronounce the names Doss and Dorsey very much alike, and Doss concluded that the man had been misdirected. He immediately notified Dorsey and then drove to his house where the two men stood guard all day and night.[32]

White opposition to the movement was pervasive; however, a number of men were particularly aggressive and antagonistic. One of these was pharmacist M. M. McFatter, widely believed to be a Klan sympathizer and described by one activist as simply "mean." Shortly after the boycott started, McFatter was involved in coercing Neal Bradley into signing an affidavit charging Henry Anderson with beating him up. Although the two black men were coworkers and, according to Anderson, friends, Bradley's affidavit alleged that Anderson beat him up for violating the boycott. Bradley later told movement leaders that he signed the document when he got drunk after three days of pressure from whites. He claimed that in exchange McFatter gave him "$25 and a pistol" and told him to "use it on anyone who annoyed him in the future." At the end of April, McFatter offered another black man "$50 to close [Shields's] mouth."[33]

The most notorious white aggressor was James Jones, a Vicksburg man who ran a used furniture business in Port Gibson. Sheriff Dan McCay described him as a "hot head," and whites and blacks alike believed his store, which "never sold a stick of furniture," was a Klan front. FBI agents who interviewed Jones reported that "he is not against the Negro because of race or creed, however, he is a strong segregationist and he does not believe in mixing the races in anything. He said he has yet to see a dove cross up with a black bird and live together, and he is sure nobody will see complete mixing of the races in the South." In a May letter to the *Reveille*, Jones wrote, "After following this communist movement in the South . . . the laxness of the people here disturbs me grossly." Decrying the "wait and see attitude of the majority of [white] people," he continued: "I intend to see at least one person tries to stop this mess without using kid gloves." Jimmy Ellis remembered, "Jones was going around to a lot of the white citizens, trying to get them to make him chief of police and he was saying that he would kill a bunch of us to put an end to this." In January 1967, Jones told FBI agents that if he were sheriff and blacks gathered at the courthouse and refused to disperse, he would instruct deputies to use machine guns to "mow them down like grass."[34]

On May 13, 1966, Jones and McFatter invited members of the United Klan of America to the regular Friday white citizens' meeting in the hopes of organizing a formal Klan group. However, most of the white business and civic community publicly opposed the Klan. Three-fourths of the 150 whites at the meeting signed a petition, drawn up by the chamber of commerce and Lions Club, stating their opposition to "outsiders [in this case the Klan] coming into Port Gibson for the purpose of settling the boycott." Sheriff McCay refused to allow the Klansmen to hold their organizational meeting in the courthouse and they were forced to reconvene at James Jones's store, where about forty whites discussed the possibility of forming a Klan Klavern and holding a rally in Port Gibson. They were ultimately unsuccessful in both of these efforts.[35]

Jimmy Allen, a Port Gibson business owner who many blacks considered quite hostile to the movement, remembered "someone trying to get the Ku Klux going" but insisted, "I wasn't the least bit interested." Talking about his efforts to oppose the Klan, Sheriff McCay, observed, "One wrong, two wrongs don't bring a right, and we had a problem as it was with the marches and things." He added, "I've never seen . . . where the Klan had done anything to help anybody." In a 1992 interview, pharmacist Q. H. McDaniel, who closed his soda fountain rather than serve blacks, said he had come to believe that he and other white merchants were wrong to fight the movement, noting, "We just didn't *do* right." He expressed regret that he did not have the courage to advocate a different response, but he insisted that he, then-mayor E. D. Davis, and several other whites who attended the Klan organizational meeting "really did everything we could to discourage it." He said he takes some solace from that action, concluding, "They *didn't* come because of that meeting. That's about the only thing *I* ever did." In fact, opposition to the Klan was so strong in Port Gibson that James Jones, who virtually everyone believed was the group's strongest supporter, felt compelled to publicly deny his association with the Klan in a letter to the editor.[36]

There is no one explanation for the anti-Klan sentiment among the majority of whites in Claiborne County, but part of it was probably related to timing. By 1966, the FBI had stepped up its efforts to infiltrate and destroy the group, and many white leaders around the state believed that violence was counterproductive. However, given that the Klan still maintained a significant presence in southwest Mississippi, including nearby Fayette and Natchez, this reason alone is not a sufficient explanation. Class was probably a factor. The vast majority of Klansmen in other areas (including Klan strongholds in Natchez and Bogalusa, Louisiana, for example) were working-class whites, many of them factory workers fearing job loss in addition to integration and electoral change. Although some whites worked in the Port Gibson factories, the community's small white population was dominated by a merchant and landowning class that generally sympathized more closely with the Citizens' Council and its strategy of economic intimidation. Port Gibson also had, by Mississippi standards, a somewhat religiously and ethnically diverse white population. The presence of first- and second-generation Lebanese immigrants, the remnants of the once-thriving Jewish community, and a strong concentration of Catholics persuaded some people to oppose the Klan. For example, McDaniel and his Catholic wife moved to Port Gibson because they found it a hospitable community. In describing his disinterest in the Klan, Jimmy Allen mentioned the organization's anti-Semitic and anti-Catholic sentiment. According to H. H. Crisler's family, the editor was prepared to use weapons against an earlier manifestation of the Klan to protect blacks and Catholics.[37]

Sheriff Dan McCay's stand against the Klan was particularly significant. At a time when the Klan and law enforcement merged in other communities, he worked aggressively to undermine its efforts to organize in the county, taking down the license plate numbers of those attending the informational meeting and making inconveniently timed personal visits to discourage them from joining. He remembered, "I tried to explain to them that . . . it wasn't ever gon' help the cause." Most civil rights activists respected McCay and considered him a relatively fair man. He had once spent the night in a darkened jail cell with an emotionally disturbed black teenager accused of raping a white girl to be sure the young man was not lynched. Evers recalled that he "always spoke softly. I never heard him [say] 'Nigger.' Never heard him curse us." Activist Charles Bunton asserted, "Now look, Dan McCay wasn't no bad sheriff, I have to tell everybody that. Dan McCay wasn't no bad sheriff." Civil rights attorneys who worked in Claiborne County shared that view. One observed, "He wasn't as bad as some of them I didn't think. He was kind of between a rock and a hard place and he was trying." George Walker, who was involved in virtually every aspect of the movement, explained, "Dan was a man that tried to do what was right. . . . We knew the line and he knew the line. We didn't cross his line and he didn't cross ours." Talking specifically about McCay's response to the Klan, Walker said, "I think Dan told them something like we don't need this kind of problem in this county and I rather that you get out."[38]

Blacks' willingness to defend themselves also influenced whites' decision to keep the Klan out of Claiborne County. One activist insisted, "The white folks won't let [the Klan] march around here. Say that will bring too much race tension." According to James Devoual, "Some say that white folks didn't want" the Klan "because it was just gonna incite black folks to be more aggressive." He added that McCay "didn't want them in because he knew they were going to antagonize us and make us do some things." James Dorsey concurred, observing that McCay discouraged the Klan because he feared "a clash." With the movement, blacks increasingly took charge of their own destiny, and in this instance, they were unwilling to rely solely on McCay for their protection. Although blacks found him more reasonable and easier to work with than other lawmen, he still did not enforce the laws in a fully equitable manner. As Dorsey put it, blacks "couldn't count on the sheriff nor the city policemens or even, not fully, upon the FBI." Many blacks observed that the police and sheriff refused to provide help when blacks received "threats of bombs and the like." Charles Bunton asserted, "We had to have defense in this county. If you didn't, they run you out of here."[39]

To deal with persistent white harassment and inadequate law enforcement, Rudy Shields organized an informal self-defense group, eventually called the Deacons (after the Deacons for Defense and Justice) or the Black Hats (based on their informal uniform). They guarded mass meetings and homes, watched over picketers, sometimes patrolled the streets and monitored the police, and were often accused of being boycott enforcers. The immediate impetus for organized self-defense in Claiborne County came from the highway patrol attack at Alcorn, the presence of hostile, armed whites, and the escalating threats against movement activists.

In their efforts to protect the black community, the self-defense group monitored radio transmissions by Ronnie Hulbert, the radio shop owner who advocated evicting blacks and boycotting black tradesmen. Learning about the Klan organizational meeting from one of these transmissions, Deacons lined up outside the meeting in an action reminiscent of white intimidation after Bob Moses's literacy classes several years earlier. They noted who was there, and they made sure that meeting participants left without incident. Charles Payne argues that white violence declined as African Americans began to retaliate. Calling blacks' willingness to use self-defense "part of the calculus of change," he notes that "the old tradition of racist violence was coming to mean that you really could lose your life or your liberty." Julius Warner, onetime president of the self-defense group, said Mayor Davis warned that "if we didn't stop, the Klan would come in and whatnot. Well, we said we weren't gonna stop, you know, and if the Klan came in, we just have to deal with that." He believed their refusal to back down helped convince the mayor that he should work against the Klan, adding that when the mayor threatened them with the Klan, several of the Deacons told him, " 'OK bring them on in, but if you get one of us, we gon' get one of you all.' So he said, 'Yes, you all prepared.' We said, 'Yeah, we are prepared.' I guess he took them for their word."[40]

CHAPTER Twelve

Seeing that Justice Is Done

In their willingness to protect themselves and their property, Claiborne Countians were part of a long tradition of self-defense among African Americans in Mississippi and throughout the rural South. Although many people equate the civil rights movement with the nonviolent ideology articulated by Martin Luther King Jr. and epitomized by the early proponents of nonviolent direct action, community-based movements often combined nonviolent protest methods with armed self-defense. SNCC worker Bob Moses explained, "Certainly we didn't meet any people in Mississippi who were practicing nonviolence—I mean none of the people we were working with." Timothy Tyson, in his biography of Robert Williams, one of the best-known advocates of armed self-defense, and John Dittmer, Charles Payne, and Adam Fairclough, in their histories of the Mississippi and Louisiana movements, point out the pervasiveness of armed self-defense among rural blacks. According to Payne, "In rural areas particularly, self-defense was just not an issue among blacks. If attacked, people were going to shoot back."[1]

Few blacks saw any inconsistency in their involvement in a largely nonviolent movement and their reliance on arms. SNCC worker Mary King noted that "there was not necessarily any contradiction or conflict felt by a black southerner who professed nonviolence but also believed in self-defense." In Claiborne County, Marjorie Brandon was probably typical. She carried a gun but did not want to "do anybody any harm." She believed both that the movement "needed" protectors to keep whites from "doing us harm in the church" and that the movement "was nonviolent." Reverend Eddie Walls, who became NAACP president in 1969, asserted, "I always preached nonviolence. . . . The NAACP stood for that nonviolence, like Dr. King always said nonviolence. . . . But yet and still people always went prepared to take care of themselves."[2]

A number of local activists point to the ways that Charles Evers's belief in self-defense shaped the movement. J. L. Sayles explained, "We kinda like Martin Luther King. He was nonviolent and that's the way they wanted to do it. But Charles [Evers] said if we can't get it one way, said we got to have it another." Dorsey made a similar point: "We were not really cut hand in glove with [Martin Luther] King. Well Mr. Evers's approach to violence . . . [was] a man could slap you on the cheek once but when he came back the second time, he had to be ready. I think that was his philosophy." In fact, Evers remained bitter for years that the national NAACP had not provided protection for his brother Medgar (who had traveled Mississippi roads with a loaded gun). When NAACP activist Vernon Dahmer was murdered in 1966, the NAACP tried not to make the same mistake with Charles Evers and paid for bodyguards to protect him. Evers wrote in an autobiography, "I don't know what the Lord told Martin Luther King, but the Lord's never once told me to turn the other cheek." He explains, "I don't consider when you defend yourself, violent. You got a right to defend yourself."[3]

Like Evers, many blacks connect their use of self-defense to white aggression and the failure of the legal system to offer protection. James Dorsey insisted that "if you are fired upon" and "you couldn't call the law, well naturally you would have to act in self-defense." James Devoual put the Deacons' efforts to protect NAACP meetings in the context of the 1963 Birmingham, Alabama, church bombing that killed four girls at Sunday school: "Their primary responsibility was to guard that church, make sure didn't nothing drastic like the bombings over in Alabama occur at First Baptist Church. . . . There was a concentration of the whole black population right there on that Tuesday night. Anywhere from a 1,000 to 1,500 folk were at that location and something like a bomb, it could really . . . have taken a lot of lives." Evers testified that he asked adults to watch over the children who were picketing because "we had so many bad incidents where the whites were threatening them and said nasty things to them." A young activist recalled that she and a group of picketers felt prepared and relatively secure when a white man began shouting "all kind of vulgarities" because George Walker had told them repeatedly, "[I] don't care what they say, don't say anything. Just stick to what you doing. We'll be watching you. *We'll* be making sure no one hurts you." One man insisted that such protection was essential because "back there then, white man, if he walk up and saw you doing something he didn't like, he grab you and catch you in the collar and slap you and couldn't nothing be done about it." Jimmy Ellis explained that when James Jones, who spearheaded the Klan organizing effort, pushed some people who were participating in a march, members of the self-defense group "came out and we surrounded him and you know, he backed off then, but after a few choice curse words." Ellis concluded, "[We] found out there was strength in numbers. Because we stood up to him, he backed off."[4]

Self-defense was one of the most obvious ways that African Americans actively challenged traditional white authority, but with Rudy Shields and Charles Evers leading the way, many blacks refused to follow the old rules requiring black deference. Among Evers's and Shields's most important contributions was their posture of fearlessness and their insistence on standing up to and confronting whites. Like the stories about Shields sneaking onto plantations to encourage voter registration, blacks tell and retell stories about Shields standing up to James Jones. According to Deacon Charles Bunton, when Jones, who "had been visiting a few of these old Klan meetings," assaulted Shields, "Rudy threw that pistol in his face and knocked him down. Man, you talking about mad. They thought the police gon' do [something]—the police not going to do nothing. We still walking the street." James Miller recalled another incident when Shields walked right up to Jones during a march and backed him away from the crowd, even though Shields was unarmed and Jones was carrying a rifle. Shields testified about a similar confrontation when Jones tried to intimidate a group of picketers: "[Jones] put a gun to my head and said he was going to kill me, but then he got scared and backed up. Then some other blacks came up to picket and he pulled a gun on them. I went to my car and got my rifle and he put his gun up."[5]

Shields's willingness to confront whites had a big impact on local blacks. Charles Bunton explained that Shields "broke up a lot of the white scary stuff. Like white people scared black people, he broke up a lot of that." He added, "People had got a little nerve there. Rudy had brought them nerve here. You couldn't scare no black people after what Rudy did." Jimmy Ellis remembered that Shields "used to tell us all the time, they are just like you and me, they put their pants on one leg at a time." Herman Leach, who worked with Shields in Yazoo City, said that he once wrote an article about how "freedom came to town on Rudy's shoulders." It was Shields's challenge of both white formal and informal power that initially captured Leach's attention; before Shields began working in the community, blacks feared both the police chief and the sheriff. However, "when Rudy came to town, he treated them just like they were every day people. You know. He wasn't concerned about them raising their voices at him, and telling him what he couldn't do. He knew his rights. That's what we wasn't

Organizer Rudy Shields (center) and a group of activists facing off against Sheriff Dan McCay (far left) and other lawmen, during an Alcorn demonstration, April 1966. Courtesy Mississippi Cultural Crossroads.

familiar with: the laws, and what the rights were." Similarly, Leach remembered that unlike local blacks who "had the understanding that you don't go" in certain places, Shields went wherever he wanted.[6]

An organizer who came to Claiborne County long after Shields had moved on, recalled that people were still telling "stories of his standing up to white folks." She said he was a "person of just mythical proportions," and people talked about him "like Robin Hood, standing up to the sheriff of Nottingham." Rick Abraham heard similar stories around the state and believed that Shields used this type of confrontation as "a conscious strategy." He explained, "[Rudy] wanted to be an example. He understood that people needed to overcome their fear. And I don't know if Rudy was afraid or not in a lot of these situations. . . . But I always had the impression from what he said to me that he was very conscious that, you know, he needed to show that people could stand up to these folks and should stand up to them and he did." In fact, according to Abraham, Shields cultivated a reputation for being crazy, believing it helped protect him. When others were beaten in jail, whites would leave Shields alone, "because they thought he was crazy and unpredictable." If Shields was afraid, he kept it from the people he worked with. Fayette activist Lillie Brown claimed, "He wasn't afraid of no man. I don't even know if he feared God. He was just ideal." Moreover, she insisted that "Rudy Shields *shield* a lot of us, because we threatened. We were being threatened by whites." A Port Gibson movement worker said that Rudy "wasn't scared of white folks, but see, we was. *Definitely* scared of white folks." Bunton made a similar point, "He didn't care if he live or die. See that's the way you had to be at that time. He did a lot, he got a lot of things straight around here. Scared the white folks, that's what he did. Cause he carried a pistol. Any time you carried a pistol, white folks scared of you." Leesco Guster explained, "If you want the truth, I don't think you would have found anybody that would have had the guts he had to go out like that. And then, to be factual about it, I wouldn't have just followed anybody."[7]

Shields and Evers regularly defied conventions. A white merchant testified in 1966 that when she referred to Shields as "boy," he responded angrily and told her "he was . . . no damn boy, he was a God damn man." The testimony of a white man who witnessed this exchange exemplifies how unwilling whites were to acknowledge the depths of black distress over their continuing use of derogatory terms. He said, "She called him a boy. He told her he wasn't no damn boy; he was a God damn man. He used that expression for no more than calling him a boy." During his courthouse speeches, Evers explicitly trampled on southern racial mores by calling white merchants and officials by their first names. Marjorie Brandon's son Carl recalled that during a June march to the courthouse, one of the Hudson brothers was standing in front of his Piggly Wiggly store smoking a cigar and listening to Evers's speech. When Evers asked white merchants: "You all want to know when we gon' lift the boycott?" and answered, "Whensoever hell freezes over, that's when we'll lift it," Hudson's cigar "just turned to flip in his mouth." Brandon remembered another incident during the Alcorn demonstrations when Evers was in his car. "All the highway patrolmen [were] standing on the cattle guard and [Evers] pulled up to them, stopped, and they kind of hesitated to move and he accelerated and then they just started clearing out of his way." Brandon noted, "Little things like that really got a lot of encouragement." A minister's comments about Evers at a 1969 mass meeting also suggest the importance of such actions: "God almighty sent a man to Claiborne County when we were running scared, getting knocked on the head. . . . How many men would stand on the courthouse steps and say the things he says?"[8]

Following Shields's and Evers's lead, blacks individually and collectively began to challenge white authority and act more assertively. Thelma Crowder recalled that when white women canceled their dressmaking orders and asked her to return their material, she "told them no, I wasn't gonna bring it—they want it, they come to my house and get it." When a store owner threatened to call the sheriff after Ann Marie Collins asked other blacks not to patronize her business, Collins responded, "Call your God Dam sheriff, I am not scared of him." When a white man who was "looking for Negro girls" fired a shotgun in the air, a crowd of blacks disarmed him. According to rumor, they also roughed up and stripped him of his hat and pants. George Walker recalled that when Ronnie Hulbert used "racial slurs" like "put a coon on the moon" in his shortwave radio broadcasts, blacks "would come back on the radio and say, 'Okay, we waiting, come on. The moon is not too high tonight.' We would always come back at him with some kind of thing. He'd know we was on the radio and he'd soon shut up."[9]

On May 23, 1966, about a week after black men stood watch outside the Klan organizational meeting, thirty-four black high school students were arrested for protesting at Alcorn's commencement ceremony. Angry about the poor treatment of those arrested during the March demonstrations at Alcorn and concerned about the young people, movement activists responded quickly. George Walker drove around beeping a distinctive and widely recognized car horn and explained the situation as people came out of their houses. He remembered, "In a matter of minutes the courthouse was just like black birds out there, covered before they could bring them down from Alcorn. It was covered, just waiting on them to get here. Time they got here, they released them to the parents and they gon' [on] home. And once that was over, everybody went back home." As Walker's vivid description illustrates, white officials quickly acceded to the demands of the angry crowd of African Americans. According to another participant, the students "were released . . . after the parents came down and made a ruckus." Highway patrol investigators reported that Calvin Williams warned that if "there were further arrests, that the Negroes would march on the courthouse until those arrested were released."[10]

Charles Evers insists that using this type of informal pressure was one of the things that distinguished him from Roy Wilkins, the head of the NAACP. He explains that Wilkins "always wanted to go through the courts. He'd say, 'Citizenship is rooted in law and must be secured by law.'" Observing that "I'd grown up in Mississippi," Evers offers a different perspective: "I knew our state courts weren't worth a damn. I might hire a white lawyer to represent me in a personal case, but I wasn't dumb enough to depend on a white judge to grant me my civil rights. No way. I said, let's boycott, go into the streets, anything short of violence to get justice. The NAACP never wanted to hear that."[11] The Port Gibson crowd's success in forcing the students' release illustrates how blacks could hold the formal systems of power accountable, not through electoral politics or even appeals to higher authority, but through their own assertive, collective actions.

Less than a week later, William Foster, a white man particularly hostile to the movement, cursed and threatened two black children, fifteen-year-old Clara Truitt and her eleven-year- old brother, Earl Truitt. Foster, a Port Gibson resident who worked at the Le Tourneau factory in Vicksburg, was aggressive and notorious for his harassment of blacks in general and movement activists in particular. He made at least one threatening visit to the home of black children who were desegregating schools. On Sundays, he patrolled a formerly segregated laundromat, once telling the black women washing clothes that they had ten minutes to move over to what had been the black side, yelling, "You god-damned niggers think you're going to take over now." A Lawyers' Committee attorney described him as "demented and dangerous," and at least one Le Tourneau employee believed that Foster was responsible for movement-related firings at that factory.[12]

On Saturday, May 29, in the midst of his harassment campaign, Foster leaned out of his truck window and yelled to the Truitt siblings, "You black bitches I'll kill you." Incensed, Rudy Shields and other movement activists took the children to the city police and insisted on an arrest. When the police claimed they needed a warrant and that they could not do anything until Monday, Shields took Clara Truitt to Sheriff McCay, who let her swear out an affidavit. Shields then returned to the police and again insisted that they arrest Foster. This time, surrounded by other activists, Shields added a warning, telling the police, "If you don't get him and arrest him yourselves, we'll find him on our own." Shields's implied threat worked, and police arrested Foster, suggesting that the possibility of black vigilante action could force some response from the white-controlled legal establishment. However, it was a limited victory. Foster was immediately released on bond and was later acquitted, while Rudy Shields and Calvin Williams were both charged and convicted of "disturbing the peace" for their role in pushing for Foster's arrest.[13]

By June 1966, a significant number of Claiborne County activists had been convicted of, or were facing, charges related to their involvement in the civil rights movement. Dozens of people were awaiting trial for demonstrating at Alcorn. Thomas Watts was appealing reckless driving and concealed weapon convictions. Several others had agreed to pay small fines rather than appeal minor charges, like breach of peace. A number of men had been arrested, and several were convicted, for boycott-related activity. Calvin Williams was still fighting the charges related to his encounter with the police chief and others on Main Street. Both Shields and Williams had been convicted for their role in pressuring police to arrest William Foster after his verbal attack on the Truitt siblings and were appealing. In mid-June, Shields was convicted of trespassing and cursing, charges related to picketing in Pattison, and of assaulting Emerson Davis, the black man who flaunted his refusal to observe the boycott. Thomas Watts's two brothers were charged in the same assault, though it is not clear whether they were convicted. In a related incident, another man was convicted of carrying a concealed weapon after Sheriff McCay found his gun in a locked box in the trunk of a friend's car.[14]

Over time, Lawyers' Committee attorneys successfully appealed most of these and other civil rights convictions. One of their most important victories was ending the practice of excluding blacks from juries. According to one attorney, it "took a big hammer out of white establishment when they couldn't take leaders of the movement and throw the key away."[15] It is important to keep in mind, though, that from the first movement-related arrests in March 1966 until January 1967, when the first jury discrimination appeal was decided, there was no guarantee that convictions would be overturned. Those who were arrested had to face the very real possibility of fines and/or jail terms.

While white officials struggled to slow the movement, several events in early June highlighted what was at stake. The June 7 Democratic primary focused national and state attention on Claiborne County's impending political transformation. Large numbers of newly registered blacks voted for the first time and gave two MFDP congressional candidates a decisive majority over white incumbents, Senator James Eastland and Representative John Bell Williams. With only about half of the eligible black population recording votes, MFDP candidates Clifton Whitley and Ed King outpolled their regular Democratic Party counterparts 1,639 to 1,220 and 1,725 to 1,227, respectively. Nearby Jefferson and Wilkinson counties had similar results, and the state legislature responded with plans to dilute black voting strength in the three counties. Speaking at a Claiborne County mass meeting in July, Ed King told the crowd that "the strong Negro vote" in the last election "shook white Mississippians very badly." On June 4, just days before the primary election, James Meredith (who had earlier desegregated the University of Mississippi) began a solitary "March against Fear" from Memphis to Jackson. After Meredith was shot on the second day, civil rights organizations gathered in Memphis and continued the march. The Louisiana-based Deacons for Defense and Justice provided protection for marchers, and, together with Stokely Carmichael's (Kwame Touré's) highly publicized use of the phrase "Black Power!," generated considerable controversy and media attention. Many whites feared black self-defense and failed to grasp the nuances of black power, considering it reverse racism with "violent implications."[16]

While the Meredith March was drawing intense scrutiny and prompting wide-spread fears of race war, tension escalated between blacks and whites in Claiborne County. In early June, when Shields was arrested and charged with assaulting Emerson Davis, a highway patrolman noted that there were "some 50 to 60 Negroes congregated in front of the courthouse." On June 20, Daniel Giles, who Ronnie Hulbert had detained through a citizens' arrest, was convicted of disturbing the peace, fined $50, and sentenced to ten days in jail. Meanwhile, Hulbert was acquitted of charges that he had made a false citizens' arrest. The judge involved in the cases justified both decisions by "mumbling a bit more about how much violence had been going on recently in Port Gibson" and asserting that it "would have to stop." Alluding to both trials at a courthouse speech the next day and directing his comments at white lawmen, Evers pointed out that "white people have done everything in this county they wanted to do, but you never fine any of them and never arrest any of them." He said, "We are sick and tired of the lily-white justice you have been giving us." Referring to Hulbert, he asked the crowd of blacks, "Do you know who made the arrest? A known cluck." He insisted, "Ain't nobody scared of Ronnie. Tell Ronnie he ain't nothing but a coward. He needs to become a man." Evers also evoked the specter of black retaliation, saying, "Tell Ronnie don't be picking up no more Negroes. If he picks us up, we are going to pick him up." Pointing to black numerical domination, he concluded, "We aren't going to take any more, white folks. We have taken all we are going to take."[17]

At a mass meeting that night, Evers used particularly aggressive rhetoric that was loudly and consistently applauded by the approximately 500 blacks in attendance. He touched on a number of his usual themes, including the black electoral majority and plans to replace white elected officials. He articulated some of the issues at the heart of the ongoing battles over power, including whites' usurpation and occupation of public venues. For example, he contested Jimmy Allen's right to park cars from his dealership on the sidewalk, forcing pedestrians and marchers to walk in the street, maintaining, "This street doesn't belong to Allen. It belongs to the City of Port Gibson. That is all of us." Similarly, he challenged white citizens' practice of holding Friday-night antimovement meetings in the ostensibly public courthouse, announcing, "From now on, we are going to be in on everything that is done in this county. There ain't going to be no rest. We ain't going to let you sit behind the desk and make decisions no more. This is our courthouse. You can have meetings in it. We are going to have them too. If there is going to be one more meeting held in here, we are coming in."[18]

Evers delivered this speech as the Meredith March approached its destination in Jackson and white lawmen worried about an armed uprising by black Mississippians. A June 25 highway patrol report about the Deacons protecting the Meredith March described the situation as "extremely explosive. It is like a powder keg. Everybody in the group has guns and shells and they say they are going to use them. A riot may or could erupt at any moment." A highway patrol investigator writing about the June 21 mass meeting in Claiborne County noted that, despite the large crowd and summer heat, the church windows were closed and the men guarding the church were carrying arms. In this setting, after speaking out against Hulbert's bullying and exclusive white claims to public space, Evers warned the white community, "We will remain nonviolent as long as you let us remain nonviolent. But when you put your hand on us, we are coming back at you." He drew applause from the assembled blacks as he continued. "We are going to turn our other cheek no more. If you slap one of us, we will knock [the] hell out of you. We are not going to bother you, and you don't bother us."[19]

In the context of the Meredith march and continuing white hostility, the Claiborne County self-defense group became more proactive, initiating a campaign of psychological warfare that included adopting the name Deacons for Defense, wearing the uniform of black hats and pants that they became known for, and spreading rumors designed to intimidate whites. Some of the Claiborne County men had attended the Meredith March final rally in Jackson, and they were consciously linking themselves to the Louisiana Deacons, who were the best-known and the most institutionalized instance of African American self-defense.

Founded in Jonesboro, Louisiana, in 1964 to protect movement workers and black communities when local lawmen would not, the Deacons typically worked closely and shared goals with movement activists. Even those who belonged to national organizations that were pledged to nonviolence typically embraced the Deacons and found the presence of armed black men "reassuring." The organization spread from Jonesboro to Bogalusa, a factory town on the Mississippi/Louisiana border, after police refused to provide protection for CORE workers being threatened by a Klan mob. The Bogalusa Deacons quickly grew into an aggressive and disciplined armed force gaining national publicity as they protected movement leaders and meetings, patrolled black neighborhoods, monitored the police and Klan, and returned fire in "a visible and highly effective manner." They began trying to expand into Mississippi even before the Meredith March. In August 1965, they encouraged Natchez blacks to form a chapter and held an informational meeting for several hundred people in Jackson. After NAACP activist Vernon Dahmer was killed in Hattiesburg in 1966, they showed up and offered to help. None of these efforts produced formally affiliated Deacons chapters, but blacks in southwest Mississippi did follow the Deacons' model and use their name, acknowledging a spiritual connection and benefiting from their reputation.[20]

Evers, always wary of any potential threat to his leadership, opposed the Louisiana Deacons' organizing efforts in southwest Mississippi. Testifying about the Port Gibson self-defense group in the 1970s, Evers made a distinction between adopting the name and actually affiliating with the Deacons: "I didn't know anything about the Deacons organizing. I knew they *called* themselves the Deacons." He recalled that when the Louisiana Deacons tried to organize in Fayette, "I told them, 'We don't need you here. We've got our own folks. Now, get the hell out of here.'" Explaining his opposition, Evers said, "We couldn't control these people coming in. . . . I deputy who I could control. If I couldn't control them, I left them alone." A Sovereignty Commission informant reported that when the Deacons held their informational meeting in Jackson in August 1965, Evers displayed a gun hidden underneath his coat and "stated that there was no need in calling on the Deacons to come here since there were plenty of them already here." In addition to reflecting Evers's antipathy to organizational competition, Evers's comment illustrates how the term "Deacon" was coming to represent black armed self-defense. In an essay on the Louisiana Deacons, Christopher Strain writes that they "became—in a theoretical sense—a mind-set, a broad concept of empowerment and self-protection." Bogalusa Deacon Charles Sims made a similar observation, insisting, "Any time a Negro and a white man have any kind of round up and the Negro decide he going to fight him back, he's a Deacon."[21]

Black men involved in the Port Gibson self-defense efforts connect calling themselves Deacons with escalating white aggression and explain that they adopted the name to keep whites off-balance and prevent violence. Rudy Shields, for example, testified, "I made up the matter about the Deacons as a scheme to keep the black communities from being attacked." He explained, "We were catching a lot of hell from white racists," and "we used the word Deacons to frighten off the Klan." Another participant remembered, "Well Rudy Shields started the Black Hats. He named us the Deacons. We knowed we was the Black Hats, but he named us the Deacons."[22]

Shields accurately anticipated that a chapter of the Deacons would concern whites more than the homegrown, informal self-defense efforts already in place. SNCC worker Hollis Watkins told historian Akinyele Umoja that during a confrontation between movement activists and armed whites, "hearing the name 'Deacons of Defense' invoked was almost as effective in scattering the mob as the guns." On July 20, a Sovereignty Commission informant observed that in Port Gibson, black men were wearing black helmets, like the blue ones worn by the police, and blacks were spreading rumors that "these workers were with the Black Panthers' group and the 'Deacons.'" A local activist told the informant that they were "false" rumors solely intended to "scare" whites and that the "police and all of the white merchants [are] afraid." In addition to the name change, the use of black hats as a uniform enhanced the self-defense group's visibility and made members appear ominous to whites. In fact, whites' use of the names Deacons and Panthers interchangeably—referring either to the Lowndes County Freedom Organization, whose emblem was a Black Panther, or the California based Black Panther party inspired by southern self-defense groups—to describe the Claiborne County group suggests that blacks were quite successful in stimulating white fears.[23] In response to the new uniform, the name change, the rumors, and the presence of guns, white lawmen intensified their policing and investigative efforts.

On Tuesday, June 21, a highway patrolman noted the presence of "armed Negroes" guarding the church during the weekly mass meeting in Port Gibson. A Sovereignty Commission investigator reported that at the next meeting "three or four Negroes stepped out of the dark and all of them were armed with shotguns or rifles." They intercepted "a local officer [who] approached the church to issue a ticket." The report concluded that "no arrest was made for pointing and aiming, etc., as the policeman was on private property." Describing a similar incident, reporter Bill Minor wrote that "in the rear of a Negro church outside Port Gibson, the white investigator of the Sovereignty Commission found himself surrounded by 15 armed young Negroes who had been made more militant by an imported member of the 'Deacons for Defense.' " In July 1966, Sheriff McCay informed the FBI that "a group of Negroes in Port Gibson" was wearing "black straw cowboy type hats during the day and black steel helmets during the night hours." He reported that "these Negroes [were] holding a close order drill and carrying rifles and other guns." The FBI, which characterized the Bogalusa Deacons as a "black vigilante group," kept close tabs on all the self-defense groups who used the name. Ken Dean, a white Baptist minister who headed the Mississippi Council for Human Relations (MCHR), wrote a colleague that blacks in Port Gibson "have organized some kind of militant group. They wear black cowboy hats and jackets, carry firearms and train in the open." He concluded, "This has the FBI and kind shook."[24]

Already uneasy, whites grew more concerned when Deacons wearing black hats were part of a July 3 crowd that pressured lawmen to arrest Emerson Davis for threatening Rudy Shields. Davis, who was routinely ridiculed and harassed by blacks for violating the boycott, had accused Shields and three other men of beating him up in June. In the July 3 incident, Davis attempted to shoot a .38 pistol at Shields as Shields was driving past him on Main Street. Several observers heard a click, but the gun malfunctioned. Shields drove directly to the police station, where he and his companions tried to convince several officers to disarm Davis and charge him with attempted murder. Instead of letting Shields sign a complaint, auxiliary policeman Bobby Wade threatened him with his nightstick and did nothing when Emerson Davis joined the group and pointed his gun at Shields, telling the police, "If you let me, I'll kill the son of a bitch now." With the police refusing to take Shields's complaint or disarm Davis, Shields asked, "Are you going to let him kill me?" Surrounded by the crowd of blacks, he warned the officers, "If you let him kill me, my people will retaliate." Still unable to convince the lawmen to arrest Davis, Shields and his companions went to Calvin Williams's house and, by telephone, arranged a meeting with Mayor Davis and Police Chief Doyle. At this meeting on Main Street, Shields swore out an affidavit against Davis. At the same time, the mayor encouraged others to "file charges against Rudy," and Emerson Davis complied. Eventually, as in the incident involving William Foster, who threatened two children, the crowd's insistence and Shields's implied threat led to Davis's arrest. However, he was quickly released and eventually acquitted, while Shields was arrested and convicted of threatening Davis.[25]

Although all of the witnesses agreed that Davis initiated the contact, whites publicly asserted that he was acting in self-defense when he threatened to shoot Shields. Moreover, the police allowed Davis to keep his unregistered weapon, although white officials were aggressively disarming black men associated with the movement during this period. Circuit Court Judge Ben Guider justified one confiscation, saying, "During a time of tension, the carrying of firearms must be strongly discouraged." In September 1967 a white man suggested to FBI agents that Mississippi create a law making it illegal for members of the Deacons to possess weapons. This was probably unnecessary since the same report noted that three Wilkinson County Deacons had been arrested for "illegal possession of weapons" under a law which made it "illegal to bear arms when the purpose is to put the law in the hands of private citizens." The district attorney who approved these arrests also gave the highway patrol "authority to disarm all members of the Deacons for Defense and Justice."[26]

Whites were almost certainly behind Davis's attack on Shields. Shields testified: "[Davis told] me he had been paid $300 by the merchants to kill me . . . because they were getting tired of me and the boycott." Although he did not actually witness any of the events, Melvin McFatter recalled that "there were some white people that gave guns to these old [black] people who ended up shooting some people." He added, "There were a couple nasty incidents." One former Deacon claimed that it was Melvin's father, M. M. McFatter, who "gave Emerson Davis the pistol." McFatter had previously offered to pay a black man to attack Shields and had given another black man a gun, ostensibly to defend himself. In a later incident, a Sovereignty Commission investigator noted, McFatter "handed Emerson [Davis] a new .38 pistol and told him to use it." Other evidence suggests that there was widespread white support for Davis's attack on Shields. Police officer Wade refused to disarm Davis even when he was pointing the gun at Shields, and a number of whites later testified on Davis's behalf, including James Jones, who acknowledged that he "hoped Emerson was going to shoot Rudy then and there."[27]

African Americans responded to this collusion by making it clear that if laws (and lawmen) did not protect them, they would safeguard themselves. One of Shields's attorneys stressed that when Shields told police that blacks would retaliate if Davis was allowed to kill him, "Shields's language was directed not at Davis but at the police officer for the purpose of invoking the machinery of the law." Calvin Williams made a similar point to the mayor after Davis attempted to shoot Shields, asserting that activists would "protect themselves" since "the police would not." George Walker explained that Mayor Davis believed "we were trying to take the town over. So we had to go to the mayor and tell him we weren't taking the town over, we were just seeing that justice is done."[28]

Whites present at the July 3 encounter between Shields and Davis were preoccupied by the crowd, especially the men wearing "black helmets." Sovereignty Commission investigator Andy Hopkins described the situation as "explosive," reporting that "8 to 12 Negro men wearing black helmets, which is characteristic of the Black Panthers," gathered during the confrontation. Hopkins insisted that Deacon Calvin Williams was "extremely dangerous" and observed that Williams and Shields were "drilling young local Negro men in a military type of drill." Moreover, the uniforms and rumor campaign appear to have influenced whites' perceptions. Although none of the Deacons ever wore clothes with a black panther on them, a white observer told Hopkins that he saw a black panther "emblem either on their clothing or their helmets" and Hopkins argued that "there is a very good chance that this is an attempt to organize a chapter of the panthers." He concluded that Claiborne Countians "are sitting on a highly explosive situation that could erupt and turn into a minor revolution at any time."[29]

Historian Christopher Strain observes that many whites perceived the Deacons "as gun-slinging vigilantes." A white lawyer questioning a former Deacon in the 1970s implied that Deacons wanted to "hunt whites" and "shoot highway patrolmen." George Walker recalled, "We were called something like the Ku Klux Klan." Contrary to whites' perceptions, however, the Deacons were an explicitly defensive organization. Charles Sims stresses that their purpose was "to prevent violence, not to start it." Port Gibson Deacon Charles Bunton explained that it "wasn't our aim to kill anybody, just to protect the people that we need to protect." Julius Warner, onetime president of the Deacons, made the same point: "We let them know that we were not out there to instigate anything or start anything. We were really out for protection and were not going to let them start anything. So we were there really to keep order." Shields testified that he told members of the organization "not to fire on anyone unless attacked first" and added that one reason he bought walkie-talkies for the group was to prevent people from getting "trigger happy." He insisted that Deacons doing guard duty contact him before taking action. George Walker also emphasized the Deacons' peacekeeping function, observing, "We were there to make sure that no crosses were burn, no KKK come in the county, and this kind of stuff." Referring to three civil rights workers who were murdered during the 1964 Summer Project, Walker once told Sheriff McCay that Deacons were monitoring lawmen because "we do not want another Neshoba County."[30]

Whites' perception of the Deacons as violent actually served the organization (and other armed defenders) well. In Port Gibson, whites acted more cautiously after the self-defense group established its presence. One activist explained that "there was not a whole lot of harassment because I think that the police respected these guys" and they "were pretty effective." Calvin Williams described an incident where armed Deacons "stepped out of bushes" and confronted lawmen who "leveled a shotgun" at a car carrying visitors to a Claiborne County mass meeting. He asserted that "after a few displays" like that, the Deacons became unnecessary. Charles Bunton argued that when large numbers of blacks began voting there was little violence at the polls because "we had them so covered with the Deacons . . . that the [white] people were scared to pull a lot of stuff."[31]

In July 1966, Shields and the Deacons escalated their campaign of psychological warfare, spreading rumors that blacks were going to destroy the downtown area and creating a fake Deacons minutes book, which the sheriff, according to plan, confiscated during an arrest. The minutes book—with entries starting on June 30, just over a week after investigators first reported guns at civil rights meetings, and ending on July 18—referred to inflated memberships, imaginary weapons caches, and nonexistent national ties. Shields testified later that "we made false records, and I suggested we let those records fall into the hands of the sheriff." He explained that he did this "to let the white community know they could no longer drive in the black community and shoot it up at night." Another Deacon contended that Shields planted the minutes book "so they could know that we did have an organization. . . . [Shields] said, 'Hell that is the only way that they will believe, here in Port Gibson, Mississippi, that black folks was for real.' " Here, again, whites appeared to accept the rumors at face value. Just as some reported seeing the nonexistent panther emblems, the Sovereignty Commission's investigator mistakenly claimed that "it is a known fact that these Negroes . . . have an arsenal of guns and ammunition stored at the . . . Negro Masonic lodge." Commission investigators made similar reports about blacks in nearby areas, and, in general, such rumors reappeared whenever the racial status quo was threatened.[32]

Shields testified that one entry in the fake minutes book was intended "to fool the sheriff and the white community into thinking that I was going to Chicago to buy weapons, so as to get them to stop attacking us." Observing that whites "were very worried" because of the rumors, NAACP president James Dorsey insisted, "It wasn't no stockpile at all. There were no truth in that." He added, "We didn't have those many weapons. Only the patrolmen and high sheriff had those." George Walker laughed at the idea that they had a stockpile of weapons and added, "I found out, any time you got a rebellious group, they think you going to stockpile stuff. We didn't have nothing. We didn't have no money." Walker bought his gun from Sears and found it hard to afford ammunition: "I didn't have 'bout no more than 'bout 15, 20 bullets. Didn't have no money to buy them high priced bullets. Bullets cost you about 20 cents each."[33]

During the week of July 19, many white merchants responded to widespread rumors that blacks were going to burn the downtown area by setting up armed guards. According to Melvin McFatter, "There was a persistent rumor that something akin to [the Watts riot in] Los Angeles was about to take place." In retrospect, he believed it was a "ruse put out by black leaders" to "get the white people upset" but recalled that whites thought blacks "were just going to come down through town and, you know, break out windows, set fire to buildings and just lay the town to waste." That night, he, a high school friend, and his father stayed "in the back of our store armed to the teeth." White merchant Bill Lum recalled Sheriff Dan McCay's warning about the same rumors: "Dan McCay called me one afternoon and says, 'Bill,' says, 'I hear that . . . they gon' march on the town tonight.' I said, 'Yeah, I hear about it.' He says, 'I also hear you plan to stay in your store tonight.' . . . And I said, 'That's right.' I said, 'I've got every gun I have and all the ammunition I have, right here by me . . . and I will be here to protect my property.' He says, 'Well, I have to warn you that I can't protect you, and they plan to burn you out tonight.'" One hundred and fifty highway patrolmen were in Port Gibson that night to protect white merchants, but there was no fire. A Sovereignty Commission informant reported that NAACP leader Walter Griffin told him, "They had put out that the Negroes were going to tear up the town," but "they were just trying to scare the people." Noting that "whites were shook up" over the rumor, Alexander Collins told the informant, "One thing about these people down here, we can put out anything, and with all that is going on all over the state, they will believe it."[34]

In this charged atmosphere, Sheriff McCay met with Rudy Shields, Calvin Williams, Alexander Collins, and Tullos Brown before the July 19 NAACP meeting and informed them that Port Gibson's aldermen were changing the local gun laws. McCay explained that no one would be allowed to carry weapons openly, and he asked the civil rights leaders to remove guns from their meetings. Speaking for the group, Shields agreed, and later that day a highway patrol investigator observed Shields sending home several people who arrived at the meeting with weapons. Shields assured another patrolman that "the meeting would be peaceful and that no weapons would be allowed." Though they acceded to McCay's request, Calvin Williams and Charles Evers expressed skepticism. Williams told the audience that night that "the Sheriff wanted the Negroes unarmed" to make it easier to "keep them in their place," and Evers told the crowd, "They asked us to leave our guns at home; they would like to shoot us all down."[35]

This change in the gun law was a direct response to black self-defense and, although it was clearly intended to disarm blacks, it was a victory for the movement. White officials' assertion that they would disarm both whites and blacks was a dramatic departure from typical Mississippi practice. Dorsey remembered that before the movement, "Whites would ride with their rifles and shotguns on the back of their pickups, [but when] blacks started doing the same thing, that sort of frightened them." Although some blacks were doubtful about whether whites would be evenhanded in applying the law, most had enough faith in Sheriff McCay that they were willing to give it a chance.[36] There is no evidence that the law was actually used to disarm anyone, but the meeting between civil rights leaders and the sheriff appears to have helped diffuse the growing tension. At the same time, after working full time in Claiborne County for about five months, Rudy Shields moved on to organize in other southwest Mississippi communities and in Ferriday, Louisiana, just across the river. Although Shields never lived in Port Gibson again, he stayed in contact with his closest allies and continued to visit mass meetings. More important, many of those he worked with carried on the traditions he had started, involving people in activism and standing up to whites.

Meanwhile, even with the new gun laws in place, the Deacons continued to protect the black community and monitor white lawmen, essentially establishing themselves as a parallel law enforcement structure. George Walker compared the organization to the "police department" and claimed the Deacons were "help[ing] the sheriff." Another man recalled, "We was supposed to be something like the state troopers." The Deacons were careful to learn and follow the law. Charles Bunton noted that the members spent a lot of time talking about "what was legal and what wasn't legal." Historian Christopher Strain insists that the Louisiana "Deacons were attuned to" and careful to stay "within the law." In a sense, the Claiborne County movement first achieved its demand for black lawmen with the creation of the Deacons rather than through white appointments (which never lasted long and rarely met with the approval of the black community). Not only did the Deacons essentially act as lawmen, at least five eventually held jobs in law enforcement and two others were the first blacks to run for sheriff.[37]

Long before they moved into these formal roles, however, the Deacons settled into a routine of shadowing the community's white lawmen and cultivated a working relationship with Sheriff McCay, an association that almost certainly helped minimize "miscommunication and misunderstanding." In fact, McCay even gave Deacons advice about which weapons they could carry legally and encouraged several blacks, including Marjorie Brandon and James Dorsey, to defend themselves. George Walker explained that when the Deacons had problems that they "would go to his office and set down and talk to him about it. He would give us his opinion and what he was going to take and we would tell him what we wasn't going to take and it was a borderline in there where we would respect each other." He added, "We had some clashes with his deputy, . . . but when it was brought to Dan's attention, he saw that it didn't happen anymore. He told [his deputies], . . . 'Just don't bother them.' "[38]

According to Walker, one of the problems with McCay's deputy occurred when Shields returned to Port Gibson for a visit and tried to avoid being arrested on an outstanding warrant. The Deacons set up an elaborate decoy and escape plan to move Shields into and out of First Baptist Church, since they knew whites would not bother him during the meeting. Their plan worked; Shields was able to attend the meeting and leave the county with no problems. However, the workers who attended the meeting with him were stopped twice as they were leaving. During the second stop, George Walker, who was one of the Deacons providing an escort, approached Deputy Sheriff Cline Williams to see what the problem was. Williams started pulling his weapon and told Walker to get back into his car. Walker remembered: "I say, 'You can go on and shoot me, . . . but I don't have a gun. I want to talk with you.' I say, 'I just want to know why you keep stopping this car. Police stopped it down there, now why you want to stop it up here?' " When Walker refused to budge, the deputy instructed the entire group to return to the courthouse. Once there, Walker said, "Then here come all these people to the courthouse. Had the courthouse full." The presence of a large black crowd convinced white lawmen to quickly release the visitors, who, with their Deacon escort, left the county with no further trouble. Angry about the harassment, Deacons Walker, Calvin Williams, and Julius Warner were waiting for Dan McCay when he arrived at work the next morning. They insisted that his deputy stop "harassing the people who came to our meetings," and, according to Walker, McCay said, " 'I'll see to that.' And he did."[39]

The Deacons were important not only for the concrete protection they offered the black community but also for what they represented in challenging the assumption that whites could attack blacks with impunity. Writing about the Bogalusa Deacons, scholar George Lipsitz notes, "Their discipline and dedication inspired the community, their very existence made black people in Bogalusa think more of themselves as people who could not be pushed around." James Miller described the Port Gibson Deacons as "very impressive," adding that "to be a Deacon was to be respected." James Devoual called them "an elite organization of black *men*" who were "warriors." They were "folk that were gonna stand there in the event of something violent. Some type of violence broke out, they were willing to stand there and kind of sacrifice themselves." He concluded, "All of your better-known black males at the time . . . just wound up Deacons." One of the picketers protected by Deacons said they were "heroes to me. I figured anything . . . that would go on wrong with any black person, that a white person had perpetrated, that the Deacons would take care of it."[40]

Like the best-known movement leaders, the Deacons for Defense were all men. Throughout the civil rights movement, women carried weapons and defended their homes, but historians Akinyele Umoja, Christopher Strain, and Timothy Tyson all argue that armed self-defense became equated with "manhood." This was particularly true, according to Umoja, "when the functions of armed Black resistance became more organized and specialized." In this context, he says, self-defense became "patriarchal." There is no evidence to support the claim by several Claiborne County men that women were welcome in the organization and the group was all male. James Miller emphasized the importance of the Deacons' masculinity: "Prior to that, you never saw black men in positions of authority, you know, postulating their manhood." Before the movement, he observed, black men were confined to "the cotton field [and] working in the stores, that kind of thing." But Deacons "were black men who were taking charge of their own destiny and the destiny of black folks, and more importantly the destiny of this community."[41]

The Deacons' presence also signaled the end of whites' absolute authority and suggested a reversal of power. By actively challenging the practices that had reinforced white supremacy, the Deacons defied decades-old traditions and power hierarchies and helped transpose the ever-present climate of fear. The Deacons' self-defense and willingness to take up arms created space for non-violent protest and political activism. Moreover, in the process, they inspired many other blacks and provided a vehicle for the movement to achieve, at least in part, a number of goals without having to wait for court decisions or electoral victories.

CHAPTER Thirteen

Our Leader Charles Evers

Charles Evers's highly visible involvement in the local civil rights movements in southwest Mississippi, especially Claiborne County, enhanced his reputation and changed his relationship with the national NAACP. With his newfound success in building large NAACP branches and with the national press featuring his role in successful voter registration campaigns, the NAACP's top leaders began to view Evers in a far more positive light. Although many of the old conflicts persisted, they became convinced that Evers could help the NAACP become the dominant civil rights organization in Mississippi and regain its place of national prominence.

In an April 1966 letter to NAACP head Roy Wilkins, Gloster Current combined information about an upcoming trip to Claiborne County with details about thriving voter registration and membership drives in southwest Mississippi, concluding that the NAACP's method of "handling Mr. Evers is going to prove fruitful after all." After his visit, Current wrote Evers that the mass meeting he attended in Claiborne County "was fruitful, stimulating and indicated what a great job you are doing." Current urged Evers to take care of himself and authorized him to hire temporary help so he could rest for several weeks. This concern was clearly associated with Current's excitement over the organization's expanding numbers, and he enthused to Evers, "At the rate you have been going our membership in the rural areas should be tremendously increased." Current wrote NAACP state president Aaron Henry that the Port Gibson meeting made it "apparent how effective our work has been in southwest Mississippi. The audience was overflowing and the spirit was high." Moreover, he asserted that Evers "is our best hope for completion of the task in Mississippi," writing, "Frankly, I believe we have reached the point in our relationship with Charles that he is proven quite valuable to us." Less than a year after he had made a case for firing Evers, Current had reversed his position and was now concerned about keeping Evers on the payroll, especially in light of rumors that the American Federation of Labor (AFL) was offering Evers a voter registration job.[1]

When a Fayette policeman shot a black man at the end of May, the NAACP's Mississippi lawyer Jack Young initially feared Evers would say something the "Association would later have to eat." Instead, he saw Evers calm an angry crowd. He wrote to Current, "I do not feel that there is any likelihood that any violence will occur because Charles has the people in Fayette *completely under his control and domination.* If he said, 'march,' they march. If he said 'be quiet,' they are quiet. I believe that they would burn the town if he said burn the town." After seeing Evers's popularity in Fayette, Young characterized him as "Our Leader" and argued that Evers "is a great influence for good." He concurred that the NAACP needed to keep him on the staff, writing, "In my opinion, the prestige of the National . . . because of Charles' work in Adams, Jefferson and Claiborne Counties, is at an all time high, and that under the circumstances, it would be disastrous for us if he chose to leave at this time." In order to keep Evers, the NAACP gave him a pay raise, an assistant, and control of a previously autonomous voter registration office. Writing Evers in June to confirm this new arrangement, Current referred to the "heartaches and difficulties of the past three years" and to the "misunderstandings and adjustments we all had to make," but he concluded that "under your leadership the state of Mississippi and especially the NAACP has been going forward. . . . We now stand on the threshold of victory." Several weeks earlier, Current was brimming with excitement about the NAACP's Mississippi memberships, led by the almost 1,200 new Claiborne County members. He wrote to the organization's publicity director, "The NAACP is the dominating organization in Mississippi, numerically and spiritually."[2]

As soon as Evers began bolstering the NAACP's membership and reputation, the national staff began to give him more latitude and to overlook actions that violated the organization's policies. However, he remained inconsistent, individualistic, opinionated, and controversial. In February 1966, for example, he was threatened with a libel suit when he implied that the Fayette sheriff was making money from bootleg liquor. He was able to talk his way out of trouble by meeting privately with the sheriff. According to an NAACP lawyer, when they emerged from their meeting, the sheriff no longer intended to sue and expressed "the

opinion that Mr. Evers was a fine up-standing young man who was only interested in serving his people."[3] Other problems were more troubling and persistent, especially accusations that Evers used civil rights boycotts to make money
and that he encouraged violence to enforce boycotts.

From selling sandwiches and loaning money to students during his college
days to associating with the Chicago underworld, Evers was always on the
lookout for money-making ventures. He was part owner of stores in Jackson and
Natchez at the time that he was leading boycotts in those communities, and in
1967 he opened a shopping center in Fayette that drew black customers from
around the area, including some who were boycotting white stores in their home
communities. In 1965, as part of its ongoing efforts to disrupt the civil rights
movement, the Sovereignty Commission taped Evers encouraging Fayette blacks
to shop at the Woodlawn grocery store in Natchez and then, using the speech as
evidence, "exposed" Evers's connection to the store. The commission wrote and
planted articles in several newspapers and prepared a speech that Fayette's
representative delivered before the Mississippi legislature.[4]

This publicity prompted a flurry of activity within the NAACP. In late January
1966, a board member wrote Roy Wilkins that she was "extremely concerned"
about the "legal implications" of Evers's actions. In February, the organization's Committee on Branches specifically recommended that as long as Evers's
NAACP work entailed boycotts, he should either avoid involvement in business
or resign. A Jackson NAACP activist who was a longtime critic of Evers sent
newspaper clippings about Evers's business holdings to the president of the
NAACP, writing, "You can see that Mississippi is without proper leadership." In
a March letter, Roy Wilkins informed Evers that the NAACP Executive Committee had decided that he "should divest himself of competitive business enter-
prises while he is an employee engaging in boycotts." Expressing impatience that
Evers had failed to respond to earlier queries, Wilkins stressed that Evers must
immediately send the NAACP an explanation of his business connections in
Natchez. After more than three weeks, Evers sent a terse reply: "The store is not
being used for my personal gain, since the Natchez boycott is over and has been
settled." Evers essentially evaded the issue; he did not address his practice of
encouraging Fayette boycotters to spend money in his Natchez store, and he
ignored the fact that the boycott in Natchez had been called on and off repeatedly
over the previous months. Influenced by Evers's recent achievements and his
value to the organization, the national NAACP let the matter drop and Evers
continued to pursue profit even when that meant operating businesses at the
same time he was leading boycotts.[5]

The NAACP leadership also ignored complaints that Evers promoted violent boycott enforcement, though they occasionally admonished him when he made comments advocating retaliatory violence against whites. In August 1966, Jackson NAACP member Falba Ruth Conic complained to Gloster Current that Evers "has shown incompetence and ineptness since his appointment and is therefore a discredit to the Association." Referring specifically to a Greenville speech, she wrote, "The latest example of his unfitness was his recent encouragement of violence against other Negroes who did not wish to honor a boycott." She added that, since the national office had not "discharged him" or even "rebuked him in a public statement," she "assumed that it endorses his administration." She concluded that she would "sever my connections with the NAACP" if its "new policy is one of threats of violence and vandalism . . . because it has sunk to the level of the bigoted organizations, black and white, that it has hypocritically denounced." In his reply, Current insisted that "it has never been the NAACP policy to use threats of violence or to uphold vandalism" and argued that Conic had failed to "substantiate" her complaint against Evers. After brushing aside the issue of boycott enforcement, Current praised Evers for "carrying on his late brother's work under severe handicaps and with great courage." In an indication of the relationship between positive national publicity and the organization's tolerance for Evers's controversial actions, he directed her to the August 22, 1966, issue of *Newsweek*, which included Evers on a list of top Negro leaders.[6]

Despite Current's response, it is likely that he was aware that Conic's complaint was grounded in truth; throughout this period, Evers's speeches consistently threatened consequences for blacks who violated boycotts and Mississippi newspapers regularly made and reported accusations about violent boycott enforcement. NAACP president James Dorsey maintained that the national office disapproved of Evers's "methods" and explained that on several occasions "the national people came down" and talked "to us about what a good civil rights organization was and what the NAACP stood for." Ed King insisted that Evers used violence to run the Port Gibson boycott and said he believed the "NAACP knew it" but "would not try to control Charles or had given up on trying to control him."[7] Despite evidence of Evers's questionable tactics, the NAACP's national leaders once again chose to defend him or look the other way as the price for a strong organizational presence in Mississippi.

Evers's position with the national organization was reinforced by his stature among white liberals. When Evers began working for the NAACP, he capitalized on distress over Medgar's murder to forge relationships with powerful national figures, independent of the NAACP. In his memoir, he explained, "I began knocking on people's doors, saying I was Medgar's brother and wanted a favor.

They'd let me in." He added, "I met many Negroes in those first years who I wouldn't have met but for Medgar's murder. I also got closer to Nelson Rockefeller. All these people were so outraged by Medgar's killing and wanted so bad to do *something* for civil rights that they were happy to do the little things I asked." During Charles Evers's first two years working for the NAACP, when he offered the organization little more than the Evers name, the NAACP's staff was troubled by Evers's independent connections to white liberals. In addition to giving him a potential power base outside the organization, Evers publicly acted on these ties, even when it meant openly disregarding his employers. For example, NAACP leaders reprimanded Evers when he campaigned for Bobby Kennedy in 1964 in direct defiance of NAACP policy and threatened to fire him in early 1965 after he endorsed another liberal white Democrat.[8] By 1966, however, when Evers was staying closer to home and his southwest Mississippi successes were reflecting positively on the national organization, top officials were pleased by his national visibility and flourishing reputation among white liberals.

Evers's standing with the NAACP and white liberals was reinforced by his importance in an emerging political coalition of moderate Mississippi whites and blacks who were trying to create a Democratic Party alternative to both the MFDP and the Mississippi Regulars. According to Charles Payne, although "they represented a wing of the movement, not the whole of it," this "group was repeatedly successful at presenting itself to opinion-makers and policy-makers outside the state as the new face of the freedom movement in Mississippi." After the MFDP's 1964 Atlantic City Challenge, many white liberals became increasingly antagonistic toward SNCC and its organizational offspring, including COFO, the MFDP, and the Lowndes County Freedom Organization (LCFO) in Alabama, which were focusing more and more on black nationalism, political alternatives to the Democratic Party, economic critiques of American capitalism, and opposition to the Vietnam War.[9] For white liberals troubled by calls for Black Power and by the far-reaching critique of American society that SNCC and other radical civil rights organizations were voicing, Evers, who publicly supported integration, praised mainstream American institutions, and was outspoken in his criticism of SNCC and Black Power, was an appealing alternative. Moreover, Evers's visible accomplishments with voter registration (and the potential for translating them into black electoral power within the framework of a moderate ideology, the national Democratic Party, and mainstream America) offered a seductive contrast to SNCC's disillusionment, and to the problems highlighted by Martin Luther King's ineffectual attempt to organize in Chicago and the increasing number of urban riots. Evers offered white liberals reassurance that the movement had succeeded, and he did so without threatening their status quo.

Evers was an immensely talented man, and many of the same attributes that made him effective in rural Mississippi helped him establish his national reputation. SNCC worker Lawrence Guyot, who chaired the MFDP in 1965 and 1966, explained, "Here's a guy who could think on his feet, who was courageous, [and] who had the blessings of being [the brother of] a slain hero." An author profiling Evers compared the "Evers charm" to the "Kennedy charm," writing that "it is strikingly similar in its force." He explained that when meeting Evers, "vitality is the word that comes to mind, and then, power," but he added that Evers also possessed "courage and strength, humor and intelligence" combined with "tremendous energy and magnetic personal appeal." Another writer described Evers's speeches as "an awesome blend of reprimand and forgiveness, mockery and cajolery: he threatens and he pleads." Barbara Sullivan, who worked on Evers's 1971 campaign for governor, said that though she and other members of Evers's campaign staff grew disillusioned with his politics, he could still draw them in. Even if "it was a speech we had heard twenty-five times already, we would still find ourselves being totally sucked up into the emotion of the moment and he'd have us right in the palm of his hand." Noting that he had "incredible presence and charisma" and that "he was smart, in a very operative kind of way," she insisted that he had the "ability to know something about the person he was speaking with and to play to them. It was uncanny, and I think that's part of what made him charismatic. He could read an individual or a crowd and connect with whatever he perceived to be your interest in him. And, he could play to it. He was just amazing."[10]

When Stokely Carmichael's use of the term "Black Power" coincided with the decisive majority vote by Claiborne and Jefferson County blacks in the June 1966 Democratic primary, Evers quickly capitalized, boosting his national reputation. In subsequent months, newspapers increasingly praised Evers and acted as if he was *the* representative of the Mississippi civil rights movement. In a July 1966 *New York Times* article, reporter Roy Reed insisted that "one immediate and unintentional effect of the militant march, with its suggestions of 'Black Power,' was to raise the political stature of Charles Evers and the NAACP." Noting that Evers denounces "Black Power" because "it suggests black domination," Reed contrasted him favorably with those leaders affiliated with SNCC who, he wrote, "tend to be more militant." Pointing to the strong black electoral showing in southwest Mississippi in the June primary, Reed called Evers the "most effective Negro leader in the state." He concluded, "Unlike some younger Negro leaders, Evers repudiates all black government for predominantly Negro counties."[11]

Subsequent media coverage was similar and often invoked Evers's views to criticize Black Power, Stokely Carmichael, SNCC, the MFDP, and the LCFO. In an August article for *Reporter* magazine, Henry Hurt referred to Black Power as an "alarming cry" but then noted that "Mississippi's Negro leadership has been generally immune to the appeals of the extremists." The rest of the article focused almost exclusively on Evers, as if he alone was "Mississippi's Negro leadership." Observing that Evers opposed Black Power because it advocates "black supremacy," Hurt added that "Evers is almost contemptuous of groups that favor all-black anything." Like Roy Reed, Hurt combined a discussion of Evers's "political control over three Mississippi counties" (including his "absolute control over the Negro vote in Jefferson county") with Evers's opposition to all black slates. Hurt's article also alluded to but then glossed over criticism of Evers's business practices, observing that "Evers, always a good businessman himself, has done very nicely with a food store he purchased during a previous series of boycotts."[12]

In addition to using Evers to critique SNCC and other proponents of Black Power, national journalists frequently cited Evers's political dominance in southwest Mississippi as a hopeful alternative to black-oriented third-party efforts, including those of the MFDP and the LCFO. One of the most obvious examples of Evers's control came in the 1966 congressional race. In the June primary, Claiborne County blacks voted overwhelmingly for the MFDP candidate Clifton Whitley, giving him a 1,639-to-1,224 countywide lead over runner-up James Eastland. In the November election, however, when Whitley ran as an independent, Evers swung his support to Republican Prentiss Walker. Eastland's vote total stayed relatively consistent, Whitley's dropped from 1,639 to 120, and Prentiss Walker led with 1,671 votes. According to James Dorsey, most people "were willing to follow Mr. Evers whatever he said at that particular time. They felt like they should do it."[13]

Journalists Rowland Evans and Robert Novak described Evers as "THE political power in southwest Mississippi" and "the new South's first Negro political boss," not just "a responsible civil rights leader." They added, "It is of major significance that Evers, an advocate of biracial moderation, succeeded where prophets of Black Power failed." In contrast, the authors referred to the MFDP's electoral losses and "their self-defeating theory of black separatism."[14] Like most journalists, Evans and Novak presumed that it was inherently preferable for blacks to work with whites and to vote for white candidates. They criticized the MFDP's third-party strategy as "self-defeating," despite the fact that the MFDP candidate ran on a platform that addressed major problems facing black Mississippians. Simultaneously, they praised Evers's advocacy of Prentiss Walker, whom they described as "a white supremacist" with Klan support. Given their analysis of Walker's politics, it is hard to see how voting for him was an effective strategy for black Mississippians.

Ed King observed that during the late 1960s "Evers's national credibility was enormous." He argued that liberals were receptive to Charles Evers because of "his brother's name" and because "he would run around with them, talking about what an integrationist he was." Recalling situations before 1964 when Evers "attacked SNCC for being interracial," King insisted that Evers's talk of integration was insincere and a calculated part of his opposition to SNCC. He explained, "When [SNCC and CORE have] gone way off into Black Power and separatism, he can talk to the northern press about black and white together and we're not extremists like them." He added, "The northern press loved that." Lawrence Guyot made a similar observation, explaining that Evers had "the support of the Rockefellers, the Kennedys, you name it" because he was "the alternative to the Freedom Democratic Party" and because he aggressively proclaimed that he was an "integrationist."[15]

Because liberals found much of what Evers espoused reassuring, most accepted him at face value and ignored his inconsistencies and the ways that some of his statements and beliefs overlapped with the tenets of Black Power that they found so disturbing. White liberals were bothered by self-defense when it was part of a Black Power ideology, but appeared to accept it from Evers. Roy Reed wrote in July 1966, "While other civil rights leaders debate the effectiveness of nonviolence, Mr. Evers has reached a solution that seems to satisfy him and his followers. He carries a pistol everywhere." White liberals also overlooked Evers's occasional advocacy of violent retaliation against whites. Historian Adam Fairclough notes that during the Meredith March, Martin Luther King Jr. and Evers had an encounter in Philadelphia, Mississippi (where three civil rights workers had been killed two years earlier) that "held a special significance for King, for he often referred to it when arguing against violence." Fairclough writes, "At one of the evening rallies, King related, Evers had orated on the need for blacks to fight back with guns, evoking an excited response from the audience. But King had interrupted him, pointing out that Medgar's killer . . . was living close by: 'If you're that violent, why don't you go up the highway to Greenwood and kill the man who killed your brother?' " Although Evers had no response for King, he continued to make similar comments. In August 1966, at the height of his national popularity as a spokesman for interracial cooperation, he told a Harlem audience, "If a pin scratches a Negro any more in Southwest Mississippi we are going to hunt them down till hell freezes over!" He was rebuked by Roy Wilkins, who was sharing the platform, but his comments appear to have had little impact on white liberals' embrace of him. Evers reversed himself and parroted King's words to him a few years later when he was traveling with a white writer who was doing a story for *Harper's Magazine*. In this context, he attacked those who the writer referred to as black "advocate(s) of violence." According to Evers, "They say to kill, but you don't see *them* shooting anybody. The white people have sat back and let the racists advocate violence and do violence. We're not going to do that."[16]

Evers's talk of interracial cooperation and power sharing was probably just as duplicitous and certainly illusory. In southwest Mississippi, away from the spotlight and oratory, whites clung to power. A few who wanted to stay in office appealed to black voters, but whites and blacks remained polarized. Evers's much-publicized talk of biracial government and integration in southwest Mississippi was at best unrealistic, and at worst an accommodation to white supremacy. White liberals and the national media who accepted Evers and his commentary at face value were embracing what they wanted to believe and overlooking many of the contradictions that lay just beneath the surface. Moreover, like the NAACP, most failed to press Evers about his questionable decisions and tactics and seemed willing to accept his abuses of power.

At the same time that Evers was securing his future with the NAACP and emerging as a favorite among white liberals, white Mississippi political leaders like Sovereignty Commission director Erle Johnston had begun to realize that some changes in race relations were inevitable. At the same time, they perceived the NAACP and Evers as more acceptable than SNCC and its organizational legacies. Adam Fairclough notes that in Louisiana "by the second half of the 1960s the NAACP had acquired a certain legitimacy in the eyes of many influential whites." He explains that "key people of influence in the state finally admitted that black insurgency would not go away, and they preferred to deal with the NAACP rather than CORE." In July 1966, *New York Times* reporter Roy Reed suggested that Evers's "repudiation of 'Black Power' and his reluctant association with the [Meredith] march gave him increased acceptability among white [Mississippi] leaders."[17]

As early as the fall of 1964, Gloster Current told a meeting of civil rights activists that Evers "has rapport" with white officials in Jackson. During the Natchez movement in late 1965, law enforcement officers relied heavily on Evers to control other blacks, once releasing him from jail to convince a crowd of protesters to go home. Evers testified later that "when people are angry and confused, I lead them on a march to get that steam off. The policemen in the towns where I have marched know that it is best not to stop them but just to let them walk it off." In December 1965, the Natchez police chief actually expressed concern that Evers was out of town because he feared that without him no one could "control the Negro civil rights workers." In the 1990s, white leader Jimmy Allen insisted that Evers "wasn't as bad as some of the others," and a white Port

Gibson merchant observed that Evers and Sheriff Dan McCay "worked pretty well together." He explained, "Charles Evers is no fool. I mean you could reason with Charles Evers better than you could with some of these others. You could talk to him."[18]

Port Gibson whites felt much less kindly toward Evers in the midst of the 1966 mass movement. But even as they fought Evers and the movement, whites around the state clung to their old patterns, preferring to deal with the black community through a single leader, and Evers was the obvious choice. His influence extended from crowd control to electoral politics. In particular, white Mississippians took note of his ability to influence black voters and his willingness to support a white supremacist in the November 1966 general election. Ed King argued that for whites who were confronting new black electoral power, Evers's ability to direct blacks' votes was reassuring. They preferred, he said, to pay off "a few bosses who could control the vote."[19] Ultimately, white Mississippians found it easier to negotiate with Evers than to respond more directly to the broad-based concerns of a diffuse black community. Moreover, Evers's overriding commitment to most aspects of the status quo and his active pursuit of political power and economic gain made him particularly receptive to bargaining with those in power.

In November 1966, Erle Johnston asked Ken Dean of the Mississippi Human Relations Council to set up a secret meeting with NAACP leader Roy Wilkins so they could explore areas of mutual concern. Johnston, who had initially hoped to convince Wilkins to fire Evers or at least make him control Rudy Shields, was disappointed when Wilkins insisted that he "had no control over Evers." However, the two men discovered a shared antipathy to other civil rights groups. In fact, Wilkins defended Evers to Johnston by pointing out that he "is the only man in Mississippi who can keep SNCC out" and insisted that Evers "is important to Mississippi just for the reason of controlling SNCC and not letting them gain a foothold."[20]

By the end of 1966, the NAACP and the Sovereignty Commission were also united in their opposition to the Child Development Group of Mississippi (CDGM), an award-winning Mississippi Head Start group that many associated with SNCC. The NAACP was a critical component of a coalition that developed Mississippi Action for Progress (MAP) as an alternative. Erle Johnston wrote in his memoir, "As strange as it may seem, unwittingly the NAACP (and Evers) and the Sovereignty Commission were working toward the same goal: to get rid of CDGM. . . . The Commission wanted them out because they stirred up trouble and turmoil. Evers wanted them out because he wanted to extend his control and power." In a letter asking Mississippi's NAACP branch presidents to support MAP in its battle with CDGM, Current ignored the substantive issues of programming and ideology and highlighted instead the past activism of NAACP activists and MAP founders Aaron Henry and R. L. T. Smith. He also emphasized the integrated nature of the MAP coalition, writing, "This marks one of the few times that such men of prominence of both races have agreed to work together on behalf of Negro advancement."[21]

A month later, Current wrote Evers about Wilkins's recent trip to Mississippi, and his comments again illustrate the NAACP's concern with organizational prominence and reveal their eagerness to work with powerful white Mississippians. Current praised Evers extensively, referring to recent national publicity and lauding him for his connections to white supremacists. Undoubtedly influenced by the NAACP's fight against CDGM and Wilkins's meeting with Johnston, he wrote, "The fact that the atmosphere has changed decidedly in favor of our organization and that the white power structure is no longer trying to destroy the Association but rather in some instances trying to assist is a wonderful tribute, first [to] the sacrifices of Medgar and secondly to your own ingenuity and efforts."[22] In this instance, the NAACP, Evers, the Sovereignty Commission, and other white segregationists were united in purpose as they tried to supplant CDGM. Although Evers and white Mississippians remained largely antagonistic as 1966 drew to a close, their mutual embrace of practical politics and their shared opposition to other civil rights groups opened the door to future collaboration.

In fact, on January 26, 1967, less than a month into the new year, Evers announced a settlement of the Port Gibson boycott. Although both the NAACP and white officials claimed victory, Port Gibson whites, especially merchants, made several significant concessions. The town hired a black police officer who was acceptable to the black community, dismissed minor charges pending against movement activists, and desegregated the hospital and public accommodations. Most important, merchants hired fifteen black clerks and "all business and public authorities" agreed to address blacks with courtesy titles.[23]

It is not entirely clear what precipitated this agreement after ten months of futile or nonexistent negotiations, but all of the parties stood to gain by bringing the boycott to a close. The merchants, for example, were under significant financial duress. Four months earlier, Erle Johnston observed that the Port Gibson boycott "[is] quite effective and is beginning to take its toll on white merchants." The Piggly Wiggly grocery store earned a $29,000 profit in 1965 but lost more than $10,000 in 1966. Owner James Hudson testified, "The boycott nearly paralyzed our business. It knocked two-thirds off our sales the first month and it stayed that way for six or eight months." The Jitney Jungle, George Ellis Food Store, and M&M grocery suffered decreases of between $13,000 and $19,000 in income, and only M&M realized any profit. Virtually all of Port Gibson's white merchants suffered losses and several went out of business, including Klan supporter James Jones.[24]

Whites had become increasingly divided about how to respond to the boycott. A number of merchants felt the rest of the white community was not offering them adequate support. Ronnie Hulbert complained that many whites did not "realize how serious" the boycott was and urged "all white citizens" to attend the Friday night meetings, because "this thing effects everyone, not just Main Street in town!" Farmer Mott Headley explained that during the boycott, some of the "people that had stores in town" told him, " 'Ya'll ought to uphold us. You ought to not hire them, you ought to not let them fish in your lake now.' But I say, 'Well, look, these people that I got hired, I been working in the fields with them ever since I was a child. . . . As far as me stopping them from working, hell I got to have somebody to help me. I'm putting up hay, or I'm doing this and that.' What am I supposed to do, cut off my nose to spite my face?" Insisting that it "wasn't my problem really," he concluded, "I'm sure this happened to most of the farm people" because the merchants "were hurting and they wanted support."[25]

There were also divisions among the merchants; some were increasingly willing to compromise, while others insisted on holding out to the bitter end. In mid-May 1966, James Jones asserted to the FBI that "many of the merchants, being financially secure, are content to passively await the outcome of the boycott and may eventually benefit because of their competitors failures." Certainly affluence helped protect some of the community's most elite white merchants. For example, Jimmy Allen had inherited considerable wealth and was financially secure no matter how his business fared. In fact, his car dealership had been losing money long before the boycott started, a trend that continued from 1960 to 1972. Nate Jones thought there was "emotionally great pressure" on merchants to take a hard line because whites believed being conciliatory was "giving in. That [was] something that they don't like." Erle Johnston observed that Canton, Mississippi, merchants who wanted to end a boycott "with some token concessions" were thwarted by the "local Citizens' Council, [which] refused to let them budge." Port Gibson pharmacist Q. H. McDaniel explained that he did not consider meeting the NAACP's demands because "I didn't want to buck anybody. . . . I think probably we took what we considered the easiest way out, which was wrong." Furniture store owner Morris Sherman was one of the merchants most interested in making concessions. In September 1966, he sought help from MHRC head Ken Dean, indicating that he was prepared to "do almost anything" to end the boycott. Sovereignty Commission investigator Leland Cole reported that few whites shared Sherman's willingness "to give the Negroes all demands." In fact, Dean recalled that, along with fellow Jewish merchants Henry and Harris

Marx, Sherman felt isolated and "afraid that if he did too much that he would be ostracized."[26]

Ironically, M. M. McFatter was the first merchant to hire a black clerk in response to the boycott. Supportive of the Klan, investigated by the FBI for voting rights violations, and involved in several altercations with movement activists, McFatter appeared to epitomize antagonistic white resistance, but he was also extremely independent-minded and a shrewd businessman. Despite his antipathy to black voting, he rented the top floor of his pharmacy to federal registrars. When McFatter's chief business competitor, Meyer-Marx Drugstore owner Pete Jordan, angered African Americans and was belatedly added to the boycott list, NAACP leaders told McFatter they would lift the boycott from his store if he hired a black clerk. He agreed and later observed, "I really mopped up for the rest of the time the boycott was on." On the recommendation of Charles Evers and NAACP leader Alexander Collins, he hired movement activist Faye Davis, although he had recently told black leaders that he did not believe blacks were capable of being clerks. He explained later: "We didn't know any that could make change or that were smart enough to be nice to customers." McFatter quickly changed his mind, and years later he considered Davis "a family friend," explaining, "I drew a good one." Even after he sold the pharmacy, he continued to employ her to collect rent for him. Though Davis later described McFatter as "a nice guy" and said that she enjoyed working for him, she was very clear about his reasons for hiring her: "He always wanted to make money and I guess he got real smart. . . . He say, 'Well I'm a hire me somebody.' Because he always have had black people working in his store for different things. . . . But he never had a clerk until he hired me."[27]

McFatter was the only merchant to break ranks and negotiate an individual deal with the NAACP, but as their losses mounted, other merchants searched for ways to end the boycott and save face. In the first week of January 1967, Alderman Jimmy Allen wrote Governor Paul Johnson, who he had just hosted during a holiday hunting trip, asking him to permit Sovereignty Commission investigator Leland Cole to devote himself to ending the boycott. Another merchant pleaded with Governor Johnson to "withhold" antipoverty program Head Start funds (earmarked for a predominantly black program in Claiborne County because whites refused to participate) "until a proper attitude and relationship can be obtained." She wrote, "Port Gibson is in such a bind we had hoped something could be done to hold up these funds until a solution could be found to end this crippling boycott. Some of our white people are leaving. Some have had to close (or are going to) their business for lack of trade." She concluded, "The merchants have tried every thing they know to do—can you help us?"[28]

The black community was also experiencing conflict, especially around boy-cott enforcement. Most blacks appear to have accepted enforcement when it was restricted to threats, intimidation, peer pressure, and property damage, but some people, including a few important leaders, expressed reservations when it in-volved beating people and shooting at homes. Evan Doss Jr. recalled that these differences caused "some tension" because "some blacks . . . did not want to see a lot of violence" against those who violated the boycott. According to NAACP president James Dorsey, most people were initially sympathetic to enforcement. However, he maintained that "when they saw the result, most of them changed" and that "the boycott would have been just as effective, even more effective, without these methods." Leesco Guster, who armed herself to defend her house, distinguished between pressuring boycott violators, which she approved of, and shooting at them, which she did not.[29] The black community supported self-defense and accepted mild harassment of boycott violators but did not condone widespread or extensive violence.

The Deacons were widely associated with violent boycott enforcement, though their exact role is hotly contested and somewhat ambiguous. Since Deacons maintained a highly visible presence on the streets and came to represent black aggressiveness, whites assumed they were responsible for all of the physical attacks and property destruction. Some Deacons did, in fact, play an active role in punishing boycott violators; however, a number of known boycott enforcers had no ties to the Deacons and some of the best-known Deacons, like George Henry Walker, were never connected to any public allegations of boycott enforcement.[30] In August 1966, the arrest of three Deacons for shooting into the home of boycott violator James Gilmore crystallized opposition to violent enforcement. Though the men denied the shooting and were never convicted, many African Americans believed that they were guilty.[31]

This incident and mounting concern about violent enforcement coincided with the Deacons' new tendency to get involved in personal conflicts, especially in support of NAACP board member Calvin Williams. Williams was widely admired for his commitment and courage, and his forceful personality had pro-pelled him into movement leadership. Yet many found him abrasive and bossy. In 1969, George Walker told a historian that many people "personally disliked" Williams but would "follow Calvin's words . . . because he has been a movement loyalist." When Rudy Shields left Port Gibson for Ferriday, Louisiana, Williams assumed leadership of the Deacons and began using the group to bolster his authority within the movement. After Nate Jones opposed Williams's decision to post armed Deacons on the roof of Collins Barbershop, Williams "threatened" Jones at a mass meeting and then sent four Deacons to "whup" him. Jones diffused the situation and argues that Williams was "misleading those Black Hat boys." They "thought I was getting in the way of their leader, Mr. Calvin Williams." In fact, Jones sees the entire incident in terms of Williams's drive for power, observing that Williams "was taking over the NAACP in a smart way and I challenged him." Deacons also threatened Alexander Collins and broke a window in his barbershop when he stopped allowing them to meet in his yard.[32]

Williams's push for power, the Deacons' use of coercive tactics against NAACP board members Nate Jones and Alexander Collins, and the controversy over violent enforcement precipitated a split between the Deacons and the NAACP's leadership. In a heated private meeting, the NAACP Executive Board told the Deacons they would no longer back the group or provide bond when Deacons were arrested. In a subsequent mass meeting, Dorsey publicly characterized the Deacons as violent and announced a policy change directed at Calvin Williams, that "people who were affiliated with the Deacons could not hold an office" in the NAACP. Dorsey later explained that the division was necessary because the "Deacons believed in violence and arms" and because they wanted to "take over" and "dictate policies." It is difficult to know the exact result of this conflict, but many of the men who called themselves Deacons remained active in the movement. In addition, the NAACP's declaration that they would no longer supply bond was probably more an effort to control behavior than an ultimatum. In discussing the alleged shooting at the Gilmore house, for example, Leesco Guster said, "I didn't approve of the shooting, now, though we did go bond for them." Moreover, though Calvin Williams's daily presence in the movement declined in September when he began commuting to a job in Louisiana, he remained an important leader.[33]

These cracks in black unity and intensifying white desperation probably contributed to the January boycott settlement, but Charles Evers and the Sovereignty Commission actually struck the deal. Erle Johnston liked to think of the Sovereignty Commission as a racial troubleshooter, and white leaders around the state wanted to improve Mississippi's national image by reducing visible racial conflict wherever possible. Though Johnston supported the status quo and worked hard to undermine civil rights activism, he was often more willing than local whites to make token concessions to blacks. Charles Evers's own preference for cutting deals made him an ideal confederate. Over the years, Evers's critics repeatedly accused him of yielding too quickly and of making deals for empty settlements. A Sovereignty Commission informant reported that during the Natchez boycott, one SNCC worker told another "not to let Charles Evers make any compromise with the local officials." According to historian John Dittmer, once Evers did make a deal to settle the Natchez boycott, "more militant blacks" believed that "Evers had compromised at a time when the movement could have demanded more and gotten more." Evers was happy to acknowledge his willingness to compromise, explaining in his memoir, "I'm always ready to deal." By January 1967, Evers's ability to mobilize blacks for protest was well known and he had little to gain from continuing the boycott. A successful settlement, however, would highlight his power and reinforce his national reputation. (For example, a June 1967 *New York Times* article noted that Evers "has been able to bring white authorities to yield to Negro grievances.")[34] Rudy Shields's early-January return to Port Gibson, which coincided with increased picketing and friction in the community, provided an additional impetus for settling the boycott. It appears that Evers was feeling threatened by Shields's independence and influence, while the Sovereignty Commission and FBI worried about Shields's affiliation with the Deacons.

Despite these diverse reasons for compromise and Evers's early-January offer to discuss a settlement, whites opened the New Year with repression, not negotiation. Working with white leaders, Sovereignty Commission investigator Leland Cole, who George Walker observed "was just constantly stirring up the people in the community," initiated a high-pressure campaign designed to undermine the boycott. He targeted the Deacons because he and other whites remained convinced that they were responsible for boycott enforcement and that without coercion the boycott would fall apart. White officials tried to "break the backbone of the organization by arresting them as often as possible for violation of every law on the book including spitting on the sidewalk" in order to "try and run them out of bond money and property." The state attorney general contributed with information "regarding laws that can be enforced," and white lawmen cast a wide net, targeting most of the black community. In less than two weeks, "over 30 cases were tried in the Mayor's court," including ones involving speeding, defective tail lights, DWI, and other traffic and parking violations, as well as assault and battery, resisting arrest, disturbing the peace, and disobeying a law officer.[35]

The tensions generated by this repression exploded into street-level conflict on Saturday, January 14. The police chief reported to the FBI that his force was "extremely busy" breaking up "small groups" of "Negroes [who were] congregating on the street corners." Emerson Davis, the notorious boycott violator, fired a gun at and slightly grazed Will T. Holmes, an unarmed black man. The police department's first response was to arrest Holmes, not Davis. They also blamed the incident on Shields, speculating that he put Holmes up to "taunting Davis." (After the shooting, pharmacist M. M. McFatter gave Davis a "brand new .38 pistol" and told him "next time, don't miss.") Later that day, McFatter and

Klan supporter James Jones "started tussling with some of the Negroes" and Jones was arrested for striking "a Negro" who would not "move out of his way." Several other people were arrested, including Shields for either "civil disobedience" or "inciting to riot." Whatever the charges, they were dropped as soon as Shields appeared in court, though white officials dredged up old charges and held him for several weeks without bond.[36]

Leland Cole maintained that he used this coercive campaign and information that Evers was taking boycott-related kickbacks to pressure Evers to end the boycott, but there is nothing to support these assertions. Several years later, another Sovereignty Commission investigator discovered that Cole's "evidence" of kickbacks was fabricated. Moreover, the merchants, rather than Evers and the NAACP, made concessions. In fact, the NAACP continued what it called a selective buying campaign against owners of the Piggly Wiggly, Jitney Jungle, M&M grocery, George Ellis Food Store, Western Auto, and other merchants who refused to hire black clerks. Perhaps more than anything else, Cole's claims provided cover for the merchants to maintain the illusion of victory. The appearance that they had won was important enough to Port Gibson's white leadership that, when the *New York Times* and newspapers in Jackson, New Orleans, and Memphis characterized the settlement as an NAACP victory, they complained forcefully to Erle Johnston. Johnston, who was a former newsman, responded by writing and peddling a report of the settlement "from the Mayor's point of view." In it, he quoted Mayor Davis insisting that "the boycott has accomplished nothing except to create tensions" and that "we have merely returned to the same status that existed prior to the boycott." Johnston enlisted a highway patrolman to distribute copies of his story to news outlets in Memphis, New Orleans, and around Mississippi. When most of the newspapers failed to carry the story the next morning, Johnston followed up with personal calls to several editors. At his urging, three papers gave it prominent coverage over the weekend, and on Monday, Cole reported that "all officials and merchants were extremely happy with the publicity." Bill Minor, a reporter who had covered the boycott settlement as an NAACP victory, devoted a 1993 column to the incident after he accessed previously confidential Sovereignty Commission files. He concluded, "What becomes obvious . . . is that I had blown the cover of the local white officials who had been negotiating with Evers, but who did not want it to appear that they had yielded to any of the blacks' demands."[37]

It is not clear how most blacks felt about ending the boycott. Evers apparently made the decision by himself (without even consulting the NAACP Executive Board) and presented it to those attending the January 24 mass meeting for their rubber stamp. Cole reported that a few people booed Evers's announcement.

Dorsey thought a more significant breakthrough was imminent and the boycott should have been continued. However, most blacks were probably happy with the agreement. It brought decent jobs for about two dozen people, offered the promise of courteous treatment, and made shopping easier. Moreover, blacks had already begun to see the possibilities for implementing other changes through new federal laws and electoral politics. Almost fifty black students were halfway through their first year of desegregating the formerly whites-only public schools. In November 1966, longtime Pattison activist Floyd Rollins had become the county's first black political candidate since Reconstruction. He lost his bid for a seat on the school board, but blacks registered a decisive county-level majority in opposing segregationist congressmen James Eastland and John Bell Williams, making it clear that black voters were going to change the county's political landscape.[38]

CHAPTER Fourteen

Charles Evers's Own Little Empire

After the January 1967 boycott settlement, Charles Evers's presence in Claiborne County declined, but his reputation and political influence remained linked to the community. From August 1966 into the 1970s, most of the considerable national news coverage and virtually every profile of Evers mentioned his ties to the Claiborne County movement. During that same period, Evers developed increasingly strong connections to the white establishment. In fact, the Port Gibson boycott settlement inaugurated a mutually beneficial relationship between Charles Evers and the Sovereignty Commission that added to his growing power in Mississippi politics and bolstered his national prominence. The 1967 commission files are filled with details about conversations, negotiations, and deals involving Evers, the commission, and southwest Mississippi communities. After they were able to reach a compromise to end the Port Gibson boycott, Sovereignty Commission director Erle Johnston recognized Evers as a valuable ally in his efforts to "reduce the chances of racial agitation whenever and wherever possible."[1] For Johnston, Evers was an ideal collaborator because he was willing to negotiate and because he had more influence with blacks than any other single person, especially in southwest Mississippi.

This relationship was a two-way street that Evers used to his benefit as well. By 1967, Evers's ability to initiate strong local mass movements and his willingness to openly confront well-known white segregationists had earned him considerable popularity among blacks. These successes and the high numbers of blacks registered to vote had propelled him into the limelight and provided him with a strong constituency and considerable political potential. He no longer needed to engage in confrontational protest to secure his reputation, and he preferred to emphasize black political power and concentrate on building his own economic base. The Sovereignty Commission was able to help Evers maintain his reputation—among blacks and northern liberals alike—by convincing local whites to make minor concessions. Ed King contended that he would hear "one or two days in advance that the Sovereignty Commission was going to help settle" a boycott and "wanted Evers to get credit." He believed that "the white power structure, including the Sovereignty Commission, probably helped settle things because they wanted Evers to look good." Commission investigator Leland Cole alluded to this practice in his report on the Port Gibson settlement when he claimed to be making concessions to bolster Evers's reputation, writing, "I could not use him to help . . . other areas if he lost face with all the Negro people." Cole concluded that "Evers can be dealt with in a firm manner and problems in other parts of the state can be solved."[2]

In fact, almost immediately after the Port Gibson boycott resolution, Evers and the commission worked together to end another boycott in nearby Woodville (Wilkinson County). In March 1967, Evers and the commission conspired again, and Evers postponed a threatened school boycott intended to protest an unpopular black principal in Hazlehurst (Copiah County). In the period between these boycott negotiations, Natchez NAACP activist Wharlest Jackson was killed by a Klan car bomb and Evers and Johnston discussed ways to minimize the possibility for black retaliatory violence. Johnston apprised Evers of the deployment of National Guardsmen and praised him for "having marches to give his people an outlet for their emotions." On several other occasions, Johnston encouraged Evers to support particular candidates in local and state elections. In April 1967, he tried to convince Evers to back a white candidate in Wilkinson County. Although Evers refused because he was already supporting a black candidate in the race, Johnston reported that Evers "stated if we had spoken several weeks ago, he would have gone along with the change." A few months earlier, at Johnston's suggestion, Evers had agreed to "scatter the Negro vote in the first primary" of the governor's race.[3]

In the 1970s, Evers testified that Johnston was "a pretty good man. Off the record, he's pretty good. I think he's a pretty nice fellow." According to Evers, Johnston "had a job to do . . . and I had one to do, too." He added that "we sort of had a thing going." Johnston's comments about Evers were similar though less flattering. In February 1967, Ken Dean of the MHRC reported to his parent organization that Johnston claimed he had "made an unofficial ally of [Evers].

He's just a monkey. He tells me that I'm too hard on him and we joke a bit. I tell you he's just a monkey, we play along with him." In his memoir, Johnston notes that Evers "became a very practical disciple of racial progress" and that the two developed a " 'behind-the-scenes' relationship of understanding and trust." His retrospective analysis mirrors comments he made in a March 1967 memo to Governor Paul Johnson. After observing that "the NAACP, under the leadership of Charles Evers, has established a political and economic base in Southwest Mississippi," Johnston reassured the governor that "Evers has shown signs of being more reasonable in approaching problems of that area than in prior months."[4]

Fearing that scrutiny would bring condemnation and maybe destroy the collaboration, Johnston explained in his memoir that neither he nor Evers revealed "to our respective associates what we were doing." In fact, after Johnston publicized some of the organization's negotiations with Evers in a lengthy report released in conjunction with his resignation in 1968, journalist Bill Minor wrote, "It is probably unthinkable to many in Mississippi that the Sovereignty Commission has maintained open communication links with Negro leaders like Evers." However, Minor accepted Johnston's claim that "this has been a vital part of the effectiveness of the cooling off efforts behind the scenes." Investigator Leland Cole was less cautious about keeping the relationship secret, and in March 1967, Johnston reprimanded him for telling "people in your territory, 'We have Charles Evers in the palm of our hand.' " Johnston told Cole, "Whether the report is true or not, I would much prefer that you never make any such statement because it might jeopardize some of our trouble shooting procedures. You may say at any time that we have a communication with Evers, but I would not go any further than that." Despite Johnston's efforts, Evers's dealings with the white power structure were not particularly secret, at least within the movement community. After asserting that Evers was "conclusively identified with the state Sovereignty Commission," a SNCC organizer observed that "people were talking about that later in retrospect, but we knew that early on." In July 1967, MFDP chair Lawrence Guyot told a reporter that he disagreed "with Evers's tactic of dealing covertly with whites," and when Evers was running for Congress in 1968, a Tougaloo College student criticized him for the way he "dealt with the power structure in Natchez." The author of a 1968 profile of Evers also noted this connection, writing, "For some time at least a few local and state officials have believed that he can be trusted, that his word is good; and they have in effect and in fact worked with him to try to make orderly and peaceful a transition they now know is inevitable."[5]

The relationship was not, as Cole had implied, entirely one-sided, and the attempts at compromise did not always go smoothly. Whenever Evers and the commission entered into negotiation, they were each backed by the implicit (or, in some cases, explicit) threat of a more coercive alternative. For its part, the Sovereignty Commission periodically replicated its Port Gibson strategy of using systematic arrests and excessive bonds in an effort to undermine protest and picketing. In May 1967, when negotiations with Evers failed to end a boycott in Hazlehurst, Erle Johnston reported that Cole "will use his own methods of removing the strong-arm goons off the streets. (He will use the same tactics that were successful at Port Gibson.)" A few months later, Cole used the same strategy in Hattiesburg. Under his direction, local lawmen arrested eighty-six blacks, and Cole reported that, "with the concealed weapon charge and other charges used, approximately $12,000 in property bonds were taken."[6]

When Shields began working in the Delta town of Belzoni, Johnston assigned Cole to follow him because of Cole's past success "in getting Shields arrested and jailed for law violations." After a meeting that included city officials, city police, a state senator, a highway patrolman, and two FBI agents, Cole reported that the men present "voted to turn the police department and the problem of Shields over to me." Cole added, "The mayor will act as ex-officio justice of the peace in order to get larger bonds from those arrested under state laws." Within days, he had made twenty-three arrests, prompting a movement newsletter to report that "a state investigator has come in and pretty much taken over local law enforcement here . . . and, among other things, engineered a number of arrests on phony charges."[7]

While the Sovereignty Commission used this strategy of wholesale arrests to try to control activism, Evers used the threat of boycotts, Rudy Shields, and the Deacons for leverage. Early in 1967, when Shields was released from jail in Port Gibson, he moved to Hazlehurst. Over time, his ties to Evers became increasingly strained, but in the short term, the two men replicated their Port Gibson alliance, with Shields doing day-to-day organizing work in other southwest Mississippi communities. By this time, the Sovereignty Commission had become fixated on Shields. In fact, widespread white antipathy toward the movement centered on Shields, and many whites believed that he was almost solely responsible for boycotts and movement activism. In January 1967, Port Gibson Klan supporter James Jones told FBI agents, "The present situation would be non-existent if it were not for [name deleted] and Rudy Shields." A few months later, Cole reported that in Copiah County "Shields was the one the local people resented the most," and a local lawyer wrote Johnston, "I still believe the key to the whole situation here is Shields." In his memoir, Erle Johnston equated Shields with boycotts, claiming that "when Shields got out of the boycotted areas, things gradually returned to normal."[8]

Meanwhile, the FBI opened a file on Shields in August 1967, and the Sovereignty Commission records are filled with information about attempts to arrest or neutralize Shields. During the August 1967 primary election, Johnston assigned Cole "to follow Shields during election day and watch him closely for any violation of law that would justify a complaint." The next month, Johnston told Cole that if Shields showed up, he should "find some reason to get him behind bars." In late 1967 and 1968, white officials in Brookhaven and Belzoni requested help to get "Shields off the streets" and to "counteract" his work. When Cole was assigned to work in Belzoni, he made it his mission to "run Shields out." A few weeks later, he had arrested Shields and reported to Johnston, "Finally, after over a year, we have a felony charge on Rudy Shields." After addressing two other possible felony charges, Cole wrote, "It looks like we may finally have him in a corner." By 1968, this obsession with Shields triggered a new Mississippi law, nicknamed the Rudy Shields law, banning secondary boycotts—that is, boycotts against white merchants that were intended to pressure political officeholders. No surprisingly, Shields was the first person arrested under this statute, though Cole's hopes for neutralizing him were premature. In the 1970s, the commission was still trying to get Shields behind bars and was considering a plan to set him up on drug-related charges.[9]

Given their belief that Shields was the primary cause of black protest, local whites and commission employees continually urged Evers to control or remove him, and this quickly became and remained a major point of contention between Evers and the commission. In May 1967, Johnston reported telling Evers that "if he persisted in backing up Shields, then we were through." Several weeks after assuring Johnston that he would remove Shields from Copiah County, Evers reversed himself. Cole and the commission responded by breaking off negotiations, arresting Shields for "an old fine that very night," and initiating a campaign of coercive arrests. In this instance, it is difficult to know whether Evers was using Shields as a negotiating tool and changed his mind or whether he was simply unable to control Shields. Ed King insisted that at times Evers purposefully downplayed his influence on Shields, explaining that the Sovereignty Commission "could talk with Charles," but "Charles is often acting like he can't control that hothead Rudy, this sort of thing." Concluding that Evers "rarely missed a chance to show off a better side," a reporter described a similar scenario. He wrote that Evers once "sat back and allowed an 'outsider,' [almost certainly Shields] young and sharply militant to lash the white leadership. Then Evers quietly led the mayor aside and offered the town a choice: 'work with me—or that wild youngster over there.' "[10]

Though Evers definitely used whites' concern about Shields to his advantage, the two men did develop very real differences. As early as July 1966, the FBI reported that Evers was disavowing Shields, and by late 1967, the two men were clearly moving in different directions. Their eventual falling out was probably triggered by Evers's intensifying ties to the Sovereignty Commission, his preference for negotiation, and his willingness to settle for superficial change. Harry Bowie, a black minister who moved to Mississippi after participating in the 1964 Summer Project, explained that Evers "dumped" Shields when Evers became "establishment" and no longer needed him. FDP activist Lawrence Guyot made a similar claim that Shields helped "create legitimacy for Evers" within the black community but that when Evers no longer had to compete with other civil rights groups, like SNCC and the MFDP, he perceived Shields as a threat. He added that Evers and the Sovereignty Commission also decided that anyone "associated with the Deacons" had to go.[11]

As long as Shields and the informal Deacons groups that he organized supported Evers's decisions, they bolstered his standing with whites by making him appear reasonable and by implying that there was a more ominous possibility. However, as an alternative source of leadership, they were a potential threat to Evers. Despite his overwhelming popularity, local blacks did occasionally oppose him, particularly when he tried to limit boycotts and confrontational behavior. When Evers agreed to a settlement ending the Woodville boycott in February 1967, Cole reported that in a meeting surrounded by armed Deacons, "there were many objections" and it took Evers "two rounds of voting," to secure agreement. Evers clashed with the Woodville Deacons again in September when, according to an FBI report, "approximately twenty-five armed members of the Deacons . . . drew their weapons on a white individual who had aimed a rifle at the participants" in an NAACP march. The highway patrol sent in more than sixty officers who essentially disarmed the black community. Rather than challenge the legality of this crackdown, Evers told a highway patrol investigator that "he regretted his people had acted as they did," explaining that "this was a bad mistake and that it happened due to a lack of strong leadership."[12]

Shields was typically more aggressive and confrontational than Evers, especially as Evers's close ties to whites began to temper his actions. Several other incidents indicate the friction between Evers and Shields. In August 1967, when the black masonic lodge in Hazlehurst was burned down, Shields held a closed meeting for black men to discuss plans for guarding buildings and being more assertive in self-defense. According to a local white lawyer, this effort ended when Evers "got in touch with Shields and told him to disband the meeting." Even before this, Sovereignty Commission files described instances in which Shields led marches and sit-ins in defiance of Evers's orders. In May 1967, Johnston reported that Evers "agreed that Shields had become too obnoxious." Testifying about the Claiborne County movement in the 1970s, Evers asserted that "we got rid of" Shields because he "was active in some things that we just really didn't approve of." Evers claimed he told Shields, "Our movement is nonviolent. And the weapons we're using now is more effective than a gun. We can't win with guns. If that's the way you feel, you get the hell out of here." Moments later, when he was pressed about this, he backtracked, acknowledging, "There were certain people, responsible citizens, who did have guns. The sheriff knew it. We told him." Implying this was somehow different than Shields's use of guns, Evers concluded, "But they were local people who had some sense . . . and they were just to keep anybody from throwing bombs at us." More revealing and significant is Evers's objection to Shields's independence. He testified that he told Shields, "Now, Rudy . . . you either take orders the way we do or you don't do at all."[13]

By the end of 1967, Evers and Shields were clearly at odds. Part of their conflict centered on the on-again, off-again boycott in Hazlehurst. The boycott was initiated in May 1967 when Evers was in the hospital. Without Evers present, Johnston observed that "the more militant group seemed to dominate" and Hazlehurst blacks voted for a boycott even though "Evers's chief committeemen were opposed." By June, Cole reported that the boycott was over and "the Negro leadership has gotten back into the right hands since Rudolph Shields has left town." His assessment was premature, and, by September, Johnston observed that the boycott was back on, with Shields and local activist Dudley Stewart "back in control." The subsequent negotiations suggest that Shields was working to keep the boycott alive, while Evers was trying to broker a settlement. When Johnston first asked Evers for help in ending the boycott, Evers refused, saying he would "not interfere." Johnston interpreted this "as a sign he is acknowledging he has lost some of his prestige and authority." However, after merchants made an offer that Shields rejected, they called Evers with the same proposal. Evers "tentatively agreed" to their terms and successfully promoted the settlement at the next NAACP meeting, although he "had a little difficulty in getting the local crowd to go along." Johnston's white contact in Hazlehurst wrote that "Shields is not too happy and would like to stir up a stink," but "Evers does seem to be in control."[14]

Shields and Evers were involved in a similar conflict in Brookhaven at the end of November. Shortly after he had started organizing there, Shields "angrily walked out" of a meeting when the NAACP Executive Committee accepted a compromise settlement with white merchants. When Shields and other local activists tried to keep the boycott going, Brookhaven NAACP officials "called Charles Evers and told him to get Shields out of Brookhaven." A couple of months later, Shields had relocated and begun organizing in the Delta town of Belzoni. For the first time, Shields was working in Mississippi outside what was considered Evers's territory of southwest Mississippi. After initially assuming that Evers had sent Shields to Belzoni, Leland Cole reported that "Shields is here on his own and not under Charles Evers." By 1971, Evers had openly split with Shields, publicly calling him a "troublemaker" and insisting to Jackson mayor Russell Davis that Shields "does not speak for the black community." He even encouraged Davis to "run Shields out of town if he makes trouble." A few years later, when Evers was asked if he was acquainted with Rudy Shields, he laughed and said yes but that "didn't last long" and "I just didn't get involved where Shields was." Although most people believe that the two men had a connection dating back to their days in Chicago and that Evers had actually encouraged Shields to come to Mississippi, Evers downplayed his ties to and former reliance on Shields, asserting dismissively, "I told him he could volunteer, but we had nothing to pay him. We get many such volunteers."[15]

That Evers's relationship with Shields deteriorated is not surprising since Evers's history in the Mississippi movement is one of friction. In 1968, a journalist observed that "the Evers approach to life has sometimes alienated civil rights leaders; he has little appreciation for the niceties of cooperative association." Both Evers and his sister-in-law Myrlie Evers make it clear that they did not get along very well, and his clashes with Roy Wilkins, Gloster Current, and other top NAACP staff are well documented. Prior to the 1964 MFDP challenge, Evers was the only civil rights activist in Mississippi who did not cooperate with the SNCC-COFO coalition, and his dispute with them intensified in subsequent years as he gained in stature. Evers also had problems with Jackson's NAACP leaders, who were among his most persistent critics.[16]

Even after the tension between Evers and his NAACP bosses began to ease, his conflict continued with NAACP staff and volunteers in Mississippi. In June 1966, when the national NAACP transferred the state's voter registration office to Evers's control, Gloster Current gave Evers detailed instructions about how to handle the staff he was inheriting. Implying that he feared Evers would fire or alienate his new employees, Current wrote, "Both persons have experience and can work quite well if properly utilized. I do hope you will be gracious in handling the transfer." A few months later, Current reported that Evers had become "distressed with Aaron Henry" and was even pushing to replace the very popular state NAACP president who had been working with the organization far longer than Evers. Evers's inability to work cooperatively with others persisted, and in January 1967 he sent a terse note informing Current that he had fired his assistant, Allen Johnson. Evers offered no explanation, though he had hand-picked Johnson just six months earlier and Johnson continued to have widespread support around the state and in the national office.[17]

The break between Evers and Shields fit Evers's pattern of being unable to sustain cooperative relationships. It was also closely tied to their divergent leadership styles, tactical approaches, and personal goals and motivations. Ed King came to believe that Shields moved to Mississippi "out of the most noble purposes" and not "to share in the gravy and corruption and loot that Charles was getting." Rick Abraham, who met Shields after his split with Evers, summed up the differences between the two men in similar ways, concluding that Shields "wasn't after recognition or credibility and he wasn't looking for a well-paying career in public office. And I think Charles Evers was." According to King, "Rudy gradually saw through what Charles was doing" and by 1967 and 1968 "was refusing to do some things that Charles wanted because he didn't think they would work, didn't think they were right." King insisted, for example, that Shields "would never have organized a boycott to force blacks to shop at his own liquor store or his own grocery store or something like that."[18]

Abraham also contended that "Rudy did not profit from his leadership of the people," pointing out that "the people he worked with were poor. Rudy stayed poor." Actually, Shields and Evers both had symbiotic relationships with local people, but while Evers pursued profit and expanding influence, Shields eked out a subsistence living. Shields testified in 1973 that "in the 8 years I have been in Mississippi, I have never been employed. Each community supports me." He explained, "I help people . . . and they support me." Asked how Shields survived financially, a Port Gibson activist said, "Well what we would do back in that time, people would just take up little donations and give money to him because he was not on a salary from anybody or anything. So, the communities, more or less would sponsor [him]." When he was arrested, blacks lined up to pay his bond. Fayette activist Lillie Brown described driving through Port Gibson and being flagged down by Matt Ross, who told her, "Hell, they got Rudy in jail, Mrs. Brown. And I don't know why they put him in there because he ain't going to stay no longer than I can get there and put the pen in my hand." In Yazoo City, Shields lived in a donated shack that doubled as the NAACP office. When he died penniless at his sister's home in Chicago, his Yazoo City friends honored his wishes and raised the money to have his body transported back to Mississippi for burial in his adopted home. His supporters gather every year to celebrate his life and pay their respects, even though they cannot afford to buy a marker for his grave.[19]

Even aside from the issue of profiting from the movement, Shields's day-to-day organizing work in communities gave him a perspective and approach to change that was almost antithetical to Evers's. Abraham explained that Shields started out as "the soldier out there" doing "the work that Charles Evers actually got credit for" but then "became a leader in his own right." Unlike Evers, who presumed that change came through "having a powerful leader," Abraham continued, "Rudy's vision was that" change "trickles up from the grassroots to the top." As a result, Shields favored working for "small local victories" that would help people gain the "power and confidence and knowledge" necessary to "really participate in the system" and "start influencing the decisions that affect their lives." Ed King, who initially thought Shields was a "hoodlum thug" who simply did Evers's bidding, came to appreciate Shields's commitment to working with people on the process of change. Implicitly criticizing Evers, he insisted that Shields did not think "[you had] to just use the people for their own good." Abraham explained that Shields was troubled by Evers's "compromises" and "alliances," arguing that one of the most important things about Shields's leadership was his belief that "someone has to be out there on the cutting edge taking strong positions and representing the folks that other folks, other people, leaders, sometimes forget about." He concluded, "Mississippi needed Rudy Shields, and he . . . was willing to fight when a lot of people were giving up the fight or being fooled into thinking they didn't need to fight any more."[20]

The conflicts between Evers and Shields closely paralleled the long-standing differences between Evers and the organizations affiliated with the SNCC-COFO tradition. Lawrence Guyot explained that Evers "never had any inhibitions about saying" that his approach to the civil rights movement was to "involve as few people as possible in . . . the decision-making, and make as much money as possible." Ed King maintained that Evers presumed that "a leader does" things "for the people and they're grateful. And you tell them what they do, need to do, and you deserve any of the spoils of war." Port Gibson NAACP president James Dorsey acknowledged that the organization's executive board was not democratic and that members typically made decisions only after Evers had provided guidance. He explained, "On the one hand [Evers] would try to make you think that he wanted you to have a mind of your own, but on the other hand he always wanted to stay in command of things." Another longtime NAACP activist asserted that "Charles has taken many decisions from the local leaders." Evers's control was reinforced by his popularity because "the masses thought that . . . he was always right" and the executive board could not generate support for any decision that Evers opposed. Evers described his ability to control decisions: "Like a lawyer leads his witness, you lead them into it. In most cases if you've done your homework they'll vote for it, don't worry."[21]

Evers was also willing to use coercion. According to historian John Dittmer, in 1965 when Evers decided to end the Natchez boycott, he squelched opposition and "NAACP bouncers" refused to allow his critics to speak. Dittmer writes, "[Evers] announced the terms and called for an end to the boycott. There had been no advance notice that this critical subject would be on the agenda, and Evers permitted no discussion of the agreement before taking a vote. . . . Evers had put his prestige on the line, and after a voice vote, the chair of the meeting declared the boycott was over." Noting that Evers demanded "total control," Ed King recalled that Evers once told him, "Black people have been ordered around all their lives by white people. Now it's time for black people to order them around." Minister Harry Bowie made an almost identical point, explaining that Evers "believed that blacks were afraid and he wanted to make them choose whether to be afraid of white or black folks. He used enforcement and other methods to force blacks to switch the focus of their fear." Jack Chatfield, who spent several months in Port Gibson in 1969, concluded that within this framework, Evers remained the "undisputed commander," while an FDP worker who moved to Claiborne County in the late 1960s acknowledged, "I wouldn't dare argue with a man like Evers. Here in the southwestern counties he has the power." He added, "The people here don't know but one organization—the NAACP. And they don't know nothing about who runs it except Charles Evers."[22]

Activists influenced by SNCC shared this view and generally opposed the kind of top-down, individualistic leadership that Evers epitomized, instead emphasizing a process of local, indigenous empowerment. Lawrence Guyot and Ed King underscored that the MFDP wanted to create an issue-oriented electorate that would use "democratic structures to strengthen people and to make changes." Lawyers' Committee attorney Bob Fitzpatrick contrasted the "Evers-type politics," which he perceived as "the quick hit, the quick fix, from the top," to the MFDP perspective, which was that "the only way we'll succeed long term is" by "empowering people" and building "from the bottom up." Reflecting that "maybe I'm still a little idealistic," Fitzpatrick explained that there was a very different movement culture in the Delta away from Evers. "Meetings were different. Everybody spoke" and "little people were leaders."[23]

In addition to disagreeing with his "autocratic" approach, Evers's critics thought he was "a power maniac" with "questionable" motives. One man insisted, "There's just nothing there. There's no principle. It's all self-aggrandizement. It's all self-promotion." A SNCC organizer explained that "Charles is for me first. His commitment to change would be tempered by that." A Fayette critic complained that "Charles Evers is just getting rich off his Brother's name," explaining, "All these white folks do is offer Charles Evers a pretty good size of money and he will get just like them and he has." She added, "If Charles Evers had been the man his brother was he would have been dead but he is a pig. But if he see when he can get a piece of money he will sell everybody. And all he is looking for now is being elected again and if that happen it will be a whole lots of hungry people here in Jefferson Co." A Port Gibson woman said, "He say he was trying to help black folk. I don't know. (Laughter.) He was probably working for himself. (Laughter.)" Another movement supporter, who praised Evers's "nerve" and acknowledged his importance to the local movement, believed that "Charles Evers would take money from white people." He added, "I believe he was the kind that would do whatever it would take to keep him up front and kind of eat cheese with white people too. Play both sides." In fact, Sheriff Dan McCay acknowledged that Evers "would get around with me somewhere" and say, "All that stuff I'm saying, don't pay no attention to it. That's what they want to hear. I'm gonna tell them what they want to hear."[24]

In 1967, Evers fueled the ongoing criticism of his money-making ventures when he opened a combination NAACP office and shopping center in Fayette, what one journalist called "a handsome complex of businesses." In 1968, one Tougaloo student criticized him for building a "personal empire in Fayette." Another student "accused him" of using boycotts to get "fat," arguing that Evers's Fayette businesses were "taking money out of the community and putting it in his own pocket." A 1968 *New York Times* magazine profile of Evers pointed to his success as a "small-town entrepreneur," noting that "few civil rights leaders are as openly and happily in pursuit of the dollar." The author observed that "some of the most bitter criticism of Evers has stemmed from his performance as a businessman" and the fact that "he opened his stores in unseemly proximity to the time when white competitors were being hit by the boycotts he had initiated." A critic told the reporter, "The trouble with Charles is that he's something of a hustler. He's not putting everything out on the table any of the time and he always has an eye out for things that will help Charles as much as the movement." Scholar Charles Payne explains that though "no one doubted his nerve," many found him "abrasive and egotistical" and believed he was "opportunistic— exploiting the popularity of a martyred brother, opening a grocery store of his own when white stores were being boycotted, using poverty funds as a form of patronage to build his own political machine, [and] making alliances with powerful politicians with segregationist records."[25]

Evers himself said that "Medgar sought after justice, I sought after money," something his critics would undoubtedly agree with. Payne notes that Evers "has responded to charges of opportunism by claiming that his critics don't understand pragmatic political and economic development." Evers repeatedly defended himself against those who accused him of profiting from boycotts. When a reporter observed in 1968 that Evers "profits from the civil rights movement" and his "affluence is in strong contrast to the economic status of so many well-known civil rights leaders," Evers responded: "If we had more Negro leaders as independent businessmen, they could fight harder and it would be less likely for them to be bought off by the power structure." He noted, "I'd hear whispers: 'Charles Evers is lining his own pockets, selling out civil rights.' Well, sure I was making money! I'm always a businessman. But I'd never sell out civil rights." He insisted, "I never started a boycott to help my own stores, but I'd been in business all my life, and I stayed in business during our boycotts."[26]

Evers publicly claimed that his business activity strengthened his movement work or was irrelevant to it, but his private comments reinforce the conclusion that making money was his priority. When Lawrence Guyot tried to bridge the divide separating Evers from the MFDP, serving as his campaign manager in the 1968 congressional race, Evers told him: "The difference between me and you is you are interested in [helping people] and I'm interested in making money." He made a similar comment to Fannie Lou Hamer, who came to national attention during her televised testimony at the 1964 Democratic convention. When they were both delegates to the 1968 Democratic convention, he told her that "she shouldn't be working for nothing." In a recent memoir, Charles Evers's sister-in-law Myrlie Evers-Williams implies that he tried to profit from his brother's death by falsely claiming he was supporting Medgar's family. She contends that "Charles had moved himself front and center in the wake of Medgar's murder" and accepted paid speaking engagements, telling audiences that "I have two families to take care of now, mine and my brother's." She reports that Evers told her "how gullible people were" and that she eventually responded by threatening, "If I ever hear you say to anyone . . . that you are taking care of your brother's family, I am going to call a press conference and denounce you publicly."[27]

Allegations that he mishandled funds followed Evers throughout his career. In September 1967, for example, Erle Johnston noted that the Mississippi Voters League, financed by the United Auto Workers, had split with Evers because "he refused to make an accounting [of funds] and insisted that he be given cash instead of checks." Evers's own description of how he handled the money that came into Fayette after he was elected mayor in 1969 was similar. He wrote, "Since '69, big money had been flowing into Fayette, care of Charles Evers, and I wasn't always careful how I accounted for it." As always, however, he scoffed at the idea that he was profiting: "But stealing money, lining my own pockets at the expense of my people? Never." A Fayette activist who was very critical of Evers insisted that that is exactly what he did. In a 1969 letter to northern supporters, she wrote that people in Fayette "can't see what he has been doing with the money he went out and fund raise for." About a year later, she said that Evers had used the donations from around the country to "build for his self" and that when a woman asked "him to let her have some milk for her little boy until her husband came home and he tell her he didn't credit his mother." In a follow-up letter, she reported that Evers "is saying he has to got to go fund raising his money is getting low."[28]

Evers's portrayal of himself was very similar to the portrait painted by his critics, and they differed most, not in the details, but in the interpretation. As Charles Payne points out, "What was selling-out from one perspective was just moving on from another, becoming a part of the structure so that one could change it even more." This belief, that the entire point of the movement was to "open up the system," epitomized Evers's approach. In 1967, he told one reporter, "They say I want to become a member of the white man's world. Of course, I do—that's what my brother died for." He asserted, "I believe in working on the inside, not the outside." Another reporter observed that "for Evers, the transition from civil rights to politics was natural and inevitable."[29]

Evers's desire to wield influence and be part of the system is clearly evident in his acceptance of the role of political boss. Although the national NAACP disapproved of Evers's pre–Voting Rights Act endorsements of big-name northern Democrats, they were less troubled by his post–Voting Rights Act political influence. In 1966, a reporter wrote that Evers "has assumed political control over three Mississippi counties, and his influence is steadily increasing." Other reporters referred to Evers as a "political boss" and as "a combination benevolent society and big-city-styled boss." Newspapers regularly highlighted Evers's political influence and described southwest Mississippi as "Evers's fiefdom," and Evers's "political enclave." Scholars make a similar assessment, calling southwest Mississippi Evers's "political empire," his "power base," and his "enclave of counties." In an effort to explain Evers's overwhelming influence, an MFDP leader suggested in 1967, "The people are tired; they want a strongly disciplined political machine with one big leader like Charles Evers (Mississippi NAACP chief) that they can look up to and follow." Whether or not this analysis was accurate, many insist that Evers was consciously setting out to direct black voters through unscrupulous machine-styled politics. Ed King, for example, argued that Evers based his approach on "Chicago corrupt models." Emphasizing Evers's dominance, one reporter described southwest Mississippi as Evers's "satrapy," while another referred to Evers's "tammany-styled politics." In 1967, Evers told reporters that "we want the Negroes' vote in Mississippi to count," explaining, "That doesn't necessarily mean that we want them to vote for all Negro candidates, but we want their vote channelled."[30]

By successfully cultivating a quiescent voting bloc that would follow his guidance, Evers was able to make deals with Erle Johnston and other white leaders and throw his weight behind particular candidates, including white supremacists. An obvious example was his successful 1966 effort to direct black votes away from the MFDP's Clifton Whitley and toward white supremacist Prentiss Walker. Whites in Mississippi and around the country embraced Evers's control, especially since he was willing to support white candidates. One journalist called this strategy "ostensibly biracial." However, since Evers agreed to back white candidates even when they resisted offering "concessions to Negroes" and cooperated with white Democrats even though they refused to "reciprocate openly," he essentially traded personal influence and prestige for the fundamental interests of his constituents.[31]

After establishing his ability to channel black votes in southwest Mississippi, Evers used this base for several high-profile personal campaigns—for a congressional seat in 1968, mayor of Fayette in 1969, and governor in 1971. Although he lost all but the mayoral race, his strong showings bolstered his overall political standing. For example, in the 1968 congressional campaign, Evers carried five counties, including Claiborne, Jefferson, and Wilkinson, to lead the first primary. Although he lost in a runoff, his campaign was featured in national newspapers and magazines, with one reporter noting that he had "developed an important bloc of votes which he can, presumably, deliver." Roy Wilkins wrote Evers that his "excellent showing" in the congressional campaign "enhanced your personal prestige, and reflected great credit upon" the NAACP. According to political scientist Leslie McLemore, the state's white moderates, who had worked with Evers and Aaron Henry to supplant the MFDP and the COFO-affiliated Head Start group, initially feared that if Evers "were beaten badly" he would lose "his influence with the white power structure" and "be destroyed politically." Instead, Evers proved that he could turn out the black vote. McLemore notes, "Five months later, with a large bloc of Black voters in view, suddenly they were willing not only to be identified publicly with Blacks but also to make real political concessions."[32]

Evers used that influence to secure a prominent place in the uneasy coalition that made up the 1968 Loyalists Democrats. The participants, which included white moderates, members of the NAACP, and the remnants of the MFDP, had little in common except their shared desire to unseat the white supremacist Mississippi Regulars. Evers's selection as national committeeman for the Loyalist Democrats provides a vivid example of his pursuit of power and his dominant style. The MFDP and NAACP partisans had worked out a preconvention agreement that included the selection of Robert Clark, an MFDP member and the first

African American elected to the Mississippi legislature since Reconstruction, as national committeeman. Evers defied this arrangement, and his supporters nominated him from the convention floor, triggering a celebratory eruption complete with confetti and a rock-and-roll band. An MFDP activist reported that when he tried to speak, a man "asked if I was for Charles Evers. I said no, and the mike was cut off. I tried to speak and was pulled from the stage and my jacket was ripped." Writing that "pandemonium broke loose on the convention floor," McLemore observes that "to Evers supporters that scene was a glorious and heartwarming sight, while to Clark supporters it was a depressing and vulgar display and a reminder of machine politics—a reincarnation of the politics of the 'Regular' party." These contrasting views are evident in an Evers disciple's insistence that "it is a sin before God for any man to run against Charles Evers!" and Fannie Lou Hamer's description of Evers's selection as a "ramrodding."[33]

Evers thrived on being the center of attention. He wrote in his memoir that after he was elected mayor in Fayette, he "loved being 'the mayor' so much" that he even had his wife "calling me 'the mayor.' " Campaign worker Barbara Sullivan believed that Evers was running for governor primarily because "he enjoyed the limelight." She had joined the campaign because she believed his race was "simply an organizing tool to get people to turn out for local elections and make that really successful." However, Sullivan came to see what she called Evers's "egomania," arguing that "he was very much interested in the attention from outside celebrities who would come to participate in his campaign." Evers's campaign staff had actually been banking on his ability to draw outside attention and participation, believing it would be used to support local candidates and address local issues. Instead, they found it directed solely at Evers. As a result, Sullivan says she came to question Evers's entire motivation, wondering whether "his whole campaign wasn't really intended to detract from local efforts."[34]

Though Evers lost the governor's race, he remained mayor of Fayette from 1970 to 1981, when he alienated many blacks by supporting then-president Ronald Reagan. Many believe his 1978 Independent candidacy for the U.S. Senate opened the door for conservative Republican Thad Cochran to beat out his Democratic opponent. After losing several other races, Evers won the job of Jefferson County's chancery clerk in 1991. He served one term and then in November 1995 ran as a Republican in an unsuccessful bid for a legislative seat representing Claiborne and Jefferson counties. In a July 1995 column, Bill Minor, who covered the civil rights movement for years, commented, "One thing you can always say about LeGrande Charles—wherever the money is, that's where he is. Naturally he's found his home in the Grand Old Party."[35]

In recent years, Charles Evers has periodically tried to provide legitimacy for conservative white Republicans with segregationist backgrounds. It is particularly telling that almost thirty years after he took over as the NAACP field secretary in Mississippi, his authenticity as a voice for civil rights remains dependent on his martyred brother. For example, in December 2002, after Mississippi senator Trent Lott was forced to resign his post as Senate majority leader for publicly suggesting the country would have been better off if Strom Thurmond had won his 1948 bid for president on a segregationist platform, a *New York Times* article, identifying Evers as the "brother of slain civil rights leader Medgar Evers," noted that he was one of a few blacks who expressed support for Lott and attended a reception on his behalf.[36]

Almost a year earlier, in February 2002, when civil rights groups were lining up in opposition to Charles Pickering's nomination to the Fifth Circuit Court of Appeals, Evers published an editorial in support of Pickering in the *Wall Street Journal*. In the article and at a subsequent White House reception, Evers claimed, "It's not the NAACP down there (in Mississippi) that opposes Pickering. It's the Yankees up here." Actually, as NAACP National Board chair Julian Bond noted, "Evers got that one wrong." According to a summary in the *Black Commentator*, "the Mississippi State Conference of the NAACP, 31 Black state legislators, the Black lawyers' Magnolia Bar Association, Black Congressman Bennie Thompson, and just about every African American Mississippian outside of Evers' clucking little brood on the White House lawn" opposed Pickering. SNCC worker Bob Zellner responded to Evers's *Wall Street Journal* editorial: "Many of us who have worked with this Mr. Evers over the years have learned that he is no Medgar. Mr. Charles has always known which side of the bread the butter was on and he has done quite well, thank you." Zellner insisted, "You do the Liberation Struggle no favors, Mr. Charles, when you allow those who profited by postponing sisterhood and brotherhood to masquerade as friends." The Senate Judiciary Committee rejected Pickering's first nomination, but in January 2003, President George W. Bush renominated him, prompting renewed debate between Evers and black leaders in Mississippi. *Jackson Clarion-Ledger* reporter Jerry Mitchell wrote that state senator David Jordan of Greenwood, Mississippi, "questioned the commitment of Evers, a Republican, to civil rights issues: 'Charles is a good fruit gone bad as far as the civil rights movement.'" Evers responded, "Tell him to go straight to hell. One damn thing about it—my fruit will last, and his won't."[37]

CHAPTER Fifteen

A Legacy of Polarization

While the 1967 boycott settlement bolstered Evers's prominence, it essentially ended the Claiborne County mass movement. NAACP membership declined rapidly from its high of
over 1,300 in 1966 to 781 in 1967, 400 in 1968, and 139 in 1971.
Marches and demonstrations became rare events, and attendance at Tuesday night mass meetings dropped off dramatically.[1] The selective buying campaign continued, but most
blacks returned to shop with white merchants. Black leaders
and organizers focused on using electoral politics, legal action,
and federal programs to continue the struggle for economic
opportunity and a say in the community's political and civic
life. Moreover, African Americans' hopes that the boycott settlement would mark a new era of cooperation were quickly
dashed as whites persistently refused to engage in worthwhile
discussion or consider meaningful power sharing. They repeatedly took actions and made decisions that polarized the
white and black communities.

Despite continuing white resistance, the mass movement had
wrought changes that reverberated throughout the community.
Bilbo Smith's March 29, 1967, arrest (about two months after
the boycott settlement) and subsequent legal battles provides a
glimpse of the white community's continued ability to wield
power, but it also demonstrates blacks' resolute refusal to simply acquiesce to it. When Deputy Sheriff J. D. Price showed up
to arrest Smith for reckless driving, he was cooperative but
questioned the deputy closely about the charges and asked to
see an arrest warrant. Price admitted that he did not have the

warrant with him, explaining that Smith had been charged based on an affidavit by a white man, Sam Perkins, who claimed that Bilbo Smith "tried to run" him "down with an automobile." While Smith and the deputy were talking, a small group of blacks gathered, including civil rights and union activists Elonzo Mc-Clorine and Johnny Moore; as Price urged Smith to get into the patrol car, McClorine and Moore advised Smith that he was right, the deputy needed a warrant to arrest him.[2]

While Smith and his companions discussed the need for a warrant, Price radioed Sheriff Dan McCay, who confirmed that there was an arrest warrant on file and instructed Smith to go with Price. Price then attempted to push Smith into the open back seat of the patrol car. At his trial several months later, Smith recalled his response: "I kind of shook loose, wiggled my shoulders and body, rather, away from him then. Then I told him to take his hands off of me. I was a man just like he was, he didn't have to push me or carry me in the car, I could get in. . . . I started walking slowly around the car and I told him . . . I was going, but he knowed that wasn't no way to do, to arrest a man without a warrant on those kind of charges." Smith walked around to the passenger seat in the front of the car and had one foot in before the deputy told him it was too late—he was charging Smith with resisting arrest. Smith walked a short distance away and sat talking with McClorine and Moore, while Price called Sheriff McCay, telling him that Smith was resisting arrest and that others were interfering. When McCay arrived, he and Price picked Smith up by his arms, put handcuffs on him, and walked him to the car. When Johnny Moore asked the sheriff if there "wasn't a better way to arrest a man," McCay answered by arresting him for interfering with an officer.[3]

Two weeks later in Justice of the Peace (JP) court, Smith was convicted and fined $50 and costs for resisting arrest. He appealed to the circuit court, where he had a jury trial, was again found guilty, and was sentenced to the stiffer penalty of sixty days in jail. In April 1968, however, the Mississippi Supreme Court overturned his conviction, affirming that Smith and his colleagues were right: the sheriff and deputy did need to show him a warrant. Since his arrest was not legitimate, he could not be charged with resisting. The case file closed a month later when Smith decided to plead guilty to reckless driving and pay a fine of $50 and costs rather than dispute the original charges, now over a year old.[4]

Although there was never any trial or testimony regarding Perkins's charges, it appears that he was inspired by Smith's very visible movement activism (as a Deacon, picketer, voter registration worker, and general volunteer) and was reacting primarily to an incident where Smith drove past him when he was standing in the road. Perkins's accusation probably also reflected whites' widespread frustration and sense of impotence as blacks increasingly refused to accord them the deference they were accustomed to. As whites lost their ability to control blacks through custom and intimidation, they relied more heavily on the legal system.[5] This is evident in the earlier movement-related arrests of Shields and other activists. There was a similar episode in June 1967, about three months after Smith's arrest, when white officials passed vagrancy and loitering laws in Port Gibson intended to stop blacks from picketing and congregating on the streets. (The Lawyers' Committee, representing a number of Deacons and other activists, successfully blocked these laws.)[6]

The lawmen involved in Smith's arrest displayed fears of declining authority. Price's testimony, that he told Smith to "cut out your foolishness and . . . behave yourself," suggests his initial presumption of paternalistic superiority. When Smith insisted on his rights, however, Price abandoned this stance in favor of a more aggressive, punitive one. Price perceived the group of men offering Smith advice as "interfering." Sheriff McCay made a similar determination when he arrested Johnny Moore for his question about the proper way to arrest "a man." Both men classified Bilbo Smith's questions, his refusal to allow the deputy to push him, and his insistence on walking "like a man" as "resisting arrest." During cross-examination in the circuit court trial, Smith's attorney Jonathan Shapiro questioned Deputy Price closely about how Smith's actions constituted resisting. Shapiro asked, "That certainly wasn't violence, was it? That wasn't force, or was it?" Price's response, that Smith "didn't sit down where he was supposed to," implies that Smith's failure to follow orders was in itself violent. Price's perception is particularly ironic, given that Bilbo Smith was approximately 5'5" tall, both law officers were over six feet, and McCay was 6'4" and 275 pounds. Moreover, during the trial, District Attorney T. J. Lawrence twice misspoke Bilbo Smith's name, calling him Bilbo Shields. Since Rudy Shields epitomized whites' worst fears about the changing racial order, Lawrence's slips of the tongue clearly demonstrate his assumption that Smith's actions were part of a larger challenge.[7]

While whites clung desperately to their slipping authority, African Americans were just as determined in asserting their dignity and their right to equal, respectful treatment. When Deputy Price tried to push Smith into the car, Smith shook the deputy's hands off and said, "I [am] a man." He, Elonzo McClorine, and Johnny Moore all insisted that the deputy make the arrest in a correct, courteous manner. Furthermore, when Smith was on trial, he, his lawyers, and his witnesses all carefully referred to blacks with courtesy titles, Mr. and Mrs., while the white witnesses, state lawyers, and judge involved in Smith's prosecution used first names or derogatory words like "boy" to address black witnesses and their white lawyers. When Lawrence addressed Smith as "Bilbo," Smith's lawyer objected, citing a legal precedent that required Lawrence to "address the witness as Mister and show proper respect." Judge Guider overruled him, telling Lawrence that "you can address a witness in the *normal* [emphasis added] way."[8]

In the short term, whites were very effective at making the legal system work for them. Smith's experience—being convicted in JP court and reconvicted in circuit court, where he was given a higher, punitive sentence before successfully appealing to the Mississippi Supreme Court—was somewhat typical. Moreover, even though Smith successfully appealed his resisting arrest conviction to the Mississippi Supreme Court, the experience left him pessimistic. When faced with a hearing on the original assault charges, he pled guilty and accepted a $50 fine even though he knew he was innocent and had witnesses to support him. He believed the plea was preferable to putting effort into another uncertain appeal.[9]

Smith's case illustrates the strength of white supremacy and how its hold on the legal system often made the costs of seeking an equitable application of the law so prohibitive that the laws were virtually worthless for blacks. Well into the 1960s, white Claiborne Countians largely stymied national laws and precedents. Over time, however, with access to civil rights lawyers and the support of an active movement, people like Bilbo Smith, Johnny Moore, and Elonzo Mc-Clorine had the knowledge, courage, and resources to fight capricious white authority. Though a just and race-neutral legal system was elusive, black activists were able to generate an impasse and limit whites' destructive power by standing up to local whites and accessing a higher authority.[10] Here, Claiborne County activists benefited from the southwide civil rights movement's earlier protests and legal battles. The presence of civil rights lawyers and the possibility of federal oversight helped combat some of the worst abuses and let white officials know that others were monitoring their actions. For example, in January 1967, when Sovereignty Commission investigator Leland Cole was using widespread arrests to try to break the Port Gibson boycott, he was concerned enough about the Lawyers' Committee to report that the "arrests are valid and we see that each case is built by enough witnesses to withstand the defense put up by civil rights lawyers from Jackson." Similarly, in a Mississippi Supreme Court decision on jury discrimination in Claiborne County, Justice Tom Brady, a well-known opponent of black equality, wrote, "This Court has repeatedly held that the discriminatory exclusion of Negroes from the venire [jury] is in violation of a defendant's rights under the Fourteenth Amendment. . . . We have heretofore stated that there is currently no escape from the inexorable rule which has been laid down by the United States Supreme Court in regard to the selection of juries. Wise public officials will take note and be governed accordingly."[11]

Even the presence of civil rights attorneys interrogating whites in authority represented a clear break with the past. For example, in March 1966, R. Jess Brown, one of the state's few black attorneys, questioned white elected officials about their procedures for selecting jurors. In addition to compelling them to account for their actions, his inquiry implied that they were answerable to African Americans and an authority outside Claiborne County. District Attorney T. J. Lawrence reacted angrily, repeatedly interrupting Brown and insisting there was no evidence of discrimination. He asserted that Brown's questions were themselves disruptive and that local officials had the right to "choose anyone they please[d]" to serve on juries. Judge Ben Guider responded similarly and, in one instance, characterized the Lawyers' Committee jury-discrimination case as an attack on Mississippi laws, the system for selecting jurors, and him "personally."[12] Although civil rights lawyers' sparring with white officials, Bilbo Smith's assertions of manhood, and blacks' insistence on using courtesy titles had little impact on the inner workings of the legal system, they did serve notice that blacks would publicly contest whites' authority and worldview. Together with movement lawyers and the threat of appeal, these assertions of dignity and equality before the law helped create the space and provide the protection that blacks needed to pursue justice and develop other sources of power. For example, black crowds at trials helped offset the intimidating presence of white lawmen and provided support for black defendants, witnesses, and jurors. Attorney Larry Aschenbrenner remembered that at first "black jurors were still intimidated to the point that they were afraid to vote their conscience until we really found out how to do it. We packed the courtroom and there were more blacks in the courtroom than whites and that gave those jurors more moral support."[13]

Bilbo Smith's legal battles took place as African Americans attempted to translate their new voting strength into political power during the 1967 statewide election, the first after significant numbers of blacks were registered voters. In Claiborne County, Nate Jones was charged with finding candidates for county offices. With fear of repercussions running high, he recalled that it was a difficult task. "Most black people would ask me, . . . 'If I run and lose, do you got a job to offer me?'" James Gray, a young candidate who had little chance of winning since he was competing in a majority white district, later explained that he ran because "everybody else was afraid to run." He was a single, self-employed homeowner and decided "somebody had to come out front somewhere down the line. Everybody scared, back behind the others. . . . Somebody had to start and break the ice somewhere. Everybody standing back waiting and waiting, we never go anywhere." Eventually, eight people agreed to run, including NAACP leaders Calvin Williams and Alexander Collins; Collins's wife, Geneva, a public schoolteacher; and businessman William Matt Ross, a World War II veteran and

early NAACP member who worked for the city doing street repair and maintenance. Most of the candidates were personally ambitious, somewhat independent of whites, and accustomed to a relatively high level of privilege and authority
within the black community. They campaigned in mass meetings and churches,
and the NAACP sponsored voter registration and get-out-the-vote drives. With
an approximately 3,000 to 1,600 edge in registered voters, blacks were optimistic,
and a few white candidates, including Sheriff Dan McCay, even sought support
from black voters.[14]

Few whites were willing to compete fairly, however, and instead they used
pervasive intimidation, fraud, and blacks' unfamiliarity with election procedures
to suppress black voting. Before the June 1966 primary, for example, Democratic
Executive Committeeman Bobby Gage assured federal examiners that there
would be no confusion over polling places since they had been in the same
location for years. He conveniently ignored the fact that in the past only whites
had voted, so only whites were familiar with the polling places. Moreover, most of
the polls were in "white territory," places like the courthouse, city hall, white-
owned stores, and the American Legion building (where whites held antimovement meetings). Across the state, whites abused rules and manipulated the votes
of illiterate voters. Few black voters knew the law, and black election officials and
poll watchers were initially limited in their ability to offer effective assistance.
Black officials and volunteers were vulnerable because of their inexperience and
limited access to power. As a result, they were often overwhelmed by whites, and
when they did try to intervene on behalf of black voters, they were almost always
overruled. In Claiborne County, whites threatened to foreclose on farms, kick
people off welfare, and close the Port Gibson box factory if black candidates
won.[15]

Despite these significant obstacles, many Claiborne County blacks remember
the first elections they voted in with excitement and pride. When the voting
booths closed after the August 1967 primary, they gathered outside the courthouse and then followed Matt Ross's son when he went inside, determined to
watch the vote count. Thelma Crowder explained, "We had gained courage. We
used to not be allowed around in that courthouse, but we were there in the
crowd. I wasn't afraid." They waited quietly at first and then began clapping and
cheering as it became clear that Ross and three other black candidates would be
victorious. Ross won his race for supervisor (earning him a seat on the county
governing board); Geneva Collins was elected chancery clerk in a countywide
race; Alexander Collins won a justice of the peace contest; and Leander Monroe
became coroner. Calvin Williams was the top vote-getter in the sheriff's race, but
he lacked the majority needed for victory and eventually lost to McCay in a

second primary runoff. Claiborne County blacks were more successful than most around the state in using their electoral majority to elect blacks to meaningful public offices. Although there were twenty-eight counties with black majorities, across the state only 22 of 127 black candidates won their races. In Claiborne County, Geneva Collins was one of only two blacks in the state elected to countywide office and Matt Ross was one of only four blacks in the state elected to the board of supervisors (the county policy-making body). Only Robert Clark, elected to the state legislature from a district that included two majority-black counties, claimed a more powerful office.[16]

Claiborne County African Americans continued to be relatively successful at electing black candidates. In November 1968, they were responsible for five of the seven new black elected officials in the state when four black men won district races for election commissioner and Horace Lightfoot became the first black member of the school board. But whites continued to find ways to minimize and counteract black electoral gains. After defeating the first black aldermanic candidates in December 1968, for example, white officials developed a plan to augment white voting strength in the town of Port Gibson by using federal funds earmarked for improving public services to annex scattered white households into the town limits. Black organizers argued that, by excluding several densely populated black subdivisions immediately adjacent to the town, the plan violated the Voting Rights Act's prohibitions on manipulating white voting strength. Black leaders also conducted a detailed survey that illustrated both the deficiencies in existing public services for blacks and how the city's annexation plan would extend the unequal distribution. White leaders flatly rejected African American efforts to participate in the annexation design, however, so the Lawyers' Committee filed suit to block the city's plan.[17]

During the litigation, black leaders submitted an alternative proposal that offers a glimpse of black concerns in 1968. It called for the equitable extension of existing municipal services to black neighborhoods (and listed places for additional street lights, fire hydrants, sidewalks, curbs, gutters, street widening and paving, and sewage services); the inclusion of several black neighborhoods in the annexation plan; an integrated urban-renewal authority; integration of the existing planning commission, with black representatives selected from an NAACP list; affirmative-action hiring by the police department until the force was half black; equal compensation for black firemen; and use of equal opportunity contractors for city work. On April 16, 1969, after months of legal maneuvering and attempts at negotiation, white officials simply withdrew their annexation plan. With little hope for outright victory in court, they chose to forfeit the much-needed federal funding (and with it the opportunity to upgrade the town's

services) rather than to accept and incorporate African Americans as full participants and citizens in the community. One of the Lawyers' Committee attorneys
described the result as "a bittersweet victory—we prevented the annexation but
the Town lost nearly a half a million dollars solely because of its stubbornness."[18]

The terrible costs of whites' self-defeating approach and persistent disregard
of African Americans became even clearer just a few days later on Friday, April
18th, 1969. Jesse Wolfe, a white police officer known for his brutality toward
blacks, shot and killed an unarmed black man, Roosevelt "Dusty" Jackson, while
black officer Henry "Rip" McKewon was holding him. Earlier in the day, Jackson
had argued with the two men when they had arrested one of his friends in the
juke joint where they were drinking, but he was home sleeping it off when the
officers came to arrest him. According to most accounts, Wolfe shot Jackson at
point-blank range on his front porch as Jackson was asking why he was being
arrested. And though the hospital was only five minutes away, Jackson lay in his
own blood for more than half an hour before an ambulance arrived.[19]

As word of the shooting spread, blacks began gathering at the hospital and
Jackson's home. Black leaders urged everyone to move to First Baptist Church,
where city officials promised to come provide information about Jackson's status.
Already angered that both the officers remained on the streets, armed and in
uniform, the crowd grew even more hostile and restless when the mayor and
police chief failed to show. No one in the crowd knew it, but Jackson had died in
the ambulance and Sheriff Dan McCay had called in Mississippi Highway Patrolmen who were waiting on the edge of town. When a white teenager shouted racist
insults at the crowd waiting outside First Baptist Church, a few young blacks
retaliated by throwing bricks and pushing a parked police car into the streets. At
this, the waiting patrolmen moved into town, ostensibly to restore order. Attacking with billy clubs and firing guns and tear gas, the patrolmen dispersed the
crowd, sweeping many people into the church. One of Jackson's friends remembered, "They didn't ask any questions. . . . As soon as they came in [they] just
started hitting and . . . it seemed as though . . . they didn't intend to stop. They
intended to teach us a lesson, so to speak." James Devoual recalled, "Tensions
were running really high" when the patrolmen "moved in and started establishing a perimeter around the church. Now I remember so distinctly because we, I,
had never seen a policeman in riot gear before. The shields, the face protectors,
so it was kind of an awesome sight . . . and it was just so many of them coming
down the street . . . the wave of the crowd just picked me up and put me in the
church. I never seen anything like it." Afraid to "get caught" in the church, he
planned to run right through and out a back window, "cause ain't no telling
what's gonna happen here and you just at the mercy of them." As he "started out

one of those side windows," he heard shots and saw "little old patches of glass" fall out the windows. "And that's when we got pinned in the church. So yes, we stayed in the church until Dan McCay let us out."[20]

It appears that at least one shot was fired from inside the church, hitting a patrolman in the leg. Lawmen contended that they fired in response to this, while many African Americans insist that the patrolmen opened fire first and the shot from within the church actually slowed down their attack. Whatever the impetus, the highway patrolmen shattered church windows with buckshot, filled the pews with pellets, and broke open the piano and organ. They shot one man and grazed another. They also beat several people, including Horace Lightfoot, the only black school board member. By the time they were done with him, "all his front teeth were missing, his right arm was broken, . . . his eyes were swollen and sealed shut," and he needed more than seventy stitches in his head. The highway patrol insisted that Lightfoot had been throwing rocks at them, but not even local whites believe this claim. After the shootings and beatings, the patrolmen searched everyone in the church, collected a handful of weapons, and took everyone's name, but they made no arrests and could never find a gun that matched the bullet in the patrolman's leg. One possibility is that one of the white auxiliary policemen, whose weapons were never checked, accidentally shot the patrolman.[21]

The police killing and subsequent violence highlighted the tremendous gap between whites and blacks. The mayor imposed a dusk-to-dawn curfew that was enforced exclusively against blacks, and white officials refused to fire the two officers. The day after the murder, Evers led a protest march and spoke to a mass meeting at First Baptist. Articulating the anger of the entire black community, he called for a renewed boycott of all white merchants, insisting, "The white merchants of this town are so wrapped up in the power structure here, since you love your Police Department so well, since you support them so well, we are going to let them buy your dirty clothes and your filthy, rotten groceries." According to George Walker, "The bitterness naturally took over then and that boycott shut down all over them." Another black protester explained, "People just decided this is it. . . . The whole community just kind of rallied around it. It didn't take a whole lot of organizing efforts this time. I mean, I think that was the final straw for everybody." A black woman asserted, "The magnitude of what had occurred was too great to let it die down then." Though blacks' collective outrage drove the boycott and made coercion unnecessary, Evers threatened to "break the damn necks" of anyone who violated the boycott.[22]

The Monday after Jackson was killed, several hundred African Americans marched to city hall, where Evers forcefully reiterated blacks' demand that the board of aldermen fire the policemen involved. According to one participant, Alderman Jimmy Allen responded by insisting "they run the town and that they wasn't going to turn them off." Though Jesse Wolfe was arrested and charged with manslaughter, he was immediately released on $5,000 bond, and in May 1969, a Grand Jury of thirteen whites and four blacks failed to indict him. Allen later recalled that Wolfe had a mean streak and "we'd a done much better if we hadn't never hired him." Yet in the aftermath of Jackson's death, he and the board remained defiant, refusing to consider blacks' request that they fire or discipline Wolfe, who remained on the force until he left Port Gibson for a different job.[23] A Lawyers' Committee attorney connected the murder of Jackson to the white community's unwillingness to fairly annex the town boundaries, writing, "Every plea for change presented to the white community by the black community has been rejected. Annexation. Murder. The future—Rivers of Blood—Years of Darkness."[24]

In fact, unwilling to compromise and desperate for relief from the boycott, white leaders became caught up in a larger effort to destroy the NAACP through their ties to the state leadership of the white Citizens' Council. In the process, they further antagonized the black community, ensuring lasting white-black polarization. On October 31, 1969, white merchants filed a lawsuit asking for immediate injunctive relief to end the boycott and for more than $3.5 million in losses and damages. In the litigation, *Claiborne Hardware, et al. v. NAACP, et al.*, the merchants named as defendants more than 100 Claiborne County residents, the NAACP, and the Head Start group Mississippi Action for Progress, asserting that, among other things, they used "threats, force, coercion, fraud, defamation, false representation and intimidation for the purpose of preventing people, customers and prospective customers, from trading with complainants."[25]

Inspired by earlier cases in which merchants won damages for civil rights–related boycotts, the Citizens' Council developed a strategy for using antiboycott litigation against the NAACP, and, according to Lawyers' Committee attorney Frank Parker, they "published a [sample] pleading in their magazine" to encourage people to file suits. Several Port Gibson whites later recalled that the Citizens' Council "offered to file this suit" and "engineered the thing," touting it as a "landmark case." One merchant remembered that the Citizens' Council and "some anonymous person" supplied "a great deal of money" to support the lawsuit.[26]

Port Gibson native and Citizens' Council attorney John Satterfield likely facilitated the alliance between the Council and Port Gibson's white merchants. In the months preceding the renewed boycott, he had represented Port Gibson in its unsuccessful attempt to annex white households. His law partner, Dan Shell, another Citizens' Council attorney, was one of the merchants' three lawyers. In Port Gibson, the bankers Bobby Gage and Richard Hastings, state legislator and merchant Bobby Vaughan, and Piggly Wiggly owner James Hudson orchestrated the lawsuit, arranging for the Citizens' Council funding and communicating with the attorneys. Waddy Abraham of the Jitney Jungle noted, "The bankers was the main men on our side" and the "major ones trying to break the boycott." Though a few whites were aware of the Citizen's Council's role, Abraham and most of the other merchants were not entirely clear about the lawsuit's backing or "who did the thing." Carolyn Dobbs, whose husband and in-laws were plaintiffs in the suit, later asserted, "It was never really explained to them what was going on. In fact, all they were ever told was that there was a benefactor that was promoting the suit."[27]

The bankers' behind-the-scenes work coordinating the case was consistent with their traditional leadership role in the community, and they undoubtedly set the tone for whites' overall response to the movement—including both the public face of moderation that limited extreme violence and the hardline refusal to compromise. The Gage family's influence is particularly apparent. In 1963 when rioting and widespread negative publicity accompanied James Meredith's desegregation of the University of Mississippi, Bobby Gage was among 200 businessmen who met to discuss "how to prevent further bloodshed in Mississippi." In an action that was notable enough to garner front-page coverage in the *Wall Street Journal*, they committed themselves publicly to work "for law and order and, in *effect*, for an end to defiance of the Federal courts, no matter how unpalatable any breaching of Mississippi's rigid segregation might be to them."[28]

When the Port Gibson movement began, R. D. Gage Jr. was on the first interracial committee discussing black grievances. Although Port Gibson Bank was never a boycott target and the only elective positions the Gages ever held were election commissioner and Democratic Party chair, R. D. Gage and then his son Bobby were involved in virtually all of the negotiating sessions with the NAACP. Bobby Gage dusted off his lawyering skills to defend whites accused of harassing blacks, and several black leaders remember the Gages as unyielding. Alexander Collins reported to a 1969 mass meeting that he overheard Gage saying that "a nigger will never work for him." In a 1966 effort to facilitate negotiations, Ken Dean, head of the MCHR, met with Gage and concluded that he "had no commitment whatsoever to the town as a community of people" that included blacks. Dean concluded that Gage saw blacks as an "undesirable element," "dirty people that he didn't want around." During his meeting with Dean, Gage avowed, "I don't like niggers coming in my bank. I don't have to have niggers' business and quite frankly, I don't want it. . . . I could take the money that's in my bank and deposit it somewhere and draw interest on it and I wouldn't have to have my life troubled with these niggers coming in here."[29] Though Gage was not alone in such intense hostility, as he pointed out to Dean, he was relatively invulnerable to black protest. Given that and his family's historic influence on the white community, his animosity was almost certainly a significant factor in shaping whites' antagonistic response to the movement.

A few examples from the late 1960s illustrate how deeply threatened and emotional whites felt as they fought to protect their privilege and segregated spaces. A white woman who was asked to train a "black girl" for a "white" job at the Allied Chemical plant, recalled, "I turned blood red and I think I stayed that way for several weeks. [It] just killed my soul to have to train her. I felt that she was not up to my standards and yet I was told that I had to train her and it . . . didn't sit well with me at all. I didn't eat well. I didn't sleep well for days. . . . I was so upset if anybody had said boo to me, I probably would have gone all to pieces." Whites were just as hostile when George Walker organized a group of young people to desegregate Port Gibson's churches. They were accepted at the Catholic church but rejected everywhere else. As they approached First Presbyterian Church, several men, including one with a gun, walked out to meet them. One of the participants recalled that the men told them, " 'You Niggers go on to your own church. There are two Gods, a black one and a white one.' [He said] for us to go to serve our God because we weren't coming into church there."[30]

White Claiborne Countians' response to school desegregation provides yet another example of how, despite appearing moderate on the surface, they persistently made decisions that ensured decades more of racial division. Like the equalization campaign of the late 1950s, school desegregation in Claiborne County came at the last minute and under threat of imminent federal intervention. Faced with losing federal funds (and the possibility of complete loss of control over the local schools), Claiborne County school officials initiated a freedom of choice (FOC) program in the Fall of 1966. Ostensibly intended to allow every student to attend the school of her/his choice, white officials throughout the South used it to minimize school desegregation and forestall more direct federal intervention.

Across the state, whites in some communities threatened and attacked black FOC students and their families, while others abandoned the public schools. In Claiborne County, however, there was no violence and, on the surface at least, school desegregation went smoothly as forty-nine African American students (including all six of Marjorie Brandon's children: Ken, twelfth grade; Vivian, eleventh; Carl, eighth; Maxine, sixth; Dennis, fifth; and John, second) began attending the formerly whites-only Port Gibson Elementary and High School

(PG). Despite this token desegregation, whites hardly embraced FOC. During the summer, a group of leading white citizens founded a segregationist private academy for grades one through eight and seventy-three students enrolled in this makeshift school rather than attend classes with a handful of black students. Many of the whites who stayed in the public schools harassed and isolated their new black classmates, who endured a miserable school year. Few teachers did anything to reach out to blacks, and white adults made sure that they were excluded from social events and extracurricular activities.[31]

Anecdotal and statistical evidence suggests, however, that the FOC years, from fall 1966 through spring 1970, were marked by gradual, almost imperceptible, adjustments and accommodations as the unrelenting isolation and harassment faced by the FOC pioneers slowly began to fade. In the fall of 1970, 169 African American students, 27 percent of the total student body, were enrolled in the formerly all-white schools. Two-thirds of them were returning for at least a second year, and twenty-five of them, more than half of the initial group, were beginning their fourth year. Even based solely on their familiarity with the school and their larger numbers, this final group of FOC students had an experience that was quite different from that of the first isolated group. Black students were more comfortable, faced less fear and harassment, had fewer academic setbacks, and had begun participating in some extracurricular activities.[32]

It would be a mistake, however, to describe the four-year period of FOC as an ongoing evolution toward effective school integration. There were distinct limits to interracial interactions and black participation in school activities. As far as whites were concerned, PG remained their school and Addison was the black school. The white superintendent and white-majority school board ran both school systems. Teaching staffs and bus routes remained completely segregated, and the vast majority of blacks still went to all-black schools. Increasing numbers of white students left the public schools for private academies, and those black and white students who did share a school remained largely separate, maintaining distinct communities within one building.[33]

Although whites later claimed that freedom of choice was working, when the U.S. Supreme Court ruled in October 1969 (just weeks before white merchants filed their lawsuit) that it was inadequate and that school districts must stop operating dual race-based school systems, most Claiborne County whites refused to give full-fledged integration a chance. Instead, they fled, virtually en masse, for private academies. Although a few black leaders and white school officials tried to plan for and facilitate an effective transition, the vast majority of whites were simply unwilling to send their children to majority black schools (where many of them would be taught by black teachers). The school board predicted that if all students returned to the public schools, there would be about 2,386 blacks and 449 whites, a ratio of about 80 to 20 percent. In whites' search for alternatives, they convinced Chamberlain Hunt Academy (CHA), an all-male, whites-only boarding school, to accept girls as day students. They also initiated a massive fund-raising drive that enabled them to eventually relocate Claiborne Education Foundation (which housed grades one through eight) from temporary housing about twenty miles from Port Gibson into permanent buildings next to CHA. When the schools opened in the fall of 1970, only 91 of the 2,504 students attending the public schools were white, less than 4 percent of the total and far fewer than the 449 projected by the school board. The others dropped out or transferred to private academies. Virtually all the white teachers and, many blacks believed, public school furniture, books, and supplies followed the students.[34]

After noting that "hindsight is always so much better," white teacher (and merchant M. M. McFatter's daughter) Carolyn Dobbs argued in a 1992, "You can look back and think [the] Claiborne County [public] schools and possibly Chamberlain Hunt would be better off today if we all had been able to work it out." She maintained that freedom of choice was "working beautifully and it would have worked. . . . That's something you can't recapture, just really prove, but . . . we were integrated in every way there at the school. The children were enjoying it. They were enjoying friendship. . . . That's the way it should have been and I wish it could have stayed like that." Other whites share her perception, but it is one that is clouded by white privilege. For example, a former teacher's aide who also concluded that freedom of choice was "working nicely" overstated the black/white student ratio, suggesting it was an even fifty/fifty when it was actually thirty/seventy. Her memory that the school system was beginning to integrate teaching staffs was also wrong.[35] In fact, whites who contend (well after the fact) that freedom of choice successfully achieved school integration disregard the difficult and marginalized experiences of most of the black students who participated. They also ignore the many more who remained in all-black schools. When it came to school desegregation, Claiborne County whites acted as they did in virtually every other area of public life, refusing to even consider substantive change or see blacks as full, engaged participants in community life. Though they were more amenable than whites in other parts of the state to accommodate token shifts in race relations, they were unwilling to relinquish the race-based hierarchy and traditions of dominance that had shaped the community since its founding. Consequently, whether in school choices, the annexation impasse, or the boycott-related litigation, whites persistently forfeited or squandered resources in a destructive, backward looking effort to preserve the status quo.

The vast gulf between the white and black communities grew even wider as the merchants' lawsuit wound its way through the legal system. The case took thirteen years and several trips to the U.S. Supreme Court to resolve, and the litigation itself bolstered the boycott that it was intended to stop. In the eight-month-long state court hearing, which began in late 1973, the merchants' lawyers were hostile to and aggressive with black defendants, insinuating, for example, that Thelma Crowder had a "mental" problem and asking NAACP board member Walter Griffin if he had ever had a "front lobotomy." (The judge overruled the defendants' lawyer's objection to the latter and let the question stand.) Despite such bullying, black defendants held their ground. One testified, "I haven't purchased anything since the suit was brought. I have refused to do so." Another asserted, "If the lawsuit is dropped, the boycott would end immediately."[36]

White merchants' collective testimony in *Claiborne Hardware, et al. v. NAACP, et al.* demonstrates how merchants interpreted constitutionally protected boycott activity as violent and criminal. When M&M grocery owner Murad Nasif was asked to give an example of how the defendants used violence to promote the boycott, he could not provide any specific details. Instead, he testified, "There were people who I called guards in front of my store. . . . I don't distinguish pickets and guards. I didn't see anyone stop anyone by force." Yet he still justified the lawsuit, insisting that "the defendants did something to me in that they quit buying from me." Similarly, Barbara Ellis testified, "I saw them stop any black customer who wanted to go into a white store. They would grab them and threaten them. If people went into a white store, they grabbed their purchases." When pressed, however, she backtracked. "I did not actually see any of the defendants stop customers and take goods away from them." Charles Dobbs testified that the actions of a picketer, who "stood in front of my store a day or two and advised them that the store was under boycott," were "illegal because of the tone of voice used and her attitude." A merchant who testified that two black teenagers stopped a customer from shopping in his store later acknowledged that the teenagers had simply asked the prospective customer to observe the boycott and "there was no argument or loud talking or violence." One merchant conceded, "We sued the NAACP and 148 black people just because they didn't trade with us."[37]

Despite scanty evidence, in August 1976, Chancellor George Haynes ruled that the boycott was an illegal conspiracy implemented through violence and ordered the NAACP, MAP, and 134 individual defendants to pay the owners of twelve businesses $1.25 million. He also imposed a permanent injunction against "the defendants and all persons confederating with them" that prohibited six separate types of boycott activity, including picketing, soliciting, and persuading. NAACP head Roy Wilkins issued a stinging response, asserting that racists had "substituted the black robes of a Mississippi judge for the white robes of the Klan

Thelma Crowder Wells (front left) singing on the courthouse steps, as she often did during the mass movement, at a 1982 celebration of the Supreme Court decision in *Claiborne Hardware, et al. v. NAACP, et al.,* affirming the right to use economic boycotts for political ends and overturning a 1.25 million dollar judgment against the NAACP and more than 100 African American defendants from Claiborne County. Photograph by Patricia Crosby, courtesy Patricia Crosby.

in their effort to thwart the NAACP drive to eliminate racial discrimination." He argued, "Unless this latest travesty of justice is reversed, opponents of change will have accomplished through black robes what violence, murder and intimidation were unable to accomplish." In fact, the ruling threatened to bankrupt the NAACP (and all of the local defendants), and even an appeal appeared beyond their resources.[38]

After desperate legal maneuvering and fund-raising, however, the NAACP was able to bring an appeal before the U.S. Supreme Court. Lloyd Cutler, who eventually worked for two U.S. presidents, presented the NAACP's oral argument, tracing the history of boycott protest back to the Revolutionary War and the Boston Tea Party. The American Civil Liberties Union, the National Organization for Women, the American Jewish Congress, and the AFL-CIO all filed friend of the court briefs on behalf of the NAACP and Claiborne County defendants. In July 1982, Justice John Paul Stevens, writing for an 8-0 majority (Thurgood Marshall did not take part because of his NAACP connections), found for the NAACP and its codefendants, reversing the lower court judgment and ordering the merchants to pay the defendants' legal fees. In the decision, Stevens wrote that the boycott had "elements of criminality and elements of majesty." He acknowledged the existence of some coercive enforcement and noted that merchants could sue individuals for any specific acts of violence they could tie directly to their losses, but he concluded that most boycott participants acted willingly. He wrote, "A court must be wary of a claim that the true color of a forest is better revealed by reptiles hidden in the weeds than by the foliage of countless free-standing trees."[39] The Court's decision, which established new precedent by explicitly protecting the right of individuals and groups to use peaceful economic boycotts to effect political change, is often pointed to as the last major unanimous Supreme Court victory for the civil rights movement.

While a few lawyers and leaders handled the *Claiborne Hardware* litigation, back in Port Gibson the black community continued to search for ways to achieve their vision of freedom and full citizenship. Despite the boycott's initial power, as anger over Jackson's death dissipated and it became increasingly difficult to imagine a resolution to the boycott, some blacks began to drift back to shopping with white merchants. Leesco Guster observed that the boycott "was very very strong for a long time, but you know you can hold anything on too long and it loses its effectiveness." James Devoual believed the boycott "just kind of dwindled out" because it "went on so long 'til people . . . got tired of adhering to it because of the hardships and everything that went along with it." Though some blacks grew tired of the inconvenience, others thought it wrong to target all merchants, including those who had hired black clerks. Some people also believed that boycotting was no longer an appropriate tactic and that blacks would be better served by focusing on politics. As a result, the April 1969 boycott ultimately generated more disagreement than the April 1966 one. With no official end, the boycott worked almost like a barometer for race relations, increasing in intensity whenever whites angered blacks or won favorable decisions in the *Claiborne Hardware* litigation. The boycott also took on an individual flavor as blacks resumed their long-standing prerogative to avoid shopping with unfriendly white merchants or those who refused to employ black clerks. In 1992, James Devoual asserted, "As far as an official end to the boycott, if it is, nobody told me, cause I'm still boycotting."[40]

CHAPTER Sixteen

Not Nearly What It Ought to Be

Throughout the late 1960s and beyond, the joint legacies of Evers and Shields and their contrasting leadership styles, what one person described as "Evers up on the podium, Shields down organizing," remained strong. In Evers's absence, a handful of prominent individuals replicated his authoritative and self-promoting leadership style, contributing to a culture of jealousy and competition. Thus, Evers's leadership model and the black community's continuing dependence on a handful of people for decision-making created opportunities for abuses and for accusations of greed and betrayal. These problems were exacerbated as the high hopes generated by the mass movement and the first black elected officials failed to translate into substantive changes in most people's lives. Many blacks began to believe that their leaders were, as one minister put it, in the movement "for what they could get out of it." Leaders' responsibility for bargaining with individual merchants after January 1967 exacerbated these problems and accelerated ac-cusations by providing more opportunities for a handful of men to conduct negotiations with little accountability.[1]

Alexander Collins and Calvin Williams, in particular, gener-ated considerable distrust. Both were outspoken men whose ambitions had been thwarted by white supremacy; they saw no conflict in using their movement status to consolidate their per-sonal well-being. In 1966, when the mass movement started, Alexander Collins was fifty-five years old and owner of the popular Fair Street barbershop. He was a light-skinned, finan-cially successful man, educated at Alcorn and married to a schoolteacher. One woman recalled that his family had owned land for years and that "if you was a Collins, you was considered, well, you had more." She added that he was "an independent man . . . and he carried himself like, 'When I walk in, I'm Alexander Collins and nobody else here is a Collins *but* me.'" Collins had a long history of activism; he joined the NAACP in its earliest years and successfully registered to vote in 1963, after making at least a dozen attempts.[2]

Thirty years after the movement ended, most people remembered Collins as an important movement founder but also as self-interested, arrogant, and unreliable. Some resented his vocal condemnations of those who continued to work for whites. Marguerite Thompson, who owned Thompson's Funeral Home, called him "a loud mouth" and offered his practice of arguing that blacks should quit working for whites and "depending on Mr. So and So" as an example. She noted that he could afford such sentiments since "he had his own private business." J. L. Sayles asserted, "You can't pay too much attention to him because he just talk in season, out of season. . . . He lie and tell the truth. You don't know when he lying or when he telling the truth." According to James Miller, "He would make these eloquent speeches about how black folks should do this, or this, or this, but then he would do something totally contradictory." Though few people are clear on the details, many objected to Collins's relationship with white merchant Gage Hynum, who paid him to solicit business and collect clothes for his dry cleaners. They considered those ties deceitful or inappropriate, assuming that Collins either violated the boycott or kept Hynum from being boycotted after Dusty Jackson's death in order to further his own financial interests. Based on a several-month stay in Port Gibson, historian Jack Chatfield wrote in 1969 that "Collins was thought to be money-hungry, opportunistic, and a potential subversive." He observed that his "relentless bluster, . . . his endless stream of parables taken from the Bible or his own past, and his loud, insistent voice rankled some of the younger men whose quiet, determined aggressiveness distinguished them from the old-school, pulpit style of Collins." Asked why Collins acted as he did, one woman speculated, "I reckon he figured he was just big enough to do it. That's all I could say." James Dorsey reflected, "From the first we thought he was too good to even think of anything like that. [He] turned away [from] the person that we thought him to be. . . . What he did, the risks that he took and everything. In the end, most of us was really saddened by what he did and the way he done it."[3]

Calvin Williams's abrasive manner also irritated many people, and by August 1966 he was embroiled in conflict for attempting to use the Deacons to consolidate his personal power. These problems paled against allegations that he sold the sheriff's race in the August 1967 runoff against McCay. This action was in sharp contrast to his public persona as one of the most uncompromising leaders—resisting negotiations and only reluctantly cooperating with white leaders. Reverend J. L. Sayles asserted, "He had me fooled one time. I thought he was serious in what he was talking about, but he wasn't." According to Dorsey, Williams told "certain key folk" to vote for McCay. "He was working both for and against himself. That was one of the biggest disappointments for us." Sayles recalled publicly denouncing Williams after the election: "See my name was Sayles and I said, 'Now I'm not for sale.' I said, 'You don't spell my name S-A-L-E-S.' I said, 'My name, you spell it S-A-Y-L-E-S.' . . . No I ain't for sale. You don't buy me."[4]

This type of allegation and disillusionment was commonplace by the late 1960s. Based on his study of Greenwood, Mississippi, Charles Payne argues that allegations of selling out and profiting from the movement were not uncommon and increased over time as participation expanded and became "relatively safe." At the same time, the reward structure changed so that joining the movement was "potentially worthwhile in terms of economic rewards, prestige, or political influence." Speculating that "outright dishonesty may have been less a problem than egotism," Payne concludes that "it is easy to see why some observers see the process as fundamentally a history of cooptation." He insists, however, that "it is also a history of demoralization. It simply became harder to know what to believe in or whom to trust."[5]

Collins and Williams were often at odds with each other, contributing to discord in the black community. According to Charles Bunton, "If Williams said one thing, Collins disagreed. If Collins said one thing, Williams disagreed. And it really busted up a lot of the people cause some of them was on Collins's side and some was on Williams's side. It really tore the peace." In the climate of suspicion, Bunton even wondered if their battles "might have been a bought in job, paid from the other side, to bust it up. Once you get people fussing, you can do what you want. You can take them." In addition, both men openly rejected Evers's authority after the January 1967 boycott settlement. According to George Walker, Collins "brought the idea that Charles Evers time was just about out in Claiborne County," saying things like, Evers "'wanted to come in and dictate what we supposed to been doing' and 'we got to live here' and 'that nigger he got to leave' and just back and forth." Then, Walker explained, "it fed on over to Calvin Williams." Reverend Sayles contended that ambition was at the heart of their conflict: "Yeah, it's a lot of them over there wanted the credit." Though indicative of the growing competitiveness among leaders, Collins's attack had little impact on Evers or his relationship with Claiborne County's black community. He had already begun to transfer his attention to Fayette, and he remained popular, easily outpolling every other candidate on the Claiborne County ballot during his races for congress and governor. Moreover, Evers was unchallenged when he assumed the mantle of authority after Dusty Jackson was killed. Alexander Collins told those present at a mass meeting, "We have asked Mr. Evers to come in here. For God's sake, do whatever he tells you."[6]

Not all leaders engaged in self-serving, competitive behavior, however. For example, James Dorsey shared Collins's and Williams's out-front, visible approach to leadership and participated in policy decisions and negotiating sessions with whites, but he was never a domineering leader. Moreover, no one ever questioned his sincerity or accused him of profiting from the movement. In fact, despite overwhelming support, he resigned from the NAACP presidency in 1967 to allow for "a new person at the helm." He explained later, "My function in the community, since I was a minister, was more or less from the ground level, helping folks." He chose not to run for elective office because he feared that if he did, he would lose "contact with the grassroots people." He was also unwilling to make the compromises he thought integral to politics. "I would have to call a spade a spade. I didn't believe in too much compromising, you know."[7]

Nate Jones offered a quieter type of leadership and was judicious in his use of public speaking. Very community-minded, he adopted two children, was active in church, volunteered in a range of civic activities, and was widely respected as a reliable, hardworking man. Though he was rarely in the spotlight, he was almost always in the forefront, joining the local NAACP branch as soon as he learned about it in the early 1950s, attending Bob Moses's voter registration workshops in the early 1960s, and then returning to the circuit clerk's office again and again until he passed the registration test in 1963. He was most unusual in his willingness to voice minority opinions. When Reverend Eugene Spencer tried to keep the NAACP from gaining a foothold, Jones was one of three people to publicly challenge him despite their friendship and his personal respect for Spencer.

He was also one of the only people who spoke at a mass meeting against implementing the boycott in April 1966. Jones recalled, "I wasn't so interested in just putting a boycott on. . . . I didn't know how come, but I knew it was going to be painful." His reluctance was not due to fear or a desire to be conciliatory with whites. By this time, he had already made a public stand with the NAACP, coauthored and signed the demand letter to merchants, participated in negotiations, gone to jail for marching at Alcorn, and been singled out by white leaders in their injunction against Alcorn protests. Trying to explain, he emphasized that he suspected that whites "wasn't going to give in" and that a long-lasting boycott would create difficulty for other blacks: "Where I probably could get by, I knew a lot of other people probably couldn't get by. I, my wife and I, made a speech that night when everybody [was] deciding." Jones's position was highly unusual in several ways. Most blacks who opposed the boycott did so from outside the

Community leader Nate Jones at a 1982 celebration of the *Claiborne Hardware, et al. v. NAACP, et al.,* Supreme Court victory. His sign reads, "We Won Our Rights in Port Gibson, MS. Join NAACP and Register to Vote." Photograph by Patricia Crosby, courtesy Patricia Crosby.

movement and did so as silently as possible. Moreover, as Jones explained, once "the majority say, 'put it on,' " he gave the boycott his full support.[8] The most significant aspect of Jones's position was the independent thinking that it indicates. At the time, few Claiborne County blacks, including NAACP leaders, developed and articulated perspectives that varied from Evers's.

Ironically, while many blacks grew disillusioned with leaders who were more successful at enhancing their personal status than envisioning or implementing policies that benefited the larger community, they seemed to embrace that leadership model, choosing authoritative leaders, accepting their command, and looking for them to almost single-handedly generate necessary changes. In the 1990s, James Miller reflected, "I'm speaking from hindsight now, but the concept was whether you're going to have one person speaking for the community or whether you're going to have diversified leadership. Now Evers did a lot of good, but I think the one bad thing that happened in the civil rights movement is . . . this concept of one man rules. That shit's still plaguing us today." Rims Barber, who worked for the Delta Ministry, explained that "there are certain expectations . . . of what we think our public officials ought to look like and do." He added, "I swear that every person black or white that runs for sheriff is male . . . and swaggers." There was, however, a competing strand among a few activists in Claiborne County, especially those who came out of the ranks of the Deacons and the high school students who worked most closely with Rudy Shields and were later influenced by the SNCC tradition (especially through their ties to the Emergency Land Fund and the Delta Ministry). As they gained confidence, skill, and access to organizers outside Evers's orbit, some began to question the authority of the community's more established leadership and to try other approaches to organizing and generating change. Ultimately, they were very effective at getting black voters to back those seeking political office, but they were largely unsuccessful at developing broad-based alternative leadership and decision-making.

The first challenge to the NAACP/Evers leadership approach came when Charles Bunton, who had worked with the MFDP in Mayersville before moving to Port Gibson, founded a Port Gibson FDP in late 1968. Asked how he organized the group, Charles Bunton said, "I got about six or seven women. You see that's where you had your workers, that's where the workers was, among the women." In fact, part of the FDP's appeal was its defiance of the local movement's gender, class, and age hierarchy. Bunton asserted in 1969 that he organized the group because "the grass roots people" felt "they didn't have a voice in the NAACP." Another participant emphasized that the organization served "the poor, uneducated people," and James Miller observed that the FDP "gave young people an avenue by which they could get involved in the political process." He explained, "Most of them were like the young kids who had came out of the NAACP movement. . . . They were looking for action. The NAACP was kind of dead. Wasn't no action happening." According to Bunton, the FDP was also a reaction against the rumors surrounding established black leaders: "Some of them NAACP members you couldn't trust. You see, you think you electing a black slate and they working for the white man over there." Ultimately, though, the FDP's challenge to the NAACP was minimal. The two organizations shared members and worked out an association that in some ways mirrored the earlier relationship between Shields and Evers. For example, the FDP initiated a door-to-door survey of black voters and took on most of the boycott picketing after Jackson's death. This was especially important since some NAACP leaders grew more cautious after merchants filed their lawsuit. The FDP was short-lived, however, and most of the members who remained active were reabsorbed into the NAACP structure.[9]

More important, the shooting of Dusty Jackson, the renewed boycott, and the 1970 mayoral race brought a number of 1966 high school activists back into the movement. Working with their mentor George Walker and former COFO activists affiliated with the Emergency Land Fund (ELF), they engaged in labor-intensive organizing around political and economic issues. One ELF staff member explained that because they believed Evers had "hampered the development of local leadership," they were "deliberately interested" in creating alternative leadership. Their first major effort came in 1970, when Jimmy Smith, a twenty-four-year-old Alcorn graduate who was enrolled in a Ph.D. program at the recently desegregated University of Mississippi, ran for mayor on a slate with three black aldermanic candidates. Their platform called for racial cooperation, job creation, medical care, housing, extension of city boundaries to include black subdivisions, recreation facilities, improved government services, police reform, and expanded use of federal programs. Though it was clearly aimed at the black community, which had been traditionally underserved in these areas, the platform was one of the first in which black candidates spelled out policy goals that moved beyond an uncomplicated racial appeal. With help from a handful of white Syracuse University volunteers, George Walker and James Miller, who dropped out of Alcorn for a semester to work full time on the campaign, spearheaded an aggressive voter registration drive that included door-to-door visits, transportation, and babysitters. They generated peer pressure by printing the names of unregistered blacks in a mimeographed newspaper, the *Black Times*. In just weeks, they cut the number of unregistered blacks to under seventy, and by the December election, black voters held a 650 to 485 majority within the town limits.[10]

Despite these efforts, whites resolutely held their ground using the now familiar tactics of intimidation, harassment, and procedural manipulation. The Draft Board called Smith and several other draft-age black activists to active duty. Blacks who were buying furniture on credit reported that whites told them "if this election goes the wrong way, . . . we're gonna have to come and take that furniture." Nancy Larraine Hoffman, a Syracuse volunteer, recalled how a white poll watcher tried to intimidate Violet Walls, a blind black voter. The poll watcher, who was a "very powerful individual in appearance and in personality," marked Walls's ballot, put "his huge hand around" her wrist, and tried to force her ballot into the ballot box. Hoffmann remembered "sitting there in terror and [watching as] this frail little blind woman somehow found the strength to *rip* her arm away from this man." Walls waved her ballot in the air and while all the observers could see that the poll watcher had selected the white mayoral candidate, she insisted, "I want a vote for Jimmy Smith. I told the man. I want to vote for Jimmy Smith. My ballot ain't marked the right way, somebody's done me wrong." In addition to this type of coercion, James Miller recalled that the all-white election commission, led by Bobby Gage, "did all kind of crazy stuff," using their control over the rules to aggressively disallow ballots. Miller explained, "If you voted on the ballot for Jimmy Smith and you voted for one of the aldermen, the ballot would be thrown out and that kind of crap. Or if you vote for two of the aldermen and didn't vote for the mayor, the ballot would be thrown out. Those kind of tactics."[11] None of the black candidates won, though Jimmy Smith came close, losing to the incumbent mayor by fifty-two votes.

The core of organizers who worked on Smith's campaign was more successful the following year when they helped Evan Doss Jr., whose father had organized box factory workers and played a visible role in the 1966 mass movement, win the countywide election for tax assessor. During his campaign, Doss promised to establish a "fair and equal tax for all county residents," and when he took office, the organizers initiated an effort to reassess and equalize the community's property tax system. In keeping with their pattern, whites reacted with fierce opposition. The outgoing tax assessor specifically warned Doss not to alter the existing assessments, and the board of supervisors (composed of Matt Ross and four white men) drastically cut Doss's operating budget to roughly half that of comparable counties. Doss, James Miller, and several other employees and volunteers discovered that there were no records of any previous assessment, no established method for determining property value, and no property list for each property owner as required by state law. In other words, people were "taxed at rates that had been arbitrarily established at some point in history and never altered. There were absolutely no documents on file to support any of the property values listed on the tax roll." Moreover, the rates were inconsistently applied, and in "most cases the lowest percentages were being applied to the properties of the county's wealthiest citizens." Doss and his associates determined that blacks were being inequitably taxed and estimated that the overall assessment was about two-thirds of the correct value.[12]

In what became a protracted battle, the county supervisors thwarted every attempt Doss made to implement tax reform. When appeals to the governor and State Tax Commission failed, Doss and his staff, with help from the Emergency Land Fund and the Delta Ministry, organized a countywide petition drive to force the board of supervisors to act. In August 1974, volunteers gathered over 1,800 signatures (enough to win most county elections) and petitioned the board of supervisors to either start a reassessment or put the issue before the voters. ELF worker Jesse Morris asserted, "Claiborne County seems to be offering us an example of what we might be able to do if we could get the leadership of the struggle back in the hands of community organizers." After several months of stalling, the supervisors called a special election for November 19, 1974. With overwhelming black voter turnout and support, the referendum succeeded, and Claiborne County blacks eventually forced a measure of tax reform that was later codified into law and applied statewide.[13]

Drawing on the 1970 Smith mayoral campaign and the tax reassessment referendum process, an organization called the People's Association of Claiborne County put together a slate of twenty-one black candidates for the 1975 county elections. Implementing a detailed and labor-intensive plan, they organized volunteers to begin visiting prospective voters months before the election with the goal of reaching each person five or six times. Visits included "going over the sample ballots" to be sure each voter knew the names of black candidates and how to mark the ballots. Volunteers were also supposed to review "campaign literature," answer questions, find out who needed assistance at the polls, and set up times to take individuals to vote. James Miller devised this strategy when his research found that the biggest stumbling block to electing black candidates was not, as organizers had once thought, blacks voting for whites but rather lack of black participation. With the voting age lowered to eighteen, activists also registered hundreds of Alcorn students.[14]

The strategy of mobilizing voters and electing blacks to countywide offices and policy-making positions was highly successful. In 1975, blacks won the offices of county superintendent and county attorney for the first time. Blacks were also elected chancery clerk, circuit clerk, tax assessor, and coroner, controlling every countywide office except sheriff, which Dan McCay held on to. Two of the most important victories came in races for the board of supervisors when black candidates defeated longtime white incumbents. They joined Matt Ross, who was elected to his third term, to create the first black majority on the county governing board. Overall, blacks now held twenty-three of the thirty-two elective offices in the county.

Though the coalition of grassroots activists and charismatic leaders was successful at mobilizing the community and electing candidates, virtually everyone was disappointed with the results of black political control. A Pattison activist spoke for many when he said, "Most of what we've got now is black elected officials and black elected officials are not doing what they supposed to do for our community." Ed Cole, a Jefferson County native who organized throughout the South, argued that after black candidates were elected, "they become selfish and they begin to do things that benefit just them." Even when "good people" were elected, he observed, they "started finding reasons why things couldn't be done rather than find reasons why things could be done." According to George Walker, in the first elections "black pride was all we had going for us" so "we were willing to put these people in office and just trust them to do the right things." In the 1990s, he asserted that blacks must do a better job of choosing candidates who have "the community at heart" and who will try "to make things better for those who elected them."[15]

Both Walker and James Miller believe that a significant part of the problem came from the gap between elected officials, organizers, and the larger black community. Miller explained that most candidates "had no earthly idea of how" the campaign "structure was put together. All they did was show up and make speeches and the crowd was there. We did all the leg work." In retrospect, he believes that this influenced "what you get at the end of the process." He also contended, "The people who had the education and had the expertise got more than the people did who fueled the movement and marched in the streets, you know. I think that was a disappointment. The trickle-down theory did not work." Jimmy Ellis made a similar point, insisting that the black leaders who benefited from the increased opportunities offered by the movement turned "their backs on poor people period, black and white. They only looking out for themselves."[16] In fact, around the state, most black elected officials were relatively elite, better educated, and more financially secure than their constituents and the earliest movement activists. A few were corrupt, and many more were eager to be part of the system that had locked them out for years.

Ultimately, though, it is too simplistic to blame black elected officials for failing to bring to life blacks' hopes for transforming society. A few examples from Claiborne County illustrate the hostile and difficult environment that black officeholders encountered. First, the Lawyers' Committee had to search the nation to find a company willing to provide the required bond for the inaugural group elected in 1967. They also had to defend Matt Ross when the Sovereignty Commission convinced his defeated opponent to file suit to keep him from taking office. In addition, for the next eight years Ross served with four white men and could do little to influence county policy. Geneva Collins spent her early days in office looking over her shoulder because she feared an attack. Over time she learned that her real problem was her predecessor's obstruction. She recalled, "Many things in the office was actually hid away and wasn't turned over to me correctly. Many times I would have to work and look through books and find my way . . . but sometimes I didn't know which way to turn for the correct information. It was bad." The county board made it extremely difficult for Evan Doss to carry out his job as tax assessor, much less implement reform. In 1975, defeated white candidates were still trying to block black victors. Although by then the public schools were virtually all black, when John Charles Noble was elected the state's first black superintendent of education, the white incumbent challenged Noble's credentials and he had to battle in court for more than a year before taking office.[17]

Julia Jones, who was elected circuit clerk in 1971, pointed to a different problem. African Americans had been so thoroughly excluded from politics and public life that many had little information about elective positions. She explained, "I didn't know anything about the circuit clerk's office. We didn't know anything about county government. We hadn't been exposed to it and we didn't know anything about it." Unlike whites, the first generations of black officeholders did not have the opportunity to work in government offices before they sought elective positions, and they very rarely learned about the jobs from relatives, friends, or their predecessors. In 1967, the departing chancery clerk refused to provide Geneva Collins any assistance. In 1971, Jones had a better experience with her predecessor, Pauline Easley. Although Jones did not want to "bother" Easley, she eventually approached her and found Easley "cordial" and willing to show her "some of the things." She also got help for several weeks from one of the few blacks with government experience, a woman who had worked in the chancery clerk's office for Geneva Collins. Jones commented, "They were just like Mars. I hadn't seen them before and I didn't know what to do with them. But I did look at them and that was a step forward. . . . I learned on the job, every step of the way." Delta Ministry's Rims Barber explained that blacks also had to be wary of following customary practices—like providing jobs, gravel, road grading work, and other favors for friends. He insisted that being "on the take" was practically in the "job description" for county supervisors and "we had to teach the new guys" not to continue that tradition.[18]

Even without such difficulties, the black electorate invested too much hope in the ability of a handful of individuals to generate change. Ed Cole explained, "We never went back and were honest with people and said, 'I know I stood here in this church a bunch of nights and said that the answer to the problem was to elect Matt Ross and I thought if you elected Matt Ross that would solve the problems,

Julia Jones, who was elected the state's first African American circuit clerk since Reconstruction, showing local Girl Scouts county record books that still retain their "white" and "colored" identifications from before she took office. Jones recalled that one of her biggest pleasures in becoming circuit clerk was making the office a welcoming place for blacks. Photograph by Patricia Crosby, courtesy Patricia Crosby.

but folks it's a whole lot more complicated than that.' " Believing that voting held the key to an equitable society and encouraged by unified protest and the quick achievements of the voter registration drives, many blacks thought substantial change was imminent. Moreover, in keeping with the Evers's model, they put their faith in a savior, first Evers and later black officeholders. However, there were no quick fixes and few effective strategies for addressing the stubborn legacies of white supremacy, especially persistent economic inequities and whites' continuing disproportionate access to wealth, jobs, resources, and power. As Ed Cole asserted, "Things still ain't better. They are better in degrees but they still are not nearly what they ought to be."[19]

The movement did provide a few opportunities, opening up some jobs and giving black businesses a temporary boost. The MAP Head Start program, which was part of Lyndon Johnson's War on Poverty and closely tied to the movement, provided education, food, and medical services to poor children.

Head Start also provided employment opportunities that enabled a few people, like Marjorie Brandon and Thelma Crowder, to continue their community activism through work with young children. NAACP leaders tried to tackle high unemployment rates among blacks and the persistent job discrimination that kept blacks locked in unskilled, low-paying jobs. Their experience with the Allied Chemical Plant in 1968 was typical. Whites held all the supervisory, better-paying, more highly skilled, and easier jobs. They dominated the preferable shifts and were more likely to work in air conditioning. When the company refused the NAACP's request to implement changes, blacks filed a complaint with the Equal Employment Opportunity Commission (EEOC). Because the EEOC was underfunded and overburdened with a huge backlog, the Claiborne County complainants eventually dropped their formal charges in exchange for minor reforms. Plant management agreed to keep a chronological list of job applicants, hire several blacks who had earlier been denied jobs, end discriminatory preemployment testing, and hire a ratio of 50 to 60 percent African Americans.[20]

One of the movement's most hopeful economic undertakings was Our Mart, a cooperative grocery store that opened in March 1967 (shortly after Evers's January settlement of the Port Gibson boycott). An early board member explained that blacks wanted a place "they could come and be treated well." Eventually more than 100 people bought the $25 shares sold at mass meetings. Nate Jones, who was the first treasurer and longtime manager, recalled, "We got started on $300. That's all we had to get started on. That's the little petty cash we had to buy the bread and stuff. Got started and that Saturday, the people came in to buy and they bought all them groceries. That's the way we got started, on a shoe string, nothing." Our Mart prospered for the next decade (buying two buildings and moving onto Main Street in 1972) before it began to decline in the 1980s (in part because of personality conflicts and increasing black political divisions) and closed in 2000.[21]

Even with these piecemeal gains, blacks' economic opportunities remained grim. As they had throughout the community's history, blacks continued to have significantly lower income and higher unemployment rates than whites. In 1968, the box factory closed, and, by 1970, the county's traditional jobs in farming and the timber industry had all but disappeared. In 1979, black per capita income of $9,570 was still less than half white per capita income of $22,146. By 1989, there were only 590 manufacturing jobs and 13.6 percent of the county's labor force was out of work. The vast majority of the unemployed, 93 percent, were black. The reality was even worse because these numbers did not include people who had given up looking for work.[22]

Grand Gulf Nuclear Power Plant, which began operation in July 1985, was promoted as the answer to this dire economic situation, promising jobs and tax revenue. Many had high hopes that it would significantly improve the community's quality of life. Grand Gulf did pay millions of dollars in taxes, but that did little to change the economic conditions and daily lives of most of the community's black residents. It is particularly telling that when Grand Gulf began paying taxes (even before the plant was operational), the county board of supervisors, even with a black majority, kept the tax revenue in non-interest-bearing accounts in Port Gibson's two white-owned banks. As a result, the banks were the big winners, reaping considerable profit and tripling in value by 1981. In 1986, after the plant began operation, the state legislature took the unusual step of mandating that the power plant's tax revenue be shared with the state and forty-four counties, and Claiborne County's portion declined significantly. Years later, Nate Jones lamented, "We were really struggling to go forward. Now it looks like to me, we have become satisfied with nothing. We had a chance there, but it's gone. That chance is gone. I was talking about the money we had here, what we could have done with, especially the schools. The education for children. And we done so little."[23]

What It Is This Freedom?

The Claiborne County civil rights movement is largely invisible in popular culture and histories. When it does show up, the focus is almost universally on Charles Evers, the boycott and the *Claiborne Hardware* Supreme Court decision, and the community's rapid political transformation and high percentage of black elected officials, all of which are typically portrayed as straightforward indications of African American progress and the success of the movement (locally and nationally). If we look closely at the Claiborne County movement, however, there are several significant problems with this emphasis and interpretation. First, while Charles Evers was quite effective at inspiring people to act, he also had many shortcomings as a leader and his legacy is, at best, ambiguous. Furthermore, the legal and political successes did not automatically translate into widespread substantive change, and focusing exclusively on these changes actually conceals the recurring and unyielding barriers that blacks contended with during the movement and still face today. Finally, this top-down perspective obscures some of the most important and far-reaching implications of the movement, especially its meaning to local people.

For example, while Charles Evers's leadership was clearly important to African Americans in Claiborne and other southwest Mississippi counties, it is highly problematic to simply cast him as a heroic leader, a Moses leading his people to the promised land of voting rights and political power. He *was* courageous and charismatic, with a compelling ability to motivate black Mississippians. He was also self-serving and relied on being a power broker instead of building the strength of the larger black community. Beyond this, it is crucial to understand how his ties to Claiborne County bolstered his personal power and made him an appealing ally for powerful forces around the country.

In retrospect, it is apparent that Evers was quite good at capitalizing on opportunities. After several years of ineffectual leadership, he used the newly passed 1965 Voting Rights Act as an opening wedge to generate massive voter registration drives that transformed the political landscape of several black-majority counties in southwest Mississippi. In the process, he became a magnet for new NAACP members, producing considerable excitement and spurring action among local blacks. Evers's association with these high-profile, seemingly strong, local movements realizing tangible successes came when the national NAACP was desperate to regain prominence and a toehold in Mississippi. At the same time, white segregationists were searching for new ways to maintain the status quo and the national movement was in transition, with increasing strains between white liberals and SNCC, which had dominated the Mississippi movement through late 1964. As a result, Evers's role in and association with county-level movements, particularly the one in Claiborne County, positioned him as a key player, locally, in Mississippi, and around the nation. To many, especially movement supporters outside the state, Evers and these local movements, particularly the electoral potential of newly enfranchised black communities, appeared to be a triumphant story that epitomized the promise of the civil rights movement and represented the final step in securing full citizenship for African Americans.

Yet this was only part of the story. At the same time, Evers's authoritarian and undemocratic style hampered local leadership, and his personal goals and ambitions quickly undermined his ability to effectively speak and work for the widespread, long-term empowerment of most of the blacks who filled the ranks of the movements he led. Because he could prosper economically and politically without significantly altering the existing status quo, he saw no need to mount a substantive challenge to that status quo, even though it effectively locked out the majority of blacks. Thus, while Evers was extremely important to many local people, he ultimately used local movements as a platform for consolidating his personal power and influence. In many respects, his success was dependent on keeping others from having the same access.

Evers was able to use these local movements to enhance his power largely because, at some level, his vision and use of power appealed to the national NAACP, prominent liberals, and segregationists. This may be one of the most important things we can learn from studying Evers's relationships with local movements: while part of this history is Evers's betrayal of the people who saw him as a savior, answered his call to act, and, in the process, secured his power, it is also the story of the self-serving actions and shared interests of people who, on the surface, appear incompatible. The NAACP, segregationists, and liberals all embraced Evers because they believed he would bolster their power. The national NAACP became so caught up in organizational survival and prominence that it ignored the connections between Evers and boycott coercion and profit. Moreover, the NAACP's rivalry with SNCC and the MFDP led it (like Evers) to try to destroy civil rights competition through collaborating with the Mississippi Sovereignty Commission. Perhaps even more important, for white liberals threatened by the radical vision of SNCC and the MFDP, Evers was a safe, appealing alternative and they embraced him, despite his questionable tactics and (perhaps even because of) his unwillingness to work for a sustained, broad-based, democratic movement. At the same time, Mississippi segregationists were fairly quick to appreciate that Evers would accept personal power in place of a long-term struggle to remake Mississippi from the bottom up. In the end, it appears that a number of people and groups with divergent priorities embraced the view expressed by a reporter covering Evers's 1968 congressional campaign, that "[Evers might be] Mississippi's 'greatest hope,' and his example a paradigm for the rest of the country."[1] This assessment was almost certainly true for those already in power, but Evers failed those who remained locked out of the system, especially those African Americans throughout rural Mississippi who he used as bargaining chips after they established his legitimacy.

Evaluating the impact of legal and political changes also requires examining the intersection of the national landscape, including milestones like Supreme Court decisions and the passage of new legislation, and local action. In Claiborne County, most substantive change came through the interaction between formal structural shifts and informal challenges. The local movement was necessary because new national laws and legal precedents were inadequate by themselves in changing racial power relations. This is evident in Claiborne County whites' persistence and effectiveness in evading court decisions and legislative changes like the *Brown* decision, the 1964 Civil Rights Act, and prohibitions against jury discrimination. Determined black assertiveness and insistence were the keys to forcing southern whites' slow, reluctant acquiescence to the nation's laws and to triggering what was, at its best, intermittent federal enforcement of those laws. It is especially critical to understand the role of the federal government with some accuracy because many people unquestioningly accept the egregiously inaccurate premise of the popular movie *Mississippi Burning*: that an activist federal government was in the forefront of generating change. In fact, the opposite is closer to the truth. Moreover, as Charles Payne suggests, "legislation serves our need to render history understandable by giving us convenient benchmarks, and we may therefore be tempted to exaggerate its significance." He contends that instead of being a "watershed," the 1964 Civil Rights Act "may have been less important than the willingness of people . . . to insist that it be enforced." He argues that that insistence "is the crucial break with the past, not the legislation itself."[2]

We see the importance of local action in Claiborne County as well. In March 1966, for example, almost two years after the Civil Rights Act had formally outlawed segregation in public accommodations and work places, black movement supporter Matthew Burks was arrested, fined, and fired from his Allied Chemical job for refusing to observe the plant's informal segregation of water fountains and restrooms. Although Burks failed to integrate Allied Chemical, his willingness to defy traditional customs (and face the consequences) marked a significant shift. He and other activists put whites on notice that blacks were not going to accept segregation. Throughout this challenge, the federal government was notably absent. It had not initiated enforcement of the 1964 Civil Rights Act and, when Burks acted, did not protect his right to desegregated facilities.[3]

Like Burks, African Americans in Claiborne County and around the nation did what they could to make new laws and legal precedents meaningful in their lives. They vigorously and repeatedly claimed the rights that were promised them and *demanded* that the government act. Community-level histories of the black freedom struggle make it abundantly obvious that our government must bear responsibility for ensuring equality and that federal involvement is crucial. Yet community studies also clearly demonstrate that laws alone will never be enough to secure full citizenship rights. Legal and political victories guaranteeing voting rights and outlawing segregation were essential to altering the racial status quo in Claiborne County and elsewhere, but these structural changes were typically propelled by more intangible challenges that were just as necessary. Ultimately the movement was effective *only because* blacks defied long-standing conventions (including white control of nominally public places) and insisted on courteous treatment and respect. Finding the courage to act despite decades of fear, black people adamantly rejected the tradition of uncontested white authority and privilege. If nothing else, their actions forced the formal systems of power to begin to incorporate the appearance of equitable treatment for African Americans.

It is also important to understand the extent and nature of white resistance and, in the case of Claiborne County, see beyond the veneer of what could be construed as moderation. Before the movement, Claiborne County whites insisted over and over that they had good race relations. And in fact, they did repeatedly reject the extreme reliance on violence that plagued much of the state.

At times they did, individually and collectively, respond with relative decency to the black community. For example, though they lagged far behind white schools in resources and funding, Claiborne County's black schools were better than most in the state. This was due in part to the leadership of white men like H. H. Crisler. Though he utterly failed to see blacks as equals, Crisler believed they were deserving of humane treatment. He expected (and insisted) that blacks accept white authority, but he also believed in a form of mutual obligation that required whites to consider and "take care of" blacks as part of the community.

Similarly, black leaders like George Walker believe Superintendent Charles Sullivan made a genuine effort to create a fully integrated school system in 1970 after the Supreme Court ruled that freedom of choice was no longer an acceptable approach to desegregation. In addition, most agree that when freedom of choice started, white principal Katy Headley was determined to minimize friction and prevent violence. That she was unable to actually deter the pervasive harassment or break down the isolation and loneliness black students faced does not negate the importance of what she did accomplish. Sheriff Dan McCay's stance deserves particular notice. His open and decisive action to discourage Klan organizing was just one of the reasons that the Klan did not flourish in Claiborne County, but it was an especially vital one. Despite his personal hostility to Rudy Shields and general opposition to the movement, McCay's willingness and ability to work effectively with the black community made a difference in the outcome of the Claiborne County movement. It is notable that McCay accepted and cooperated with the armed Deacons, even as they aggressively insisted on their right to self-defense. And because of their mutual respect, neither McCay nor the Deacons backed the other into a corner or pursued a reckless strategy of escalation and confrontation.

At times there is a tendency among historians and the general public to misinterpret such relatively positive white actions and give them too much weight. As important as they were, these individual actions are only part of the story, and focusing on them can be evasive, obscuring the insidious and persistent nature of white supremacy. Collectively, Claiborne County whites were, by Mississippi standards, somewhat moderate in their response to the movement. Yet they were determined and destructive in their resistance to any meaningful changes to the status quo. They categorically refused to see blacks as equal partners, to consider power sharing, to envision a shared future. Charles Payne argues that the "tradition, in which racists are pictured as stupid, vulgar, and one-dimensional, is one of the hoariest conventions of writing about civil rights and one of the most destructive[,] . . . giving racism the face of the ignorant, the pot-bellied, and the tobacco-chewing, an image with which almost no one can identify and which easily supplants more complex and realistic images of racism."[4]

One unfortunate side effect of the pervasive stereotype of white racists as bomb-throwing, redneck Klansmen is that it allows people to characterize or perceive any milder response as reasonable or moderate. There was, however, nothing moderate or reasonable in whites' refusal to allow blacks to register to vote, to use public facilities, to serve on juries, to access the law in an evenhanded manner, to compete for jobs on an equitable basis, to enjoy basic public services (like stop signs, curbs, and adequate sewage disposal), or to be addressed with courtesy, treated with dignity, and accorded basic human respect. It is fairly easy to criticize or dismiss Klan supporter James Jones, with his hateful rhetoric and expressed desire to kill blacks, as an irrational and highly unpleasant racist. In contrast, men like H. H. Crisler and his son E. T. Crisler Sr. appear kind and considerate, with a sense of fairness. Yet all of them believed it was their prerogative to set the timetable for black freedom and they saw every black demand or assertion of full citizenship as unreasonable. Even Dan McCay, who deserves considerable credit for extending respect to black activists and defusing potentially violent situations, still insisted in the 1990s that black demands during the movement were excessive. Ultimately, it is important to resist characterizing grudging concessions made under considerable pressure as forward-thinking, legitimate attempts at cooperation.

Looking at race in Claiborne County from the Jim Crow era to the twenty-first century makes it clear that white supremacy has a resilient, pernicious ability to adapt and survive. After fleeing the public schools and then losing control over most of the county's political offices, the white community abdicated any commitment to the community as a whole. Asked to assess the movement, Nate Jones explained, "At first it was a big change. Don't look like it's been [as] much change as we thought it would [be]." In the 1980s, he particularly emphasized the continuing divisions in religion and education.

> I certainly would like to see where we could work together and have a better relationship—feeling—toward one another, and better respect toward one another. . . . I would like to see it where we would be able to live together a little better, especially on the religious part. I certainly would like to see where we could go to their church just like they is free to come to ours. White is free to come to ours anytime, and welcome. I would like to see that more than ever. Course, I would like to see the children go to school together. I would like to see that too. . . . No, I don't see any hope of it in the near future.[5]

Together, the boycott, black voting strength, and blacks' insistence on decent treatment *did* fundamentally change racial power relations. Black teacher Annie

Jones explained, "See, your strength, your vote, and that dollar can turn things around." In 1960, just fifteen blacks were registered to vote. With the break-through 1975 election, twenty-three of Claiborne County's thirty-two elected officials were black. By 1982, when the Supreme Court ruled in the *Claiborne Hardware* case, most of the NAACP's original demands had gradually come into being. Black and white clerks commonly worked side by side, and white merchants were almost universally careful to be courteous to their black customers. In 1992, merchant Bill Lum, who catered primarily to whites and never hired a black clerk, reflected that at first "it seemed strange" to have black clerks, "but you accept it now. You get used to it. I mean, it's really no problem. It doesn't bother me." On the surface, at least, there have been other visible changes. Blacks and whites now speak cordially on the streets and mingle easily in the stores. At least one white-owned restaurant is integrated, and some whites work with black elected officials and civic leaders on community and political boards.[6]

Yet this surface peace does not alter the fact that there remain significant, lasting divisions. Even with important changes and the visibility of black elected officials, Claiborne County today clearly demonstrates the persistence of eco-nomic inequality, the limitations of achieving substantive change through the existing political system, and the enduring nature of racial polarization. In 1992, James Devoual explained that whites "hold on to those traditional values that you are second-class citizens, that white folk are right, that you're not equal, you're uneducatable, that I don't care what you say, we ain't going to school with you, we ain't going to hang out with you, and we ain't going to let you be a part of the decision-making process." Former Deacon and high school history teacher Julius Warner concurred: "I think the whites here began to just tolerate blacks. I don't think it's really integration here. . . . I don't really think it has changed a whole lot. The signs have come down and you can go where you want to, but if too many go there—." Warner's voice trails off in midsentence, but the implication is clear. There is very little meaningful interaction between blacks and whites and vir-tually no sense of a shared community. In fact, most whites have chosen to withdraw as much as possible from public life. Many continue to seek and find refuge in segregated facilities. The Port Gibson swimming pool, Lake Claiborne, and Moss Wood Country Club, all private facilities built with some public resources in the wake of the *Brown* decision, remain whites-only space in 2005. Moreover, whites have not returned to the public schools. More than fifty years after the *Brown* decision, the virtually all black public and all white private systems replicate the segregation of an earlier era.[7]

It is evident that simply noting court victories and defeats, chronicling legisla-tive change, and tallying the number of black officeholders severely distorts our understanding of the movement and obscures the nuances of its challenge to white supremacy. The successes and failures of the movement are much more complex. Moreover, many of the events and issues that captured national attention and have typically occupied historians do not embody the civil rights movement's relevance to participants and communities. For most African Americans, the movement's significance is closely tied to intangibles—how it wedged open the door to full citizenship, brought a measure of courteous, dignified treatment, and forever altered their sense of self and the framework for their interactions with whites. Bernice Johnson Reagon, an activist and historian, makes the point that those who have written about the Albany, Georgia, movement "add up stuff that was not central to what happened" and as a result she does not recognize the movement she participated in. She insists that the "transformation that took place inside of the people" was far more important than the events and debates that historians focus on. For her, the defining aspect of the movement was that it gave her "the power . . . to fight and struggle and not respect boundaries that put me down."[8]

Asked what the movement accomplished, a black Claiborne County teacher responded, "Now in most places they treat you better, like in stores. They treat you like you're human." James Devoual insisted that the "whole fight was about" realizing "basic human respect." Jimmy Ellis expressed some disappointment with the movement's results but asserted that it did open "some doors." Pointing out that now blacks can go into restaurants and be served, he emphasized, "It hadn't always been that way. It took a lot of blood, sweat, and tears to get this way." According to Julia Jones, the movement made a "definite difference because . . . the children aren't afraid anymore. They used to be afraid." Evan Doss Jr. noted that with the Claiborne County movement blacks became "more knowledgeable" and began to "feel as if they were somebody." This experience of transformation, of breaking barriers and shattering myths of white superiority, is visible in the experiences of the black students who pioneered in desegregating the public schools. Ken Brandon was an honor roll student at the formerly all white Port Gibson High, and he came to understand that his success was profoundly meaningful for other blacks. He explained that his father was quite skilled in math but had never had an opportunity to "demonstrate his abilities." Ken added, "You know, here he is, 'Yes sir.' 'No sir.' 'Yes ma'am.' 'No ma'am.' You know, on a daily basis he's kind of saying [to whites], you superior to me and then all of a sudden having his son compete with them, . . . he felt real good about that." A black woman at Ken's church had a similar reaction. When the honor roll was printed in the *Reveille*, she cut out and framed the announcement, telling him, "Son, we so proud of you." Brandon concluded, "It meant so much to older people who had been told all of their lives, 'You dumb. You can't compete.' "[9]

Blacks' use of self-defense to protect against white violence is one of the most important examples of how blacks' assertiveness influenced white actions and how the movement fundamentally changed the ways that blacks and whites interacted. Despite its continuing invisibility in both mainstream depictions and historiographical overviews of the civil rights movement, black self-defense was both essential and pervasive. All over the rural South, blacks, acting individually and in groups, accepted and relied on self-defense. When it was most successful, self-defense was an effective deterrent, making white vigilantes think hard about the consequences of their actions. At times, it also helped compel action from a reluctant federal government that appeared far more likely to intervene to prevent race war than to protect black citizens under attack for trying to realize their constitutional rights. African Americans in Claiborne County supplemented their use of basic, functional self-defense with psychological warfare, playing on and manipulating whites' fears of an armed rebellion by blacks. This tactic appears to have been successful and is almost certainly what prompted Dan McCay and other whites to intervene and attempt to de-escalate the growing tension as blacks refused to back down in the face of whites' threats. Interestingly, while lawmen from outside the area were extremely concerned about what they believed was the revolutionary threat posed by the homegrown Deacons, local whites were far more fixated on the Deacons' perceived role in enforcing the boycott.

The Port Gibson boycott itself played a particularly critical role in recasting the relationships between blacks and whites. It gave voice to blacks' insistence on dignified treatment and threatened whites' entrenched authority over public space and black behavior. It also asserted blacks' refusal to be excluded from community decision-making and provided blacks with a weapon for attacking a seemingly invulnerable white community. These changes in race relations, not the few white concessions in January 1967 and the Supreme Court victory in 1982 that most people emphasize, were at the heart of the boycott's importance. With the onset of the boycott in April 1966, white merchants suddenly experienced a new reality. Instead of being in a position to offer or withhold credit and other favors, they were soliciting black customers and had to be careful not to insult or anger them. Albert Butler insisted that even as Piggly Wiggly owner James Hudson grew increasingly angry about the boycott, he began treating his black employees more respectfully. Similarly, Jimmy Allen recalled that during the boycott whites began to do the shopping for their black maids. Though his emphasis was on blacks' desire to do business with white merchants and their fear of retaliation, the very idea of whites doing the shopping for black servants suggests a major reversal. When three black women ignored picketers and went into McFatter's Drugstore in April 1966 to fill a prescription, McFatter seated the women and brought them cold drinks. At the time, white shopkeepers were removing stools and closing their businesses rather than desegregate and permit blacks to sit down and eat. Moreover, it was unthinkable for a white man to serve black women. McFatter's atypical behavior was clearly intended to reward these women for breaking the boycott. Ironically, he and other merchants could have ended the boycott entirely by offering all blacks a small measure of such courteous, respectful treatment. By 1968, several white merchants were so concerned about cultivating black customers' goodwill that they had even purchased NAACP memberships.[10]

Blacks very deliberately used the boycott to punish whites individually and collectively. When blacks learned that Harvey Stampley, whose small store had been initially exempted from the boycott, was selling meat for the Piggly Wiggly, they immediately began to boycott him. After several weeks of record sales, he was left with large quantities of newly ordered groceries and few customers. When a Ford dealer refused to let a black customer use the restroom, picketers were boycotting his business within hours. In a similar incident, Meyer-Marx owner Pete Jordan, who had also been exempt from the boycott because he employed a black clerk, cursed a black customer. In response, the NAACP "executive committee and Mr. Evers decided they would close that [store] down." This provided M. M. McFatter with his opportunity to get out from under the boycott by hiring Faye Davis. Sovereignty Commission files note that in another instance boycott negotiations were derailed in December 1966 because white officials failed to publicize the mayoral election until after it was too late for black candidates to qualify. In 1968, Claiborne County blacks expressed their outrage over the assassination of Martin Luther King by participating in a statewide week-long boycott of white-owned businesses.[11]

Because whites persistently ignored African American concerns and excluded blacks from policy decisions, the boycott became one of the few ways blacks could register their collective viewpoint. It is hardly surprising, then, that they responded to Dusty Jackson's murder with the renewed boycott. More than anything else, it was an expression of black anger. At a mass meeting the Monday after the shooting, Evers told the crowd, "There comes a time when you really don't know what to do, but you know you got to do something. . . . We've been pushed to the hilt and there ain't nowhere to go." In this context, there was no room for negotiation: the shooting, white officials' refusal to discipline the officers, and blacks' use of the boycott to articulate anger and punish whites illustrated and reinforced the vast gulf between the community's whites and blacks. When one merchant appealed to Evers for relief from the boycott by explaining that he had "complied with all the requests" and had several black employees, Evers rejoined, "'You white, ain't you?' [and] turned around and walked off." The merchant later went out of business. In 1969, observer Jack Chatfield wrote, "The boycott has gone beyond being simply an instrument in the social struggle." He argued, "The boycott itself—not its strategic aim—is the symbol of the new departure." Locked out of city government and spurned by white leaders, blacks could do little to productively influence policy or decision-making. Instead, they used the boycott to articulate their outrage and punish white merchants—because they were the most vulnerable representatives of the white community.[12]

The boycott did not end the continuing disparity in resources and power, and whites' unrelenting defiance did much to slam the door on any possibility for serious cooperative efforts to create a humane, inclusive, integrated community, something that haunts the area today. Yet, even though whites were slow to respect blacks, acknowledge the legitimacy of their grievances, or consider meaningful power sharing, ultimately they had to recognize that blacks now wielded a source of power that could hurt them. In the 1990s, pharmacist Q. H. McDaniel explained that he had participated in the *Claiborne Hardware* lawsuit because the attorneys "led us to believe that they would be able to" stop the boycott and "I wanted the boycotting stopped." In retrospect, however, McDaniel realized, "They *couldn't* do it. There was no way in the *world* they could do it, [to] *make* people do things." This was an important lesson for whites to learn, that they could not control African Americans, and it was undoubtedly one of the key changes brought by the movement. James Dorsey recalled that when the boycott first began, whites thought Evers would leave and "things would be back to normal." They were mistaken, however, and, as Dorsey explained, "things were never the same . . . after that."[13]

In many ways, the movement was a struggle over power. When it was over, blacks had gained some measure of political power, whites had essentially retained economic power, and, on a personal level, blacks and whites had negotiated new ways of interacting. But at its best, the movement was about far more, and this, too, gets buried if we look at the movement in terms of big events or judge it primarily in terms of legal and political questions. When assessing the movement's accomplishments or limitations, it is important not to overlook the commitment and vision of people who worked broadly for "freedom" and who understood that freedom meant far more than being able to vote or hold political office.

The life's work of Nate Jones represents much of what is obscured and vital about the movement. Throughout his life, Jones has demonstrated a commitment

Nate and Julia Jones, aged ninety and eighty-five, respectively, still engaged in community service in 2004. Photograph by Roland L. Freeman, courtesy Roland L. Freeman.

to something beyond himself. For him (and others), joining the movement was part of a larger responsibility to community—defined fundamentally by the needs of African Americans, but always with an eye toward a broader, more inclusive group, including blacks and whites on the basis of genuine equality. Jones explained that while serving in the segregated navy in World War II, he experienced "a little taste of freedom."[14] He spent the rest of his life trying to fully realize and expand on that freedom—for himself and for others. For him, that meant taking risks to join the NAACP and recruit others to the organization. It also meant that, despite a lifetime of friendly relations with whites, when there was a chance for a mass movement, he was willing to stand publicly and insist on African American equality, whatever the costs. At the same time, Jones never reduced the movement to a conflict between blacks and whites and he never adopted the hostile, destructive demeanor of some white racists. Throughout his movement work, Jones believed that ends and means both were important and he was known as much for the tedious work on voter registration as for his public position on the NAACP Executive Committee. Because he was not inspired by personal ambition, Jones never sought to enhance his own status. Instead, he was willing to make unpopular stands (even when that meant upsetting powerful whites or old friends) and passed up opportunities to pursue political power. Thus, while some blacks used the movement as a stepping stone to elected office and many whites fought day after day to retain as much power as they could, Jones followed up the mass movement with the same kind of commitment to community that drew him into it in the first place.

In May 2001, when people gathered to honor Jones, the event was framed around his movement leadership, yet it quickly became clear that, while his movement work might have been the most dramatic, or notable for historians, his impact on the community went far deeper and continued long after the NAACP declined and the *Claiborne Hardware* case was settled by the Supreme Court. The celebration itself was organized when Jones was unable to save Our Mart (the cooperative grocery store founded during the movement) from bankruptcy, despite making the heroic effort of coming back from retirement twice (to work long hours for no pay). And yet perhaps the real tribute to Jones's broad sense of community was that in story after story, those present kept returning to his role as a school bus driver. Years after they graduated from high school, men and women talked about the impact that he had on them—how he treated them respectfully and took time to talk to them about history, living up to their potential, and being thoughtful and concerned about others. Over ninety, Jones still farms the land he and his wife, Julia, bought after World War II and remains active in his church, working to sustain the Baptist Aid Society that provides low-cost, nonprofit burial insurance. And Jones still has an impact on young people, taking the time to speak to high school and college groups about the movement whenever he's asked. I recently met a student from Syracuse, New York, who said that hearing Mr. Nate and touring his farm was one of the best things he had ever done.[15]

The movement was fueled by people like Nate Jones, who, in the words of NAACP president James Dorsey, "fought for those things that are right, those things that are good and those things that are just."[16] Through the movement, people who had an expansive sense of community pushed hard to create opportunities and extend the boundaries of that community. They took risks and did work that was explicitly political. When they had to, they took up guns to protect themselves and their families. They also nurtured people and did the often overlooked work of sustaining the fabric of community. At its best, the movement gave people a framework and the tools they could use to expand the possibilities for building community—by standing up to oppression, fighting for freedom, and pursuing a broad-based vision of a just, humane, and inclusive world. In the process, they built on the work of those who came before and provided a foundation for those who follow.

Looking the Devil in the Eye
Who Gets to Tell the Story?

Most of the community's history holds different meaning for blacks and whites, and movement history in particular remains a highly charged topic. The divergent memories of the events surrounding Dusty Jackson's death provide just one small example of the vast differences in how African Americans and whites perceive the past. Jackson's killing and the subsequent events—the highway patrol shooting into First Baptist Church and the beating of Horace Lightfoot—were cataclysmic and unforgettable events for virtually all blacks, whether they experienced them firsthand or through the accounts of family, friends, and neighbors. As one woman said, "I didn't understand how anybody could attack a church. I thought we were safe at the church. I thought that was the one place we were safe, in our own church." In contrast, most whites have little or no memory of these events and those few who do remember them generally think of them collectively as a "riot." One white merchant, who had only a hazy recollection of the incidents, was under the erroneous impression that a black man assaulted a highway patrolman and knocked his teeth out. He concluded, "The black people had a way of creating an incident. You see, and used that. They did that everywhere. They started it really and forced the law people to do something." Similarly, Dan McCay described Dusty Jackson as a "known outlaw," and whites assumed the highway patrol presence was necessary to keep a rowdy, lawless crowd of African Americans from burning, looting, and attacking. In contrast, most blacks insist that Jackson's biggest crime was excessive drinking.

Moreover, Charles Evers berated Dan McCay and the mayor for having such poor relationships with the black community that they turned to the highway patrol rather than deal with the problem themselves. NAACP president James Dorsey also blamed McCay for abdicating his responsibility by calling in the patrolmen, given the likelihood that they would act violently.[1]

There are similar differences in how people remember the beating of Horace Lightfoot. Jimmy Allen's response is typical of whites. He characterized Lightfoot as "the wrong man" and acknowledged that he was both unjustly and viciously attacked. He said, "They grabbed Horace and they almost killed him. They beat him with butts of guns and everything. They bashed his head all in. He had some terrible scars on his head up until he died." Allen then quickly dismissed the beating as an unfortunate incident and denied that it had any connection to Lightfoot's untimely death several years later. Most African Americans, on the other hand, believe that Lightfoot never fully recovered and that the beating was a "contributing factor to his early death." Moreover, it appears that even though blacks have contradictory memories about the extent of Lightfoot's involvement in the movement, all of them share outrage over the patrolmen's attack. For example, many blacks take pains to specifically separate Lightfoot from the movement and emphasize that he was ending his work day, not attending the mass meeting or roaming the streets. Charles Evers insisted to Dan McCay, "You know Mr. Lightfoot won't harm a snake, he wouldn't march if you pulled him by his side down the street."[2] Although it is doubtful that Lightfoot could have run for office or been elected in 1968 without some movement approval or alliance, it is unquestioned that his presence near First Baptist that night was a coincidence. It appears that those who try to distance him from the movement do so to bolster claims of his innocence and to emphasize the unjustified nature of the attack. In contrast, a distinct minority of African Americans specifically attribute Lightfoot's beating to movement affiliation, and some even connect it to his status as the only black school board member, though it is unlikely that the highway patrolmen knew who Lightfoot was. In both interpretations, despite their differing emphases, blacks perceive Lightfoot's beating as an inexcusable and heinous attack on an innocent man, who either was targeted because of his activism or was an innocent victim caught in a vicious attack on the movement.

Blacks' and whites' divergent views on the community's history are important to acknowledge and understand because in the early 1990s, some civic and political leaders began trying to use the community's history to draw tourists to the area as part of a larger economic development plan. In this context, it is absolutely essential to consider who gets to tell this story and who gets to assign meaning to this history. This is especially true since there is still very little substantive, meaningful exchange between blacks and whites about their different historic experiences. Though blacks and whites share a past, they do not share an understanding of that past. So far, efforts to institutionalize and interpret the community's history appear to both reflect and perpetuate race-based divisions. Whites still presume to speak for the entire community and seem intent on using historic preservation and interpretation as a vehicle for returning to their ideal of the past. Blacks actively contest this white-dominated vision, but whites' role in establishing the framework for public history and their continuing control over resources makes it an uphill battle.

Whites' views of the community's history remain strongly influenced by their antipathy to the civil rights movement, their belief that there is no need to acknowledge it, and their certainty that any discussion of it simply exacerbates current racial tensions by dwelling on a negative period of the past. Here, whites are undoubtedly influenced by their overriding perception of the movement as a period of loss and betrayal. For many whites, especially those of the leadership class, life in Claiborne County before the movement was centered around their needs; the movement did, in some ways, shatter that world of privilege and replace it with conflict, uncertainty, and declining authority. Locked in their own reality, few whites understand or acknowledge that the movement was a direct response to centuries of oppression, that for blacks it was a hopeful, joyous time, and that it brought a necessary and partial corrective to the reality that the political, economic, and social structures of the community were arranged for the benefit of whites. Whites, then, fault African Americans for shattering their refuge in small, locally controlled, segregated public schools, for intruding in politics, and, most significantly, for carrying out the boycott that they blame for destroying the downtown. The movement also called into question whites' deeply held beliefs about good race relations and interracial friendship, challenged their right to speak for the entire community, and introduced an element of insecurity into their sense of the world. So, in many ways, whites' view of the movement as a time of loss is accurate; however, what the vast majority of whites refuse to understand is that it was specifically their loss, not a widespread loss for the community. Furthermore, most of what whites lost, they never really had (like good interracial friendships) or never had a right to (like political control based on disfranchisement). Moreover, whites fail to concede that they still benefit, especially economically, from the enduring legacy of white supremacy.

Most whites dismiss the movement as "that old mess" and look beyond it to frame the community's history around a bygone golden age of their imagination, putting forth a romanticized image represented by antebellum mansions and

General Ulysses S. Grant's oft-quoted description of Port Gibson as "Too Beautiful to Burn." For many years, the town promoted an annual "pilgrimage" that glorified a white ideal of plantation society and featured tours of antebellum homes and pageants with black women dressed up in stereotypical "mammy" attire. This view of the past, including the premise that the movement destroyed the community's good race relations, is reflected in the comments of one white woman who lamented, "I'm so sorry that you won't ever see it like it was and that my children won't see it like it was. The comfortable feeling, everybody taking care of everybody. And, no hate. . . . Race wasn't a word. I mean, it was a word, then it was either you used 'darky' or 'colored man' to designate, 'yes he's black' and this is 'white.' This sort of thing. But, I mean it wasn't a dirty word. I mean, you just describing it like somebody's blonde and somebody has dark hair. But . . . it was just a wonderful warm thing."[3]

Just as blacks challenged white control over the legal and political systems during the movement, they have contested whites' right to interpret the community's history. One of the earliest and most substantive challenges came through the development and installation of "No Easy Journey," a permanent exhibition commemorating and celebrating the Claiborne County civil rights movement. The project was sponsored and initiated by Mississippi Cultural Crossroads (MCC), a community arts and education organization that envisions African American cultural, artistic, and aesthetic traditions as central to the community and emphasizes "the unique contribution that each racial group has made and can make to the community." Although MCC has always been integrated and is a pioneer in actively working for integration, most whites perceive it as a black organization because whites do not control it.[4] "No Easy Journey," which was funded primarily by MCC, the Claiborne County Board of Supervisors, and the Mississippi Humanities Council, opened in December 1994 in the newly completed William "Matt" Ross Administration Building, home to the black-majority board of supervisors and named in honor of the county's first twentieth-century black member of that governing body. There was considerable community involvement in planning the exhibit and the opening weekend events, including a day-long forum and several showings of "What It Is This Freedom," a play based on local oral histories and performed by local residents.

The integrated community advisory board consisted of former NAACP presidents Reverend James Dorsey, Reverend Eddie Walls, and George Walker, who were all still doing community work; James Miller, high school movement activist, MCC board member, and county administrator; Carl Brandon, who spent a year integrating Port Gibson High during freedom of choice; Julius Warner, president of the Deacons and father of a daughter involved in freedom of choice;

Matt Ross, longtime NAACP member and first black county supervisor; Evan Doss Jr., first black tax assessor; James Devoual, high school movement activist and then director of a public heath clinic; Dan McCay, the sheriff during the movement and the last white person to hold countywide office before being defeated by one of his black deputies in 1979; Ruth Willis, one of the few white students who remained at Port Gibson High after the black and white public schools were combined; Melvin McFatter, whose father supported the Klan and broke ranks with other whites to hire a black clerk and end the boycott of his pharmacy; Joan Beesley, daughter of box factory owner J. C. Wheeless and wife of then-mayor James Beesley; Robert Gage IV, who inherited Port Gibson Bank and leadership status from his father; and several other community residents who were less immediately involved in the movement, either as supporters or opponents.

The work leading up to the exhibit opening facilitated some of the first meaningful conversations between those who took markedly different positions during the movement. During an advisory board discussion about locating material objects to include in the exhibit, former sheriff Dan McCay wondered aloud about the Deacons minutes book and former Deacon George Walker responded that he remembered the night McCay confiscated it during an arrest. The two men shared a laugh as they reminisced. Chad McCaa, a middle school student who attended Claiborne Education Foundation (the private academy founded to avoid integration), was one of the few whites to participate in the play "What It Is This Freedom?". And though other whites repeatedly warned his family that his involvement put him in danger (from blacks) and that he should withdraw, he did not. Chad's involvement in the play prompted him to ask his merchant grandfather, Burnice Cleveland, about the boycott. Cleveland emphasized that the boycott had hurt them as a family, but he also acknowledged that it stemmed from genuine problems. Thus Chad had the unusual experience of learning about the boycott from two perspectives: that of his grandfather, who suffered economic loss, and that of African Americans, who saw it as essential to achieving dignified treatment. Moreover, because Chad was involved, his parents and grandparents were among the few local whites who attended the play, although one of Chad's grandparents made it clear that she disapproved of the event and Chad's presence was the only reason she was there.

Dan McCay and Melvin McFatter spoke as part of the "Participant Memories" panel during the opening events. McCay discussed his opposition to the Klan and his efforts to keep the group out of Claiborne County. McFatter, who described the boycott era as a "mean and ugly time," emphasized his family's tradition of independence to explain some of his father's actions. In keeping with that tradition, McFatter seems more willing than most whites to juxtapose his understanding of white fears and reluctance to change with a recognition that the movement was necessary and that premovement race relations were actually flawed. In particular, he described how he and his father responded to rumors that blacks were going to burn the downtown by spending the night in their drugstore, armed to the teeth. He noted that despite his youthful disappointment, he is now grateful that the night passed with no violence. Interestingly, although McFatter did nothing to welcome the black students who attended Port Gibson High during his senior year, Ken Brandon remembered him with some fondness, as someone who did not engage in taunting and as the person who was willing to walk beside him at graduation; now the two men offer each other friendly greetings whenever Brandon returns to Claiborne County.[5]

The willingness of this handful of whites to engage with blacks in a relatively honest, open, and substantive manner, even if only to accept that blacks and whites experienced movement-related events differently, demonstrates the potential of a genuine examination of the community's history. Yet most whites ultimately maintained their position of animosity and refused to take part in any meaningful way. For example, although Joan Beesley and Robert Gage were both on the planning committee, neither participated. And although a few local whites interested in theater attended the opening of "What It Is This Freedom?" except for those on the program, there was essentially no local white attendance at the opening forum that included a panel of scholarly presentations, the "Participant Memories" panel (in which both activists and those who opposed the movement spoke), and a "Community Roundtable." Even the participants were generally only present for their portion. Mayor James Beesley, for example, gave a welcome and left, and Joan Beesley and Robert Gage IV came only for their part on the final panel.

The grudging nature of whites' limited participation in "No Easy Journey" is clearest when it is contrasted with their much more enthusiastic and wholehearted involvement in every aspect of an earlier Mississippi Cultural Crossroads–sponsored exhibit, "Picturing our Past," which featured the early-twentieth-century photographs of white planter Leigh Briscoe Allen (father of merchant and politician Jimmy Allen). White political and civic leaders embraced the project and helped fund it, large numbers of whites attended all of the opening events, and Mayor James Beesley opened his antebellum Church Street home for a reception. This is not surprising since "Picturing Our Past" reflected whites' vision of the past. It literally conveyed the community's history (and African Americans) through the eyes of a very wealthy and powerful white man. It is important to note, however, that despite some discomfort with the ways that Allen's photographs so

"No Easy Journey" opening panel participants (left to right) Nate Jones, Julia Jones, Melvin McFatter, Dan McCay, and Carl Brandon, with moderator Alpha Morris (far right). Photograph by Patricia Crosby, courtesy Patricia Crosby.

clearly demonstrated the early 1900s power imbalance between blacks and whites, the black-majority board of supervisors helped with the funding and other blacks participated in and supported the project. These African Americans concluded that it was important to look honestly at the past, even when it evoked unpleasant reminders of the ways that white supremacy circumscribed blacks' lives.

The differing role that Port Gibson Main Street, Inc., played in the two exhibitions is particularly telling. Founded in 1990 as a program of the National Historic Trust, Main Street's primary purpose is rebuilding the downtown and encouraging historic preservation, but it sees fostering interracial conversation and cooperation as central to its mission. The organization is integrated but, in contrast to Cultural Crossroads, was initially white-oriented and white-led. Main Street accepted MCC's invitation to co-sponsor "Picturing Our Past," and both Main Street and the white-controlled City of Port Gibson helped MCC fund the exhibit. In contrast, both entities pointedly refused to provide any financial support or other assistance to "No Easy Journey." In fact, Main Street would not even formally consider funding the exhibit, and its (white) paid staff and leading white volunteers were conspicuously absent from the opening forum. Blacks' support for "Picturing Our Past" and whites' refusal to reciprocate with "No Easy Journey" highlight how differently blacks and whites view collaborative work and how unwilling whites are to acknowledge blacks' different historic experiences. (Ironically, as "No Easy Journey" has received attention from outsiders and drawn people to the community, Main Street has come to claim it as a community strength and as evidence of racial cooperation.)[6]

In many ways, the conflicting perspectives and opinions of the white and African American communities in terms of "No Easy Journey" are not very different from the period the exhibit commemorates. There are a few important distinctions, however. Unlike thirty years ago, blacks are no longer completely locked out of public or governmental spaces and were able to marshall the resources to install an exhibit that celebrates the movement. Moreover, a few white leaders felt obligated to participate, even if only in nominal ways. Mayor James Beesley, for one, depended on black voters. More important, a growing number of white leaders have begun to realize that they need to project an image of interracial cooperation in order to be successful at promoting economic development and tourism. Unfortunately, most whites translate this into an updated version of premovement "good relations," operating within a white-dominated vision and framework. Like Gage and Joan Beesley, they might serve on a committee or attend a meeting with blacks, but they steadfastly refuse to actually look, in any realistic or complex way, at the community's history, especially in terms of race.

Even those whites involved in politics or business who, in their need to accommodate African Americans, have learned to publicly acknowledge that there were some racial problems in the era before the movement, still typically refuse to deal with specifics or concede the legitimacy of black grievances and tactics. Historian Wesley Hogan points out that during the movement there was no action that black Mississippians could take that whites in authority would consider moderate: "Only total passivity and acquiescence to all the customs and expectations of a white supremacist society was regarded as acceptable conduct."[7] That view has persisted into the present so that even in retrospect whites insist that during the movement blacks were too impatient and used inappropriate tactics. Whites' fixation on the boycott, and their characterization of it as vindictive, disruptive, unnecessary, and the key factor in ruining the downtown, is particularly telling, in that they adamantly refuse to concede that merchants and white officials could have easily ended the boycott by making minor concessions, by taking simple actions that even whites now consider routine—hiring blacks and addressing them with courtesy. Instead, whites persistently act as if they had no culpability, as if they were helpless, innocent victims. There is no meeting place between whites' acknowledgment that there were "some problems" and their bitterness toward the boycott. They insist that blacks should have negotiated, while conveniently overlooking white leaders' steadfast refusal to negotiate. Thus, even those whites who proclaim their desire to work with blacks, who are interested in promoting the community's history, and who emphasize the need to move forward on racial reconciliation remain staunchly unwilling to acknowledge the movement's centrality and meaning for African Americans, concede that it is a legitimate topic for commemorating and using to attract tourists, or even truly examine its implications for their understanding of race relations, past or current.

Whites' approach to both movement history and contemporary legacies of white supremacy (and how they differ from blacks') are evident in public comments at the 1994 panel, "Claiborne County: Where Are We Today" that was part of the "No Easy Journey" opening, and in *Cannonballs and Courage*, a 2003 history of Port Gibson. White panelists Joan Beesley and Robert Gage and black panelists Claiborne County Administrator James Miller and County Supervisor Percy Thornton took markedly different approaches in discussing the current status of the community. Miller opened the session by asserting that during the movement African Americans were "right in our position. It was wrong for us to be locked out of this, which is America." He also insisted that "if we do not speak candidly, if we do not look the Devil in the eye and deal with our situation, I don't think we'll be able to move forward." Having asserted the legitimacy of the movement, he then directed most of his comments at black elected officials, who, he asserted, had an obligation to live up to the "high moral ground" of the movement and "do the greatest good for the greatest number." Percy Thornton, who spoke next and was one of those officials, agreed that the black community needed to confront internal problems, stop blaming others, and understand that the movement was not just about getting blacks elected. However, he also insisted that whites and blacks needed to work together. In particular, Thornton urged that the schools be integrated (meaning that whites return to the public schools) "for the betterment of our community," so that young people learn to "respect each other at an early age." He argued that "white citizens of this community can't afford to sit back and say that the blacks are in charge, and let them run things, and complain from their houses. They must come out and take part in their community too."[8]

Joan Beesley followed, opening her remarks by insisting both that "it takes time to change" and that "we have come so far from where we were in the 1960s." Then, in what seemed almost like a caricature, she went on to emphasize her personal friendships with blacks, both in the past and present, as if they were a substitute for a close examination of the community's persistent racial divisions. In particular, she talked about her "best friend Dorothy," a black child who moved into the house behind hers when they were both almost five. Beesley barely acknowledged that many of the details of her story were of race-based inequalities—like Dorothy's half-days at school and then quick promotion to second grade because the black schools were so severely overcrowded. Finally, although Beesley admitted she never saw Dorothy (whose last name she does not know) between the time Dorothy left Claiborne County after her high school graduation and her death at a young age, Beesley asserted with certainty that if Dorothy were present, she would say that "memories are wonderful and we need them" but we should not use them to "hurt." In essence, Beesley utilized two of whites' long-standing strategies for evading a serious examination of race relations: she hid behind the façade of interracial "friendship" and tried to provide legitimacy for her views by articulating them through a black spokesperson (in this instance a dead woman she had known only as a child and had not seen since the 1950s). Beesley concluded by insinuating that the entire day's forum and its reflections on the civil rights movement were hurtful and exacerbated divisions. Instead of dwelling on the past, she asserted, Claiborne Countians needed to "put down burdens that make us hate each other."[9]

Robert Gage IV was the final speaker, and he opened by referring to the "important comments" made by the speakers at earlier panels (which he had not come to hear). Then he spoke in vague generalities, directing his comments almost exclusively at the black community, complaining, for example, that too many school-age children were on the streets and not in school: "If we can't educate them, train them, they can't get a job." He then went on to say that high unemployment and other community problems are "color blind" and that "you can't look at it from that stand point any more." He insisted that the world was wide open for "the minority businessman who gets his act together" and argued that, through bank loans, there had been a tremendous "transfer of wealth into the black community." Then, like Beesley, he concluded his talk by evoking the words of a black spokesperson, this time co-panelist Percy Thornton's earlier comments, that the black community needed to look at itself in the area of "values, education, and accountability." In the process, he implied that blacks were solely responsible for the community's future.

Ultimately, both white panelists were evasive, emphasized past change and current racial harmony in the most general terms, and refused to examine or concede the white community's historic role in shaping Claiborne County's contemporary problems or its responsibility for acting to improve the future. In contrast, although Thornton called on the white community to take some responsibility for the community's future, especially by integrating the schools, both he and Miller emphasized that the black community must also be accountable and identified things that blacks needed to do for the entire community's well-being. Thus, while the black commentators framed the community's past and future in terms of both blacks and whites, the whites ignored the past and placed current responsibility solely at the feet of African Americans. Though Gage was quick to use Thornton's words to criticize blacks, he completely ignored Thornton's call for school integration. Both Gage and Beesley seemed more interested in emphasizing that the community had changed than in exploring how it could continue to move forward.[10]

At the end of the program, Hollis Watkins, a SNCC worker in the audience, pointed that out, asking the white panelists why, instead of focusing on "how far we have come," they would not ask "where we should be and work toward getting us there." Beesley responded by asserting, "I no longer speak in terms of black and white. . . . 'We' are 'we' to me and we have come forward." Repeating "and we have come forward" as a refrain throughout her comments, she stressed the integrated nature of the day's events as evidence. "Twenty years ago," she said, "we would not be here in an integrated meeting, would we have been?" Interestingly, she also brought up her work with Main Street, Inc., emphasizing both its presence in the community as an integrated organization and that it had facilitated her friendship with a black woman, Lula Mae Arnold, "one of the best friends I've made in the last ten years of my life." Beesley then insisted, "Until we become friends and interact as we're doing here and talk with one another, it doesn't matter about the school system or our churches or anything. We're not going anywhere. So that's what I mean by 'we have come forward.' We are able to sit here tonight, even though we may not always agree." It is particularly ironic that Beesley would use Main Street as evidence of racial progress since the organization refused to support "No Easy Journey," or even the forum in which Beesley was making in that claim. That refusal highlights the limitations of such surface-level manifestations of racial harmony and friendship. As former governor William Winter observed while speaking at a 2003 memorial service for three civil rights workers killed in Philadelphia, Mississippi, "White folks think we've come further in race relations than black folks do. As far as we've come, we still have a lot left to do."[11]

Beesley's comments clearly illustrate how whites view shifts in form, like using courtesy titles or attending integrated meetings, especially ones led by African Americans, as breakthroughs and indications of tremendous change. In some ways they are. Yet, as Percy Thornton pointed out, they are no substitute for integrated schools or a shared commitment to the community as a whole. Being civil and sharing a platform do not address the ramifications of decades of white supremacy or the community's long-standing racial divisions. For whites, then, it seems racial progress, or good race relations, is the presence of an integrated, white-dominated organization that they can participate in without having their views of the past or present challenged in any fundamental ways. In fact, some white civic and political leaders appear to be advancing Main Street's work as a response, an antidote even, to the movement and the boycott. That is, in their view, the boycott destroyed the downtown and interracial friendships and Port Gibson Main Street is leading the way in restoring both.[12]

Main Street's role is particularly critical because the organization is closely intertwined with the Port Gibson City government. For more than a decade, the city has paid the Main Street manager's salary and provided office space, a phone, and some secretarial support. Both former mayor James Beesley and his successor, Amelda Arnold, the town's first black mayor (elected in 1999), have strong personal ties to Main Street. These formal and informal associations and the years of collaboration have translated into a symbiotic relationship between Main Street and the city. One result is that Main Street provides white leaders with a vehicle for influencing the city government, even after the recent transition to a black-majority government. The implications of this influence are evident in *Cannonballs and Courage*, a book published in 2003 to commemorate Port Gibson's 200th anniversary. Main Street employees and volunteers helped initiate the project and arranged its financial support from the city and the two local banks (whose owners include Robert Gage IV and James Beesley). Main Street personnel dominated an advisory committee (comprised of the black mayor and six whites) and were involved in hiring and guiding the book's author, directing her to local resources, and helping facilitate her research. The author herself, Mary Ellis, is a white woman related by marriage to the Ellis family, including merchants who participated in the lawsuit against the NAACP.

The almost 200-page book recognizes the presence of African Americans, concedes that blacks experienced some injustice, and includes a chapter on the civil rights movement, all of which are a testament to the changes wrought by the movement. Despite that, whites are at the center of the story, and their perspective dominates. Ellis's white point of view leaps off the pages. For instance, she refers to African Americans as "Our Black people" and calls the Civil War the "War Between the States." Ellis opens her chapter on contemporary Port Gibson by noting that after the boycott, "some of my citizens, Black and White, realized that if we did not pull together and build on what we had learned during the boycott, then the boycott would become a millstone around our collective necks and drag us . . . into a sordid, non-productive existence." However, like Gage and Beesley at the "No Easy Journey" opening, Ellis is vague about what lessons were learned; her book, in fact, is striking evidence that whites have actually learned very little. In fact, whites' perception of the community's racial history and of the civil rights movement (clearly laid out in Ellis's book) seems most notable for how similar it is to that of the whites who actively fought against the movement.[13]

Throughout *Cannonballs and Courage*, virtually every discussion of African Americans is framed in terms of whites, with an emphasis on interracial friendship and cooperation. In one case, after acknowledging that slavery was wrong, Ellis insists, however, "One must not forget that mixed with the basic evil of slavery were love, trust, and mutual protection between Black and White people." The book also features a photograph of a woman identified only as "Mammy Mary." The accompanying caption is noteworthy, claiming that Mammy Mary "embodies the love that existed between many Black and White families" and she "stayed with the Shaifer family throughout the [Civil War] and afterwards, serving in place of a mother to the young Shaifer boys." Ellis justifies her use of the word "mammy," writing, "Now I know that today many of our Black citizens find the title 'Mammy' offensive, but please take a minute and listen. As it was originally used, 'Mammy' was a title of endearment. As has happened so often, someone later turned the title into a caricature—and that was wrong—but for Mammy Mary, the title was used with love."[14]

That this is a story told from whites' perspective is also immediately evident in Ellis's handling of the civil rights movement. She persistently portrays the boycott as one of the most dire problems the community has faced, opening her chapter on the movement by asserting, "We have survived fire, floods, yellow fever epidemics, wars, and boll weevils, but the civil rights boycott in the sixties almost killed us." Ellis quickly asserts that "the purpose in remembering this chapter of our history is not to open old wounds." She attributes the "major factors causing the upheaval" to a "world problem" originating in "Biblical times," and she never actually discusses how African Americans in Claiborne County experienced the race-based inequality that prompted the civil rights movement. She implies that local whites and blacks were both victims of outsiders—black agitators "who did not really care about individuals in the community" and white "state leaders who intended to retain power no matter who got trampled." Moreover, she contends there had to be a "better way to solve our problems" (implying that blacks should have been more reasonable and engaged in negotiation), emphasizes that the boycott brought financial ruin to white merchants and the downtown, asserts that school integration caused "emotional distress" for black and white students, and features African Americans who did not support the boycott or who offered implicit criticism of school integration. (This is particularly ironic since the schools have never been integrated in any real way.)[15]

Cannonballs and Courage closes on a laudatory note, emphasizing Main Street's role in rebuilding downtown Port Gibson and in developing interracial ties and friendships. Ellis devotes sixteen pages to Main Street's history and programs, including six pages of photographs from the group's 2002 Christmas parade. Both the text and the illustrations emphasize integration and interracial interactions. For example, she highlights the experience of Lula Arnold, a black Main Street volunteer and the mayor's mother, who noted that before she got involved with the organization, she "had never visited a White person's home or had a White person visit hers, but both happened and they still do." Arnold continued, "The most important thing about working with Main Street is that when people work together on programs, they forget about race, they develop trust, and friendship results." Like Joan Beesley and Robert Gage did in their "No Easy Journey" opening forum comments, Ellis uses black spokespeople to bolster white claims of positive race relations. Moreover, like Beesley and white leaders as far back as H. H. Crisler in the 1940s and 1950s, she uses stories of interracial friendship as a substitute for a meaningful and candid examination of the role race plays in Claiborne County's past and present.[16]

Black high school students used an incident in which a white store clerk called a black teenager "nigger" to offer a contrasting view of contemporary race relations. In a dramatic presentation titled *Holla: Claiborne County Teenagers Having Their Say*, the students drew on the experiences of cast member Parris Walker to develop a scene in which they reenacted and then interpreted this incident and what followed. They portray Parris reporting the racist insult to his grandfather, movement stalwart George Henry Walker, who "went over and had a few words with him." On stage, Parris explains, "Now whenever I go into that store, he says: 'Do you need help, *sir?*' or 'Here you go, *sir.*' or 'Would you like a receipt, *sir?*'" Though the store clerk responds to George Walker's insistence that he address Parris respectfully, the students doubt the clerk's sincerity. Every time Parris says the word "sir," the rest of the cast drowns him out, asserting, "What he really means is '*nigger.*'" They end the scene with their perception of the community's current racial divisions: "separate churches, separate foods, separate neighborhoods, separate stores, white pool and black pool, white school and black school, "Nigger and Honky."[17]

The students' portrayal of these events speaks to what the movement did and did not change. As Parris's experience suggests, blacks can insist that whites conform to certain standards of courtesy, but many whites do so only grudgingly, and many blacks suspect that even apparently friendly interracial interactions mask deep-seated white hostility. The underlying tensions these teenagers identify are unlikely to change as long as meaningful integration and power-sharing remain elusive. And yet, despite persistent divisions, there are some things that the movement changed forever. One change is that now African Americans, including high school students working with a cultural arts organization, can publicly assert a vision of their community at odds with the one put forth by white leaders.

Notes

Abbreviations

ARP	Annie Rankin Papers, Coleman Library, Tougaloo College, Jackson, Mississippi
CHT	*Claiborne Hardware, et al. v. NAACP, et al.* testimony, Mississippi Supreme Court storage, Jackson, Mississippi
EKP	Ed King Papers, Coleman Library, Tougaloo College, Jackson, Mississippi
FBIP	Federal Bureau of Investigation Papers (In author's possession through Freedom of Information Privacy Act)
IAL	*i ain't lying* (Mississippi Cultural Crossroads, Lorman, Mississippi)
IHLP	Institutions of Higher Learning Papers, Mississippi Department of Archives and History, Jackson, Mississippi
IWAP	International Woodworkers of America Papers, Southern Labor Archives, Pullen Library, Georgia State University, Atlanta, Georgia
JCN	Jack Chatfield 1969 interview notes
JDP	Justice Department Papers (in author's possession through Freedom of Information Privacy Act)
MDAH	Mississippi Department of Archives and History, Jackson, Mississippi
MSCS	Mississippi Supreme Court storage, Jackson, Mississippi
NAACPP	National Association for the Advancement of Colored People Papers, Manuscript Division, Library of Congress, Washington, D.C.
NLRB Hearing	National Labor Relations Board Hearing in Port Gibson, Nov. 26, 1945, NLRB Case No. 15-C-1020, National Labor Relations Board Papers, National Archive, College Park, Maryland
NYT	*New York Times*
PBJP	Paul B. Johnson Jr. Papers, McCain Library, University of Southern Mississippi, Hattiesburg, Mississippi
PGR	*Port Gibson Reveille*
RBP	Rims Barber Papers, Coleman Library, Tougaloo College, Jackson, Mississippi
SCP	Sovereignty Commission Papers, Mississippi Department of Archives and History, Jackson, Mississippi

SCRLR   Southern Civil Rights Litigaton Records, on microfilm, Coleman
               Library, Tougaloo College, Jackson, Mississippi
SEFP   Southern Election Fund Papers, Alderman Library, University of
               Virginia, Charlottesville, Virginia
SRCP   Mitchell F. Ducey, ed., *Southern Regional Council Papers, 1944–1968*
               (Ann Arbor, Mich.: University Microfilms, 1984)
U.S. v. Miss.   U.S. Commission on Civil Rights, *U.S. v. Mississippi* transcript,
               vols. 1 and 2
USM   University of Southern Mississippi Center for Oral History and Cultural
               Heritage, Hattiesburg, Mississippi
WPA   Works Progress Administration

Preface

1. Alex Waldauer, Jan. 19, 2004, Geneseo King Day Celebration, speech in author's possession.

2. David Dennis in Moses and Cobb, *Radical Equations*, vii–viii; *Mississippi Burning*, dir. Alan Parker.

Chapter One

1. [WPA], *Claiborne County [WPA Project]*, 93–94; Hoffman, "Small-Town Southern Jewish Experience"; *Mississippi Stockman Farmer* 5 (Oct. 1950): 20; Mississippi Power & Light Company, "Mississippi Statistical Summary."

2. [WPA], *Claiborne County [WPA Project]*, 15, 16; Foner, *Reconstruction*, 352; Morrison, *Black Political Mobilization*, 35–45; Posey, *Against Great Odds*; Dunham, *Centennial History of Alcorn A&M College*.

3. Foner, *Reconstruction*, 558–63; [WPA], *Claiborne County [WPA Project]*, 131, 184.

4. Lane and Cole, *Soil Survey*, 53; McMillen, *Dark Journey*, 111–53; Cobb, " 'Somebody Done Nailed Us.' "

5. Foner, *Reconstruction*, 86, 106–8; McMillen, *Dark Journey*, 3–32; Disharoon interview.

6. Annie Holloway Johnson interview, 36–38.

7. *PGR*, June 22, 1944; Annie Holloway Johnson interview; Durham interview, 16.

8. Moore interview, 10–13; Katie Ellis interview, 5–6; Camphor interview; Annie Holloway Johnson interview, 45–47.

9. Galloway interview, 8–9; Jesse Johnson interview, 36–37.

10. Katie Ellis interview, 30–31; Walker interview, *IAL*, 37, 36, 40; Buck interview, *IAL*, 40–41.

11. Annie Holloway Johnson interview, 36–38; Lucas interview, *IAL*, 19–20.

12. Eugene Spencer interview, 7; Waites interview, 29–33; Anonymous no. 3 interview.

13. McMillen, *Dark Journey*, 126; Woodruff, "African-American Struggles for Citizenship," 35.

14. McMillen, *Dark Journey*, 230–31; Sayles interview; *PGR*, Jan. 14, May 27, 1943; Dec. 28, 1944; Jan. 4, 1945.

15. David Crosby, " 'Piece of Your Own,' " 46–51.

16. Freeman, *Communion of the Spirits*, 90–98; Hystercine Rankin interview, USM, 4.

17. Freeman, *Communion of the Spirits*, 90–98; Litwack, *Trouble in Mind*; David Crosby, " 'Piece of Your Own,' " 46–51.

18. McMillen, *Dark Journey*, 28; *PGR*, July 4, Aug. 15, 1940; Feb. 5, 1942; Jan. 20, Apr. 13, Aug. 24, Nov. 30, 1944; Oct. 30, 1947; Jan. 19, 1950; Mar. 15, 22, 29, May 17, Dec. 27, 1951; Sept. 25, Oct. 2, Dec. 25, 1952; Apr. 9, Dec. 10, 1953; Feb. 4, Dec. 30, 1954; Jan. 6, Oct. 6, 1955; Jan. 15, 1959; Aug. 30, 1962; Devoual interview; Ernest Kennedy Brandon interview; *Mississippi Stockman Farmer* 5 (Oct. 1950); Powledge, *Free at Last?*, 31.

19. Fairclough, *Race & Democracy*, 41; James Miller Feb. 1994 interview; McMillen, *Dark Journey*, 24; "STOP! READ! THINK! CONCENTRATE!" Nov. 1944, IWAP; George Walker, JCN, 17; Marguerite Thompson, JCN, 17. In one striking oversight, titles referring to the black women who founded a "colored" PTA slipped through. See *PGR*, May 21, 1953.

20. Watson interview, USM, 35; Collins, Evans, and Grigsby interview; Ezekiel Rankin interview, USM, 27; Devoual interview.

21. Stewart interview; Julia Jones 1992 interview.

22. Ernest Kennedy Brandon interview.

23. Devoual interview; Miller interview, *IAL*, 14; Marjorie Brandon 1992 interview; Carl Brandon interview.

24. James Dorsey 1992 interview; *PGR*, Nov. 9, 1944; Nov. 6, 1952.

25. Moses and Cobb, *Radical Equations*, 25; Ezekiel Rankin interview, USM, 33; Ezekiel Rankin interview; Nathaniel Jones 1992 interview.

26. Nathaniel Jones 1992 interview; Julia Jones 1992 interview; Marjorie Brandon 1992 interview.

Chapter Two

1. Sullivan, *Days of Hope*, 117, 132, 136; Bartley, *Rise of Massive Resistance*, 14–15.

2. Cobb, " 'Somebody Done Nailed Us,' " 919; Sullivan, *Days of Hope*, 132; *PGR*, Dec. 5, 19, 1940; July 3, 1941; Aug. 27, 1998; [WPA], *Claiborne County [WPA Project]*.

3. David Crosby, " 'Piece of Your Own,' " 46–54; U.S. Bureau of the Census, *U.S. Census of Population: 1930*; Lane and Cole, *Soil Survey*; Jesse Johnson interview, 43; Aikerson interview, 45; Katie Ellis interview, 10, 12, 36–37; Annie Holloway Johnson interview; Matthew Page interview; Walker 1992 interview; Wells interview; McMillen, *Dark Journey*, 307.

4. Galloway interview, 13, 16.

5. Estella Parker interview, 16–17; James Dorsey 1980 interview, 36–38.

6. Durham interview, 7; Pauline Spencer interview, 13; Eugene Spencer interview, 13; Katie Ellis interview, 5–6; David Crosby, "Tenant Purchase Program," 7.

7. James Dorsey 1980 interview, 36–38; Annie Holloway Johnson interview, 60–61.

8. Eugene Spencer interview, 16–17; Waites interview, 1–3, 11–12; Richard Jefferies interview, 19; Katie Ellis interview, 30–31; Durham interview, 1–2, 4–6; Annie Holloway Johnson interview, 30–35.

9. Long interview; Katie Ellis interview, 29–30.

10. O'Brien, *Color of Law*, 102; James Dorsey 1992 interview; Ezekiel Rankin interview.

11. Miller interview, *IAL*; Ross interview; Nathaniel Jones (with Julia Jones) June 1996 interview; Nathaniel Jones 1992 interview; Julia Jones (with Nathaniel Jones) June 1996 interview; James Dorsey 1992 interview.

12. Miller interview, *IAL*, 12; Nathaniel Jones 1992 interview; Nathaniel Jones (with Julia Jones) Aug. 1996 interview; Ross interview; James Dorsey 1992 interview.

13. *PGR*, Apr. 20, Oct. 19, 26, 1944; Daniel, "Going Among Strangers," 889.

14. Woodruff, "Pick or Fight," 80; Cobb, " 'Somebody Done Nailed Us,' " 916; Newman interview, 14–20; *PGR*, Aug. 24, 31, 1944.

15. *PGR*, July 6, Sept. 7, 1944.

16. According to a U.S. census, 109.4 percent of the black population between the ages of twenty-one and sixty-five was in the workforce in 1930. By contrast, only 74.8 percent of the white population in that age group was in the workforce (U.S. Bureau of the Census, *U.S. Census of Population: 1930*). Lillie Brown quoted in Harris, "Historical Analysis," 87; *PGR*, Oct. 19, 1944; Aug. 23, 1945; Sept. 24, Oct. 15, 1953; Sept. 9, 16, Oct. 14, 1954; Jane Ellis interview, USM, 4.

17. *PGR*, Oct. 5, 1944; Aug. 27, 1998; NLRB Hearing, 92, 110–11, 262–63, 368, 402, 404.

18. NLRB Hearing, 36–37, 149–50; Jim Rowan, Oct. 27, 1944, Written and Witnessed by Harry Koger, IWAP.

19. NLRB Hearing, 92, 106–8, 110–11, 222–24, 262–63, 264, 368.

20. *PGR*, Oct. 26, 1944; NLRB Hearing, 40–43, 143, 183, 408C–408D, 409.

21. NLRB Hearing, 218–19, 243–44; "STOP! READ! THINK! CONCENTRATE!," IWAP.

22. Regional War Labor Board, Directive Order, June 28, 1945, Mailed July 5, 1945, IWAP.

23. NLRB Hearing, 155, 162, 174–75, 466; National Labor Relations Board, *Decisions and Orders*, 341.

24. Leatha Doss to Sir, Oct. 20, 1945; E. E. Benedict to Leatha Doss, Oct. 24, 1945; Transcript of Evidence, Hearing before Mississippi Unemployment Commission, May 17, 1946, IWAP.

25. Sullivan, *Days of Hope*, 222–23.

26. Handwritten notes on the back of notice: by J. H. Bare, Mayor, and M. M. Montgomery, Sheriff, May 6, 1946; and Luther Buie to George Bentley, May 11, 1946, IWAP.

Chapter Three

1. U.S. Bureau of the Census, *U.S. Census of Population: 1930*; U.S. Bureau of the Census, *U.S. Census of Population: 1940*; U.S. Bureau of the Census, *U.S. Census of Population: 1950*; *PGR*, Nov. 12, 1964; *Mississippi Stockman Farmer* 5, Oct. 1950; McMillen, *Dark Journey*, 152; Claiborne County Area Development Association, *Comprehensive Overall Economic Program*, 14, 16, 34, 35; Brief on Behalf of Port Gibson Veneer, National War Labor Board, Atlanta, IWAP; Watson interview, USM, 7; *PGR*, Aug. 27, 1998.

2. Brandon interview, *IAL*, 31; Rankin interview, *IAL*, 61–73; Smith interview, *IAL*, 25; Sayles interview; Ezekiel Rankin interview, USM, 12; Young interview.

3. *PGR*, May 10, 1956; Gibson interview, *IAL*, 3–11; Headley interview; Joan Beesley interview; Jane Ellis interview, USM, 4.

4. Warner interview; Walker 1992 interview; NLRB Hearing, 106–8, 416; No Title, List of Employees, Hotel Vicksburg Stationery, n.d., IWAP.

5. Ezekiel Rankin interview, USM, 12; Aikerson interview, 17–18; Duffin interview, *IAL*, 13.

6. *PGR*, Aug. 27, 1998; NLRB Hearing, 93, 371, 427; Watson interview, USM, 7; NLRB Hearing, 435; Brief on Behalf of Port Gibson Veneer, National War Labor Board, Transcript of Evidence, May 17, 1946, Hearing before Mississippi Unemployment Commission, 14, IWAP.

7. Long interview; Annie Holloway Johnson interview; Nathaniel Jones interview, *IAL*, 51–52; Duffin interview, *IAL*, 13; James Miller 1999 interview.

8. Dorsey interview, *IAL*, 59; Aikerson interview, 36–37; Page interview, *IAL*, 5–6; Waites interview, 23–24.

9. Trimble interview, *IAL*, 22; *PGR*, Aug. 27, 1998; Lum interview; McLendon interview, *IAL*, 11; Nelson interview.

10. Long interview; Atlas interview; Nathaniel Jones (with Julia Jones) Aug. 1996 interview; Hystercine Rankin interview, USM, 15.

11. Headley interview; *PGR*, Sept. 3, 1998; Rosalie Abraham interview; Albert Butler interview.

12. Anderson interview; Nathaniel Jones (with Julia Jones) Aug. 1996 interview; NLRB Hearing, 93.

13. *PGR*, Jan. 18, 1940; Melvin McFatter interview; McMillen, *Dark Journey*, 28.

14. U.S. Bureau of the Census, *U.S. Census of Population: 1960. General Social and Economic Characteristics, Mississippi*; U.S. Bureau of the Census, *U.S. Census of Population: 1960*, vol. 1, *Characteristics of the Population*; Shannon, *Toward a New Politics*, 2–3, 43–44; Pyles interview; Minor interview; Harris, "Historical Analysis," 53; see also Mars, *Witness in Philadelphia*, 40–41.

15. *PGR*, June 29, July 6, Nov. 30, 1944; May 13, 1948; June 25, Aug. 2, Oct. 4, Dec. 13, 1951; June 12, Aug. 21, Dec. 11, 1952; Dec. 17, 1953; July 15, 1954; Feb. 13, 1955; Aug. 27, 1998; Joan Beesley interview.

16. [WPA], *Claiborne County [WPA Project]*, 370–71; *PGR*, Aug. 27, 1998; Mississippi Cultural Crossroads, "Picturing Our Past."

17. *PGR*, Dec. 10, 1942; Dec. 7, 1944; Aug. 8, Dec. 5, 1946; Dec. 9, 1948; Aug. 10, Dec. 7, 1950; Dec. 4, 1952; Aug. 6, 1953; Dec. 14, 1961; Aug. 27, 1998.

18. *PGR*, Sept. 11, 1941; June 1, Aug. 3, 1944; June 6, 27, July 25, 1946; July 31, 1947; Sept. 9, 16, 1948; July 21, 1949; Dec. 13, 1951; Sept. 11, 1952; May 14, July 2, Aug. 27, 1953; May 20, July 15, Oct. 21, 28, Nov. 11, 1954; May 24, 1956; Oct. 17, Nov. 28, 1957; Dec. 11, 1958; Apr. 25, Aug. 8, 1963.

19. *PGR*, July 20, Aug. 3, Aug. 10, 1950; Sept. 25, Oct. 9, 1952; Apr. 23, 1959; Jimmie Person interview; Allen interview.

20. *PGR*, Mar. 31, Apr. 21, 28, 1955; June 13, 1957; Warner interview; Allied Chemical Plant File, SCRLR.

21. *PGR*, July 15, Aug. 26, Dec. 23, 1954; July 26, 1955; Oct. 17, 1957; Oct. 1, 1964; Port Gibson Swimming Pool File, SCRLR; Atlas interview; Allen interview.

22. *PGR*, Jan. 29, 1953; Feb. 4, Apr. 1, June 11, 1954; Mar. 1, 1956; Union's Comments on Panel Report, June 5, 1945, IWAP; Andrew B. James, "An Environmental Health Survey," Enlargement of Boundaries File, SCRLR.

23. *PGR*, Aug. 8, 1946; July 1, 29, 1954; Dec. 14, 1961.

24. Headley interview.

25. Williams interview; *PGR*, May 25, 1950; July 12, 1951.

26. *PGR*, May 29, 1947; July 28, 1949; Aug. 3, Mar. 23, 1950; July 26, 1951; Jan. 8, 1953; Feb. 13, 1975; Aug. 27, 1998; *Jackson Clarion-Ledger*, Feb. 11, 1975.

27. *PGR*, Oct. 5, 1944.

Chapter Four

1. Julia Jones 1992 interview.

2. Ruby Jefferies interview, 39–40; Miller interview, *IAL*, 12; James Miller 1996 interview; Sullivan interview.

3. Marjorie Brandon 1992 interview; Ernest Kennedy Brandon interview.

4. Stewart interview; James Dorsey 1992 interview.

5. Mississippi Power & Light Company, "Mississippi Statistical Summary"; McMillen, *Dark Journey*, 27; Williams interview; Freeman, *Communion of the Spirits*, 94; Ernest Kennedy Brandon interview; Julia Jones 1992 interview; Atlas interview.

6. Reagon, "Songs Are Free," 16:50; Welch interview, *IAL*, 20–21; Breckinridge interview, *IAL*, 3–4.

7. *PGR*, Mar. 29, 1951; Walker interview, *IAL*, 48.

8. Anderson interview, *IAL*, 8; Nathaniel Jones (with Julia Jones) Apr. 2001 interview; Nathaniel Jones (with Julia Jones) May 2001 interview; James Dorsey 1992 interview.

9. Eugene Spencer interview, 25–26.

10. Reagon, "Songs Are Free," 10:30, 12:07, 17:47; James Miller 1996 interview.

11. Smith interview, *IAL*, 27–28; Rankin interview, *IAL*, 62; Long interview.

12. *PGR*, Aug. 13, 1942.

13. Sayles interview; U.S. Bureau of the Census, *U.S. Census of Population: 1960. General Social and Economic Characteristics, Mississippi*; U.S. Bureau of the Census, *U.S. Census of Population: 1960*, Vol. 1, *Characteristics of the Population*.

14. Owings and Ainsley, *School Survey*, 63, 70, 72, 80–88; James Dorsey Feb. 1994 interview; Walker 1992 interview; James Dorsey 1992 interview; Ross interview.

15. Walker 1992 interview.

16. Ezekiel Rankin interview, USM, 5; Nathaniel Jones interview, *IAL*, 49; Walker interview, *IAL*, 3; James Miller Feb. 1994 interview.

17. Julia Jones interview, *IAL*, 41; Dungee interview.

18. See Michele Mitchell, " 'The Black Man's Burden': African Americans, Imperialism, and Notions of Racial Manhood, 1890–1910," *International Review of Social History* 44

(1999): 81 n. 14. Worth Long similarly observes that the Claiborne County blacks who were served by Alcorn College "were coming into the middle." He explained, "I'm not really talking about black middle class, I can't formulate that in the rural economy of that time, but into what was not the bottom" (Long interview).

19. *PGR*, Sept. 12, 1940; Mar. 5, Nov. 12, 26, Dec. 10, 1942; Nov. 18, 1943; Jan. 27, Feb. 24, 1944.

20. *PGR*, Sept. 17, 1942; Jan. 20, 27, 1944.

21. *PGR*, Jan. 20, 27, 1944.

22. U.S. Bureau of the Census, *U.S. Census of Population: 1930*; U.S. Bureau of the Census, *U.S. Census of Population: 1940*; U.S. Bureau of the Census, *U.S. Census of Population: 1950*; U.S. Bureau of the Census, *U.S. Census of Population: 1960. General Social and Economic Characteristics, Mississippi*; U.S. Bureau of the Census, *U.S. Census of Population: 1960*, Vol. 1, *Characteristics of the Population*; *PGR*, July 14, 1955; Watson interview, USM, 34; Davis interview; James Miller Feb. 1994 interview.

23. *PGR*, May 10, 1956; Smith interview, *IAL*, 31; Watson interview, USM, 34.

24. James Miller Feb. 1994 interview.

25. U.S. Bureau of the Census, *U.S. Census of Population: 1930*; Lane and Cole, *Soil Survey*; [WPA], *Claiborne County [WPA Project]*, 187; *PGR*, Dec. 16, 1943; David Crosby, "Piece of Your Own," 54; O'Brien, *Color of Law*, 61.

26. Rankin interview, *IAL*, 64, 71; White interview, *IAL*, 60; Woodard interview, *IAL*, 49; Green interview, *IAL*, 45; Mackey interview, *IAL*, 40; Collins, Evans, and Grigsby interview; Nathaniel Jones 1992 interview.

27. Williams, "Mississippi and Civil Rights," 171; Ashmore, *Negro and the Schools*, 152–53; *Memphis Commercial Appeal*, Mar. 15, 1953; *PGR*, Aug. 13, 1942; June 13, Nov. 9, 1944.

28. *PGR*, Nov. 9, 1944.

29. *PGR*, Sept. 27, Oct. 18, 1945; Feb. 21, June 13, 20, 1946; July 10, 1947.

30. *PGR*, June 19, 26, July 10, 1947.

31. Woodruff, "Mississippi Delta Planters," 284; *PGR*, Sept. 21, 1950; Nov. 20, 1952; Aug. 20, 1953; Jan. 26, Mar. 1, Apr. 25, June 7, 1956; Jan. 24, 1957.

32. Myrdal, *American Dilemma*, 720–21, 770; Black and Black, *Politics and Society in the South*, 82, 83; Eskew, *But for Birmingham*, 69; Fairclough, *Race & Democracy*, 304; Chestnut, *Black in Selma*, 44–45; Myrlie Evers, *For Us, the Living*, 148, 149.

33. *PGR*, Nov. 17, 1960; Eugene Spencer, JCN, 5; Eugene Spencer interview; Hal C. DeCell to J. P. Coleman, July 28, 1958, SCP.

34. Eugene Spencer interview, 15–17, 25.

35. Allen interview.

36. *PGR*, June 3, 10, July 8, 1948; Eugene Spencer interview, 29.

37. Sullivan, *Days of Hope*, 141; Nathaniel Jones 1992 interview; Collins, Evans, and Grigsby interview; A. L. Hopkins to Director, June 27, 1960, SCP.

38. Nathaniel Jones (with Julia Jones) June 1996 interview; Collins, Evans, and Grigsby interview; *PGR*, Nov. 11, 1943.

39. Katie Collins 2001 interview. I believe the following belonged to the NAACP during the late 1930s and early 1940s: Bass (or Bazil) Brown, Alexander Collins, Dan Curry, A. N. Dorsey, James Dorsey, Lemuel Dotson, Annie Holloway, Jesse Johnson, Roscoe Johnson, Ernest Jones, Sarah Jones, Eddie Lee, A. L. Martin, Dan Newman, Flint (or William) Owens, Floyd Rollins, Eugene Spencer, Carl Thompson, and Marguerite Thompson. For A. E. "Eddie" Lee, Roscoe Johnson, Reverend A. L. Martin, Bass Brown, Daniel Newman, Dan Curry, Jesse Johnson, Lemuel Dotson, Alex Collins, and Eugene Spencer, see Ernest Jones, JCN, 63–64. For Ernest Jones, Daniel Newman, Flint Owens, Floyd Rollins, Alex Collins, Jesse Johnson, and Roscoe Johnson, see Roscoe Johnson, JCN, 61; for A. N. and James Dorsey, see James Dorsey 1992 interview. On the existence of a branch before 1951 charter drive, see Nathaniel Jones 1992 interview. Dorsey mentioned attending meetings at First Baptist Church, which coincide with those of the 1940s group (Eugene Spencer interview, 26). For Thompsons and Rollins, see Page interview, *IAL*, 8–9. For Rollins, see Walker 1992 interview; for Daniel Newman information, see Daniel Newman, JCN, 64. See also Katie Collins 2001 interview.

40. James Dorsey 1992 interview; Marguerite Thompson, CHT, 167; Hopkins to Director, June 27, 1960, SCP; *PGR*, Mar. 5, 1942; Jan. 20, Feb. 24, Apr. 13, Nov. 9, 1944; Jan. 25, 1945; Jan. 15, 1952; Dec. 3, 10, Feb. 12, May 7, 21, 27, 1953; Apr. 14, 1955; Jan. 8, 15, 1959; Jan. 14, 1960; Jan. 31, 1963.

41. Dittmer, *Local People*, 34; Gloster Current to Ernest Jones, Mar. 28, 1952, and Mabel W. Spencer to Muriel Outlaw, Sept. 30, 1952, NAACPP.

42. In addition to the fifty-nine names on the charter, sources suggest that there were at least fourteen other members during roughly the same time period (Nov. 22, 1951, Claiborne County Charter, NAACPP). Marjorie Brandon 1992 interview; Ernest Kennedy Brandon interview; Nathaniel Jones (with Julia Jones) June 1996 interview; Camphor interview; Page interview, *IAL*, 8–9; Ernest Jones, JCN, 63; Zack Van Landingham to Director, Mar. 18, 1959, and Virgil Downing report, Jan. 30, 1961, SCP; *PGR*, Mar. 5, 1942; Jan. 20, Feb. 24, Apr. 13, Nov. 9, 1944; Jan. 25, 1945; Jan. 15, 1952; Feb. 12, May 7, 21, Aug. 27, 1953; Jan. 6, Apr. 14, 1955; Feb. 7, 1957; Jan. 8, 15, 1959; Jan. 14, 1960; Jan. 31, 1963.

43. Nathaniel Jones (with Julia Jones) June 1996 interview; Nathaniel Jones 1992 interview; Ernest Kennedy Brandon interview; Marjorie Brandon 1992 interview; Marjorie Brandon 1996 interview.

Chapter Five

1. Myrlie Evers, *For Us, the Living*, 145; Dittmer, *Local People*, 58.

2. Dittmer, *Local People*, 45–46, 50–52, 60; Payne, *I've Got the Light of Freedom*, 34–35; McMillen, *Citizens' Council*.

3. *PGR*, May 20, May 27, 1954; Jan. 26, 1956.

4. Eugene Spencer, JCN, 7; Jesse Johnson, JCN, 18; D. A. Newman to NAACP, Aug. 28, 1956, NAACPP; Ezekiel Rankin interview; Minor interview.

5. *PGR*, Oct. 10, 17, Nov. 14, 21, 28, 1957; Apr. 10, May 8, Oct. 16, 1958; July 2, 1959;

May 19, 1960; Van Landingham to Director, Mar. 18, June 1, 1959; Albert Jones to file, June 22, 1960; A. L. Hopkins to Director, June 27, 1960, all SCP; Minor interview.

6. Morris, *Origins of the Civil Rights Movement*, 33; Eugene Spencer interview, 26; Page interview, *IAL*, 9–10.

7. Ernest Jones, JCN, 63–64; Jesse Johnson, JCN, 17–18; Dan Curry, JCN, 1; Nathaniel Jones (with Julia Jones) June 1996 interview; Nathaniel Jones 1992 interview; Julia Jones interview, *IAL*, 43–44.

8. Annual Report of Branch Activities, 1961; Ernest H. Jones to NAACP, May 12, 1963; Report on Memberships and Freedom Fund Contributions from Mississippi Branches, Jan. 1–Oct. 15, 1963, all NAACPP.

9. James Dorsey 1992 interview; Davenport interview, USM, 11; Nathaniel Jones (with Julia Jones) June 1996 interview.

10. *U.S. v. Miss.*, 1:451–52, 585–87; 2:910–24; J. Harold Flannery to Henry Putzel Jr., Apr. 6, 1959; Gordon A. Martin Jr. to John Doar, June 21, 1962; Doar to Burke Marshall, July 9, 1963; Marshall to FBI Director, July 9, 1963, all JDP; Eugene Spencer interview, 27–28; Dittmer, *Local People*, 52–53.

11. *U.S. v. Miss.*, 2:910–24; Nathaniel Jones 1992 interview; Affidavit by Claiborne County Negro, Feb. 24, 1959; Port Gibson Negro to William P. Rogers, [Mar. 10, 1959]; Doar to Marshall, Apr. 19, 1962; Marshall, "Discrimination of Voter Registration in Claiborne County, Mississippi," July 9, 1963, all JDP; William Matt Ross, CHT, 929; Odessa Ross, CHT, 908; Willie Wilson interview; Gibson interview, *IAL*, 10.

12. William Owens, CHT, 685; *U.S. v. Miss.*, 2:910, 914; Eugene Spencer interview, 28.

13. *U.S. v. Miss.*, 1:451–52, 586; J. Harold Flannery to Henry Putzel Jr., Apr. 6, 1959; Doar to Marshall, July 9, 1963; Marshall to FBI Director, July 9, 1963, all JDP; James Dorsey 1992 interview; M. M. McFatter interview.

14. *U.S. v. Miss.*, vol. 1, 451–52, 586; Eugene Spencer interview, 28.

15. Page interview, *IAL*, 8–9.

16. The names of these complainants are not available; however, there is convincing evidence that Spencer and Holloway Johnson were among them. See Feb. 24, 1959, affidavits by Claiborne County Negroes; Port Gibson Negro to William P. Rogers, [Mar. 10, 1959]; J. Harold Flannery to Henry Putzel Jr., [Apr. 6, 1959], all JDP; Eugene Spencer interview, 27; and Hopkins to Director, June 27, 1960, SCP.

17. W. Wilson White to FBI Director, Apr. 21, 1959; Henry Putzel to J. Harold Flannery, May 18, 1959; White to FBI Director, May 25, 1959; William J. O'Hear to White, July 10, 1959; Putzel to Flannery, July 21, 1959; Flannery to Chief, July 28, 1959, all JDP.

18. *PGR*, Oct. 17, 1957; June 25, 1959; May 19, June 16, 1960; General Legislative Investigating Committee Report, Apr. 12, 1960; Jones to file, June 22, 1960; Erle Johnston to Russell Fox, May 17, 1963; Mississippi State Sovereignty Commission Minutes, July 19, 1963, all SCP; Allen interview; Minor interview; Minor, *Eyes on Mississippi*, 313.

19. *PGR*, Jan. 14, 1954; June 9, 1955; Sept. 26, Nov. 7, 14, 1957; Mar. 13, 1958.

20. Van Landingham to Director, June 1, 1959; Hopkins to Director, June 27, 1960, both SCP.

21. Van Landingham to file, July 6, 1959; Hopkins to Director, June 27, 1960; Virgil Downing report, Jan. 30, 1961; A. L. Hopkins report, July 18, 1961, all SCP.

22. Van Landingham to Director, Mar. 18, 1959; Albert Jones report, Aug. 11, 1960; R. A. Segrest to Jones, Aug. 18, 1960, all SCP; *PGR*, July 29, 1965.

23. Watson interview, USM, 32; Hopkins to Director, June 27, 1960, SCP.

24. Hal C. DeCell to J. P. Coleman, July 28, 1958; Van Landingham to Director, Mar. 18, 1959, both SCP; *PGR*, Sept. 30, 1965.

25. Claiborne County Schools, List of School Employees, 1961–62 Term, Aug. 1961, SCP; Nathaniel Jones (with Julia Jones) June 1996 interview; *PGR*, May 22, 1958; Mar. 26, 1959.

26. Medgar Evers report, [Mar. 1957], NAACPP; Sansing, *Making Haste Slowly*, 144.

27. DeCell to Ney M. Gore Jr., Mar. 5, 1957, DeCell to Gore, Mar. 7, 1957, DeCell to Gore, Mar. 14, 1957, SCP; Medgar Evers report, and Letter to "The Friends of Alcorn A&M College," NAACPP; Sansing, *Making Haste Slowly*, 144; minutes, Mar. 9, 1957, IHLP.

28. O. W. Moses interview.

29. Ibid.; Van Landingham to File, May 5, 1960, SCP; *Evers v. Birdsong* file, SCRLR.

30. Dungee interview; O. W. Moses interview; Dittmer, *Local People*, 38–40; *Jackson Daily News*, Aug. 12, 1954; *PGR*, Mar. 28, 1957.

31. *PGR*, Mar. 14, 1957; Dungee interview; O. W. Moses interview; minutes, June 27, Apr. 18, 1957, IHLP; *Pittsburgh Courier*, Mar. 16, 1957; Van Landingham to Director, Jan. 26, 1959, SCP.

32. Dungee interview; J. D. Boyd, "The Role and Scope of Alcorn A. & M. College in Higher Education in the State of Mississippi," 1965, IHLP; *PGR*, May 11, 1958; May 11, 1959; Nov. 24, 1960; Aug. 17, 1961; Aug. 29, 1964; Dunham, *Centennial History*, 79.

33. Downing report, Sept. 27, 1963, SCP.

34. O. W. Moses interview.

35. *PGR*, Oct. 29, 1959; *AAUP Bulletin* (Sept. 1962), 248, 251; Dungee interview.

36. O. W. Moses interview; Dungee interview.

Chapter Six

1. Robert Parris Moses 2001 interview; Bob Moses to SNCC Executive Committee, [Aug. 1963], *Student Nonviolent Coordinating Committee Papers, 1959–1972* (Sanford, N.C.: Microfiling Corp. of America, 1981); Nathaniel Jones Aug. 1991 interview; Nathaniel Jones (with Julia Jones) June 1996 interview; Nathaniel Jones, quoted in Regina Devoual, "HTK— Voting Rights in Mississippi," 6.

2. John Doar to FBI Director, Apr. 3, 1961, JDP; *U.S. v. Miss.*, 2:910–24; Wells interview.

3. *U.S. v. Miss.*, 2:910–24; Wells interview; Henry, *Aaron Henry*, 105.

4. "U.S. Sues to Widen Mississippi Voting," *NYT*, Aug. 29, 1962; Doar to Burke Marshall, Apr. 19, 1962; FBI Director to Marshall, July 9, 1963, both JDP; Virgil Downing report, Jan. 30, 1961, SCP; "Burke Marshall's Statement before hearing of Civil Rights Commission," Voter Education Project Papers, in *SRCP*; Nathaniel Jones 1992 interview.

5. *PGR*, June 7, 1962; Marshall to Robert D. Gage III, Apr. 24, 1962; Doar to Marshall, Apr. 19, 1962; Marshall to file, June 16, 1962, all JDP.

6. *PGR*, Aug. 30, 1962; FBI Director to Marshall, July 9, 1963, JDP; Headley interview.

7. Pauline Easley to Marshall, Nov. 30, 1962, JDP; *U.S. v. Miss.*, 2:917.

8. Thomas R. Kendrick, "A Town in the Lee of the Race Storm: Mississippi's Port Gibson Lives in Segregated Peace—Now," *Washington Post*, July 19, 1964; Headley interview. See also Lum interview.

9. *U.S. v. Miss.*, 1:22–24; 2:919–24, 1294–96.

10. Albert Jones report, Aug. 11, 1960; Jones to Easley, Jan. 16, 1961; A. L. Hopkins report, Mar. 20, 1961; Downing report, Sept. 18, 1961, all SCP; Erle Johnston to Investigators, Feb. 8, 1965, PBJP.

11. Payne, *I've Got the Light of Freedom*, 130–31, 141; McArthur Cotton, "Plans and Budget—3rd Congressional District," EKP; Long interview; Sellers interview; Robert Parris Moses 2001 interview; Houze interview.

12. R. L. Morgan to Paul Johnson, Apr. 22, 1964; T. B. Birdsong to Johnson, Apr. 24, 1964, both PBJP; minutes, June 27, Aug. 20, 1964; Nov. 1965, all IHLP; *Evers v. Birdsong* file, SCRLR.

13. Minutes, June 27, Aug. 20, 1964; Nov. 1965, all IHLP; Informant report, Jan. 7, 1965; Johnston to file, Jan. 12, 1965; Special Report, Jan. 16, 1965; Johnston to Herman Glazier, Jan. 14, 1965, Jan. 17, [1965]; Handwritten note on Johnston to Glazier, Jan. 14, 1965, all PBJP.

14. James Dorsey 1992 interview; Walls interview, USM, 8–9; McClorine interview; Sayles interview; W. Wilson White to FBI Director, May 25, 1959, JDP; Henry, *Aaron Henry*, 105; Van Landingham to file, July 6, 1959, SCP; Geneva Collins interview.

15. Dittmer, *Local People*.

16. Fairclough, *Race & Democracy*, 282–83; John Morsell to Aaron Henry, Oct. 8, 1965, NAACPP; Dittmer, *Local People*, 78, 116–20, 157–69, 274–76.

17. John Brooks to Roy Wilkins, Morsell, and Gloster B. Current, July 16, 1964, NAACPP; Dittmer, *Local People*, 178.

18. Payne, *I've Got the Light of Freedom*, 361; Charles Evers, *Have No Fear*, 7, 56, 146, 147.

19. Current to Wilkins, Sept. 9, 1963; Current to Charles Evers, July 1, 1964; Wilkins to Evers, Dec. 13, 1964; Current to Evers, Feb. 5, 1964; Current to Evers, Apr. 23, 1964, all NAACPP; Evers interview.

20. Dittmer, *Local People*, 242–302; Donald White to Wilkins, Feb. 4, 1964; R. Hunter Morey to Wilkins, Feb. 4, 1964; Current to Evers, Feb. 5, 1964; Evers to Ruby Hurley, Aug. 28, 1964; Current to Morsell, Oct. 5, 1964; Current to Evers, Oct. 23, 1964; Current to Evers, June 25, 1965, all NAACPP; McClorine interview. For an example of the Sovereignty Commission's reports on Evers's conflict with COFO, see Informant report, May 22, 1964, Report of Operator #79, August 7, 1964, SCP.

21. Current to Morsell, Oct. 5, 1964; Current to Evers, June 25, 1965; Current to Wilkins, Aug. 13, 1965, all NAACPP.

22. Current to Evers, Oct. 23, 1964; Evers to Hurley, Jan. 25, 1965; *New York Herald Tribune*, Aug. 28, 1965, all NAACPP; Dittmer, *Local People*, 353–54.

23. *Jackson Daily News*, Aug. 28, 1965; *New York Herald Tribune*, Aug. 28, 1965; *Jackson Clarion-Ledger*, Aug. 31, 1965; Current to Publicity Dept., Sept. 2, 1965; Evers Press Release, Sept. 1, 1965, NAACP; Morsell to Henry, Oct. 8, 1965, all NAACPP; Dittmer, *Local People*, 353–62.

24. Dittmer, *Local People*, 356–62; Charles Evers, *Have No Fear*, 149–50; Pyles interview; Charles Evers, CHT, 414; Informant report, Sept. 7, 1965; Informant report, Sept. 11, 1965; Informant report, Sept. 20, 21, 1965; Informant report, Sept. 27, 1965; Informant report, Sept. 30, 1965; Charles E. Snodgrass to Birdsong and A. D. Morgan, Sept. 14, 1965, all PBJP; Gene Roberts, "N.A.A.C.P. May Oust Evers as Aide in Mississippi," *NYT*, Sept. 10, 1965.

25. Dittmer, *Local People*, 314, 315–37, 341–42, 346, 347; Payne, *I've Got the Light of Freedom*, 315, 316, 340, 341, 365–66; McMillen, *Citizens' Council*, 266.

26. McMillen, "Black Enfranchisement in Mississippi," 369; Dittmer, *Local People*, 352.

Chapter Seven

1. James Miller Feb. 1994 interview; Eddie Lee Wells, CHT, 371; Julia Jones 1992 interview.

2. Ernest Brown, JCN, 42, 60; Eugene Spencer, JCN, 5; James Dorsey, JCN, 55.

3. Rick Abraham interview; Profile of Rudolph Arthur Shields, Dec. 19, 1973, Shields FBI file, FBIP; Rudy Shields, CHT, 427; "Over 100 Arrested in Natchez March," *Jackson Clarion-Ledger*, Oct. 5, 1965; A. L. Hopkins report, Jan. 3, 1966, both SCP; Charles E. Snodgrass to T. B. Birdsong and A. D. Morgan, Dec. 21, 1965; Snodgrass report, Dec. 27, 1965; Snodgrass to Birdsong and Morgan, Dec. 30, 1965; Hopkins report, Jan. 3, 1966, all PBJP; Gloster Current to Evers, Jan. 21, 1966, NAACPP; Walker 1992 interview; Nathaniel Jones (with Julia Jones) June 1996 interview.

4. Devoual interview; James Miller Feb. 1994 interview; Walker 1992 interview; Sayles interview; Scott interview; Barber interview; James Dorsey 1992 interview; Dorothy Brandon interview.

5. Nathaniel Jones (with Julia Jones) June 1996 interview; Eugene Spencer, JCN, 5–6, 8; Rudolph Shields, CHT, 429; James Dorsey 1992 interview; James Dorsey Dec. 1994 interview; Tommy Williams, JCN, 9; F. A. White, JCN, 8; Ernest Brown, JCN, 60; Evers to Current, Jan. 14, 1966, NAACPP.

6. Eugene Spencer, JCN, 5; James Dorsey, JCN, 55; *PGR*, Dec. 23, 1965.

7. *PGR*, Dec. 23, 1965.

8. F. A. White, JCN, 8; Eugene Spencer, JCN, 5, 8; Tommy Williams, JCN, 10; James Dorsey Dec. 1994 interview; Johnston, *Mississippi's Defiant Years*, 326.

9. James Miller Dec. 1994 interview; Jim Rowan, Oct. 27, 1944, written and witnessed by Harry Koger, IWAP; Eugene Spencer, JCN, 5.

10. Eugene Spencer, JCN, 7; *PGR*, Sept. 30, 1965.

11. Eugene Spencer, JCN, 5; Nathaniel Jones, JCN, 8–9; Odessa Ross, JCN, 10; A. C. Garner, JCN, 20; Odessa Ross, JCN, 10; A. C. Garner, JCN, 20; Nathaniel Jones (with Julia Jones) June 1996 interview.

12. Nathaniel Jones (with Julia Jones) June 1996 interview; *PGR*, Dec. 23, 1965; Eugene Spencer, JCN, 5; A. C. Garner, JCN, 20.

13. *PGR*, Dec. 23, 1965.

14. Calvin Williams, JCN, 14; Calvin Williams file, SCRLR; James Miller Feb. 1994 interview.

15. Nathaniel Jones 1992 interview; Nathaniel Jones Aug. 1991 interview; Eugene Spencer, JCN, 6; George Henry Walker, JCN, 12; James Dorsey, JCN, 55.

16. Calvin Williams, JCN, 14; *PGR*, Dec. 16, 1965; Nathaniel Jones, JCN, 8–9.

17. James Dorsey Dec. 1994 interview; James Dorsey, JCN, 55; Calvin Williams, JCN, 14–15; Calvin Williams, CHT, 172; Nathaniel Jones 1992 interview; Nathaniel Jones (with Julia Jones) June 1996 interview; A. C. Garner, JCN, 20; George Walker, JCN, 12; James Miller Feb. 1994 interview; Nathaniel Jones, JCN, 9.

18. *PGR*, Dec. 30, 1965.

Chapter Eight

1. D. B. Crockett report, Oct. 13, 1964; A. L. Hopkins report, July 21–28, 1965; Charles E. Snodgrass to T. B. Birdsong and A. D. Morgan, Aug. 9, Nov. 29, 1965, all PBJP; *Jackson Clarion-Ledger*, Mar. 3, 1967, EKP; June [1966]: Report written for May, Miss. Quarterly Report [by Ken Dean], *SRCP*; *Freedom Information Service, Mississippi Newsletter*, No. 25, Aug. 11, 1967, 1, RBP; John Dittmer, *Local People*, 391.

2. Stewart interview; James Dorsey 1992 interview; James Dorsey Feb. 1994 interview; Nathaniel Jones (with Julia Jones) June 1996 interview; F. A. White, JCN, 8; Calvin Williams file, SCRLR.

3. Nathaniel Jones 1992 interview; Nathaniel Jones (with Julia Jones) June 1996 interview.

4. James Dorsey Dec. 1994 interview; James Dorsey 1992 interview.

5. Ernest Jones, JCN, 63; Calvin Williams, CHT, 172; Calvin Williams, JCN, 14.

6. James Dorsey Feb. 1994 interview; Nathaniel Jones 1992 interview; Sayles interview; Calvin Williams, JCN, 15; Eugene Spencer, JCN, 6; Chatfield, "Anatomy of a Protest Movement," 38, 59; J. C. Dunbar, JCN, 11; Nathaniel Jones (with Julia Jones) June 1996 interview; Ernest Kennedy Brandon interview; Garner interview.

7. Mercedes Wright, "Status of Withholding Patronage Campaign in Jackson, Mississippi," Aug. 9–22, 1964, NAACPP.

8. James Miller Feb. 1994 interview; Young interview; Dorsey 2001 interview; McGehee, " 'You Do Not Own What You Cannot Control,' " 12–20; Reagon, "Women as Culture Carriers," 211; James Miller 1996 interview.

9. Guster interview; Sayles interview; Gloster Current to Lucille Black, May 10, 1966, NAACPP; Ethel Warner, CHT, 873; Ernest Kennedy Brandon interview; Marjorie Brandon 1992 interview.

10. McGehee, " 'You Do Not Own What You Cannot Control,' " 15; Reagon, "Songs Are Free," 24:20; Reagon and Cluster, "Borning Struggle," 20; Sullivan interview.

11. Martin interview; Carolyn Miller interview; Ezekiel Rankin interview.

12. James Miller Feb. 1994 interview; *Vicksburg Citizens' Appeal*, Oct. 19, 1966, EKP; Ezekiel Rankin interview; Sayles interview; James Dorsey Feb. 1994 interview; Guster interview; Brown interview, USM, 36.

13. James Dorsey 1992 interview; Dorothy Brandon interview; Guster interview; McClorine interview; Nathaniel Jones (with Julia Jones) June 1996 interview.

14. John Eggleston, CHT, 653; Walker 1992 interview; Guster interview; Walter Griffin, CHT, 261.

15. Walker 1992 interview; Anderson interview; Nathaniel Jones (with Julia Jones) June 1996 interview; James Dorsey 1992 interview; Doss interview, USM, 13; Guster interview.

16. Lum interview; Guster interview; James Dorsey 1992 interview; Walls interview, USM, 11; Melvin McFatter FBI file (HQ) 44-32887, FBIP; James Dorsey Dec. 1994 interview; Nathaniel Jones (with Julia Jones) June 1996 interview; Walker 1992 interview; Current to Roy Wilkins and John Morsell, Apr. 20, 1966; *Williams, Calvin, Port Gibson v.* file; Thomas Watts file, all SCRLR.

17. Charles E. Snodgrass to Birdsong and Morgan, Feb. 7, 1966; Snodgrass to Birdsong and Morgan, Feb. 11, 1966, both PBJP; Current to Black, May 10, 1966, NAACPP; Doss interview, USM, 17; Marjorie Brandon, CHT, 473; Guster interview.

18. Wells interview; Julia Jones interview, *IAL*, 44; Julia Jones 1992 interview; Nathaniel Jones (with Julia Jones) Aug. 1996 interview; Julia Jones 1992 interview.

19. Sayles interview; Guster interview; Wells interview; Wells interview, *IAL*, 66.

20. Nathaniel H. Jones et al. to the Mayor and Board of Aldermen et al., Mar. 14, 1966, NAACPP; Calvin Williams et al. to Mayor et al., Mar. 23, 1966, SCP; Evers and Jolliff et al. to Copiah County Board of Supervisors et al., Aug. 19, 1966; Ferd Allen et al. to Mayor et al., Dec. 9, 1965, both PBJP.

21. Nathaniel H. Jones et al. to the Mayor and Board of Aldermen et al., Mar. 14, 1966, NAACPP.

22. James Dorsey 1992 interview.

23. Davis interview; Wells interview; Julia Jones 1992 interview; Artemeasie Brandon interview.

24. Mack Tisdale, CHT, 891–93, 895, 900; James Hudson, CHT, 1172–73; Dan McCay, CHT, 134; Nathaniel Jones, CHT, 181; Board of Aldermen and Board of Supervisors, Jefferson County, to Negro Citizens of Jefferson County, Mississippi, Dec. 15, 1965, Exhibit C-68, *Claiborne Hardware, et al. v. NAACP, et al*, MSCS; Johnston, *Mississippi's Defiant Years*, 326–27.

25. Devoual interview; Davenport interview, USM, 22; Leland Cole report, Sept. 26, 27, 1966; Cole report, Sept. 28, 29, 1966; Cole report, Oct. 3, 4, 1966, all PBJP; William Hay, CHT, 1167; Waddy Abraham interview; Charles Evers, CHT, 4670; Mack Tisdale, CHT, 891–93, 900; George Walker, JCN, 16; Rosalie Abraham interview, USM, 16; Atlas interview.

26. Fairclough, *To Redeem the Soul of America*, 403; William Owens, CHT, 685; Charles Evers, *Have No Fear*, 156.

27. Davenport interview, USM, 3; Evers interview; James Beesley interview; Nelson interview; Waddy Abraham, CHT, 1195.

28. Mack Tisdale, CHT, 891–93; James U. Allen, CHT, 1204–5; James Dorsey 1992 interview; Aaron Henry quoted in Burner, *And Gently He Shall Lead Them*, 189; [Snodgrass], "Appraisal of the Natchez Situation," Sept. 22, 1965, PBJP; Walker 1992 interview.

29. James Dorsey Dec. 1994 interview; James Dorsey 1992 interview; A. C. Garner, JCN, 20; Rosalie Abraham interview, USM, 30.

30. Walker 1992 interview.

Chapter Nine

1. Roy Wilkins to Charles Evers, Apr. 6, 1966, NAACPP.
2. *Evers v. Birdsong* file, SCRLR.
3. Ibid.
4. Ibid.
5. James Dorsey 1992 interview; Albert Butler interview; *Evers v. Birdsong* file, SCRLR.
6. *Evers v. Birdsong* file, SCRLR.
7. Ibid.
8. Ibid.
9. Ibid.
10. Ibid.
11. Julia Jones (with Nathaniel Jones) Aug. 1996 interview; Nathaniel Jones (with Julia Jones) Aug. 1996 interview; Warner interview; Willie Wilson interview; *Evers v. Birdsong* file, SCRLR.
12. *Evers v. Birdsong* file, SCRLR.
13. Ibid.
14. Nathaniel Jones (with Julia Jones) Aug. 1996 interview; McCay interview.
15. *Brandon v. Alcorn* file, *Evers v. Birdsong* file, SCRLR.
16. *Evers v. Birdsong* file, SCRLR; Sellers interview. For a fuller discussion of student efforts to protest at Alcorn, see Emilye Crosby, "Common Courtesy," 101–47.
17. Minutes, Apr. 12, 1966, IHLP; James Dorsey 1992 interview; James Miller Feb. 1994 interview; Nathaniel Jones 1992 interview; Scott interview; Anderson interview; Snodgrass report, Mar. 14, 1966, PBJP.
18. McCay interview; Warner interview.

Chapter Ten

1. Charles E. Snodgrass to T. B. Birdsong and A. D. Morgan, Mar. 30, 1966; Snodgrass to Birdsong and Morgan, Apr. 1, 1966, both PBJP; Walter Griffin, CHT, 244; Anonymous no. 3 interview.

2. Snodgrass to Birdsong and Morgan, Apr. 4, 1966, PBJP; Jimmy Ellis, CHT, 742; Melvin McFatter interview; James Hudson, CHT, 99; Walker 1992 interview; Rudolph Shields, CHT, 431.

3. PGR, Apr. 7, 1966; *Evers v. Birdsong* file, SCRLR; James Hudson, CHT, 100–1, 1174; Waddy Abraham, CHT, 1191–92; Dan McCay, CHT, 134.

4. Warner interview; Gloster Current to Roy Wilkins and John Morsell, Apr. 20, 1966; "Time to Dig," Aug. 8, 1966, both NAACPP; Thomas Watts file, SCRLR.

5. Marjorie Brandon 1992 interview; Alex Warner, CHT, 881; Katie B. Wells, CHT, 362; Sullivan interview.

6. Marjorie Brandon 1992 interview; Snodgrass report, Mar. 14, 1966; Snodgrass memo, Apr. 1, 1966, both PBJP; *Vicksburg Citizens' Appeal*, Sept. 21, Oct. 19, 1966, EKP.

7. Devoual interview.

8. James Dorsey 1992 interview; James Miller 1996 interview; King interview.

9. James Dorsey Feb. 1994 interview; Carl Brandon interview; Devoual interview.

10. Scott interview; Devoual interview; James Miller Feb. 1994 interview; Jimmy Ellis interview.

11. Albert Butler interview; James Miller Feb. 1994 interview.

12. James Miller Feb. 1994 interview; Scott interview; Martin interview; Devoual interview.

13. Devoual interview; Carolyn Miller interview; James Miller 1996 interview; Carl Brandon interview.

14. Marjorie Brandon, CHT, 474; Murriel Cullins, CHT, 1113; Quitman H. McDaniel Jr., CHT, 1164; Walter Griffin, CHT, 241; Julia Jones (with Nathaniel Jones) Aug. 1996 interview; Ross interview; Charles Evers, CHT, 415.

15. Devoual interview; *Shields v. Mississippi* file and *Smith, Bill B., MS v.* file, SCRLR; James Miller Feb. 1994 interview; Sayles interview; Bunton interview.

16. Wells interview, *IAL*; Wells interview; *PGR*, Jan. 14, 1960; Jan. 31, 1963.

17. Nathaniel Jones (with Julia Jones) Aug. 1996 interview; Guster interview; Standley, "Role of Black Women," 187.

18. Elmo James Scott Jr., CHT, 264, 272–74; James Whitney, CHT, 284–85, 293; Warner interview; Ernest "Tullos" Brown, JCN, 41; Le Tourneau Corporation file, SCRLR; Ernest "Tullos" Brown, CHT, 991; Barbara B. Ellis, CHT, 147.

19. Jimmy Ellis, CHT, 756; R. L. T. Smith, CHT, 1228; Albert Butler interview; Sayles interview; Annie Jones interview, USM, 34.

20. Snodgrass to Birdsong and Morgan, Apr. 1, 1966, PBJP; Charles Evers speech, June 21, 1966, *Claiborne Hardware, et al. v. NAACP, et al.*, MSCS; Charles Evers, *Evers*; Charles Evers, *Have No Fear*, 187; Evers interview.

21. *Mississippi Free Press*, Dec. 28, 1963; Johnston to Glazier, July 2, 1964, SCP; King interview.

22. Lee, "Passionate Pursuit of Justice," 383; *NYT*, June 7, 1965. Although Payne does not say this, Rudy Shields almost certainly organized the Spirit (Payne, *I've Got the Light of Freedom*, 323–27). Herman Leach, who worked with Rudy Shields in Yazoo City, Mississippi, reported that Shields organized boycott enforcement groups called "the Spirit" (Herman Leach interview, USM, 16–17).

23. Marjorie Brandon 1992 interview; Ferd Allen, CHT, 798; William Matt Ross, CHT, 919; Evers interview; Anonymous no. 3 interview.

24. James Dorsey 1992 interview; Gray interview; Charles Evers, CHT, 403; Marjorie Brandon 1992 interview; Charles Evers, *Have No Fear*, 187; Laura Cullins, CHT, 1101–4;

Murriel Cullins, CHT, 1109; Willie Myles, CHT, 1078–79; Jasper Coleman, CHT, 1080; Guster interview; Scott interview; George Walker, JCN, 13; Watson interview, USM, 23–24; James Bailey Jr., CHT, 328; Martin interview.

25. Barber interview; Rick Abraham interview; Celia Anderson interview; Julia Jones (with Nathaniel Jones) Aug. 1996 interview; Nathaniel Jones (with Julia Jones) Aug. 1996 interview; Willie Wilson interview; McCay interview.

26. James Miller 1996 interview; Carolyn Miller interview; Dungee interview; Watson interview, USM, 23–24.

27. Doss interview, USM, 14; James Dorsey 1992 interview; Devoual interview; Melvin McFatter interview; Willie Wilson interview; Sayles interview.

28. James Miller Feb. 1994 interview; Emerson Davis, CHT, 1096–98.

29. Scott interview; Warner interview; James Dorsey 1992 interview; Melvin McFatter interview; McCay interview; Murriel Cullins, CHT, 1116; Emerson Davis, CHT, 1091–92; *Shields, Port Gibson v.* file and *Alexander v. Mississippi* file, SCRLR.

30. Marjorie Brandon 1992 interview; Charles Evers, CHT, 4695; Laura Cullins, CHT, 1101–4; Murriel Cullins, CHT, 1109.

31. Guster interview.

32. Nathaniel Jones (with Julia Jones) Aug. 1996 interview.

33. Vera Smith, JCN, 32–33; Warner interview; Scott interview; FBI report, May 19, 1966; Racial Demonstration, Port Gibson, Mississippi, May 13, 1966, Port Gibson Racial Matters, FBIP; James Dorsey, JCN, 57.

34. George Walker, JCN, 13; "Brief for Petitioners," *Claiborne Hardware, et al. v. NAACP, et al.*, 8, 28–29, MSCS; Dan McCay, CHT, 139; Arthur Wyatt, CHT, 591–92; Jasper Coleman, CHT, 1081; Willie Myles, CHT, 1078–79.

35. James Miller Feb. 1994 interview; Anderson interview; Director to file, May 2, 1969, SCP.

36. Charles Evers, CHT, 4685; Guster interview; Hystercine Rankin interview, USM, 21; Marjorie Brandon 1992 interview.

Chapter Eleven

1. *Shields v. Mississippi* file, SCRLR.

2. Anonymous interview no. 3; Jane Ellis interview, USM, 20; *PGR*, May 19, 1966; James Miller Feb. 1994 interview.

3. Branch, *Pillar of Fire*, 37; M. M. McFatter interview; Charles Evers, *Have No Fear*, 202.

4. Mars, *Witness in Philadelphia*, 212; Walker 1992 interview; Nathaniel Jones (with Julia Jones) Aug. 1996 interview.

5. Allen interview; Barbara B. Ellis, CHT, 150; Lum interview; Albert Butler interview.

6. Blackwell interview; Nathaniel Jones (with Julia Jones) Aug. 1996 interview; Jimmy Ellis interview.

7. Albert Butler interview; James Dorsey 1992 interview; Warner interview; Devoual

interview; James Dorsey Feb. 1994 interview; Thompson Webb interview; Annie Rankin to Freedom Friends, Mar. 4, 1967, ARP; Davenport interview, USM, 8.

8. *PGR*, Apr. 28, 1966.

9. Albert Butler interview; James Dorsey Dec. 1994 interview; Henrietta Dorsey interview; Shaifer interview, USM, 14; James Hudson, CHT, 96, 108, 111, 1178; Charles Groves, JCN, 33; Hudson interview.

10. Charles Evers, CHT, 4669, 4682, 4697; Guster interview; Charles Groves, JCN, 33; James Dorsey Dec. 1994 interview; Albert Butler interview.

11. Allen interview; Waddy Abraham interview; James Hudson, CHT, 105; Quitman H. McDaniel Jr., CHT, 1163.

12. *Williams, Calvin, Port Gibson v.* file, SCRLR; James Dorsey Dec. 1994 interview; Fairclough, *Race & Democracy*, 326.

13. Lum interview; *PGR*, Apr. 7, 21, 28, May 19, 1966.

14. *PGR*, Apr. 7, 28, 1966; Allen interview; McCay interview.

15. McCay interview; Murad Nasif, CHT, 1188; Rosalie Abraham interview, USM, 32; Lum interview; Charles Evers, CHT, 4680; Evers interview; Marjorie Brandon 1996 interview.

16. *PGR*, Apr. 21, 28, 1966; Waddy Abraham, CHT, 1195–96; Sullivan interview; Rick Abraham interview.

17. Guster interview; Walls interview, USM, 33; Hopkins report, July 7, 1966, PBJP.

18. Wells interview, *IAL*, 67–68; William Matt Ross, CHT, 920; Odessa Ross, CHT, 915; Horace Lightfoot, CHT, 600.

19. *Evers v. Birdsong* file, Le Tourneau Corporation file, SCRLR; Artemeasie Brandon interview; Dorothy Brandon interview; Nathaniel Jones 1992 interview; Frank Davis quoted in Blank, *How to Become Sheriff*; Murad Nasif, CHT, 1188; James Hudson, CHT, 1173.

20. James Dorsey 1992 interview; Wells interview, *IAL*, 67–68; Guster interview.

21. Barkan, *Protesters on Trial*, 31; Bob Moses quoted in Cagin and Dray, *We Are Not Afraid*, 148; Ann Marie Collins file; George Lee Weddington file; *Shields, Port Gibson v.* file; *Shields v. Mississippi* file; *Shields and Williams v. MS* file; *Shields, Rudy, MS v.* file, all in SCRLR.

22. *Shields, Rudy, Port Gibson v.* file, *Shields, Rudy, MS v.* file, SCRLR; Charles Groves, JCN, 33–34.

23. *Watts, Thomas, MS v.* file; Daniel Giles file; *Shields, Rudy, MS v.* file, all in SCRLR.

24. *Shields and Williams v. MS* file; *Alexander v. Mississippi* file; *Watts, Thomas, Miss. v.* file, all in SCRLR.

25. *Shields v. Mississippi* file; *Smith, Bill B., MS v.* file; Daniel Giles file; Ann Marie Collins file; *Shields, Rudy, Ms. v.* file; *Shields, Rudy, Port Gibson v.* file; *Shields and Williams v. MS* file, all in SCRLR.

26. Dan McCay, CHT, 139; Melvin McFatter interview; Tom Scarbrough report, Jan. 14, 1966, PBJP; Johnston to Jimmy Walker, *Fayette Chronicle*, Dec. 27, 1965, SCP.

27. James Dorsey 1992 interview; James Dorsey Dec. 1994 interview; Charles Evers, June 21, 1966, speech, *Claiborne Hardware, et al. v. NAACP, et al.*, MSCS.

28. Marjorie Brandon 1992 interview; Dorothy Brandon interview; Calvin Williams, JCN, 16; Melvin McFatter FBI file (HQ) 44-32887.

29. Mars, *Witness in Philadelphia*, 102; James Beesley interview; Jimmy Ellis, CHT, 759–60, 762–63; James Bailey Jr., CHT, 328–29; Alexander Collins, CHT, 215; Calvin Williams, CHT, 177; James Dorsey 1992 interview; Rudolph Shields, CHT, 436–37; Leesco Guster, CHT, 503; John Eggleston, CHT, 654; McClorine interview; Robert Butler Jr., CHT, 816.

30. Warner interview; Matt Ross interview; James Dorsey 1992 interview; Guster interview; Calvin Williams, CHT, 177; James Dorsey 1992 interview; Calvin Williams Jr. interview; McClorine interview; Robert Butler Jr., CHT, 816.

31. Artemeasie Brandon interview; Marjorie Brandon 1996 interview; Ernest Kennedy Brandon interview; Marjorie Brandon 1992 interview.

32. Tisdale interview, USM, 8; James Dorsey 1992 interview.

33. Melvin McFatter FBI file (HQ) 44-32887; Anderson interview; Henry Anderson file, SCRLR.

34. Warner interview; Walker 1992 interview; McCay interview; United Klans of America, Incorporated, Racial Matters–Klan, Nov. 4, 1966, Claiborne County Racial Matters, MS, 157-JN-6101, FBIP; Report about James Jones, Jan. 25, 1967, Claiborne County Racial Matters, MS, 157-JN-6101, FBIP; *PGR*, May 5, 1966; Jimmy Ellis interview; Report about James Jones, Jan. 25, 1967, Claiborne County Racial Matters, MS, 157-JN-6101, FBIP.

35. Charles E. Snodgrass to T. B. Birdsong and A. D. Morgan, May 16, 1966, PBJP.

36. Allen interview; McCay interview; McDaniel interview, USM, 9; *PGR*, May 5, 1966.

37. McMillen, *Citizens' Council*, 266; Nelson, *Terror in the Night*; D. B. Crockett report, Oct. 13, 1964, PBJP; Cobb, "'Somebody Done Nailed Us,'" 920; Davis, *"Deep South Reencountered"*; Johnston, *Mississippi's Defiant Years*, 70–71; Allen interview; McDaniel interview, USM, 5, 9; *PGR*, Aug. 27, 1998.

38. McCay interview; James Dorsey 1992 interview; Walker 1992 interview; Scott interview; Dan McCay, speaking at "Time for a Change" forum, Dec. 3, 1994 (videotape); Johnny Yarborough file, SCRLR; Evers interview; Bunton interview; Aschenbrenner interview; Shapiro interview.

39. Scott interview; Devoual interview; James Dorsey 1992 interview; James Dorsey Dec. 1994 interview; Bunton interview. Both names of the self-defense group were adopted in June 1966, but I follow local custom and use them to refer to the self-defense group throughout its history (Jimmy Ellis, CHT, 732, 759–60; Rudolph Shields, CHT, 432, 436–37; Warner interview; James Whitney, CHT, 292; Nathaniel Jones 1992 interview; Robert Butler Jr., CHT, 813; James Odom, CHT, 776).

40. Walker 1992 interview; Walker 1994 interview; Payne, *I've Got the Light of Freedom*, 205–6; Warner interview.

Chapter Twelve

1. Robert Parris Moses 1983 interview; Payne, *I've Got the Light of Freedom*, 204; Dittmer, *Local People*; Fairclough, *Race & Democracy*; Tyson, *Radio Free Dixie*.

2. King, *Freedom Song*, 91; Jodie "Preacher" Saffold in Rural Organizing Cultural Center, *Minds Stayed on Freedom*, 64; Marjorie Brandon 1992 interview; Walls interview, USM, 23. See also McClorine interview.

3. Sayles interview; James Dorsey 1992 interview; Henry E. Briggs to Wilkins, Jan. 17, 1966; John Morsell to Briggs, Mar. 16, 1966, both in NAACPP; Charles Evers, *Have No Fear*, 36; Evers interview.

4. James Dorsey 1992 interview; Devoual interview; Charles Evers, CHT, 4699–700; Carolyn Miller interview; Scott interview; Jimmy Ellis interview.

5. Bunton interview; James Miller Feb. 1994 interview; Rudolph Shields, CHT, 435; see also McLawrence Bailey, CHT, 351.

6. Bunton interview; Jimmy Ellis interview; Leach interview, USM, 5.

7. Sullivan interview; Rick Abraham interview; Brown interview, USM, 19; Scott interview; Bunton interview; Guster interview.

8. *Shields v. Mississippi* file, SCRLR; Sayles interview; Allen interview; Charles Evers speech, June 21, 1966, *Claiborne Hardware, et al. v. NAACP, et al.*, MSCS; Chatfield, "Port Gibson, Mississippi," 47; Carl Brandon interview; Mass Meeting, May 6, 1969, JCN, 78.

9. Wells interview, *IAL*, 67–68; Anne Marie Collins file and Elza Williams file, SCRLR; Walker 1994 interview.

10. Alcorn Commencement Arrests file, SCRLR; Walker 1992 interview; Vera Smith, JCN, 36; Charles E. Snodgrass to T. B. Birdsong and A. D. Morgan, May 25, 1966, PBJP.

11. Charles Evers, *Have No Fear*, 83.

12. *Shields and Williams v. MS* file and LeTourneau file, SCRLR; Artemeasie Brandon interview.

13. *Shields and Williams v. MS* file, SCRLR.

14. Alcorn Commencement Arrests file, *Watts Thomas, Miss. v.* file, Anne Marie Collins file, *Shields, Rudy, Port Gibson v.* file, Lawrence Bailey file, George Lee Weddington file, *Port Gibson v. Calvin Williams* file, Henry Anderson file, *Smith, Bill B., MS v.* file, *Shields and Williams, v. MS* file, *Alexander v. Mississippi* file, *Shields, Port Gibson v.* file, *Shields v. Mississippi* file, SCRLR.

15. Aschenbrenner interview.

16. *Jackson Clarion-Ledger*, June 9, 1966, EKP; U.S. Commission on Civil Rights, "Voting in Mississippi," 71; Snodgrass to Birdsong and Morgan, July 20, 1966, PBJP; *PGR*, June 9, Sept. 1, 1966; Parker, *Black Votes Count*, 59; Dittmer, *Local People*, 389–97.

17. Snodgrass to Birdsong and Morgan, June 6, 1966, PBJP; Daniel Giles file, SCRLR; Charles Evers speech, June 21, 1966, *Claiborne Hardware, et al. v. NAACP, et al.*, MSCS.

18. Charles Evers speech, June 21, 1966, *Claiborne Hardware, et al. v. NAACP, et al.*, MSCS.

19. MHP report, June 25, 1966; Jimmie Felder report, June 21, 1966, PBJP; Charles Evers speech, June 21, 1966, *Claiborne Hardware, et al. v. NAACP, et al.*

20. Fairclough, *Race & Democracy*, 342–43, 345; Lipsitz, *Life in the Struggle*, 94–95; Sims quoted in Raines, *My Soul Is Rested*, 417–21; Sims quoted in Grant, ed., *Black Protest*, 336–43; CES [Snodgrass] report, Sept. 27, 1965; E. F. Ray to Snodgrass, Jan. 27, 1966;

Birdsong and Morgan to Snodgrass, Feb. 4, 1966, all in PBJP; Umoja, "Eye for an Eye," 200–201; *Vicksburg Citizens' Appeal*, Sept. 20, 1965, EKP; FBI report, Oct. 25, 1965, Deacons of Defense and Justice, Incorporated, Racial Matters, FBIP; James Whitney, CHT, 293.

21. Charles Evers, CHT, 4699–700, 4705, 4710; Informant report, Aug. 27, 1965, SCP; Strain, " 'We Walked Like Men,' " 61; Sims quoted in Grant, ed., *Black Protest*, 342.

22. George Walker, JCN, 44; Calvin Williams, JCN, 16; Jimmy Ellis, CHT, 761; Charles Evers, CHT, 4710; Rudolph Shields, CHT, 432, 433, 436; James Whitney, CHT, 292–93. See also Elmo Scott and Roosevelt Henry, JCN, 70; Nathaniel Jones 1992 interview; and Camphor interview.

23. Umoja, "Eye for an Eye," 206; Guyot interview; Informant report, July 20, 1966, Port Gibson, PBJP; Rudolph Shields, CHT, 436; Robert Butler Jr., CHT, 813; Jimmy Ellis, CHT, 733; Scott interview; James Odom, CHT, 776; Barbara B. Ellis, CHT, 146.

24. Hopkins report, July 7, 1966, PBJP; Bill Minor, "Sovereignty Unit's Role in Race Relations Bared," *New Orleans Times-Picayune*, May 5, 1968, SCP; "Rudolph Arthur Shields: Racial Matters," Aug. 29, 1967, FBIP; "FBI–Deacons for Defense and Justice File (157-2466)," in O'Reilly, *Racial Matters*, 394 n. 24; Ken Dean to Ed Stanfield, July 7, 1966, SRCP.

25. *Shields, Port Gibson v.* file, *Shields, Rudy, MS v.* file, SCRLR; George Walker, JCN, 44; Rudolph Shields, CHT, 434; Jimmy Ellis, CHT, 762–63; Scott interview.

26. *Watts, Thomas, Miss. v.* file, SCRLR; FBI Report, Sept. 6, 1967, Woodville and Centreville, Mississippi, Sept. 2, 4, 1967, Claiborne County Racial Matters, FBIP.

27. Rudolph Shields, CHT, 439; Melvin McFatter interview; Scott interview; James Dorsey Dec. 1994 interview; Leland Cole report, Jan. 5, 1967, PBJP; *Shields, Rudy, MS v.* file, SCRLR.

28. *Shields, Rudy, MS v.* file, SCRLR; Hopkins report, July 7, 1966, PBJP; George Walker, JCN, 44.

29. *Shields, Rudy, MS v.* file, SCRLR; Hopkins report, July 7, 1966, PBJP; Barbara B. Ellis, CHT, 146.

30. Strain, " 'We Walked Like Men,' " 45, 50–51; James Whitney, CHT, 304; Walker 1992 interview; *Vicksburg Citizens' Appeal*, Sept. 20, 1965, EKP; Walker 1994 interview; Sims quoted in Grant, ed., *Black Protest*, 343; Bunton interview; Warner interview; Rudolph Shields, CHT, 432–33, 438; Walker 1992 interview.

31. A. C. Garner, JCN, 21; Garner interview; Calvin Williams, JCN, 15–16; Bunton interview.

32. Hopkins report, July 7, 1966, PBJP; Rudolph Shields, CHT, 432–33; James Dorsey Dec. 1994 interview; James Whitney, CHT, 296, 305; Jimmy Ellis, CHT, 738; Henry Anderson, CHT, 673–79; Scott interview; Cole report, Oct. 21, 1966, SCP. Adam Fairclough (*Race & Democracy*, 80) writes that in 1942, whites in New Orleans believed "that blacks had acquired hidden caches of arms and planned a 'race uprising.' "

33. Rudolph Shields, CHT, 432–33; James Dorsey Dec. 1994 interview; Walker 1994 interview.

34. Melvin McFatter interview; Lum interview; Hopkins report, July 7, 1966, PBJP; Informant report, July 20, 1966, PBJP.

35. Snodgrass to Birdsong and Morgan, July 20, 1966, PBJP.

36. Restricted, Port Gibson, July 20, 1966, PBJP; James Dorsey Dec. 1994 interview.

37. Walker 1992 interview; Walker 1994 interview; Scott interview; Bunton interview; Strain, " 'We Walked Like Men,' " 49–50. For similar arguments about the Deacons serving as a parallel law enforcement group and examples in other places, see FBI report, Mar. 28, 1967, no. 157-3290, FBIP; FBI Report, Mar. 28, 1966, no. 157-2466, Deacons of Defense and Justice, Inc., Racial Matters, FBIP; and Umoja, "Eye for an Eye." Calvin Williams and Robert Butler ran for sheriff. George Walker and Nathaniel Minor became deputy sheriffs. Jimmy Ellis became a constable and judge. James Whitney and Julius Warner worked for the sheriff's department as jailers or dispatchers. See McCay interview; Walker 1992 interview; Johnston to file, Sept. 8, 1966, PBJP; Watson interview, USM, 30–31; James Miller Feb. 1994 interview; Albert Butler interview; Charles Groves, JCN, 34; and *Shields, Rudy, Ms v.* file, SCRLR.

38. James Miller 1996 interview; George Walker, JCN, 44. See also A. C. Garner and Roosevelt Henry, JCN, 50; Walker 1992 interview; Walker 1994 interview; Hopkins report, July 7, 1966, PBJP; and Cole report, July 21, 22, 24, 25, 26, 1967, PBJP.

39. Walker 1992 interview.

40. Lipsitz, *Life in the Struggle*, 96; James Miller 1996 interview; James Miller Feb. 1994 interview; Devoual interview; Carolyn Miller interview.

41. Umoja, "Eye for an Eye," 188–89; Strain, " 'We Walked Like Men,' " 54; Tyson, "Robert F. Williams," 551; Elmo Scott and Roosevelt Henry, JCN, 71; James Whitney, CHT, 295; James Miller 1996 interview.

Chapter Thirteen

1. Gloster Current to Roy Wilkins and John Morsell, Apr. 20, 1966; Current to Charles Evers, Apr. 28, 1966; Current to Roosevelt Henry, Apr. 28, 1966, all NAACPP.

2. Jack Young to Current, May 28, 1966; Current to Evers, June 13, 1966; Current to Henry Lee Moon, May 18, 1966, all NAACPP.

3. Barbara Morris to Jack Young, Feb. 10, 1966; Barbara A. Morris to Robert I. Carter, Feb. 25, 1966, both NAACPP.

4. *Vicksburg Citizens' Appeal*, Feb. 8, 1967, EKP; Erle Johnston to Tom Scarbrough, Jan. 11, 1966; Tom Scarbrough report, Jan. 14, 1966; Editorial for *Fayette Chronicle*, [Jan. 1966], all PBJP; Scarbrough to Johnston, Jan. 11, 1966; Rep. Geoghegan to House of Rep. [Jan. 1966]; "Evers Denies He Promoted Boycott for Personal Gain," *Jackson Daily News*, Jan. 19, 1966; Hopkins report, Mar. 4, 1966, all SCP; Johnston to Herman Glazier, Jan. 17, 1966, Lawrence Guyot papers in author's possession.

5. Maria L. Marcus to Wilkins, Jan. 28, 1966; Current to Morsell, Feb. 10, 1966; Myrtle Johnson to Kivie Kaplan, Feb. 11, 1966; Wilkins to Evers, Mar. 4, 1966; Evers to Wilkins, Mar. 28, 1966; Current to Henry, Apr. 28, 1966, all NAACPP.

6. Gene Roberts, "N.A.A.C.P. May Oust Evers As Aide in Mississippi," *NYT*, Sept. 10, 1965; "Civil Rights Leaders Look at Genesis of 'Black Power,'" *Jackson Clarion-Ledger*, Aug. 25, 1966, SCP; Falba Ruth Conic to Current, Aug. 13, 1966; Current to Conic, Aug. 19, 1966, both NAACPP.

7. Current to Henry, Apr. 28, 1966, NAACPP; "Evers Calls for Beating of Negroes," *Jackson Clarion-Ledger*, July 26, 1966, SCP; Robert Beals in *PGR*, May 12, 1966; James Dorsey Dec. 1994 interview; King interview.

8. Charles Evers, *Have No Fear*, 136; Current to Morsell, Oct. 5, 1964; Current to Evers, June 25, 1965, both NAACPP.

9. Payne, *I've Got the Light of Freedom*, 341, 375–77; Dittmer, *Local People*, 314–18, 325, 340, 341–43, 348–51.

10. Guyot interview; Robert Canzoneri, "Charles Evers: Mississippi's Representative Man?" *Harper's*, July 1968; Walter Rugaber, "The Brothers Evers," *NYT Magazine*, Aug. 4, 1968; Sullivan interview.

11. Roy Reed, "Negroes and Liberal Whites Score Big Gains in Mississippi," *NYT*, July 17, 1966.

12. Henry Hurt, "Boycott and Ballot," *Reporter*, Aug. 11, 1966, 23–27.

13. *Jackson Clarion-Ledger*, June 9, 1966, EKP; *PGR*, June 9, Nov. 10, 1966; James Dorsey Dec. 1994 interview.

14. Rowland Evans and Robert Novak, "New South's First Negro Political Boss," *World Journal Tribune*, Nov. 16, 1966, 37.

15. King interview; Guyot interview.

16. Reed, "Negroes and Liberal Whites Score Big"; Fairclough, *To Redeem the Soul of America*, 325–26; "Civil Rights Leaders Look at Genesis of 'Black Power'"; Canzoneri, "Charles Evers." See also Don McKee, quoted in *Jackson Clarion-Ledger*, Aug. 25, 1966.

17. Fairclough, *Race & Democracy*, 408; Reed, "Negroes and Liberal Whites Score Big."

18. Forman, *Making of Black Revolutionaries*, 401; [Snodgrass] report, Sept. 22, 1965; Charles E. Snodgrass to T. B. Birdsong and A. D. Morgan, Dec. 27, 1965, both PBJP; "Over 100 Arrested in Natchez March," *Jackson Clarion-Ledger*, Oct. 5, 1965, SCP; Charles Evers, CHT, 403; Allen interview; Lum interview.

19. Evans and Novak, "New South's First Negro Political Boss," 37; *Mississippi Independent: Community Newspaper*, Apr. 28, 1967, EKP; King interview.

20. Johnston, *Mississippi's Defiant Years*, 294–95; Wilkins and Johnston meeting, Nov. 12, 1966, *SRCP*.

21. Johnston, *Mississippi's Defiant Years*, 291; Current to Mississippi Branch Presidents, Oct. 14, 1966, NAACPP.

22. Current to Evers, Nov. 18, 1966, NAACPP.

23. "Jobs for Negroes Won by NAACP Unit in Miss," NAACPP; *New Orleans Times-Picayune, Memphis Commercial Appeal*, Jan. 27, 1967, SCP; Leland Cole report, Jan. 18–24, 1967, PBJP; Nathaniel Jones (with Julia Jones) June 1996 interview; Alexander Collins, CHT, 217; James U. Allen, CHT, 1206; Allen interview; James Hudson, CHT, 121; James Hudson notes, *Claiborne Hardware, et al. v. NAACP, et al.*, 754, MSCS; Barbara B. Ellis,

CHT, 143; Anonymous interview no. 2; Julia Jones, CHT, 539; William Matt Ross, CHT, 927.

24. Johnston to file, Sept. 8, 1966, PBJP; James Hudson, CHT, 107; McDaniel interview, USM, 7; Jan. 25, 1967, Report about James Jones, Claiborne County Racial Matters, MS, 157-JN-6101, FBIP. Yearly profit figures were determined from merchant tax returns and financial information; see *Claiborne Hardware, et al. v. NAACP, et al.*, MSCS.

25. *PGR*, Apr. 28, 1966; Headley interview.

26. May 19, 1966, "Racial Demonstration, Port Gibson, Mississippi, May 13, 1966," Claiborne County Racial Matters, MS, 157-JN-6101, FBIP; James U. Allen, CHT, 1211; Allen interview; Nathaniel Jones (with Julia Jones) June 1996 interview; Johnston, *Mississippi's Defiant Years*, 331; McDaniel interview, USM, 8; Cole report, Sept. 26, 1966, PBJP; Dean interview.

27. Davis interview; M. M. McFatter interview.

28. James U. Allen to Paul Johnson, Jan. 6, 1967; Mary B. Cressman to Johnson, Jan. 24, 1967, both PBJP.

29. Doss interview, USM, 15–16; James Dorsey, JCN, 57; Guster interview; Leesco Guster, CHT, 345.

30. For evidence about people who were involved in enforcement activity but who were never associated with the Deacons, see, for example, Martin interview; James Bailey, CHT, 328–35; McLawrence Bailey, CHT, 347–58; and Lawrence Bailey file, *McLawrence Bailey, PG v.* file, and *Bailey, James, PG v.* file, all SCRLR. For a general discussion of the Deacons and enforcement, see Scott interview; Warner interview; Robert Butler interview; Walker 1992 interview; Devoual interview; Gray interview; Umoja, "Eye for an Eye," 212–14; Rudolph Shields, CHT, 436; Elmo Scott and Roosevelt Henry, JCN, 70; A. C. Garner and Roosevelt Henry, JCN, 50; Guster interview; A. C. Garner, JCN, 21; Whitney, Bailey, and Scott file, SCRLR; Robert Butler Jr., CHT, 816; and King interview. It is impossible to conclusively prove that someone was never accused of or involved in boycott enforcement. However, it is clear that there is little or no evidence to connect some Deacons with violent boycott enforcement. Most Deacons were never formally charged with acts of violence. Moreover, only a few of them were informally accused, even in court testimony intended to demonstrate that their violence made the boycott effective. Similarly, in more than 100 oral histories, many of which include discussions of the Deacons and enforcement, no one connects George Henry Walker, Calvin Williams, or Julius Warner (who was identified by some as president of the organization) to violent enforcement. In addition, Emerson Davis, the most notorious boycott violator, testified, "I never had any trouble with George Henry Walker [and] Calvin Williams" (Emerson Davis, CHT, 1093).

31. Rudolph Shields, CHT, 435; A. C. Garner and Roosevelt Henry, JCN, 50; Guster interview; Nathaniel Jones 1992 interview.

32. Elmo Scott and Roosevelt Henry, JCN, 70; James Dorsey, JCN, 57; A. C. Garner, JCN, 22, 50; Nathaniel Jones (with Julia Jones) Aug. 1996 interview; George Walker, JCN, 47, 69; James Dorsey Feb. 1994 interview; Watson interview, USM, 41; Marjorie Brandon 1996 interview; Calvin Williams, JCN, 15; Snodgrass to Birdsong and Morgan, July 20, 1966, PBJP; Rudolph Shields, CHT, 432–33.

33. Leesco Guster, JCN, 1; A. C. Garner, JCN, 50; George Walker, JCN, 68–69; James Dorsey, JCN, 56; Guster interview; Calvin Williams, JCN, 13–14.

34. Informant report, Oct. 10, 1965, SCP; Dittmer, *Local People*, 361; Charles Evers, *Have No Fear*, 156; *NYT*, Jan. 27, 28, 1967.

35. Walker 1994 interview; Cole report, Jan. 5, 6, 9, 11, 12, 13, 15, 16, 1967, PBJP; *PGR*, Jan. 19, 1967.

36. *Shields, Rudy, MS v.* file; Davis, Alfred Lee, file, both SCRLR; FBI report, May 17, 1968, Rudolph Arthur Shields file, FBIP; Cole report, Jan. 5, 6, 9, 11, 12, 13, 15, 16, 1967, PBJP.

37. "Jobs for Negroes Won by NAACP Unit in Miss.," 1966 State Report, NAACPP; *New Orleans Times-Picayune, Memphis Commercial Appeal*, Jan. 27, 1967; *Jackson Clarion-Ledger*, Jan. 28, 1967; "Port Gibson Back to Normal Mayor Declares," *Jackson Daily News*, SCP; Walter Griffin, CHT, 224; Charles R. Dobbs, CHT, 1181; *Shields, Rudy, Port Gibson v.* file, SCRLR; Johnston to file, Jan. 30, 1967; Johnston to Glazier, Jan. 27, 1967, both PBJP; Bill Minor, "Managing the News Was Frightening," Columbus, Mississippi, *Commercial Dispatch*, Oct. 28, 1993.

38. Dorsey Dec. 1994 interview; Port Gibson High Yearbook for 1966–67, in author's possession; *PGR*, May 12, 26, June 16, Aug. 18, 25, Sept. 1, 8, Nov. 10, 1966.

Chapter Fourteen

1. Henry Hurt, "Boycott and Ballot," *Reporter*, Aug. 11, 1966, 23, 26, 27; *NYT*, Sept. 11, 1966, 64; Rowland Evans and Robert Novak, "New South's First Negro Political Boss," *World Journal Tribune*, Nov. 16, 1966, 37; *NYT*, Jan. 27, 1967, 21; Jan. 28, 1967, 12; "New Mississippi Center Offers Voting Advice in Rights Drive," *NYT*, [May 15, 1967]; *NYT*, June 25, 1967, 54; *Washington Post*, July 17, 1967, EKP; *NYT*, Aug. 10, 1967, 1, 20; Aug. 11, 1967, 34; Aug. 29, 1967, 23; Robert Canzoneri, "Charles Evers: Mississippi's Representative Man?" *Harper's*, July 1968; Walter Rugaber, "The Brothers Evers"; "Report on Mississippi State Sovereignty Commission (1964–1967)," [Jan. 1968], both PBJP.

2. "New Mississippi Center Offers Voting Advice in Rights Drive," *NYT*, [May 15, 1967], EKP; King interview; Bowie interview; Leland Cole report, Jan. 18–24, 1967, PBJP.

3. Cole report, Feb. 13, 1967; Johnston to file, Mar. 1, 1967; Cole report, Apr. 21, 1967, all PBJP; Ken Dean, Memorandum for Council Files, Feb. 20, 1967, SRCP; Johnston, *Mississippi's Defiant Years*, 339–40.

4. Charles Evers, CHT, 4696–97; Ken Dean, Memorandum for Council Files, Feb. 20, 1967, SRCP; Johnston, *Mississippi's Defiant Years*, 232, 293; Johnston to Paul Johnson, Mar. 13, 1967, SCP.

5. Johnston, *Mississippi's Defiant Years*, 232; Johnston to Cole, Mar. 31, 1967; Bill Minor, "Sovereignty Unit's Role in Race Relations Bared," *New Orleans Times-Picayune*, May 5, 1968, both SCP; Long interview; *Washington Post*, July 17, 1967; "Evers Criticized by Students," Feb. 9, 1968, both EKP; Canzoneri, "Charles Evers."

6. Johnston to file, May 23, 1967, PBJP; Cole report, July 21–26, 1967, PBJP.

7. Cole report, Feb. 19, 1968; *Freedom Information Service*, Mar. 8, 1968, both EKP; Informant report, Mar. 13, 1968, SCP.

8. David Bethea report, Mar. 24, 1967; Cole report, Mar. 29, 30, 1967, both PBJP; Davis, Alfred Lee, file; *Shields, Rudy, Ms v.* file, both SCRLR; Report on James Jones, Jan. 25, 1967, Claiborne County Racial Matters, MS, FBI file 157-JN-6101, FBIP; Cole report, Apr. 12–14, 1967; Harry O. Hoffman to Johnston, May 17, 1967, both SCP; Johnston, *Mississippi's Defiant Years*, 296.

9. "Rudolph Arthur Shields: Racial Matters," Aug. 29, 1967, FBIP; Johnston to file, Aug. 8, 1967; Erle Johnston to file, Sept. 5, 1967; Cole to Johnston, Nov. 30, 1967, all PBJP; Johnston to file, Feb. 6, 1968; telephone report from Cole to Johnston, Feb. 9, 1968; Cole report, Feb. 26, 1968; Fulton Tutor report, Oct. 19–24, 1970, all SCP; "Brief for Petitioners," *NAACP, et al. v. Claiborne Hardware, et al.*, 11, MSCS; Rick Abraham interview; Rick Abraham, "Rudy Shields [*sic*] Work in Mississippi" (in author's possession).

10. Johnston to file, May 4, 1967, SCP; Johnston to file, May 11, 1967; Cole to Johnston, May 29, 1967, both PBJP; King interview; Walter Rugaber, "The Brothers Evers," *NYT Magazine*, Aug. 4, 1968.

11. Bowie interview; September 5, 1967, Airtel to Director, FBI, from SAC, Jackson, Rudolph Arthur Shields, File number: 157-HQ-7950, FBIP; Guyot interview.

12. Umoja, "Eye for an Eye," 208; Cole report, Jan. 30–Feb. 6, 1967; Cole report, Feb. 13, 1967; Charles E. Snodgrass to A. D. Morgan and T. B. Birdsong, Sept. 6, 1967, all PBJP; Deacons for Defense and Justice, FBI file, no. 157-3290, FBIP.

13. Harry O. Hoffman Jr. to Herman Glazier, Aug. 15, 1967; David Bethea report, Mar. 24, 1967; Cole report, Mar. 29, 1967, all PBJP; Johnston to file, May 4, 1967, SCP; Charles Evers, CHT, 4701–3.

14. Johnston to file, May 9, 1967; Cole to Johnston, June 26, 1967; Johnston to file, Sept. 11, 1967; Hoffman to Johnston, Sept. 22, 1967; Hoffman to Johnston, Oct. 2, 1967, all PBJP; Johnston to Hoffman, Sept. 21, 1967, SCP.

15. Cole to Johnston, Nov. 30, 1967; Cole report, Dec. 7, 1967, both PBJP; Johnston to file, Feb. 6, 1968; Cole report, Feb. 19, 1968; "Black United's Unity Doubted by Black Mayor," *Jackson Clarion-Ledger*, Feb. 12, 1971; Informant report, Feb. 15, 1971, all SCP; Charles Evers, CHT, 401, 412, 4698, 4703; Johnston, *Mississippi's Defiant Years*, 296–97.

16. Rugaber, "Brothers Evers"; Myrlie Evers, *Watch Me Fly*, 119–20; Charles Evers, *Have No Fear*; Charles Evers, *Evers*; Current to Wilkins, Sept. 9, 1963; Donald White to Wilkins, Feb. 4, 1964; R. Hunter Morey to Wilkins, Feb. 4, 1964; Myrtle Johnson to Kivie Kaplan, Feb. 11, 1966; Falba Ruth Conic to Current, Aug. 13, 1966, all NAACPP.

17. Current to Wilkins and Morsell, June 21, 1966; Current to Evers, June 21, 1966; Current to Wilkins and Morsell, [Aug. 1966]; Evers to Current, Jan. 31, 1967; Current to Evers, Mar. 10, 1967, all NAACPP.

18. King interview; Rick Abraham interview.

19. Rick Abraham interview; Rudolph Shields, CHT, 427–28; Dorothy Brandon interview; James Whitney, CHT, 292, 300; James Miller Feb. 1994 interview; Scott interview; Brown interview, USM, 35–36; Rick Abraham interview; Rudolph Shields, CHT, 427–28; Leach interview, USM; Conversation with Akinyele K. Umoja, Dec. 1994; Rudy Shields 1984, campaign flier (in author's possession).

20. King interview; Rick Abraham interview.

21. Guyot interview; King interview; Henry Hurt, "Ballot and Bullet," *Reporter*, Aug. 11, 1966, 23–26; Roscoe Johnson, JCN, 58, 62; James Dorsey, JCN, 58; "From Reporters' Pads," JCN, 74.

22. Dittmer, *Local People*, 360–61; King interview; Bowie interview; Chatfield, "Anatomy of a Protest Movement," 50; Charles Bunton, JCN, 19, 26.

23. Guyot interview; King interview; Robert Fitzpatrick interview.

24. Sullivan interview; Lichtman interview; Guyot interview; Ken Dean quoted in Johnston, *Mississippi's Defiant Years*, 295; Long interview; Annie Rankin to Frank [Stewart] and Caroline Stewart, Jan. 18, 1968 and Annie Rankin to [Caroline] Stewart and Frank Stewart, Jan. 10, 1971, both ARP; Watson interview, USM, 35; Landers interview; McCay interview.

25. Jerry De Laughter, "Evers Scores Northern 'Exploitation' in Look at Future for Negro," *Memphis Commercial Appeal*, Jan. 19, 1967; "New Mississippi Center Offers Voting Advice in Rights Drive," *NYT*, [May 15, 1967]; "Evers Criticized by Students," Feb. 9, 1968, EKP; Rugaber, "Brothers Evers"; Payne, *I've Got the Light of Freedom*, 360–61.

26. Charles Evers, *Have No Fear*, 104, 156, 203; Payne, *I've Got the Light of Freedom*, 360–61; Rugaber, "Brothers Evers."

27. Guyot interview; Lee, "Passionate Pursuit of Justice," 410; Myrlie Evers, *Watch Me Fly*, 119.

28. Johnston to file, Sept. 11, 1967, SCP; Charles Evers, *Have No Fear*, 278; Oct. 21, 1969, [Nov. 18, 1970], Dec. 10, 1970, ARP.

29. Payne, *I've Got the Light of Freedom*, 358; *Washington Post*, July 17, 1967; "Evers at Millsaps Sees South Ahead in Race Relationships," May 18, 1967, EKP; Rugaber, "Brothers Evers."

30. Hurt, "Ballot and Bullet," 23–26; "Inside Report: New South's First Negro Political Boss," *World Journal Tribune*, Nov. 16, 1966, 37; *Washington Post*, July 17, 1967, EKP; *NYT*, June 25, 1967; Dittmer, "Politics of the Mississippi Movement," 91; Parker, *Black Votes Count*, 5, 71; McLemore, "Mississippi Freedom Democratic Party," 404–5; "Mississippi Freedom Democratic Party: The End of a Movement?" Newsletter of the New Orleans Movement for a Democratic Society, Nov. 1967, reprinted in *Freedom Information Service Newsletter*, Nov. 3, 1967; *Mississippi Independent: Community Newspaper*, Apr. 28, 1967, all EKP; King interview.

31. "Inside Report," 37; *Washington Post*, July 17, 1967, EKP.

32. "Part of the Way," *Time*, Mar. 8, 1968; "Mississippi: The Impossible Dream," *Newsweek*, Mar. 11, 1968; "Mississippi: Closer to Home," *Time*, Mar. 22, 1968; Rugaber, "Brothers Evers"; Canzoneri, "Charles Evers"; Wilkins to Evers, Mar. 13, 1968, NAACPP; McLemore, "Mississippi Freedom," 404–5, 403, 440.

33. *Freedom Information Service Mississippi Newsletter*, Nov. 8, 1968, EKP; McLemore, "Mississippi Freedom," 460–61.

34. Charles Evers, *Have No Fear*, 247; Sullivan interview.

35. Bill Minor, editorial, "Charles Evers Has Found an Unlikely Home—the GOP," *Jackson Clarion-Ledger*, July 23, 1995.

36. *Wall Street Journal*, Feb. 7, 2002; *NYT*, Dec. 31, 2002.

37. *Wall Street Journal*, Feb. 7, 2002; *NYT*, Dec. 31, 2002; John Nichols, "Unspinning the Pickering Push," *The Nation Online Beat*, Mar. 14, 2002 (<http://www.thenation.com/thebeat/index.mhtml?bid=1&pid=29>, accessed Jan. 16, 2003); *Black Commentator*, Jan. 16, 2003 (<http://www.blackcommentator.com/25/25—issues.html>, accessed Jan. 16, 2003); "Comment by Bob Zellner," Feb. 7, 2002, written for *Wall Street Journal* (in author's possession); *Jackson Clarion-Ledger*, Jan. 23, 2003.

Chapter Fifteen

1. Gloster Current, CHT, 1260; Eddie Walls, JCN, 71.

2. *Smith, Bill B. v. MS*, file, SCRLR.

3. Ibid.

4. Ibid.

5. Bilbo Smith was out of town on Easter Sunday and someone else was using the car in question that weekend. Smith did remember an earlier encounter with Perkins that he assumed was the basis for his accusation. In that incident, Perkins was standing in the middle of a two-lane road talking to the driver of a pick-up truck when Smith pulled up behind them. When the pick-up driver pulled off, Smith followed. Perkins, who was still standing in the middle of the road, yelled at Smith as he drove by (*Smith, Bill B., MS v. Smith* file, SCRLR).

6. *Shields v. Davis* file, SCRLR.

7. *Smith, Bill B. v. MS* file, SCRLR.

8. Ibid.

9. *Watts, Thomas, Miss. v.* file; *Shields, Port Gibson v.* file; *Shields v. Mississippi* file; *Alexander v. Mississippi* file; *Shields and Williams v. MS* file; *Shields, Rudy, MS v.* file; Whitney, Bailey, and Scott file; *Smith, Bill B. v. MS* file, all SCRLR.

10. I would like to thank Deseriee Kennedy, of the University of Tennessee Law School, for her thoughtful reading of an earlier draft of this material. I adopted several of her suggestions, including the use of the word "impasse."

11. Leland Cole to Johnston, Jan. 17, 1967, PBJP; Brady, *Black Monday*; *Thomas Watts v. State of Mississippi* decision, Mississippi Supreme Court, Jackson, Miss.

12. *Watts, Thomas, Miss. v.* file, SCRLR.

13. James Dorsey 1994 interview; *Watts, Thomas, Miss. v.* file; *Shields and Williams v. MS* file, both SCRLR; Chestnut, *Black in Selma*, 255–56; Aschenbrenner interview.

14. Nathaniel Jones 1992 interview; Gray interview; *PGR*, July 21, 1955; Aug. 24, 1967; *Washington Post*, July 17, 1967. Dan McCay's wife, Joyce, was the official candidate, since Mississippi prohibited sheriffs from succeeding themselves.

15. "Claiborne County," report by [Martin] Glick–[Marvin] Nathan, May 27, 1966; "Examiners for General Election, Nov. 8, 9, 10, 1966, State of Mississippi"; "In Mississippi Primary Election, June 7, 1966," Report by James P. Turner, Aug. 21, 1967, all JDP; *PGR*, Aug. 3, 1967; McClorine interview; O. W. Moses interview; Hoffmann interview; "Evers

Wants Mississippi Election Declared Invalid," Sept. 13, 1967, EKP; Mills, *This Little Light of Mine*, 184; Parker, *Black Votes Count*; Calvin C. Williams FBI file, FOIPA No. 0371449-002, FBIP.

16. Wells interview; Ross interview; Parker, *Black Votes Count*, 30–33, 72–74; *PGR*, Aug. 10, 1967; *Freedom Information Service Newsletter*, Aug. 11, 1967, EKP.

17. *PGR*, Nov. 7, 1968; Parker, *Black Votes Count*, 31; Port Gibson Enlargement of Boundaries file, SCRLR.

18. Port Gibson Enlargement of Boundaries file, SCRLR.

19. *Jackson Clarion-Ledger*, Apr. 20, 21, 22, 23, 1969; Andrew McGrew file, SCRLR.

20. Walker 1992 interview; Walker 1994 interview; McCay interview; Headley interview; Albert Butler interview; Devoual interview.

21. Chatfield, "Port Gibson, Mississippi," 52; Allen interview; Dan McCay, CHT, 141; Walker 1992 interview.

22. Charles Evers speech, Apr. 19, 1969, *Claiborne Hardware, et al. v. NAACP, et al.*, MSCS; Walker 1992 interview; Carolyn Miller interview; Young interview.

23. Nathaniel Jones, CHT, 191; Allen interview.

24. Port Gibson Enlargement of Boundaries file, SCRLR.

25. *PGR*, Apr. 24, May 22, Nov. 6, 1969; Nov. 5, 1970; *Jackson Clarion-Ledger*, Apr. 21, 1969; *Jackson Daily News*, May 24, 1969.

26. Frank Parker interview; Lum interview; Jane Ellis interview, USM, 3.

27. Waddy Abraham interview; Lum interview; Jane Ellis interview, USM; James Dorsey 1992 interview; Dixon Pyles to James Hudson, Nov. 20, 1969; Hudson to Pyles and Betty Tucker, Nov. 21, 1969; Pyles to R. D. Gage III and Hudson, Jan. 17, 1970; "Office Conference with Gage, Louis Ellis, Hudson, Pyles, Tucker, and Shell," handwritten notes, Jan. 22, 1970; Gage to Pyles, Apr. 6, 1970; Hudson to Pyles and Tucker, Sept. 1, 1970; Office conference with Pyles and Tucker, Gore, Shell, Simmons, Gage, Vaughan, Jan. 21, 1972; Dan H. Shell to Gage, Feb. 22, 1972; Gage to Pyles, Apr. 27, 1973; Gage to Pyles, Aug. 16, 1974; Pyles to Gage, May 3, 1977; Pyles to Gage, Nov. 3, 1978; all Pyles Papers, McCain Library, University of Southern Mississippi, Hattiesburg, Miss. On Dec. 7, 1978, Dixon Pyles wrote Bobby Vaughan, "Ordinarily I would take this matter up with Richard Hastings and Bobby Gage; however, they appear to be boycotting me at the present time" (Pyles to Vaughan, Dec. 7, 1978, Pyles Papers; Dobbs interview).

28. Neil A. Maxwell, "Moderates Speak Up: 200 Top Mississippians Seek to Bar Defiance of Courts in Future," *Wall Street Journal*, Oct. 3, 1962; Johnston, *Mississippi's Defiant Years*, 170–71; "List of Mississippi Business Men," SCP.

29. Mass Meeting, May 6, 1969, JCN, 79; James Dorsey Dec. 1994 interview; Anne Marie Collins file, SCRLR; Dean interview.

30. Anonymous interview no. 2; Carolyn Miller interview; Scott interview; Norton interview.

31. Dittmer, *Local People*, 404–6; *Vicksburg Citizens' Appeal*, Jan. 4, 1967, EKP; *Port Gibson Reveille*, May 12, 26, June 16, Aug. 18, 25, Sept. 1, 8, Oct. 20, 1966; Carl Brandon interview; Ernest Kennedy Brandon interview; Melvin McFatter interview; Williams inter-

view; Warner interview; Marjorie Brandon 1992 interview; Coach Hines testimony, Raymond Hynum School Board Hearing, Oct. 15, 1966, Claiborne County Board of Education Minutes, MDAH.

32. Port Gibson High yearbooks, 1966-67, 1067-68, 1968-69, 1969-70, in author's possession.

33. Ibid.

34. *PGR*, May 7, 14, Sept. 3, 10, 1970; James Dorsey 1992 interview.

35. Dobbs interview; Norton interview.

36. Thelma Crowder, CHT, 480; Walter Griffin, CHT, 220; Rachael Ellis, CHT, 956-57; Eddie Walls, CHT, 561.

37. Murad Nasif, CHT, 1188; Barbara B. Ellis, CHT, 144-45; Charles R. Dobbs, CHT, 1182; William Hay, CHT, 1169; Shreve Guthrie Jr., CHT, 1199.

38. George Haynes, "Opinion of Court" and "Final Decree," *Claiborne Hardware, et al. v. NAACP, et al.*, MSCS; *PGR*, Aug. 12, 19, 26, Sept. 16, 23, 30, 1976; *Jackson Clarion-Ledger*, Aug. 13, 20, Sept. 12, Oct. 1, 1976; *Vicksburg Evening Post*, Sept. 26, 1976; *Jackson Daily News*, Sept. 25, 1976.

39. *NYT*, Dec. 7, 1981, July 2, 1982; *Jackson Clarion-Ledger*, Mar. 21, July 3, 1982; *PGR*, Nov. 3, 1981, July 8, 1982; *NAACP, et al. v. Claiborne Hardware, et al.*, MSCS; *United States Reports* 458 (Oct. 1981), 886-940.

40. Guster interview; Devoual interview; Rachel Wilson interview.

Chapter Sixteen

1. Devoual interview; Albert Butler interview; Brown interview, USM, 33; Rachel Wilson interview; James Miller 1992 interview; Willie Wilson interview; Sayles interview; James Dorsey Dec. 1994 interview; Hystercine Rankin interview, USM, 29-30; James Miller July 1996 interview; Doss interview, USM, 22-23.

2. Shaifer interview, USM, 21; James Miller Feb. 1994 interview; Thompson Webb interview; Hystercine Rankin interview, USM, 31; Thomas R. Kendrick, "A Town in the Lee of the Race Storm: Mississippi's Port Gibson Lives in Segregated Peace—Now," *Washington Post*, July 19, 1964.

3. Thompson Webb interview; Albert Butler interview; James Miller July 1996 interview; Sayles interview; Willie Wilson interview; Alexander Collins, CHT, 215, 219; Hystercine Rankin interview, USM, 29-30; Bunton interview; James Dorsey Dec. 1994 interview; Watson interview, USM, 24; Alberta Coleman, JCN, 34-35; FDP meeting, June 5, 1969, JCN, 27; Mass Meeting, June 24, 1969, JCN, 79; Vera Smith, JCN, 32; Katie Wells, JCN, 37-38; Chatfield, "Anatomy of a Protest Movement," 76.

4. James Dorsey Dec. 1994 interview; Sayles interview.

5. Payne, *I've Got the Light of Freedom*, 361-62.

6. Bunton interview; Walker 1994 interview; James Dorsey, JCN, 58; James Dorsey Dec. 1994 interview; Sayles interview; Mass Meeting, May 6, 1969, JCN, 78.

7. James Dorsey 1992 interview; James Dorsey Dec. 1994 interview.

8. Nathaniel Jones 1992 interview.

9. James Miller Feb. 1994 interview; Barber interview; Chatfield, "Port Gibson, Mississippi," 53; Chatfield, "Anatomy of a Protest Movement," 31; Bunton interview; Bunton, JCN, 18; FDP meeting, May 1, 1969, JCN, 23; FDP meeting, June 5, JCN, 27; James Miller July 1996 interview; James Miller Dec. 1994 interview; Garner, JCN, 22; Katie Wells, JCN, 38.

10. Sullivan interview; Hoffmann interview; *Black Times*, Aug. 4, 6, 1970; *Claiborne Hardware, et al. v. NAACP, et al.*, MSCS.

11. Hoffmann interview; *NYT*, Nov. 29, 1970; James Miller Dec. 1994 interview, 11.

12. Phillips and Huttie, *Mississippi Property Tax*, 49–51; "Reassessment in Claiborne County: What It Means," part of "Proposal To: Voter Education Project, From Claiborne County Steering Committee," Oct. 15, 1974, SEFP; Jerry De Muth, "Blacks Win Elections But Not Power," Aug. 24, 1973, RB.

13. Jesse [Morris] to John Lewis, Oct. 15, 1974, SEFP.

14. "Memo to Candidates for the Board of Supervisors, from James Miller and James Devoual, re: Proposed Strategy for 1 to 20 Nov. 4th General Election," SEFP.

15. Camphor interview; Cole interview; George Walker quoted in Devoual, "People of Claiborne County," 35.

16. James Miller Dec. 1994 interview; James Miller 1996 interview; Jimmy Ellis interview.

17. James Hudson notes, *Claiborne Hardware, et al. v. NAACP, et al.; MS ex rel Lawrence & Eaton v. Ross* file; "By Candidates-Elect (alphabetical order), Status of Public Official Bond, Applications of Elected Negro Officials," Dec. 18, 1967, Bonding and Surety, both SCRLR; *Freedom Information Service Newsletter*, Dec. 29, 1967, EKP; Geneva Collins interview; Frank Parker interview; *PGR*, Jan. 8, Feb. 26, 1976.

18. Julia Jones 1992 interview; Julia Jones, speaking at "Time for a Change," Dec. 5, 1994 (videotape); James Hudson notes, *Claiborne Hardware, et al. v. NAACP, et al.*, MSCS; Barber interview.

19. Cole interview.

20. *PGR*, Oct. 20, 27, 1966; Mar. 16, 1967; James Miller Feb. 1994 interview; James Miller Dec. 1994 interview; Anderson interview; Marjorie Brandon 1992 interview; Wells interview; Allied Chemical Plant file, SCRLR.

21. Thompson Webb interview; Nathaniel Jones 1992 interview; Julia Jones 1992 interview; Nathaniel Jones interview, *IAL*, 57; Nathaniel Jones (with Julia Jones) June 1996 and Aug. 1996 interviews.

22. Pro-Mark, Inc., *Claiborne County, Mississippi, Economic Adjustment Strategy*.

23. "Bills to Divide Grand Gulf Tax Approved," *Jackson Clarion-Ledger*, Feb. 13, 1986; "Claiborne Board to Ask High Court to Reconsider," *Jackson Clarion-Ledger*, Aug. 16, 1988; Devoual, "People of Claiborne County," 35; Nathaniel Jones Aug. 1991 interview.

Conclusion

1. Robert Canzoneri, "Charles Evers: Mississippi's Representative Man?" *Harper's*, July 1968.

2. Payne, *I've Got the Light of Freedom*, 217–18.

3. Matthew Burks file, SCRLR.

4. Payne, *I've Got the Light of Freedom*, 418–19.

5. Nathaniel Jones 1991 interview; Nathaniel Jones interview, *IAL*, 57–58.

6. Annie Jones interview, USM, 18; Lum interview.

7. Devoual interview; Warner interview.

8. Reagon and Cluster, "Borning Struggle," 23; Reagon in Carson et al., eds., *Eyes on the Prize Reader*, 143–45.

9. Watson interview, USM, 47; Devoual interview; Jimmy Ellis interview; Julia Jones interview, *IAL*, 45; Doss interview, USM, 15; Ernest Kennedy Brandon interview.

10. Albert Butler interview; Allen interview; Melvin McFatter FBI file, (HQ) 44-32887, FBIP; Alberta Coleman, JCN, 34.

11. McCay interview; Robert Butler interview; Charles Evers, CHT, 401, 4725; Gray interview; Claiborne County Racial Matters, Aug. 27, 1966, MS, 157-JN-6101, FBIP; James Dorsey Dec. 1994 interview; M. M. McFatter interview; Johnston to file, Dec. 8, 1966, PBJP; *PGR*, April 11, 1968; Flier, Mississippi Freedom Democratic Party file, SCRLR.

12. Mass meeting, Monday night after shooting, JCN, 77; Lum interview; Chatfield, "Port Gibson, Mississippi," 55.

13. McDaniel interview, USM, 10; James Dorsey 1992 interview.

14. Nathaniel Jones (with Julia Jones) June 1996 interview.

15. Joseph Zurro, personal introduction, Jan. 25, 2005 (in author's possession).

16. *PGR*, May 10, 2001.

Epilogue

1. Carolyn Miller interview; Dobbs interview, USM, 19; Lum interview; Jane Ellis interview, USM, 22; Headley interview; Allen interview; McCay interview; Evers' speech, Apr. 19, 1969, *Claiborne Hardware, et al. v. NAACP, et al.*, MSCS; Dorsey 1992 interview.

2. Allen interview; Albert Butler interview; Charles Evers speech, Apr. 19, 1969, *Claiborne Hardware, et al. v. NAACP, et al.*, MSCS.

3. Jane Ellis interview, USM, 4.

4. Information about Mississippi Cultural Crossroads found at <http://www.mscultural. crossroads.org/About/AboutFrameset.htm> (accessed Aug. 3, 2003).

5. "Time for a Change" forum, Dec. 5, 1994 (videotape); "No Easy Journey" brochure.

6. Ellis, *Cannonballs and Courage*, 169–85; *Main Street America*, produced by PBS WNEO and WEAO, aired July 25, 2002; "Time for a Change" forum program and videotape; "No Easy Journey" brochure; "Picturing Our Past" brochure; "Then and Now: Looking Back at the Allen Collection," Oct. 5, 1991, program.

7. Hogan, "Many Minds, One Heart," 76.

8. "Time for a Change" forum.

9. Ibid.

10. Ibid.

11. Ibid.; Chris Allen Baker, "Memorial Held for Slain Trio," *Neshoba Democrat*, June 25, 2003.

12. Ellis, *Cannonballs and Courage*, 169, 171–85.

13. Ibid., 7, 9, 154–55.

14. Ibid., 62, 65, 67.

15. Ibid., 128, 131, 136, 140, 145, 163.

16. Ibid., 169, 178.

17. *Holla: Claiborne County Teenagers Having Their Say*, Constructed by Maya Gurantz and Abigail Cooper, from the writings and improvisations of the cast, performed February 25, 2003 (copy in author's possession).

Bibliography

Manuscript and Archival Material

Atlanta, Georgia
    Southern Labor Archive, Pullen Library, Georgia State University
        International Woodworkers of America Papers
Charlottesville, Virginia
    Alderman Library, University of Virginia
        Southern Election Fund Papers
College Park, Maryland
    National Archive
        National Labor Relations Board Papers
Hattiesburg, Mississippi
    McCain Library, University of Southern Mississippi
        Paul B. Johnson Papers
        Dixon Pyles Papers
Jackson, Mississippi
    Coleman Library, Tougaloo College
        Rims Barber Papers
        Aaron Henry Papers
        Ed King Papers
        Annie Rankin Papers
        Southern Civil Rights Litigation Records
    Mississippi Department of Archives and History
        Board of Education Minutes, Claiborne County (microfilm)
        Institutions of Higher Learning Papers
        Oral History Collection
        Sovereignty Commission Papers
        Subject Files
    Mississippi Supreme Court Storage
        Claiborne Hardware, et al. v. NAACP, et al.
Madison, Wisconsin
    State Historical Society of Wisconsin
        Social Action Vertical File

Washington, D.C.
  Federal Bureau of Investigation Freedom of Information Privacy Act (FOIPA) Materials
    Claiborne County Racial Matters
    Deacons for Defense and Justice
    James Jones
    Klan, Port Gibson, Mississippi
    Melvin M. McFatter
    Port Gibson Racial Matters
    Rudolph Arthur Shields
    Calvin Williams
  Justice Department FOIPA Materials
  Library of Congress, Manuscript Division
    National Association for the Advancement of Colored People Papers

Microform Collections

Ducey, Mitchell F., ed. *Southern Regional Council Papers, 1944–1968.* Ann Arbor, Mich.: University Microfilms, 1984.

Meier, August, Elliott Rudwick, and Randolph Boehm, eds. *Congress of Racial Equality (CORE) Papers Part 3: Scholarship, Educational and Defense Fund for Racial Equality, 1960–1976.* Frederick, Md., 1984.

Papers of the NAACP, Supplement to Part 4, Voting Rights, General Office Files, 1956–65. Bethesda, Md.: University Publications of America, 1996.

Port Gibson Reveille. Mississippi Department of Archives and History, Port Gibson, Mississippi.

Student Nonviolent Coordinating Committee Papers, 1959–1972. Sanford, N.C.: Microfiling Corp. of America, 1981.

Vose, Clement E., ed. *Southern Civil Rights Litigation Records for the 1960s.* New Haven, Conn.: Yale University Photographic Services, 1977.

Government Documents

U.S. Bureau of the Census. *U.S. Census of Population: 1930.* Vol. 3, *Reports by States, Showing the Composition and Characteristics of the Population for Counties, Cities, and Townships or Other Minor Civil Divisions.* Part 1, *Alabama-Missouri.* Government Printing Office, 1932.

U.S. Bureau of the Census. *U.S. Census of Population: 1940.* Vol. 2, *Characteristics of the Population.* Part 4, *Minnesota–New Mexico.* Government Printing Office, 1943.

——. *U.S. Census of Population: 1950.* Vol. 1, *Number of Inhabitants.* Government Printing Office, 1952.

——. *U.S. Census of Population: 1960. General Social and Economic Characteristics, Mississippi.* Final Report PC(1)-26C. Government Printing Office, 1961.

——. *U.S. Census of Population: 1960.* Vol. 1, *Characteristics of the Population.* Part 26, *Mississippi.* Government Printing Office, 1961.

[Works Progress Administration]. *Claiborne County [WPA Project]*. Works Progress Administration for Mississippi, 1935, 1982.

Interviews

Note: All interviews are in the author's possession and/or available at Mississippi Cultural Crossroads in Port Gibson, Mississippi. Those identified with USM are also available at the University of Southern Mississippi. Two persons asked to remain anonymous, and their interviews are identified by Anonymous no. 2 and Anonymous no. 3.

Abraham, Rick, telephone interview by Emilye Crosby, February 10, 1999.
Abraham, Rosalie, interview by Emilye Crosby, Port Gibson, Mississippi, July 3, 1992.
Abraham, Waddy, interview by Emilye Crosby, Port Gibson, Mississippi, July 12, 1992.
Aikerson, George, interview by David Crosby, Claiborne County, Mississippi, March 22, 1979.
Allen, Jimmy, interview by Emilye Crosby, Port Gibson, Mississippi, February 9, 1994.
Anderson, Celia, interview by Emilye Crosby, Claiborne County, Mississippi, April 14, 1992.
Anonymous no. 2, interview by Emilye Crosby, Claiborne County, Mississippi, May 6, 1992.
Anonymous no. 3, interview by Emilye Crosby, Claiborne County, Mississippi, April 29, 1992.
Aschenbrenner, Larry, telephone interview by Emilye Crosby, June 29, 1995.
Atlas, Gustina, interview by Emilye Crosby, Port Gibson, Mississippi, April 6, 1992.
Barber, Rims, interview by Emilye Crosby, Jackson, Mississippi, February 17, 1994.
Beesley, James, interview by Emilye Crosby, Port Gibson, Mississippi, February 15, 1992.
Beesley, Joan, interview by Emilye Crosby, Port Gibson, Mississippi, May 16, 1992.
Blackwell, Unita, interview by Emilye Crosby, Mayersville, Mississippi, July 17, 1996.
Bowie, Harry, telephone interview by Emilye Crosby, August 1999.
Brandon, Artemeasie, interview by Emilye Crosby, Claiborne County, Mississippi, May 18, 1992.
Brandon, Carl, interview by Emilye Crosby, Port Gibson, Mississippi, April 30, 1992.
Brandon, Dorothy, interview by Emilye Crosby, Fayette, Mississippi, August 5, 1992.
Brandon, Ernest Kennedy, interview by Emilye Crosby, Detroit, Michigan, September 11, 1994.
Brandon, Marjorie, interviews by Emilye Crosby, Claiborne County, Mississippi, May 4, 1992; July 23, 1996.
Brown, Lillie D., interview by Emilye Crosby, Fayette, Mississippi, July 23, 1992, USM transcript.
Bunton, Charles, interview by Emilye Crosby, Port Gibson, Mississippi, August 5, 1996.
Butler, Albert, interview by Emilye Crosby, Port Gibson, Mississippi, February 16, 1994.
Butler, Robert, interview by Emilye Crosby, Lorman, Mississippi, February 10, 1994.
Camphor, Arthur Lee, interview by Emilye Crosby and Kenzia Tisdale, Claiborne County, Mississippi, June 23, 1992.
Cole, Ed, interview by Emilye Crosby, Jackson, Mississippi, July 16, 1996.
Collins, Geneva, interview by Wanda McGowan, Port Gibson, Mississippi, August 7, 1991.

Collins, Katie, interview by Emilye Crosby, Claiborne County, April 26, 2001.

Collins, Katie, Etta Evans, and Wilhemia Grigsby (sisters), interview by Emilye Crosby, Claiborne County, September 5, 1998.

Davenport, M. K., interview by Emilye Crosby, Port Gibson, Mississippi, April 11, 1992, USM transcript.

Davis, Faye, interview by Emilye Crosby and Kenzia Tisdale, Port Gibson, Mississippi, June 25, 1992.

Devoual, James, interview by Emilye Crosby, Port Gibson, Mississippi, July 28, 1992.

Disharoon, Ben, interview by Emilye Crosby, Claiborne County, Mississippi, February 3, 1994.

Dobbs, Carolyn, interview by Aron Irby, Port Gibson, Mississippi, June 29, 1992, USM transcript.

Dorsey, Henrietta, interview by Emilye Crosby, Port Gibson, Mississippi, June 22, 1992.

Dorsey, James, interview by David Crosby, Claiborne County, Mississippi, July 14, 1980.

Dorsey, James, interviews by Emilye Crosby, Port Gibson, Mississippi, May 4–5, 1992; February 10, 1994; December 20, 1994; May 1, 2001.

Dorsey, James, telephone interview by Emilye Crosby, June 20, 1995.

Doss, Evan, Jr., interview by Emilye Crosby, Port Gibson, Mississippi, April 7, 1992, USM transcript.

Dungee, Grant, interview by Emilye Crosby, Albany, Georgia, February 1, 1994.

Durham, Emma, interview by David Crosby, Claiborne County, Mississippi, July 23, 1979.

Ellis, Jane, interview by Emilye Crosby, Port Gibson, Mississippi, June 25, 1992, USM transcript.

Ellis, Jimmy, interview by Emilye Crosby, Port Gibson, Mississippi, August 6, 1996.

Ellis, Katie, interview by David Crosby, Claiborne County, Mississippi, July 18, 1979.

Evers, Charles, interview by Emilye Crosby, Fayette, Mississippi, August 5, 1992.

Fitzpatrick, Robert, interview by Emilye Crosby, Washington D.C., May 31, 1996.

Galloway, Henry, interview by David Crosby, Claiborne County, Mississippi, July 14, 1980.

Garner, A. C., interview by Wanda McGowan, Port Gibson, Mississippi, February 20, 1992.

Gray, James, interview by Emilye Crosby, Port Gibson, Mississippi, July 1, 1992.

Guster, Leesco, interview by Emilye Crosby, Port Gibson, July 3, 1996.

Guyot, Lawrence, interview by Emilye Crosby and James Miller, Washington D.C., January 5, 1999.

Headley, Mott, interview by Emilye Crosby, Claiborne County, Mississippi, July 28, 1992.

Hoffmann, Nancy Larraine, interview by Emilye Crosby, Albany, New York, October 22, 1992.

Houze, Henry, interview by Emilye Crosby, Lorman, Mississippi, February 17, 1994.

Hudson, George, interview by Emilye Crosby, Port Gibson, Mississippi, February 19, 1994.

Jefferies, Richard, interview by David Crosby, Detroit, Michigan, August 13, 1979.

Jefferies, Ruby, interview by David Crosby, Claiborne County, Mississippi, June 28, 1979.

Johnson, Annie Holloway, interview by David Crosby, Claiborne County, Mississippi, June 13, 1979.

Johnson, Jesse, interview by David Crosby, Claiborne County, Mississippi, July 16, 1980.

Jones, Annie, interview by Emilye Crosby, Port Gibson, Mississippi, March 19, 1992, USM transcript.

Jones, Julia, interview by Emilye Crosby, Claiborne County, Mississippi, June 29, 1992.

Jones, Julia (with Nathaniel Jones), interviews by Emilye Crosby, Claiborne County, Mississippi, June 30, 1996; August 4, 1996; April 28, 2001; May 3, 2001.

Jones, Nathaniel, interview by Wanda McGowan, Port Gibson, Mississippi, August 7, 1991.

Jones, Nathaniel, interviews by Emilye Crosby, Port Gibson, Mississippi, March 12, 1992; Jauary 15, 2000.

Jones, Nathaniel (with Julia Jones), interviews by Emilye Crosby, Claiborne County, Mississippi, June 30, 1996; August 4, 1996; April 28, 2001; May 3, 2001.

King, Ed, interview by Emilye Crosby, Jackson, Mississippi, September 4, 1998.

Landers, Maurice, interview by Emilye Crosby, Port Gibson, Mississippi, July 22, 1992.

Leach, Herman, interview by Emilye Crosby, Yazoo City, Mississippi, February 14, 1994, USM transcript.

Lichtman, Elliott, interview by Emilye Crosby, May 30, 1996.

Long, Worth, interview by Emilye Crosby, Atlanta, Georgia, January 31, 1994.

Lum, Bill, interview by Emilye Crosby, Port Gibson, Mississippi, July 29, 1992.

Martin, Nathaniel, interview by Emilye Crosby, Port Gibson, Mississippi, June 23, 1992.

McCay, Dan, interview by Emilye Crosby, Claiborne County, Mississippi, May 19, 1992.

McClorine, Elonzo, interview by Emilye Crosby, Port Gibson, Mississippi, April 6, 1992.

McDaniel, Q. H., Jr., interview by Emilye Crosby, Port Gibson, Mississippi, June 27, 1992, USM transcript.

McFatter, M. M., interview by Emilye Crosby, Port Gibson, Mississippi, June 15, 1992.

McFatter, Melvin, interview by Emilye Crosby, Port Gibson, Mississippi, May 18, 1992.

Miller, Carolyn, interview by Emilye Crosby, Port Gibson, Mississippi, February 15, 1994.

Miller, James, interviews by Emilye Crosby, Port Gibson, Mississippi, February 2, 1994; December 21, 1994; July 26, 1996.

Miller, James, interview by Emilye Crosby, Washington, D.C., January 5, 1999.

Minor, Wilson "Bill," interview by Emilye Crosby, Jackson, Mississippi, February 8, 1994.

Moore, David, interview by David Crosby, Claiborne County, Mississippi, July 17, 1979.

Moses, O. W., interview by Emilye Crosby, Lorman, Mississippi, July 14, 1992.

Moses, Robert Parris, interview by Joseph Sinsheimer, November 19, 1983, 20, Joseph Sinsheimer Papers, Duke University, Durham, North Carolina.

Moses, Robert Parris, interview by Emilye Crosby, Jackson, Mississippi, May 7, 2001.

Nelson, Frances, interview by Emilye Crosby, Claiborne County, Mississippi, April 13, 1992.

Newman, Joe, interview by David Crosby, Gary, Indiana, August 11, 1980.

Newsome, Milligan, interview by David Crosby, Claiborne County, Mississippi, May 30, 1979.

Norton, Mary Ann, interview by Emilye Crosby, Port Gibson, Mississippi, May 21, 1992.

Page, Matthew, interview by Sarah Crosby, Claiborne County, Mississippi, July 9, 1983.

Parker, Estella, interview by David Crosby, Vicksburg, Mississippi, August 5, 1980.

Parker, Frank, interview by Emilye Crosby, Washington, D.C., October 15, 1992.

Person, Jane, interview by Emilye Crosby and Aron Irby, Port Gibson, Mississippi, May 27, 1992.

Person, Jimmie, interview by Emilye Crosby, Port Gibson, Mississippi, May 18, 1992.

Pyles, Dixon, interview by Emilye Crosby, Jackson, Mississippi, July 31, 1992.

Rankin, Ezekiel, interview by Emilye Crosby, Jefferson County, Mississippi, April 28, 1992.

Rankin, Ezekiel, interview by Emilye Crosby, Jefferson County, Mississippi, May 14, 1992, USM transcript.

Rankin, Hystercine, interview by Emilye Crosby, Jefferson County, May 13, 1992, USM transcript.

Ross, William Matt, interview by Emilye Crosby, Port Gibson, Mississippi, May 7, 1992.

Sayles, J. L., interview by Emilye Crosby, Claiborne County, Mississippi, May 20, 1992.

Scott, James, interview by Emilye Crosby, Port Gibson, Mississippi, June 22, 1992.

Sellers, Cleveland L., Jr., interview by Emilye Crosby, Columbia, South Carolina, January 10, 1993.

Shaifer, Evelyn, interview by Emilye Crosby, Port Gibson, Mississippi, June 23, 1992.

Shapiro, Jonathan, telephone interview by Emilye Crosby, March 4, 1999.

Spencer, Eugene, interview by David Crosby, Claiborne County, Mississippi, June 21, 1979.

Spencer, Pauline, interview by Pamela Bolden, Claiborne County, June 21, 1979.

Stewart, Ruth Juanita, interview by Emilye Crosby, Detroit, Michigan, September 11, 1994.

Sullivan, Barbara Phillips, interview by Emilye Crosby, Oxford, Mississippi, September 8, 1998.

Thompson Webb, Dolly Marguerite, interview by Emilye Crosby, Natchez, Mississippi, May 12, 1992.

Tisdale, Fred M., interview by Kenzia Tisdale, Claiborne County, Mississippi, June 28, 1992, USM transcript.

Waites, Moses, interview by David Crosby, Claiborne County, Mississippi, June 27, 1979.

Walker, George Henry, interviews by Emilye Crosby, Port Gibson, Mississippi, June 24, 1992; February 16, 1994.

Walls, Eddie, Jr., interview by Emilye Crosby, Port Gibson, Mississippi, June 24, 1992, USM transcript.

Warner, Julius, interview by Emilye Crosby, Port Gibson, Mississippi, June 29, 1992.

Watson, Gladys J., interview by Emilye Crosby, Port Gibson, Mississippi, February 4, 1994, USM transcript.

Wells, Thelma Crowder, interview by Emilye Crosby, Port Gibson, Mississippi, April 7, 1992.

Williams, Calvin, Jr., interview by Emilye Crosby, Jackson, Mississippi, February 2, 1994.

Wilson, Rachel, interview by Emilye Crosby, Port Gibson, Mississippi, June 29, 1992.

Wilson, Willie, interview by Emilye Crosby, Claiborne County, Mississippi, May 26, 1992.

Young, Bobbie, interview by Emilye Crosby, Port Gibson, Mississippi, February 11, 1994.

Published Interviews

Anderson, Celia, interview. *i ain't lying*. Mississippi Cultural Crossroads, Lorman, Mississippi, vol. 5 (forthcoming).

Brandon, Artemeasie, interview. *i ain't lying*. Mississippi Cultural Crossroads, Lorman, Mississippi, vol. 2 (Winter 1982): 29–39.

Breckinridge, Janie Clara, interview. *i ain't lying*. Mississippi Cultural Crossroads, Lorman, Mississippi, vol. 1 (Spring 1981): 3–8.

Buck, Minnie Lou, interview. *i ain't lying*. Mississippi Cultural Crossroads, Lorman, Mississippi, vol. 1 (Spring 1981): 34–45.

Dorsey, Saul, interview. *i ain't lying*. Mississippi Cultural Crossroads, Lorman, Mississippi, vol. 2 (Winter 1982): 58–60.

Duffin, Eddie, interview. *i ain't lying*. Mississippi Cultural Crossroads, Lorman, Mississippi, vol. 2 (Winter 1982): 12–25.

Gibson, Geneva, interview. *i ain't lying*. Mississippi Cultural Crossroads, Lorman, Mississippi, vol. 2 (Winter 1982): 3–11.

Green, Bernice, interview. *i ain't lying*. Mississippi Cultural Crossroads, Lorman, Mississippi, vol. 2 (Winter 1982): 43–47.

Jones, Julia, interview. *i ain't lying*. Mississippi Cultural Crossroads, Lorman, Mississippi, vol. 3 (Summer 1983): 37–46.

Jones, Nathaniel, interview. *i ain't lying*. Mississippi Cultural Crossroads, Lorman, Mississippi, vol. 3 (Summer 1983): 47–58.

Lucas, Frances Pearl, interview. *i ain't lying*. Mississippi Cultural Crossroads, Lorman, Mississippi, vol. 1 (Spring 1981): 19–23.

Mackey, Rosetta, interview. *i ain't lying*. Mississippi Cultural Crossroads, Lorman, Mississippi, vol. 2 (Winter 1982): 40–42.

McGehee, Molly. " 'You Do Not Own What You Cannot Control': An interview with Activist and Folklorist Worth Long." *Mississippi Folklife* 31 (Fall 1998): 12–20.

McLendon, Elizabeth, interview. *i ain't lying*. Mississippi Cultural Crossroads, Lorman, Mississippi, vol. 3 (Summer 1983): 3–16.

Miller, Charles, interview. *i ain't lying*. Mississippi Cultural Crossroads, Lorman, Mississippi, vol. 5 (forthcoming).

Page, Lydell, interview. *i ain't lying*. Mississippi Cultural Crossroads, Lorman, Mississippi, vol. 5 (forthcoming).

Rankin, Hystercine, interview. *i ain't lying*. Mississippi Cultural Crossroads, Lorman, Mississippi, vol. 2 (Winter 1982): 61–73.

Reagon, Bernice Johnson, and Dick Cluster. "Borning Struggle: The Civil Rights Movement: An Interview with Bernice Johnson Reagon." *Radical America* 12, no. 6 (1978): 8–25.

Smith, Sylvia, interview. *i ain't lying*. Mississippi Cultural Crossroads, Lorman, Mississippi, vol. 4 (Fall 1989): 25–35.

Trimble, Mary Lee, interview. *i ain't lying*. Mississippi Cultural Crossroads, Lorman, Mississippi, vol. 2 (Winter 1982): 20–25.

Walker, William, interview. *i ain't lying*. Mississippi Cultural Crossroads, Lorman, Mississippi, vol. 4 (Fall 1989): 36–48.

Welch, Rosa Page, interview. *i ain't lying*. Mississippi Cultural Crossroads, Lorman, Mississippi, vol. 3 (Summer 1983): 17–27.

Wells, Thelma, interview. *i ain't lying*. Mississippi Cultural Crossroads, Lorman, Mississippi, vol. 4 (Fall 1989): 61–70.

White, Lucille, interview. *i ain't lying*. Mississippi Cultural Crossroads, Lorman, Mississippi, vol. 3 (Summer 1983): 59–66.

Woodard, Gronetta, interview. *i ain't lying*. Mississippi Cultural Crossroads, Lorman, Mississippi, vol. 1 (Spring 1981): 46–49.

Books

Ashmore, Harry S. *The Negro and the Schools*. Chapel Hill: University of North Carolina Press, 1954.

Barkan, Steven E. *Protesters on Trial: Criminal Justice in the Southern Civil Rights and Vietnam Antiwar Movements*. New Brunswick: Rutgers University Press, 1985.

Bartley, Numan V. *The New South, 1945–1980*. Baton Rouge: Louisiana State University Press, 1995.

———. *The Rise of Massive Resistance: Race and Politics in the South during the 1950s*. Baton Rouge: Louisiana State University Press, 1969.

Berry, Jason. *Amazing Grace: With Charles Evers in Mississippi*. New York: Saturday Review Press, 1973.

Biondi, Martha. *To Stand and Fight: The Struggle for Civil Rights in Post-War New York City*. Cambridge: Harvard University Press, 2003.

Black, Earl, and Merle Black. *Politics and Society in the South*. Cambridge: Harvard University Press, 1987.

Bond, Julian, ed. *Black Candidates: Southern Campaign Experiences*. Atlanta: Voter Education Project, 1968.

Brady, Tom P. *Black Monday: Segregation or Amalgamation . . . America Has Its Choice*. Winona, Miss.: Association of Citizens' Councils, 1955.

Branch, Taylor. *Parting the Waters: America in the King Years, 1954–1963*. New York: Simon and Schuster, 1988.

———. *Pillar of Fire: America in the King Years, 1963–1965*. New York: Simon and Schuster, 1998.

Burner, Eric. *Gently He Shall Lead Them: Robert Parris Moses and Civil Rights in Mississippi*. New York: New York University Press, 1994.

Cagin, Seth, and Philip Dray. *We Are Not Afraid: The Story of Goodman, Schwerner and Chaney and the Civil Rights Campaign for Mississippi*. New York: Bantam, 1988.

Carson, Clayborne, et al., eds. *The Eyes on the Prize Civil Rights Reader: Documents, Speeches, and Firsthand Accounts from the Black Freedom Struggle, 1954–1990*. New York: Penguin, 1991.

Cecelski, David. *Along Freedom Road: Hyde County, North Carolina, and the Fate of Black Schools in the South.* Chapel Hill: University of North Carolina Press, 1994.

Chafe, William. *Civilities and Civil Rights: Greensboro, N.C., and the Black Struggle for Freedom.* New York: Oxford University Press, 1980.

Chestnut, J. L., Jr. *Black in Selma: The Uncommon Life of J. L. Chestnut, Jr., Politics and Power in a Small American Town.* New York: Farrar, Straus and Giroux, 1990.

Claiborne County Area Development Association. *Comprehensive Overall Economic Program for Claiborne County, Mississippi.* [Jackson, Mississippi], 1961.

Colburn, David R. *Racial Change & Community Crisis, St. Augustine, Florida, 1877–1980.* 1985. Gainesville: University of Florida Press, 1991.

de Jong, Greta. *A Different Day: African American Struggles for Justice in Rural Louisiana, 1900–1970.* Chapel Hill: University of North Carolina Press, 2002.

Dittmer, John. *Local People: The Struggle for Civil Rights in Mississippi.* Urbana: University of Illinois Press, 1994.

Dunham, Merlerson Guy. *The Centennial History of Alcorn A&M College.* Hattiesburg: University and College Press of Mississippi, 1971.

Eagles, Charles, ed. *The Civil Rights Movement in America.* Jackson: University Press of Mississippi, 1986.

Egerton, John. *Speak Now Against the Day: The Generation Before the Civil Rights Movement in the South.* New York: Random House, 1994.

Ellis, Mary H., *Cannonballs and Courage: The Story of Port Gibson.* Virginia Beach: Donning Company Publishers, 2003.

Eskew, Glenn T. *But for Birmingham: The Local and National Movements in the Civil Rights Struggle.* Chapel Hill: University of North Carolina Press, 1997.

Evers, Charles. *Evers.* Edited by Grace Halsell. New York: World Publishing Company, 1971.

———. *Have No Fear: The Charles Evers Story.* New York: Wiley and Sons, 1997.

Evers, Myrlie. *For Us, the Living.* New York: Doubleday and Company, Inc., 1967.

———. *Watch Me Fly: What I Learned on the Way to Becoming the Woman I Was Meant to Be.* Boston: Little, Brown, 1999.

Fairclough, Adam. *Race and Democracy: The Civil Rights Struggle in Louisiana, 1915–1972.* Athens: University of Georgia Press, 1995.

———. *To Redeem the Soul of America: The Southern Christian Leadership Conference and Martin Luther King, Jr.* Athens: University of Georgia Press, 1987.

Fleming, Cynthia Griggs. *In the Shadow of Selma: The Continuing Struggle for Civil Rights in the Rural South.* Lanham, Md.: Rowman & Littlefield, 2004.

Foner, Eric. *Reconstruction: America's Unfinished Revolution, 1863–1877.* New York: Harper & Row, 1988.

Forman, James. *The Making of Black Revolutionaries.* 1972. Seattle: Open Hand, 1985.

Freeman, Roland. *A Communion of the Spirits: African-American Quilters, Preservers, and Their Stories.* Nashville: Rutledge Hill Press, 1996.

Grant, Joanne, ed. *Black Protest: 350 Years of History, Documents, and Analyses.* New York: Random House, 1996.

Headley, Katy McCaleb. *Claiborne County, Mississippi: The Promised Land*. Port Gibson: Claiborne County Historical Society, 1976.

Henry, Aaron. *Aaron Henry: The Fire Ever Burning*. Jackson: University Press of Mississippi, 2000.

Hill, Lance. *The Deacons for Defense: Armed Resistance and the Civil Rights Movement*. Chapel Hill: University of North Carolina Press, 2004.

Johnston, Erle. *Mississippi's Defiant Years, 1953–1973: An Interpretive Documentary with Personal Experiences*. Forest, Miss.: Lake Harbor Publishers, 1990.

King, Mary. *Freedom Song: A Personal Story of the 1960s Civil Rights Movement*. New York: Morrow, 1987.

Kirk, John A. *Redefining the Color Line: Black Activism in Little Rock, Arkansas, 1940–1970*. Gainsville: University Press of Florida, 2002.

Levy, Peter B. *Civil War on Race Street: The Civil Rights Movement in Cambridge, Maryland*. Gainesville: University Press of Florida, 2003.

Lipsitz, George. *A Life in the Struggle: Ivory Perry and the Culture of Opposition*. Philadelphia: Temple University Press, 1988.

Litwack, Leon F. *Trouble in Mind: Black Southerners in the Age of Jim Crow*. New York: Knopf, 1998.

Mars, Florence. *Witness in Philadelphia*. Baton Rouge: Louisiana State University Press, 1977.

McMillen, Neil R. *The Citizens' Council: A History of Organized Resistance to the Second Reconstruction*. Urbana: University of Illinois Press, 1971.

———. *Dark Journey: Black Mississippians in the Age of Jim Crow*. Urbana: University of Illinois Press, 1989.

Mills, Kay. *This Little Light of Mine: The Life of Fannie Lou Hamer*. New York: Dutton, 1993.

Mills, Thornton. *Dividing Lines: Municipal Politics and the Struggle for Civil Rights in Montgomery, Birmingham, and Selma*. Tuscaloosa: University of Alabama Press, 2002.

Minor, Bill. *Eyes on Mississippi: A Fifty-Year Chronicle of Change*. Jackson, Miss.: J. Prichard Morris Books, 2001.

Morris, Aldon. *Origins of the Civil Rights Movement*. New York: Free Press, 1984.

Morrison, Minion K. C. *Black Political Mobilization: Leadership, Power, and Mass Behavior*. Albany: State University of New York Press, 1987.

Moses, Robert P., and Charles E. Cobb Jr. *Radical Equations: Math Literacy and Civil Rights*. Boston: Beacon Press, 2001.

Moye, J. Todd. *Let the People Decide: Black Freedom and White Resistance Movements in Sunflower County, Mississippi, 1945–1986*. Chapel Hill: University of North Carolina Press, 2004.

Myrdal, Gunnar. *An American Dilemma: The Negro Problem and Modern Democracy*. New York: Harper & Row, 1962.

Nelson, Jack. *Terror in the Night: The Klan's Campaign against the Jews*. New York: Simon and Schuster, 1993.

Norrell, Robert J. *Reaping the Whirlwind: The Civil Rights Movement in Tuskegee*. New York: Vintage Books, 1985.

O'Brien, Gail Williams. *The Color of Law: Race, Violence, and Justice in the Post–World War II South*. Chapel Hill: University of North Carolina Press, 1999.

O'Reilly, Kenneth. *Racial Matters: The FBI's Secret File on Black America, 1960–1972*. New York: Free Press, 1989.

Owings, Ralph S., and Raymond M. Ainsley. *School Survey: The City of Port Gibson and Claiborne County, Mississippi*. Hattiesburg: Department of Educational Administration, Mississippi Southern College, 1955.

Parker, Frank R. *Black Votes Count: Political Empowerment in Mississippi after 1965*. Chapel Hill: University of North Carolina Press, 1990.

Payne, Charles, M. *I've Got the Light of Freedom: The Organizing Tradition and the Mississippi Freedom Struggle*. Berkeley: University of California Press, 1995.

Phillips, Barbara, and Joseph Huttie Jr. *Mississippi Property Tax: Special Burden for the Poor: A Citizens' Manual for Tax Reform*. Jackson: Black Economic Research Center, 1973.

Posey, Josephine McCann. *Against Great Odds: The History of Alcorn State University*. Jackson: University Press of Mississippi, 1994.

Powledge, Fred. *Free at Last? The Civil Rights Movement and the People Who Made It*. Boston: Little, Brown, 1990.

Rabby, Glenda Alice. *The Pain and the Promise: The Struggle for Civil Rights in Tallahassee, Florida*. Athens: University of Georgia Press, 1999.

Raines, Howell. *My Soul Is Rested: The Story of the Civil Rights Movement in the Deep South*. 1977. New York: Penguin, 1983.

Rogers, Kim Lacy. *Righteous Lives: Narratives of the New Orleans Civil Rights Movement*. New York: New York University Press, 1993.

Rural Organizing and Cultural Center. *Minds Stayed on Freedom: The Civil Rights Struggle in the Rural South: An Oral History*. Boulder, Colo.: Westview Press, 1991.

Salter, John R., Jr. *Jackson, Mississippi: An American Chronicle of Struggle and Schism*. Hicksville, N.Y.: Exposition Press, 1979.

Sansing, David. *Making Haste Slowly: The Troubled History of Higher Education in Mississippi*. Jackson: University Press of Mississippi, 1990.

Shannon, Jasper Berry. *Toward a New Politics in the New South*. Knoxville: University of Tennessee, 1949.

Strain, Christopher B. *Pure Fire: Self-Defense as Activism in the Civil Rights Era*. Athens: University of Georgia Press, 2005.

Sullivan, Patricia. *Days of Hope: Race and Democracy in the New Deal Era*. Chapel Hill: University of North Carolina Press, 1996.

Sullivan, Patricia, and Armstead L. Robinson, eds. *New Directions in Civil Rights Studies*. Charlottesville: University of Virginia Press, 1991.

Theoharis, Jeanne F., and Komozi Woodard, eds. *Freedom North: Black Freedom Struggles Outside the South, 1940–1980*. New York: Palgrave, 2003.

——. *Groundwork: The Local Black Freedom Movement in America*. New York: New York University Press, 2004.

Tuck, Stephen G. N. *Beyond Atlanta: The Struggle for Racial Equality in Georgia, 1940–1980*. Athens: University of Georgia Press, 2001.

Tyson, Timothy. *Radio Free Dixie: Robert F. Williams and the Roots of Black Power*. Chapel Hill: University of North Carolina Press, 1999.

Articles

Chatfield, Jack. "Port Gibson, Mississippi: A Profile of the Future?" *New South* 24 (Summer 1969): 45–55.

Cobb, James C. "'Somebody Done Nailed Us on the Cross': Federal Farm and Welfare Policy and the Civil Rights Movement in the Mississippi Delta." *Journal of American History* 77 (December 1990): 912–36.

Crosby, David. "'A Piece of Your Own': The Tenant Purchase Program in Claiborne County." *Southern Cultures* 5 (Summer 1999): 46–51.

Crosby, Emilye. "Claiming the Law: Struggles Between the Claiborne County, Mississippi, Civil Rights Movement and White Resistance." *Arkansas Review: A Journal of Delta Studies* 33 (August 2002): 91–103.

——. "'Coming Back At You': Challenging White Supremacy in Port Gibson, Mississippi." *Mississippi Folklife* 31 (Fall 1998): 21–27.

——. "'The lady folk is a doer': Women and the Civil Rights Movement in Claiborne County, Mississippi." In *Black Women in the Old World and New*, edited by Rae Ferguson, Catherine Higgs, and Barbara Moss, 189–204. Athens: Ohio University Press, 2002.

Daniel, Pete. "Going Among Strangers: Southern Reactions to World War II." *Journal of American History* 77 (December 1990): 886–911.

Devoual, Regina. "The People of Claiborne County." *Southern Exposure* 10 (April/May 1982): 35–38.

Dittmer, John. "The Politics of the Mississippi Movement, 1954–1964." In *The Civil Rights Movement in America*, edited by Charles Eagles, 65–93. Jackson: University Press of Mississippi, 1986.

Eagles, Charles W. "Toward New Histories of the Civil Rights Era." *Journal of Southern History* 66 (November 2000): 815–55.

Kincaid, John. "Beyond the Voting Rights Act: White Responses to Black Political Power in Tchula, Mississippi." *Publius* 16 (4)(1986): 155–72.

Lawson, Steven F. "Freedom Then, Freedom Now: The Historiography of the Civil Rights Movement." *American Historical Review* 96 (April 1991): 456–71.

McLemore, Leslie Burl. "Protest and Politics: The Mississippi Freedom Democratic Party and the 1965 Congressional Challenge." *The Negro Education Review* 37 (July–October 1986): 130–43.

McMillen, Neil R. "Black Enfranchisement in Mississippi: Federal Enforcement and Black Protest in the 1960's." *Journal of Southern History* 43, no. 3 (1977): 351–72.

Michele Mitchell. "'The Black Man's Burden': African Americans, Imperialism, and Notions of Racial Manhood, 1890–1910." *International Review of Social History* 44 (1999): 77–99.

Reagon, Bernice Johnson. "Women as Culture Carriers in the Civil Rights Movement: Fannie Lou Hamer." In *Women in the Civil Rights Movement: Trailblazers and Torchbearers, 1941–1965*, edited by Vicki L. Crawford, Jacqueline Anne Rouse, and Barbara Woods, 203–17. Brooklyn: Carlson, 1990.

Russell, J., Carl Alette, Henry Tomes, "General Conditions of Academic Freedom and Tenure at Southern University." *AAUP Bulletin* 54 (Spring 1968): 22.

Standley, Anne. "The Role of Black Women in the Civil Rights Movement." In *Women in the Civil Rights Movement: Trailblazers and Torchbearers, 1941–1965*, edited by Vicki L. Crawford, Jacqueline Anne Rouse, and Barbara Woods, 183–202. Brooklyn: Carlson, 1990.

Strain, Christopher B. "'We Walked Like Men': The Deacons for Defense and Justice." *Louisiana History* 38, no. 1 (1997): 43–62.

Tyson, Timothy. "Robert F. Williams, 'Black Power,' and the Roots of the African American Freedom Struggle." *Journal of American History* 85 (September 1998): 540–70.

Umoja, Akinyele O. "The Ballot and the Bullet: A Comparative Analysis of Armed Resistance in the Civil Rights Movement." *Journal of Black Studies* 29, no. 4 (1999): 558–78.

——. "1964: The Beginning of the End of Nonviolence in the Mississippi Freedom Movement." *Radical History Review* 85 (2003): 201–26.

——. "'We Will Shoot Back': The Natchez Model and Paramilitary Organization in the Mississippi Freedom Movement." *Journal of Black Studies* 32, no. 3 (2002): 271–94.

Woodruff, Nan Elizabeth. "African-American Struggles for Citizenship in the Arkansas and Mississippi Deltas in the Age of Jim Crow." *Radical History Review* 55 (Winter 1993): 33–51.

——. "Mississippi Delta Planters and the Debates over Mechanization, Labor, and Civil Rights in the 1940s." *Journal of Southern History* 60 (May 1994): 263–84.

——. "Pick or Fight: The Emergency Farm Labor Program in the Arkansas and Mississippi Deltas during World War II." *Agricultural History* 64 (Spring 1990): 74–85.

Dissertations, Theses, and Papers

Chatfield, Jack. "Anatomy of a Protest Movement: Conflict and Consensus in a Deep South Civil Rights Organization." M.A. thesis, Columbia University, 1973.

Crosby, David L. "The Tenant Purchase Program in Claiborne County, Mississippi, 1939–1980." Paper in author's possession.

Crosby, Emilye. "Common Courtesy: The Civil Rights Movement in Claiborne County, Mississippi." Ph.D. diss., Indiana University, 1995.

Davis, Jack. "*Deep South* Reencountered: The Cultural Basis of Race Relations in Natchez, Mississippi, Since 1930." Ph.D. diss., Brandeis University, 1994.

Devoual, Regina. "HTK—Voting Rights in Mississippi: Toward Parity for Black Voters." Paper in author's possession.

Harris, Johnny L. "A Historical Analysis of Educational, Economic, and Political Changes in Fayette, Mississippi, from 1954 to 1971." Ph.D. diss., Florida State University, 1972.

Hill, Lance E. "The Deacons for Defense and Justice: Armed Self-Defense and the Civil Rights Movement." Ph.D. diss., Tulane University, 1997.

Hoffman, Kenneth Ross. "The Small-Town Southern Jewish Experience: Port Gibson, Mississippi, A Case Study." M.A. thesis, Tulane University, 1993.

Jeffries, Hasan Kwame. "Freedom Politics: Transcending Civil Rights in Lowndes County, Alabama, 1965–2000." Ph.D. diss., Duke University, 2002.

Lee, Chana Kai. "A Passionate Pursuit of Justice: The Life and Leadership of Fannie Lou Hamer, 1917–1967." Ph.D. diss., University of California, Los Angeles, 1993.

McLemore, Leslie Burl, "The Mississippi Freedom Democratic Party: A Case Study of Grass-Roots Politics." Ph.D. diss., University of Massachusetts, 1971.

Miller, James Edward. "The Transformation of the Political Process in Claiborne County, Mississippi, 1967–1983." M.A. thesis, University of Massachusetts, 1987.

Strain, Christopher Barry. "Civil Rights and Self Defense: The Fiction of Nonviolence, 1955–1968." Ph.D. diss., University of California, Berkeley, 2000.

Umoja, Akinyele O. "Eye for an Eye: The Role of Armed Resistance in the Mississippi Freedom Movement." Ph.D. diss., Emory University, 1997.

Williams, Kenneth H. "Mississippi and Civil Rights, 1945–1954." Ph.D. diss., Mississippi State University, 1985.

Miscellaneous Documents

AAUP Bulletin. September 1962, pp. 248, 251.

Blank, Donald. *How to Become Sheriff When Poor & Black in Segregated Mississippi.* New York: Filmakers Library, 2002.

Hogan, Wesley. "Many Minds, One Heart: The Student Nonviolent Coordinating Committee and the Dream for a New America." Draft in author's possession.

"Holla: Claiborne County Teenagers Having Their Say." Constructed by Maya Gurantz and Abigail Cooper, from the writings and improvisations of the cast, performed February 25, 2003. Copy in author's possession.

Chatfield, Jack, notes, from Chatfield's 1969 master's thesis research. In author's possession.

Lane, Henry C., and William A. Cole. *Soil Survey of Claiborne County, Mississippi.* U.S. Department of Agriculture Soil Conservation Service with Mississippi Agriculture Experiment Station, series 1960, no. 3, July 1963.

Main Street America. Produced by PBS WNEO and WEAO, aired July 25, 2002. In author's possession.

Mississippi Power & Light Company. "Mississippi Statistical Summary of Population, 1800–1980." February 1983.

Mississippi Stockman Farmer 5 (October 1950).

National Labor Relations Board. *Decisions and Orders of the National Labor Relations Board*, Vol. 59, November 1, 1944–January 13, 1945.

"No Easy Journey." Brochure. In author's possession.

Owings, Ralph S., and Raymond M. Ainsley. *School Survey: The City of Port Gibson and Claiborne County, Mississippi*. Department of Educational Administration, Mississippi Southern College, Hattiesburg, Mississippi, 1955.

Mississippi Cultural Crossroads. "Picturing Our Past." Brochure in author's possession.

Pro-Mark, Inc. *Claiborne County, Mississippi, Economic Adjustment Strategy* (September 1990). In author's possession.

Reagon, Bernice Johnson. "The Songs Are Free." Videorecording. Princeton, N.J.: Films for the Humanities & Sciences, 1997.

"Then and Now: Looking Back at the Allen Collection." Program, opening forum for "Picturing Our Past," October 5, 1991. In author's possession.

"Time for a Change." Program, opening forum for "No Easy Journey," December 5, 1994. In author's possession.

"Time for a Change." Videotape, opening forum for "No Easy Journey," December 5, 1994. In author's possession.

U.S. Commission on Civil Rights. *United States v. Mississippi* transcript, vol. 1–2.

———. "Voting in Mississippi." 1965.

Acknowledgments

Many of the most rewarding aspects of writing this history have come through my connections to other people. I am repeatedly encouraged by and appreciative of the help so many have offered and for the ways that so many have embraced this project. Despite the fact that I've written and edited hundreds and hundreds of pages, now that I'm faced with the daunting task of actually articulating my thanks and acknowledging the invaluable contributions of so many, I find that the words are elusive and inadequate in conveying the extent of my appreciation.

I have been fortunate to experience an extensive community of teachers, friends, scholars, and activists who have offered much. I would like to acknowledge my college history professors, especially Peter Rachleff, Jim Stewart, Norm Rosenberg, and Emily Rosenberg; my Indiana University dissertation committee, Richard Blackett, John Bodnar, David Nordloh, and Steven Stowe; the staff at the *Journal of American History*, especially Susan Armeny and the late Barbara Tarrant; Debbie Gershenowitz, Paul Murphy, Sarah Vosmeier, and Mary Ann Wynkoop, good friends at Indiana University and since; Cynthia Blair, Bill Jackson, Michele Mitchell, Mary Rose, Hannah Rosen, Gail Shirley, Patricia Sullivan, and others at the Woodson Institute; the participants in the 1997 Houston Black History Workshop, organized by Richard Blackett and Linda Reed; the 1999 "Black Women in the Old World and New" Rockefeller conference at the University of Tennessee, organized by Rae Ferguson, Catherine Higgs, and Barbara Moss; and the Summer 2000 NEH Institute titled "The Civil Rights Movement: History and Consequences" led by Patricia Sullivan and Waldo Martin.

Wanda McGowan and Akinyele Umoja have epitomized the best in scholarly collaboration as we have all studied southwest Mississippi. Adam Fairclough and Paul Hendrickson shared research gems. Charles Bolton and Stephanie Millet helped with transcribing interviews. Jack Chatfield graciously sent me his M.A. thesis and thirty-year-old research notes on Claiborne County and has been just as charitable with his enthusiasm and encouragement. Julian Bond, Lawrence Guyot, Desiree Kennedy, and Charles Payne read and offered insightful critiques of earlier drafts. In the spirit of the SNCC organizers she writes about, Wesley Hogan struck up a conversation with me as we headed to a program at the National Civil Rights Museum in Memphis. We've been friends ever since, and she seemed to give me just what I needed to finish this book. I am also fortunate to be in conversation with Hasan Kwame Jeffries, Tiyi Morris, Todd Moye, Robyn Spencer, Jeanne Theoharis, Akinyele Umoja, Komozi Woodard, and other scholars examining the historiographical implications of local movement studies and the role of self-defense in the modern black freedom struggle. Like them, Leslie Brown always gives me something to think about and, even better, something to laugh about.

I have received extensive assistance from librarians and archivists, including Odelle Dawkins, Robert Dinwiddie, Jan Hillegas, Clarence Hunter, Jeff Rogers, Anne Webster, and others at the Library of Congress; the McCain Archives at the University of Southern Mississippi; the Mississippi Department of Archives and History; the National Archives; the State Historical Society of Wisconsin; and Tougaloo College's Coleman Library. This book would not have been possible without the financial support of Indiana University, the Woodson Institute at the University of Virginia, the National Endowment for the Humanities Fellowship for College Teachers, the Geneseo Foundation, and the Nuala McGann Drescher Affirmative Action Leave program of the State University of New York State and the United University Professors. I would like to thank Chuck Grench and others at UNC press who made the publication of this book possible. In particular, I appreciate the help of Patricia Sullivan and Waldo Martin, editors of the press's John Hope Franklin series on African American History and Culture.

A number of people at SUNY-Geneseo have facilitated this project. Mary Ann Stopha and others at CIT have been patient as they have indulged my insistence on using an outdated word-processing program. Harriet Sleggs and the interlibrary loan staff have gone above and beyond in helping me access materials from around the country. Barb Rex-Mckinney has been a constant help, with everything. Over the years, Susan Bailey, Sue Ann Brainard, Rose-Marie Chierici, Kate Conway-Turner, Joe Cope, Christopher Dahl, Carol Faulkner, Tze-ki Hon, Maria Lima, Kathy Mapes, Beth McCoy, Ren Vasiliev, Helena Waddy, and Jim Williams have variously offered support, feedback, and friendship. When I arrived at Geneseo just out of graduate school, the late Randy Bailey was an ideal colleague—consistent, kind, helpful, and decent—and I miss him. I am particularly grateful for the friendship of Celia Easton and Paula Henry, who have been generous with their time and insights and unwaveringly kind and supportive.

Since fall 1995 I've found considerable pleasure in working with Geneseo students. Rachel Gyore, Michelle Kleehammer, Stephanie Ellis, and the late

Jennifer Wachunas provided me with a wonderful welcome. Another delightful group has raised my spirits and engaged my mind as I've worked to finish this project. Peter Anderson, Laura Auerhahn, Christopher Bruce, Sarah Buzanowski, Jackie Chessen, Jared DePass, Gregory Fair, Jacqueline Jones, Michael Kaiser, Justin Levy, Christopher Machanoff, Patrick O'Neill, Marykate Russo, Jen Sahrle, Natalie Stachowski, Gregory Stoneberg, Stephen Stringer, and Alex Waldauer have given me a sense of being part of a community of people committed to studying movement history because it matters to us in our lives today. Several other students, including Frank Cafarella, Missy Frye, Ryan Irwin, Margaret Needham, Nicole Pleten, Jennifer Sahrle, and Ben Valentin, made direct contributions to this work, doing research and reading papers, chapters, and manuscript drafts. At the beginning of my second year at Geneseo, Joanna DiPasquale asked me to direct her honors thesis. I undoubtedly got the better end of that deal. She is a brilliant scholar, and only her openness and excitement kept me from being overly intimidated by her formidable intellect and capacity for hard work. Despite a daunting schedule, for years now she has been one of my most consistent, helpful, and perceptive readers. She always asks terrific questions, the kind that make me go "duh!" and "ah ha" and leave me enormously grateful for her insight.

I join the legions of people thanking John Dittmer. We all look to his groundbreaking work, *Local People*, that provides the base for anyone studying the Mississippi movement or doing community studies. More than that, he has been unfailingly patient, encouraging, and helpful as he has read many, many versions of this work—from the earliest dissertation chapter drafts through its various evolutions. John always asked the questions and provided the suggestions I needed to move forward, without ever overwhelming me with all that I had left to do. I am grateful to him for that and for his friendship and our conversations about Mississippi.

In very different ways, Roland Freeman and Worth Long have taught me a lot about pursuing the things I value and taking my place in the world. Everyone in my college dorm knew Roland from his early morning phone calls and the posters of his photographs that covered my walls. When those posters were in tatters from years of moving and rehanging them, Roland gave me a new set, and they still cover my walls. Throughout the time I've known him, he has modeled the kind of craziness that suggests anything is possible. When I started this project, he immediately offered his photographs and since then has done all he could to hurry me along. For his part, Worth asked questions, listened patiently to my floundering answers, and even, occasionally, answered questions. Despite failing vision, he continued to read (or listen to) and comment on this work in its many manifestations. During one weekend visit, we waded through chapter after chapter until together we came up with titles that seemed to work.

How can I even begin to express my appreciation for Richard Blackett? He's got to be the funniest, most consistent, helpful, and absolutely best mentor and friend that any graduate student, any person, could ever have. At the end of my first year of graduate school, he and Cheryl left their sons Victor and Peter (when they were five and three) in my care while they were out of the country for a week. They returned, early, to find the two boys under the back steps digging up the gas line. Richard has never let me forget it, but, as I have often repeated, they were quiet! Supported by the Blacketts' expansive generosity, Richard's Indiana graduate students, Gwen Crenshaw, Priscilla Dowden, Rae Fergeson, Ron Gifford, Lynn Hudson, Jeffrey Ogbar, Richard Pierce, and Liann Tsoukas, developed close bonds. I am thankful for their friendship, support, and camaraderie, and for being enveloped in that community in graduate school and beyond. Though Richard insists that he's done with us when we graduate, our version, that he's stuck with us forever, seems to be holding sway. His invitation to share an earlier, much longer, version of this manuscript with his fall 2001 University of Houston African American history seminar was an unparalleled gift. What fun to be back in a Blackett class! His students were quite helpful and extremely generous with their comments, questions, and enthusiasm. Best of all, I got to go to dozens of holiday parties with Richard and Cheryl. As Richard often said, "Eh?"

I would especially like to recognize and thank the many people of Claiborne County who have shared their time, memories, insights, and help. They include all who did interviews with me and whose names and stories are found throughout this book. In addition, Kendra Hall, Kennsie Tisdale, Aron Irby, and LaTrina Holmes transcribed tapes, the Claiborne County board of supervisors hired them, and Melvin McFatter used his lawyers' credentials to help me get access to legal records. Geraldine Nash and the Crossroads Quilters answered questions, gave suggestions, told me who was kin to who and who to ask what questions, and, of course, gave me directions for getting around the back roads of Claiborne County. Mississippi Cultural Crossroads, a nonprofit cultural arts organization that Charles Payne characterized as a freedom school, has been dedicated to preserving Claiborne County histories and cultural traditions since its founding in 1979. I have benefited tremendously from a wide range of MCC's programs, including their early oral history publication, *i ain't lying*, "No Easy Journey" (the exhibition commemorating the movement, which I was fortunate to be able to help with), and their periodic public humanities forums exploring, race, culture, and history. Among the most important for me were the 1994 opening for "No Easy Journey" and the 2004 "Telling the People's Story" on oral history. MCC is a crossroads in many ways and facilitated my connections with other people, including Akinyele Umoja and Paul Hendrickson, who wandered through doing their own research. Several other Claiborne Countians have been absolutely integral to this work, including Gustina Atlas, James Dorsey, Nate Jones, James Miller, and George Walker. Ms. G. and James, especially, have embraced and believed in this project and provided immeasurable help. And who can blame them for refusing to read another version that isn't actually a book? I'd also like to recognize and offer thanks to the outstanding teachers of the Claiborne County Public Schools who got me started years ago, especially Gustina Atlas, Harold Liggans, Cynthia Patton, Julius Warner, Pearl Wilson, the late Percy Thornton, and the late Mason Denham.

My parents probably initiated this project when, after moving to Mississippi in 1973, they sent me and my sisters Sarah and Jessica to the public schools. They also provided some of the evidentiary base for this book through their own work collecting oral histories. Leaving nothing to chance, they specifically pointed me to the "Port Gibson Boycott" during my early years in graduate school. Over the years, they have answered a seemingly endless stream of questions, dug up information, and commented on drafts up until the last minute. As I write this, my father is working on a map, my mother is looking for a picture, and I'm sure I'll have something for Sarah to do before the day is over. I am grateful for my family's help and our conversations as we've all come to a new understanding and appreciation for the place we think of as home.

Michele Mitchell has been a friend since the day we met at the Woodson Institute in Virginia. I greatly appreciate her concrete help, but far more than that, I treasure our talks and visits, her insights and compassion, and her presence in my world. I met Janis Forbes in the early months of this project and she's been a good friend and enthusiastic supporter throughout. I have much to thank her for, including concerts and conversation, bribery and distraction, and even a slightly premature "it's done" gift. Lastly, I'd like to thank Kathy Connelly, who has shared my life throughout this project. She's endured story after story after story and read draft after draft after draft after draft. She's also created space for me to write, fixed footnotes, and traveled with me to Mississippi any number of times. Most important, she's held out her own vision of what was possible and consistently demanded that this be not just "good history," but a "good story," one that lives up to the best of the education I got riding the Alcorn school bus. For her, and all those back home who don't understand what's been taking so long, here, finally, is "our book."

Index